Challenged Sovereignty

Challenged Sovereignty

The Impact of Drugs, Crime,
Terrorism, and Cyber Threats
in the Caribbean

IVELAW LLOYD GRIFFITH

UNIVERSITY OF
ILLINOIS PRESS
Urbana, Chicago, and Springfield

Library of Congress Cataloging-in-Publication Data
Names: Griffith, Ivelaw L., author.
Title: Challenged sovereignty : the impact of drugs, crime, terrorism, and cyber threats in the Caribbean / Ivelaw Lloyd Griffith.
Description: Urbana, Chicago : University of Illinois Press, [2024] | Includes bibliographical references and index.
Identifiers: LCCN 2023032353 (print) | LCCN 2023032354 (ebook) | ISBN 9780252045660 (cloth) | ISBN 9780252087776 (paperback) | ISBN 9780252055386 (ebook)
Subjects: LCSH: Sovereignty. | National security—Caribbean Area. | Caribbean Area—Politics and government. | Terrorism—Caribbean Area. | Crime—Caribbean Area. | Caribbean Area—Foreign relations.
Classification: LCC JC327 .G738 2024 (print) | LCC JC327 (ebook) | DDC 320.1/509729—dc23/eng/20230808
LC record available at https://lccn.loc.gov/2023032353
LC ebook record available at https://lccn.loc.gov/2023032354

Contents

Preface and Acknowledgments

Every book—whether a scholarly work, a novel, or other—has a genesis, and in many cases there is an interesting story about that genesis. This book is no different. The story about its genesis began one day in August 2011 when Erica Williams Connell and I finally spoke after she had left two voicemails and Carole Boyce Davies had left one to the effect that Erica would be trying to reach me with an invitation and she, Carole, hoped I could accept it.

Erica is the daughter of the late Eric Eustace Williams, distinguished scholar-historian, who was also the founding—and a long-standing—prime minister of Trinidad and Tobago. Since her father's death in 1981, she has dedicated her life to preserving his intellectual legacy through the Eric Williams Memorial Collection, which is housed in several institutions in Trinidad and Tobago and the United States, and the annual Eric Williams Memorial Lecture Series. The lecture series began in 1999 as a partnership with the African–New World Studies Program (now African and African Diaspora Studies [AADS] Program) of Florida International University (FIU) and the consulate general of Trinidad and Tobago in Miami. Then in its second decade, the series grew to become a major annual fixture on South Florida's public intellectual calendar. Carole, now the Frank H. T. Rhodes Professor of Humane Letters and professor of Africana Studies and Literatures in English at Cornell University, was the cofounder of the series, along with Erica. She was then the director of the African–New World Studies Program and professor of English at FIU. Incidentally, the lecture series moved from FIU in 2021 to the University of Texas at Austin.

Erica's invitation was for me to deliver the Thirteenth Eric Williams Memorial Lecture, which I did on October 28, 2011. My lecture was preceded by a list of distinguished speakers who addressed weighty academic and policy issues that crossed disciplinary and geographic boundaries. They were the late John Hope

Franklin from Duke University; the late Kenneth Kaunda, former president of Zambia; Sir Hillary Beckles, vice chancellor of the University of the West Indies; Mia Mottley, then–attorney general, now prime minister of Barbados; Cynthia Pratt, former deputy prime minister of the Bahamas; Beverly Anderson-Manley, former first lady of Jamaica and veteran journalist; Angela Davis of the University of California, Santa Cruz; Robert Fatton of the University of Virginia; MacArthur Genius author Edwidge Danticat; scholar-musician Hollis "Chalkdust" Liverpool of the University of the Virgin Islands; the late Colin Palmer of Princeton University; Joseph Inikori of the University of Rochester; Verene Shepherd of the University of the West Indies; Arnold Rampersad of Stanford University; Portia Simpson Miller, former prime minister of Jamaica; and P. J. Patterson, former prime minister of Jamaica. Speakers who followed me included Rachel Manley, prizewinning poet and professor at Lesley University; Reginald Dumas, retired ambassador from Trinidad and Tobago and former U.N. special adviser on Haiti; Rawle Gibbons of the University of the West Indies; musician Willard Harris, aka "Lord Relator"; Kenney Davis Anthony, former prime minister of St. Lucia; and Carol Anderson, the Charles Howard Candler Professor and chair of African American studies at Emory University.

The Thirteenth Lecture was delivered at a momentous time. Williams, renowned scholar and statesman, was born on September 25, 1911. Thus, the year 2011 was his birth centennial. The milestone was celebrated with intellectual celebrations in Trinidad and Tobago, at Oxford University (his alma mater), the University of London, the University of Havana, and elsewhere. The Thirteenth Lecture was part of the centennial celebrations. As well, a three-part documentary titled *Inward Hunger: The Story of Eric Williams* premiered in Port-of-Spain, Trinidad, in September of that year. The year 2011 also was the fiftieth anniversary of the publication of Williams's seminal essay "Massa Day Done," in March 1961. In addition, it had been a little over forty years since Williams's critical role in lowering Venezuela's jingoistic decibel regarding Guyana, through mediation that led to the June 1970 Protocol of Port-of-Spain, which froze the territorial controversy between the two nations for twelve years.

Moreover, the year 2011 marked thirty years since the March 29, 1981, death of Williams, a visionary of the highest order, notwithstanding the brickbats leveled after his death. As I told the FIU audience, Williams was diminutive in physical stature but a towering giant as scholar and statesman. The year 2011 also marked almost seventy years since the publication in 1944 of his scholarly masterpiece, *Capitalism and Slavery*. With copious evidence, the study masterfully debunked many historiographical and political myths about British motives and practices in relation to slavery and its abolition. The book so offended British academic and political sensibilities that it took two decades for British authorities to come to terms with having it published in Britain, despite the platitudinous embrace of academic freedom and free speech. Other than in English, the book appears in Spanish, Portuguese, Russian, Turkish, Korean, French, Chinese, Italian, Japanese, and Dutch. Williams himself was versatile linguistically, and he was said to have worked with ease and eloquence in English, Latin, Spanish, and French.

Undoubtedly, Williams was an eminent Trinidadian statesman. But he was not just a nationalist; he also was a regionalist. Toward the end of the public lecture, I invoked the name of Bob Marley, another regionalist, and I identified some connections between the two of them. Marley was no scholar or statesman, but he certainly was eminent and a purveyor of hope and pride, as was Williams. Marley died the same year as Williams—in 1981; Williams in March and Marley in May. Marley once asserted, "The greatness of a man is not in how much wealth he acquires, but in his integrity and his ability to affect those around him positively." As I suggested to the audience, whether or not he knew it, Marley was talking about Williams. A great and complex man, Williams affected people and nations around him positively (and negatively) while alive, and he has been doing so decades after his death. Were he alive to see his beloved nation and region contend with the drama of drugs, the crucible of crime, and the trauma of terrorism and cybersecurity, he certainly would have influenced how his nation and the region have responded to them.

Williams was one of seventy-three leaders worldwide and just three from the Caribbean—the others being from the leaders of the Dominican Republic and Guyana—invited in 1969 to send messages to the historic Apollo 11 lunar landing; it is still on the moon. He wrote two sentences: "The Government and the people of Trinidad and Tobago acclaim this historic triumph of science and the human will. It is our earnest hope for mankind that while we gain the moon, we shall not lose the world." Thinking of the second sentence, during the lecture I expressed the hope that as the leaders, peoples, and partner nations of the contemporary Caribbean contend with our Problems Without Passports (PWPs), we do not save our states and lose our civilization.

The public lecture was titled "Drugs and Crime as Problems without Passports in the Caribbean: How Secure Is Security, and How Sovereign Is Sovereignty?" I found the aspects needing attention so complex and absorbing that I ended up writing more than one hundred pages. Of course, this was too much for the lecture itself. The part that I used ended up being thirty pages. My presentation was followed by perceptive questions and comments, some of which raised important issues not addressed in the speech or only cursorily so, although many of the issues were developed or referenced in the prepared text. Understandably, having researched and written a considerable amount for the occasion, I was inclined to have the material published. But I envisaged doing so in an occasional paper, not a book. Importantly, too, the lecture focused on just two

PWPs—drugs and crime. As well, the proposition about challenged sovereignty was developed subsequently.

This book builds on some of my earlier studies, notably *The Quest for Security in the Caribbean* (M. E. Sharpe, 1993) and *Drugs and Security in the Caribbean: Sovereignty Under Siege* (Pennsylvania State University Press, 1997) as well as the edited volume *Caribbean Security in the Age of Terror* (Ian Randle, 2004). The impetus for it came mainly from the interest generated at the lecture at FIU and, more significantly, after the lecture was posted on the web at FIU and York College and circulated by two friends to their electronic networks. One of those friends was Norman Girvan, professor emeritus of international relations at the Institute of International Relations, University of the West Indies, in Trinidad and Tobago and former secretary-general of the Association of Caribbean States. The other is David Lewis, vice president of Manchester Trade, a business consulting firm based in Washington, D.C., and of the Caribbean Policy Consortium. Most of the positive feedback came through email and phone conversations with several individuals. So, over time, I became convinced of the wisdom of addressing some of the issues that were raised during the lecture and in conversations afterward. An occasional paper could not suffice for this; a book was needed.

My wife, Francille Waveney Griffith, gave a fillip to the book idea. For several years since my 2004 book, she had poured cold water on suggestions or questions from friends about "the next book." She had good reason to do so; not only did such pursuits take me away from the family, even when I was working at home, but as I assumed increasingly challenging administrative roles over the years, she worried, and quite rightly so, about my adding to already substantial scholarly and administrative portfolios. Thus, it was a pleasant surprise when, out of the blue one evening in July 2012 while we were on a business trip in San Francisco, California, Francille asked, "So when are you going to write that new book?" I concealed my pleasant surprise at the change of heart, but I recognized that implicit in her question was both permission and ownership: permission to trade some family time for the time required to research and write another book, and ownership in that she was signaling a willingness to invest some of her own time and creative energy in the project. Francille had come to appreciate over the years of our almost four decades of partnership that not only does "mi casa es su casa" apply to us, but "mi libro es nuestro libro" does too.

This book has enabled me to pursue many pleasant intellectual and social journeys, with many kind and generous journey assistants, whom I now gratefully acknowledge. My thanks are extended to Erica Williams Connell and Jean Muteba Rahier for the invitation to deliver the lecture and to Rosa Henríques, then-administrative assistant in the AADS Program for managing the logistics for the event; Avis Lau Quan, my secretary while I served as provost and senior vice president at York College, CUNY, for her invaluable assistance as the book project progressed; and librarians at York College, Fort Valley State University, and the University of Delaware. Gratitude is also extended to librarians George Lutz and Mary Robinson of the Freeport Memorial Library, and IT specialist David Chan. My thanks, too, to several individuals at the University of Illinois Press (UIP) for shepherding the project through the various pre-contract and publication phases. Notable here are Larin McLaughlin, former senior acquisitions editor; Dawn Durante, senior acquisitions editor, who is now editor-in-chief at the University of Texas Press; editor in chief Daniel Nasset; and acquisition editors Alison Syring and Dominique Moore. Notable, too, are senior editor Tad Ringo and copyeditor Jill R. Hughes.

This project was placed on hold for much of the time I spent at Fort Valley State University and while I was at the University of Guyana. Appointment as a Distinguished Visiting Scholar at the University of Delaware for the 2019–2020 academic year enabled me to resume work and complete the book. Thus, I am deeply grateful to the two individuals who facilitated that appointment: the late Babatunde Ogunnaike, the William L. Friend Chaired Professor of Chemical Engineering, and David Redlawsk, the James R. Soles Professor and Chair, Department of Political Science and International Relations. Thanks, as well, to Barbara Ford of the Department of Political Science and International Relations at the University of Delaware for her assistance.

I also appreciate the suggestions from the UIP reviewers of the book proposal and the sample chapters and, later, of the book manuscript. Clifford Griffin of North Carolina State University was one of the proposal reviewers who elected to be identified; many thanks! The reviewers offered thoughtful critiques and suggestions, some of which enabled me to improve the book's organization and analysis. Several friends and colleagues aided with the provision of data and data sources. They include Dale Erskine, former director of prisons and correctional services of Guyana; Hilary Herman, then director of corrections of St. Lucia; Major Gen. (ret.) Eddie Dillon, then chief of defense staff of the Trinidad and Tobago Defense Force; Lt. Colonel John Nurse, superintendent of prisons of Barbados; then-Commissioner of Police Owen Ellington of the Jamaica Constabulary Force; Sheridon Hill of the Trinidad and Tobago Police Service; Brig. Gen. (ret.) John Sandy, then-national security minister of Trinidad and Tobago; Professor Michael Sharpe of York College/CUNY; and Marcia Manning, secretariat manager of the Association of Caribbean Commissioners of Police.

Allow me to record my indebtedness to several close friends and colleagues whose constructive comments on various chapters have led to a much-improved work. They include Anthony Maingot, professor of sociology emeritus at Florida International University; Georges Fauriol of the Caribbean Policy Consortium and the Center for Strategic and International Studies; Aubrey Armstrong of Aubrey Armstrong Associates; Anthony Bryan of the Caribbean Policy Consortium and the Institute of International Relations at the University of the West Indies; Holger Henke, director of the Sir Arthur Lewis Institute of Social and Economic Studies at the Mona Campus of the University of the West Indies; Fitzgerald Yaw, former director of strategic initiatives at the University of Guyana, now with Guyana Development Initiative—the Porter Project; Humberto García-Muñiz of the University of Puerto Rico; Scott MacDonald of the Caribbean Policy Consortium and Smith's Research and Gradings; and Dion Phillips, professor of sociology emeritus at the University of the Virgin Islands.

At one stage this book was in jeopardy of non-completion. The sections completed before June 2019 had been on a flash drive that had journeyed with me from New York to Georgia and back to New York and then to Guyana and then back to New York. It was corrupted, and efforts at home and by the IT specialists at the University of Delaware and at MIT to recover the files were futile. I am particularly thankful to Terrence Blackman of Medgar Evers College, CUNY, and MIT, who elicited the assistance of his colleagues at MIT in the recovery quest. But my dejection was supplanted by elation when, on the advice of two friends in Georgia who once had a similar file corruption experience, I secured the assistance of the Microsoft Store in recovering parts of some documents from the laptop on which the writing had been done. I owe a debt of gratitude to those friends: the late Dr. Claudette Heyliger-Thomas and Professor Kelwyn Thomas of Morehouse School of Medicine.

I am immensely grateful to my dear wife, Francille, for motivation and social permission to pursue the project and help with many of its aspects. Thanks, too, to our daughter, Shakina Aisha Griffith, who assisted with the bibliography and provided helpful comments on some of the chapters. As well, my thanks are extended to our son, Ivelaw Lamar Griffith, whose encouragement and motivation to complete the project were invaluable, especially when it appeared that early files were irrecoverable and that I would have to begin the project anew. This book has been long in the making. And although aspects of the drugs, crime, corruption, and the horrible prison conditions uncovered were disquieting, researching and writing about them was invigorating. My hope is that readers will find value in what they read here. But to anyone who is skeptical about its worth, I commend Toni Morrison's words of wisdom: "If there's a book that you want to read, but it hasn't been written yet, then you must write it."

Acronyms and Abbreviations

CARICOM	Caribbean Community
CARICOM IMPACS	CARICOM Implementation Agency for Crime and Security
CARPHA	Caribbean Public Health Agency
CBSI	Caribbean Basin Security Initiative
CCJ	Caribbean Court of Justice
CDB	Caribbean Development Bank
CEPI	Coalition of Epidemic Preparedness Innovations
COI	Commission of Inquiry
COVAX	COVID-19 Vaccines Global Access
CTO	Caribbean Tourism Organization
GAVI	Global Alliance for Vaccines and Immunization
GCI	Global Cybersecurity Index
GDF	Guyana Defense Force
IDB	Inter-American Development Bank
INCSR	International Narcotics Control Strategy Report
ISIS	Islamic State in Iraq and Syria
JCF	Jamaica Constabulary Force
JDF	Jamaica Defense Force
MENA	Middle East and North America
MSEZ	Multilateral Security Engagement Zone
OAS	Organization of American States
OECS	Organization of Eastern Caribbean States
PAHO	Pan American Health Organization
PWP	Problems Without Passports
SoE	State of Emergency

RSS	Regional Security System
SOUTHCOM	United States Southern Command
TG	Tivoli Gardens
TTDF	Trinidad and Tobago Defense Force
TTPS	Trinidad and Tobago Police Service
UNODC	United Nations Office on Drugs and Crime
UWI	University of the West Indies
WHO	World Health Organization
ZOSO	Zone of Special Operations

Challenged Sovereignty

Contexts and Concepts

1

Probing Problems Without Passports

Our world is more interdependent than ever. Borders have
become more like nets than walls, and while this means
that wealth, ideas, information and talent can move freely
around the globe, so can the negative forces shaping
our shared fates. The financial crisis that started in the
U.S. and swept the globe was further proof that—for
better and for worse—we can't escape one another.
—Bill Clinton, "The Case for Optimism"

It is true that criminal activities surged and became global
in the 1990s. But thinking about international illicit trade
as just another manifestation of criminal behavior misses
a larger, more consequential, point. Global criminal
activities are *transforming the international system*,
upending the rules, creating new players, and configuring
power in international politics and economics.
—Moisés Naím, *Illicit: How Smugglers, Traffickers,
and Copycats Are Hijacking the Global Economy*

In the preface to the *World Drug Report* of 2000, the late, respected U.N.
secretary-general Kofi Annan observed, "Globalization offers the human race
unprecedented opportunities. Unfortunately, it also enables many anti-social
activities to become 'problems without passports'" (Annan 2000, i). Drugs,
crime, terrorism, and cyber threats are among the Problems Without Passports,
hereafter called PWPs. The PWPs are transnational issues that disdain political
authority and territorial boundaries of states and threaten the safety and security of individuals and groups within states, thereby impacting the sovereignty
of states. The term "Passports" is hugely symbolic, as passports are the official
travel instruments that states use to facilitate legal ingress and egress, thereby

exercising authority over their sovereign jurisdictions. This book examines the manifestation of drugs, crime, terrorism, and cyber threats as PWPs in the Caribbean and the way in which they undermine the authority of Caribbean states, presenting a circumstance of *challenged sovereignty* in the process.

Drugs, crime, terrorism, and cybercrime surely are not the only PWPs of concern to the international community.[1] This is evident from the coronavirus pandemic that has ravaged the global commons, with its myriad deleterious consequences for societies rich and poor, large and small, and geopolitically potent and impotent (see Al-Marashi 2020; Nye 2020; Marder 2020). In his March 3, 2020, *New York Times* op-ed, a philosopher at Spain's University of the Basque Country captured this reality trenchantly in noting that we live in an interconnected world, where borders are porous, more like living membranes than physical walls (Marder 2020). Indeed, in September 2018, long before the advent of the pandemic, two scholar–policy wonks called attention to this harsh reality chillingly: "Consider that it takes only one infected carrier of bird flu to escape screening or detection at a train station or airport to transform a local health crisis into a global pandemic. As there are over 60 nonstop flights between China and the United States daily, with an estimated total of 30,000 passengers traveling between the two countries each day, this possibility is more than a remote and existential threat" (Monaco and Gupta 2018).

According to the Johns Hopkins University Coronavirus Resource Center, as of March 10, 2023, the world had endured 676,609,955 COVID-19 infections, which represents more than three times the 2023 population of Brazil and seventeen times that of Canada, and had suffered 6,881,955 fatalities, about the populace of Libya and five times that of Bahrain, because of it. The United States has the dubious distinction of being the country affected the most, with 103,804,262 infections and upward of one million deaths—1,123,836, to be exact.[2] In addition, speaking at a press conference in March 2021, World Health Organization (WHO) director general Tedros Adhanom Ghebreyesus revealed that "the COVID-19 pandemic has caused more 'mass trauma' than World War II" (Feuer 2021). In relation to the Caribbean, as we shall see in chapter 8, the pandemic has exacerbated the condition of challenged sovereignty. In June 2021, *Time* magazine reported that life expectancy in the USA fell by almost two years between 2018 and 2020, the steepest decline since 1943, when World War II was raging (see Szabo 2021). Surely, it fell elsewhere. Thus, the pandemic's global dimensions and collaborative imperatives have been evident. In fact, noted scholar-statesman Henry Kissinger (2020) captured some of the vicissitudes thus: "No country, not even the U.S., can, in a purely national effort, overcome the virus. Addressing the necessities of the moment must ultimately be coupled with a global collaborative vision and program. If we cannot do both in tandem, we will face the worst of each."

Yet, as former U.S. president Bill Clinton and influential thinker Moisés Naím rightly suggest in the epigraphs to this opening chapter, the PWP connections are not just functional; the contemporary global arena has a structural feature—interdependence—that makes it impossible for any state or society, in whatever part of the world, to escape the impact of significant international practices and pursuits, whether licit or illicit, and whether by design or default. The nature and impact of these PWPs are such that the very interstices of our global commons are affected, in both structural and functional terms. Their combined impact is such that they are "upending the rules, creating new players, and configuring power" nationally and internationally, to quote Naím. As will be seen below, this "upending" has both local and global implications. In addition to pondering some relevant local-global implications, this chapter delineates the aims of this study and then outlines the nature and scope of each of the following chapters.

Local-Global Nexus

What the former top U.N. official called PWPs the late respected scholar James Rosenau called "interdependence issues," positing:

> Where political agendas used to consist of issues that governments could cope with on their own or through interstate bargaining, now these conventional issues are being joined by challenges that by their very nature do not fall exclusively within the jurisdiction of states and have rendered the Frontier increasingly porous. Six current challenges are illustrative: environmental pollution, currency crises, crime and the drug trade, terrorism, AIDS, and the flow of refugees. . . . Since these challenges are fueled by shrinking social and geographic distances, such problems can appropriately be called "interdependence" issues. (Rosenau 1997, 71)

Quite notably, he also suggested, "Given their diffuse, boundary-crossing structure, these types of issues are spawning a whole range of transnational associations that are furthering the density of the multi-centric world and, as a result, are likely to serve as additional challenges to the authority of states" (72).

Common Features and Cross-Continental Connections

There is copious evidence from across the global commons that the authority of states is increasingly being challenged by these PWPs or "interdependence issues," and this study provides incontrovertible evidence of this in relation to the Caribbean. Whether they are called PWPs or "interdependence issues," these challenges share several common features. Transnationality is one of them; PWPs cross national and regional spaces, paying little regard to physical, political, or legal boundaries; they neither seek nor respect passports. Multidimensionality is a second feature; interdependence issues have political, security, and other implications, and they span class, age, gender, and other categories. There is broad agreement across governmental, international governmental, and international nongovernmental constituencies about these features and about the severity of the challenges presented by the PWPs under discussion.

In the first respect, the annual *International Narcotics Control Strategy Report* (*INCSR*), which is published by the U.S. Department of State, makes this abundantly clear. On the international governmental side, *The World Drug Report*, which now is produced annually by the U.N. Office on Drugs and Crime, provides clear evidence of this. With regard to the international nongovernmental constituency, so does *The Alternative World Drug Report*, first published in 2012 by the Count the Costs initiative, which was launched in 2011 to commemorate the fiftieth anniversary of the 1961 U.N. Convention on Narcotic Drugs.[3] In relation to terrorism, *Country Reports on Terrorism*, which is produced by the U.S. Department of State, and the *Global Terrorism Index*, which is published by the Australia-headquartered Institute for Economics and Peace, are among reports that highlight the local-global nexus and the clear and present dangers involved. As for cybersecurity threats, the *Global Threat Intelligence Report*, produced by the Nippon Telegraph and Telephone Corporation; the *Global Threat Report*, which is published by CrowdStrike, a global cybersecurity firm; and the *State of Cybersecurity*, presented by the Computing Technology Industry Association, based in Illinois, are among reputable annual assessments that highlight the depth and breadth of the challenges faced by local and global constituencies.

The "flatness" of the world to which Thomas Friedman referred in his seminal book, *The World Is Flat*, involves not just technology, trade, transportation, communication, and other "positives" but also human trafficking, drug trafficking, the sale of human organs, and other transnational criminal "negatives." Indeed, quite ominously, his remark "Globalization 3.0 makes it possible for so many more people to plug and play, and you are going to see every color of the human rainbow take part" (2005, 11) is increasingly being played out in relation to drugs, crime, and other PWPs, as the studies cited above and other works show. For instance, *Transnational Crime and Global Security* captures many other PWPs, including maritime piracy, trade in antiquities, environmental crimes, and sex trafficking (see Reichel and Randa 2018).

Not unexpectedly, the local-global nexus involved in these PWPs long predated our current period, the second decade of the twenty-first century. One example from the 1990s that crossed the continents of Africa, Asia, and Europe will suffice; it was provided by Louise Shelley, a respected expert on the subject: "The drugs (hashish) originated in Pakistan and were delivered to the port of Mombasa (Kenya), where they were added to a cargo of tea and shipped to Haifa (Israel) by way of Durban (South Africa). At Haifa, the cargo was put on to a ship of a company that ships to Constanza (Romania) every fifteen days. From there, it was to have been shipped by an Israeli-Romanian company to Italy, via Bratislava (Slovakia)" (Shelley 1995, 472–73). As well, Shelley explained that the head of the network was a German citizen of Ugandan origin who worked for a Romanian company. This complex network was disclosed only because the perpetrators were apprehended in Constanza.

Closer to the present, the arrest on July 8, 2019, in São Paulo, Brazil, of two members of the 'Ndrangheta, a criminal organization headquartered in Calabria, in southern Italy, that traces back to the sixteenth century, further highlights the increasingly close partnership between the Italian mafia and Brazil's PCC (Primeiro Comando da Capital [First Capital Command]) and provides further evidence of transcontinental criminal links.[4] Brazilian federal police arrested Nicola and Patrick Assisi in São Paulo on suspicion of drug trafficking. Nicola Assisi is allegedly the 'Ndrangheta's main contact in South America and worked with the PCC to smuggle cocaine into Europe. *InSight Crime* investigations revealed that those arrests are only the most recent indications that the two groups closely coordinate drug trafficking activities. For instance, Brazilian authorities found that the head of the 'Ndrangheta's Pelle clan, Domenico Pelle, traveled to São Paulo at least twice between 2016 and 2017, during which he supposedly met with Gilberto Aparecido dos Santos, reportedly the top lieutenant of incarcerated PCC leader Marcos Willians Herbas Camacho. Quite notably, drug seizures in Brazil during the first six months of 2019 increased by more than 90 percent. Much of the cocaine seized was destined for Europe, where the 'Ndrangheta purportedly controls trafficking routes across considerable parts of that continent (Neves and Betancur 2019).

The discovery of the failed arms trafficking attempt in Senegal in January 2022 also revealed cross-continental dynamics in which the country's customs agency seized three containers of weapons worth US$5 million from a Guyana-flagged cargo vessel, the *MV Eolika*. The ship, with a Ukrainian crew, had made a refueling stop in Dakar, having made stops earlier in Italy and the Canary Islands. Inconsistencies in their customs declarations led to investigations that resulted in the detection of the weapons, which were destined for the Dominican Republic. Law enforcement investigations in Guyana later revealed that the ship's registration had been granted by the International Maritime Safety Agency of Guyana, a company that had been decertified in 2021 by the country's maritime regulatory agency, the Maritime Administration (MARAD) of Guyana (*Guyana Times* 2022).

Closer to our unit of analysis—the Caribbean—two arms-trafficking cases from the late 1980s also highlight the criminality local-global nexus; together, they crossed the continental divides of Asia, Europe, and North America. In the first case, a ten-ton shipment of arms with an estimated value of J$8 million (US$52,160) arrived in Jamaica on the way to Colombia in December 1988. The consignment, from the Heckler and Koch firm of West Germany, included 1,000 G3A3 automatic assault rifles, 250 HK21 machine guns, and 10 sixty-millimeter commando mortars with 600 high-explosive rounds. The planned operation involved Germans, Englishmen, Panamanians, Colombians, and Jamaicans. Interrogation of some of the conspirators in January 1989 revealed that the arms were destined for the Revolutionary Armed Forces of Colombia (FARC). The operation had been underwritten by Colombian cocaine dealers who financed FARC. The arms had been paid for from the proceeds of a special drug shipment made earlier to Europe. The affair ended later that month when the arms were placed on a Colombian military aircraft and sent to Bogotá. The foreigners were extradited, and the Jamaicans were held on several charges.

Even more dramatic was the case involving Antigua-Barbuda. In December 1989 the Colombian police killed two Medellín cartel leaders: Gonzalo Rodríguez Gacha and his son Freddy. One of the raids made on the cartel's properties uncovered hundreds of Israeli-made Galil rifles, with ammunition. Colombia sought an explanation from Israel. The disclosure by Israel that the weapons had been part of a larger sale to the Antigua-Barbuda Defense Force (ABDF) led to a Colombian diplomatic protest to Antigua-Barbuda. As the matter developed, it became clear that both domestic and foreign aspects had to be probed.

Consequently, there was an extensive public inquiry by British jurist Louis Blom-Cooper. He uncovered an unbelievable scheme involving Israelis (one posing as an agent of the Antiguan government), Antiguans, Panamanians, Colombians, and United States citizens. The weapons had been shipped from Haifa, Israel, to Antigua. They never actually entered Antigua; while the first ship was in port, they were transferred to another ship and taken to Colombia, the real destination. The twin-island Antigua and Barbuda was merely the cover. Incidentally, the arms smuggling was only part of a larger scheme; the other part was to create a mercenary training outfit using the ABDF as organizational cover.[5]

Intelligence reports and the seizures of drugs and arrest of traffickers have revealed numerous instances of drugs shipped from South America to Europe or Africa and back to the Caribbean for onward movement to the United States. Actually, Nigerians once cornered the circuitous trafficking market, moving drugs from South America to Africa to Europe—or to Europe and then

Africa—and then to the Caribbean for onward shipment to the United States, or from South America to Europe and directly to the Caribbean and then to North America. Consequently, trafficking suspicions were raised in parts of Latin America whenever foreigners of African descent were seen at airports or seaports or in remote parts of the country. Elsewhere I recounted the full details of my experience in this regard in Ecuador in the mid-1990s (Griffith 1997, 90–91). Here are the core aspects of the experience.

I had gone to Quito for a European Union–Rio Group conference on security in November 1996 and was heading back to the United States the day before Thanksgiving. After checking in at the American Airlines ticket counter at the Mariscal Sucre International Airport, I headed toward the immigration control area. Two undercover narcotics police officers then approached me. They discreetly flashed their badges, introduced themselves, asked for my passport, and then "invited" me for an "inspection" in the airport's police outpost. They took possession of my luggage and led me to the police outpost, which was ensconced in the mezzanine of the building. I was "handed over" to the commanding officer on duty, a boyish but courteous individual who appeared to be in his mid- to late twenties. He took the passport and examined it. There was a distinct facial expression of relief when he saw that it was a United States passport. (There was an additional expression of relief later when he saw my official conference invitation letter.)

The commanding officer posed five questions: Where did I live? How long had I been in Ecuador? Did I go outside of Quito? Where had I stayed in the city? Was I there as a tourist, or for business? My responses were: Miami. Three days. No, only Quito. Hotel Oro Verde. Business. Next they conducted a body search—thankfully, not a strip search. This was followed by the luggage search. I had only two pieces of luggage: a flight attendant's bag and a briefcase. Two of the officers started searching them simultaneously. However, I objected and insisted on the right to observe the inspection of each piece one at a time. I was not prepared to risk having any drugs "found" in my luggage. The commanding officer readily agreed, and the search proceeded uneventfully. Afterward I asked the commanding officer why I had been singled out for the inspection. He was diplomatic in explaining some of the then fairly new realities of circuitous drug smuggling through Ecuador. It was obvious to me that smuggler profiling was in play; I am of African descent, was traveling lightly, and was taking the first flight of the day to Miami. Thus, my presence sent a red flag up their counternarcotics flagpole.

Undoubtedly, the globalization bonds have been tightened since the 1990s, constraining the ability of many states and societies to resist entanglements. This has increased their vulnerability to a myriad of internal and external challenges. Suzette Haughton's splendid analysis of the Jamaican situation is instructive, and not just for Jamaica: "As Jamaica's case firmly depicts, increased and cheaper accesses to communication, transportation, and information technologies continue to be the core processes making it easy for drugs to enter external markets. These aspects of globalization have caused law enforcers not to win the overall war on drugs, though some successes have been registered including the arrest of Jamaican drug kingpins" (Haughton 2011, 221).

These PWPs or interdependence issues present a myriad of difficulties for states the world over. However, for states that are small and subordinate, such as those in the Caribbean, they often do more than precipitate "anti-social activities"; they also undermine security and sovereignty. In fact, as Jarat Chopra and Thomas Weiss once contended, "Whether the power structure of sovereign states ever accurately reflected textbook characteristics, sovereignty is no longer sovereign; the world has outgrown it" (Chopra and Weiss 1992, 104). Thus, the harsh reality is that sovereignty is not sovereign. Indeed, as will be argued later, the sovereignty of Caribbean countries had already been compromised—from their birth as nations. The threats posed by drugs, crime, and other PWPs have been exacerbating their vulnerability, pushing their ships of security into turbulent seas and presenting a circumstance of challenged sovereignty. Thus, sadly, the Caribbean, a region of small and subordinate states, is a good candidate for empirical analysis of these interdependence issues that confront states and societies the world over. The following section outlines the approach to pursuing this undertaking.

Aims and Approach

In contributing to the analysis of the PWPs in the Caribbean, this study offers an appreciation of contemporary drugs, crime, terrorism, and cyber realities and explains their impact on security and sovereignty. It provides a regional assessment of the interrelationships and the implications of those interrelationships for state sovereignty in the region. In pursuit of this overall objective, this study does the following:

- Outlines relevant conceptual perimeters of the notions of vulnerability and security.
- Probes some relevant conceptual aspects of sovereignty and postulates the notion of challenged sovereignty.
- Examines some contemporary manifestations and consequences of four Problems Without Passports—the drug phenomenon, crime, terrorism, and cyber threats.
- Analyzes the impact on security and sovereignty of the linkages between drugs and crime, with special attention to the 2010 Christopher "Dudus" Coke saga in Jamaica and the 2011 State of Emergency in Trinidad and Tobago, controversial cases with region-wide salience.

- Probes the nexus between geonarcotics and geopolitics, focusing on Suriname, where the 2010 election of a former coup maker, who also had the dubious distinction of being the world's only head of state with a drug trafficking conviction and sentence (in absentia), prompted concerns about the prospects of a narco state being established in Suriname.
- Ponders the following consequential question: "How secure is security, and how sovereign is sovereignty in the Caribbean?"

Literature and Lacuna

As might be expected, there is a mixed profile of book-length scholarly works on the PWPs under consideration over the last few decades in terms of number and analytic heft. For instance, there is *Crime and Criminal Justice in the Caribbean* (Harriott, Braithwaite, and Wortley 2004); *Caribbean Drugs: From Criminalization to Harm Reduction* (Klein, Day, and Harriott 2004); *Caribbean Maritime Security* (M. Morris 1994); *Security Problems and Policies in the Post-Cold War Caribbean* (Rodríguez Beruff and García Muñiz 1996); *Drugs and Security in the Caribbean* (Griffith 1997); *From Pirates to Drug Lords* (Desch, Domínguez, and Serbin 1998); *Security in the Caribbean Basin* (Tulchin and Espach 2000); *The Political Economy of Drugs in the Caribbean* (Griffith 2000); *Caribbean Security in the Age of Terror* (Griffith 2004); *Crime, Delinquency, and Justice* (Deosaran 2007); *Policing the Caribbean* (Bowling 2010); *Cocaine Trafficking in the Caribbean and West Africa in the Era of Mexican Cartels* (Figueira 2012); *Gangs in the Caribbean* (Seepersad and Bissessar 2013); *Crime, Violence, and Security in the Caribbean* (Izarali 2018); and *Managing New Security Threats in the Caribbean* (Chami et al. 2022). Interestingly, too, although *The Military of the Caribbean* (Phillips 2022) is not an examination of any of the PWPs per se, the author shows how the armed forces in the region have been used to battle two of them—notably, drugs and crime.

This outstanding body of work is complemented by equally exceptional country-specific studies, such as *Cocaine and Heroin Trafficking in the Caribbean: The Case of Trinidad and Tobago, Jamaica, and Guyana* (Figueira 2004); *The Cuban Connection: Drug Trafficking, Smuggling, and Gambling in Cuba from the 1920s to the Revolution* (Sáenz Rovner 2009); *Drugged Out: Globalization and Jamaica's Resilience to Drug Trafficking* (Haughton 2011); *Crime and Security in Trinidad and Tobago* (Randy Seepersad and Dianne Williams 2016); and *Citizenship on the Margins* (Y. Campbell 2018). Expectedly, the Caribbean also has featured in works on the Americas or on Latin America, such as *The Future of Inter-American Relations* (J. I. Domínguez 1999); *Transnational Crime in the Americas* (Farer 1999); *The Political Economy of the Drug Industry* (Vellinga 2004); *Trafficking, Organized Crime, and Violence in the Americas Today* (Bagley and Rosen 2017); and *Transnational Organized Crime in Latin America and the Caribbean* (Ellis 2018). Moreover, as indicated earlier, there are many reports by governmental agencies and international organizations.

The studies cited above probe one or a few of the PWPs under discussion. This work fills a lacuna in becoming the first single-authored study to examine the four most troubling PWPs in the Caribbean—drugs, crime, terrorism, and cyber threats—and their implications for security and sovereignty in the region. It is guided by the view that understanding the dynamics of security and sovereignty in the contemporary Caribbean requires pondering the clear and present dangers presented by these PWPs, which fall within the realm of nontraditional security. This is not to suggest, though, that traditional security matters, such as territorial disputes and geopolitics, are no longer relevant.

As is explained fully in chapter 2, my approach to security views it as *protection and preservation of a people's freedom from external military attack and coercion, from internal subversion, and from the erosion of cherished political, economic, and social values.* Thus, security is multidimensional, with military, political, and other dimensions, and it requires paying attention to both traditional issues, such as territorial disputes and geopolitical anxieties, and nontraditional ones. With regard to sovereignty, the point also is made in the same chapter that sovereignty is viewed from many lenses: as international legal sovereignty, Westphalian sovereignty, and domestic or positive sovereignty, among other things. I contend that however viewed, sovereignty in the Caribbean is negatively impacted—that the combined impact of the PWPs has created a condition where security is undermined and sovereignty is challenged.

Security is viewed as being concerned both with threats to the political and territorial integrity of the state, also called national defense, and with the well-being of individual and corporate citizens—known also as public security or citizen security. Several Caribbean nations face traditional security challenges, especially border and territorial disputes. Jamaica, Guyana, Suriname, Haiti, Bahamas, Dominican Republic, Belize, Antigua-Barbuda, and Dominica are among countries with such disputes.[6] But both perception and reality have changed over the decades such that nontraditional challenges, drugs and crime among them, are more salient now for most Caribbean countries than the traditional ones.

Commendation and Condemnation

To be sure, there is consensus among scholars, policy makers, and security practitioners across the region that PWPs constitute the most significant nontraditional threats. Thus, the assertion by Jorge Domínguez in 1998 still is salient decades later: "The most common sources of insecurity in the Caribbean affect the quotidian experiences of ordinary people" (Domínguez 1998, 2). The combination of fear and frustration of ordinary citizens over their experiences with drugs and crime was voiced powerfully and candidly by Lady Allen, the wife of the Jamaican governor-general in April 2013, when she declared, "Yesterday (Tuesday, April 11) morning when I woke up I didn't want to be a Jamaican. I must be honest with you. And the reason is, there is a security [officer] I had at King's House when I went there by the name of Sergeant Simpson. He was one of the best security persons I have met and when I got the news that he was gunned down, I didn't want to be in Jamaica anymore" (Hines 2013). As might be expected, her remark created a firestorm, with citizens and groups voicing both condemnation and commendation over her candor. Understandably, Lady Allen's sentiment is shared by citizens across the region.

A few days later the firestorm winds shifted with some utterances by then–minister of national security Peter Bunting. In his April 13, 2013, speech to the Thirteenth Annual Prayer and Thanksgiving Service for the country's security forces, the minister observed:

> I think that after 15 months I am convinced that the best efforts of the security forces, by itself, will not solve the crime problem in Jamaica. But it is going to take divine intervention, touching the hearts of a wide cross section of the society and using as the instruments of divine intervention the Ministers' Fraternals, the academics, the business community, those persons who work in the NGO (non-governmental organization) community, those of us who are in political service—all to try to make an impact, to touch the hearts and minds of our fellow Jamaicans. . . . I am going through a kind of a dark night of the soul. (*Jamaica Observer* 2013)

The firestorm that erupted led the minister to clarify what he really meant, prompted calls for his resignation, and evoked strong views from political, corporate, and civic sections of the society (see Nelson 2013).

Understandably, part of the firestorm caused by the utterances of Lady Allen and Minister Bunting derived from the fact that, although citizens sympathized with them on a personal, human level, their expressions revealed a certain amount of fatalism that undermined citizens' confidence in their authority individually—although Lady Allen exercised more symbolic than substantive authority—and in the authority of the state that they represented. Of course, this reality has region-wide resonance.

Clearly, the changing dynamics of nations' clear and present dangers are not limited to the Caribbean; real-world circumstances have necessitated redefinition of concepts, policies, and programs elsewhere too. For instance, in relation to the Americas, the final U.S. Institute for National Strategic Studies *Strategic Assessment* before the turn of the current century offers some prescient observations: "The international security system emerging in the Americas at the end of the [twentieth] century de-emphasizes the need to balance power against other states, perfect military deterrence, or seek collective defense arrangements against threats from outside the hemisphere. This approach to security has been eclipsed by threats to the domestic order challenging the state's ability to hold the country together and to govern" (U.S. Institute for National Strategic Studies 2000, 178). Moreover, they discerned three categories of threats: (1) natural disasters; (2) domestic threats, such as poverty, socioeconomic inequality, crime and violence, and illegal migration; and (3) threats from private actors, including terrorists, international organized crime, including the trafficking of drugs, weapons, and humans, and private armies.

The Rest of the Book

This book examines some of the multidimensional and localized issues relative to the Caribbean that cut across the second and third categories identified in the *Strategic Assessment* in the manner outlined below.

Chapters and Constituencies

Chapter 2 pursues two main tasks. First, it clarifies the contextual usage of the terms "vulnerability," "security," and "sovereignty." Second, it postulates the notion of "challenged sovereignty." Overall, the chapter sets the conceptual foundation for the rest of the book. Chapter 3 analyzes some of the contemporary manifestations of the drama of drugs. First, I offer a brief explanation of the geonarcotics framework, for two reasons. The first is to reintroduce the framework as a useful heuristic device to study the drugs phenomenon. The second is to enable readers to understand the conceptual milieu in which I am probing drugs as a PWP, although I do not purport to offer an empirical application of the geonarcotics framework. I then explain how the region's physical and social geography conduces to trafficking.[7] This is followed by a summary portrait of the contemporary reality and then by a discussion of some legalization and decriminalization endeavors by several nations and by the CARICOM (Caribbean Community) Commission on Marijuana.

Next, chapter 4 examines the crucible of crime, which severely affects the everyday experiences of ordinary citizens and the essentials of statehood. The focus is on homicides, as these are the ultimate crimes and have powerful public security, economic, and other consequences. I demonstrate there that States of Emergencies have allowed for powerful spotlights to be shone on both criminality and challenges to state authority by criminals. I also probe some of the economic and social costs involved and a number of the civilizational implications, including the horrible conditions of some prisons, and the corruption and impunity of some public authority officials.

The PWPs under consideration vary in the period of time over which they have presented themselves as clear and present dangers in the Caribbean region. Drugs and crime have had a decades-old impact; terrorism and cyber challenges have been of more recent vintage. Chapter 5 examines the nature and scope of the terrorism and cyber challenges, which have geopolitical and geoeconomic ramifications. Special attention is paid to Trinidad and Tobago in relation to the terrorism PWP, as this twin-island republic once was considered the epicenter of terrorism-related dynamics in the region. The vulnerability to cyber threats is demonstrated and several cyberattacks are identified. Chapter 6 delves into two controversial cases where guns and gangs featured prominently and that pushed countries to the edge of their security and sovereignty precipices: the 2010 Christopher "Dudus" Coke saga in Jamaica and the 2011 State of Emergency in Trinidad and Tobago. Indeed, it was the dramatic nature and aftermath of these two cases that initially prompted me to ponder the question that is addressed in chapter 8: "How secure is security, and how sovereign is sovereignty in the Caribbean?"

The penultimate section, chapter 7, examines the situation in Suriname, where Desi Bouterse's return to power in May 2010, this time democratically, raised anxieties in some quarters about matters in the realm of both geonarcotics and geopolitics. After detailing the political resurgence of Desi Bouterse in the context of Suriname's political system, the chapter examines some of the country's geonarcotics involvement. I explain why the speculation that Bouterse would facilitate Suriname becoming a narco state was implausible and examine the dynamics of Suriname's relationship with Guyana in relation to their maritime and territorial disputes. Finally, I discuss Bouterse's November 2019 conviction for the murder of fifteen political opponents in 1982 and his political demise following the May 2020 elections.

The final chapter considers the question "How secure is security, and how sovereign is sovereignty in the Caribbean?" I conclude that the drugs, crime, terrorism, and cyber challenges present threats that undermine the security and sovereignty of Caribbean states, and I show the manifestations of this. One is by contributing to increased violence that challenges the monopoly on the use of force, creates climates of fear, and stresses and stretches military, police, and judicial capabilities. A second is by enabling criminal entrepreneurs to violate sovereignty by penetrating territory with impunity and undermining normal internal governance by necessitating the introduction of extreme governance measures, such as States of Emergency, which restrict civil and political rights.

In light of the significance of the Christopher "Dudus" Coke case and the centrality of the extradition treaty between Jamaica and the United States to the case, I thought it useful to provide the text of that treaty. Curiously, although there has been considerable media publicity across the world and many official statements within and beyond Jamaica about the Christopher Coke saga, the treaty that has been a key element of the saga has been a publication rarity.[8] It appears as the appendix. It also is noteworthy that, as stated by President Ronald Reagan in his April 17, 1984, ratification Letter of Transmittal to the U.S. Senate, "The Treaty is the first modern United States extradition treaty within the Caribbean region." As such, it has served as a model for treaties with other Caribbean nations and, indeed, as a model for agreements with countries in other regions.

Of course, Jamaica is not the only Caribbean nation with an extradition treaty with the United States. Moreover, it is not the only Caribbean state that has had extradition disagreements with the United States. It is reasonable to suggest that given the scope and severity of the drug and crime threats, extradition treaties will continue to be needed, and parties to them likely will disagree about aspects of their execution occasionally. As well, although Caribbean countries do have extradition treaties with nations other than the United States, the United States is both the most significant nation with which Caribbean countries have counternarcotics and counter-crime engagements and the one with the most extensive set of treaties on those matters. Thus, I consider it valuable to name the countries that have extradition treaties with the United States as of June 2022, with some basic details.[9] The countries appear in table 1.1.

The nature and implications of the issues examined in this book, their national security salience, the attention to both policy and operational matters, and the book's region-wide geographic ambit combine to make this study appealable to various constituencies. Students, scholars, and policy makers within and outside the Caribbean interested in the region's PWPs and security constitute one community. Military and law enforcement practitioners in the Caribbean and in the United States, Canada, Britain, the European Union, and China—countries with national security interests in the region—comprise a second audience. Scholars and policy wonks across the Americas who are concerned with security and sovereignty matters in the Caribbean and in other small states comprise a third group. Additionally, the book should interest policy and operational staffs in nongovernmental organizations and international agencies—such as the U.N. Office on Drugs and Crime, the Organization of American States, and the Caribbean Community Implementation Agency for Crime and Security (IMPACS)—that worry about PWPs and state sovereignty in the region and elsewhere. The book also should attract the interest of policy and operational personnel of U.S. government entities with mandates and missions related to the security of the region. Notable here is the U.S. Southern Command. As well, this book likely will attract the attention of students and professors in security studies programs within the region, such as at the Caribbean Military Academy, based in Jamaica, and those outside it, such as at the William Perry Center for Hemispheric Defense Studies, in Washington, DC.

TABLE 1.1 Bilateral Extradition Treaties between Caribbean Countries and the United States

Country	Date Signed	Entered into Force
Antigua and Barbuda	June 3, 1996	July 1, 1999
Bahamas	March 9, 1990	September 22, 1994
Barbados	February 28, 1996	March 3, 2000
Belize	March 30, 2000	March 27, 2001
Cuba	April 6, 1904	March 2, 1905
Dominica	October 10, 1996	May 25, 2000
Dominican Republic	June 19, 1909	August 2, 1910
Grenada	May 30, 1996	September 14, 1999
Guyana[a]	December 22, 1931	June 24, 1935
Haiti	August 9, 1904	June 28, 1905
Jamaica	June 14, 1983	July 7, 1991
Saint Kitts and Nevis	September 18, 1996	February 23, 2000
Saint Lucia	April 18, 1996	February 2, 2000
Saint Vincent and the Grenadines	August 15, 1996	September 8, 1999
Suriname[b]	June 2, 1887	July 11, 1889
Trinidad and Tobago	March 4, 1996	November 29, 1999

Notes: (a) Executed by the United Kingdom of Great Britain, of which Guyana was then a colony; (b) Executed by the Kingdom of the Netherlands, of which Suriname was then a colony.

Source: U.S. Department of State, Extradition Treaties, https://www.state.gov/treaties-in-force/.

In applying his Fragmegration Theory to the Caribbean, James Rosenau observed that "hurricanes are not the only intruders" (see Desch, Domínguez, and Serbin 1998). His remark resonates more powerfully now in the early 2020s than when it first was expressed in the late 1990s. Indeed, most Caribbean countries have reason to worry equally about "the 'enemy' within" and "intruders" from the outside. Over the last few decades, the region has been living some incredible PWP experiences, in both negative and positive terms. The Christopher "Dudus" Coke affair has been one of the negative experiences. It was a political-security volcano that reverberated beyond the geographic confines of Tivoli Gardens, as will be seen in chapter 6. Drugs-driven corruption and police impunity also are among the negatives. One positive was the dismantling in September 2019 of the drug syndicate based in the Dominican Republic with the arrest of César Emilio Peralta, known as "El Abusador," and two dozen other major operatives. Also noteworthy is the sentencing in Florida in February 2022 of eight members of a notorious Puerto Rico–based drug trafficking organization to a combined fifty-six years in prison (see Asmann 2019; U.S. Department of Justice 2022). Initiatives by CARICOM IMPACS also warrant entry on the positive side of the balance sheet.[10]

Perhaps many readers of this book will have read about or been witness to some of the developments considered here, although others will not have connected the sundry security and sovereignty dots in ways that allow appreciation of the gravity of the region's overall situation. In addition to bearing witness, I have had the opportunity to interpret some of the developments in media interviews and academic lectures in the United States and the Caribbean over the years. Plus, the invitation to deliver the Thirteenth Annual Eric Williams Memorial Lecture at Florida International University, where I once served as a professor and a dean for more than a decade, provided an opportunity to ponder some of the drugs and crime issues. We turn next to the theoretical and conceptual underpinnings of this study, which I hope readers find as much pleasure in reading as I derived in writing it.

2

Understanding Security and Sovereignty

It is almost no longer controversial to say that traditional
conceptions of security were (and in many minds still
are) too narrowly founded. That advance does not,
however, mean that consensus exists on what a more
broadly constructed conception should look like.

—Barry Buzan, *People, States, and Fear*

All this adds up to a world that is not fully sovereign. But nor
is it one of either world government or anarchy. The world
35 years from now will be semi-sovereign. It will reflect the
need to adapt legal and political principles to a world in
which the most serious challenges to order come from what
global forces do to states and what governments do to their
citizens rather than from what states do to one another.

—Richard Haass, "Sovereignty"

Political scientist James Rosenau once counseled, "We need to start afresh,
to relax in our gardens, emulate [Isaac] Newton and ponder the scene around
us, allowing ourselves to be puzzled by those recurring patterns that seem self-
evident but that somehow have never been adequately explained" (Rosenau
1980, 237). The wisdom of this observation extends beyond the arena of foreign
policy, where the observation first was made, to security studies and other
arenas. Indeed, it should be welcome by scholars in every social science field.
Rosenau's comment assumes added value when one is dealing with an area with
significant "real world" policy implications regarding security and sovereignty,
and where the changing dynamics of domestic and international politics have
so affected the terms of intellectual engagement that rethinking of core concepts
and central assumptions is not merely desirable but necessary.

The decolonization movement that followed the end of World War II gave a boost to the rethinking about "sovereignty," and the end of the Cold War witnessed significant efforts to redefine "security" as a core concept, as Barry Buzan infers in the first epigraph to this chapter. Moreover, globalization dynamics, including Problems Without Passports, and technological innovation prompted rethinking about the status of "sovereignty," such that Richard Haass predicts its progressive denudement. Many scholars continued, and some began, to do precisely what Rosenau suggested—revisit concepts and theories, reexamine threats and vulnerabilities, review puzzles and patterns, and re-estimate the utility of and necessity for extant strategies. Adopting Rosenau's advice, this chapter clarifies the use of the term "vulnerability" and explains the contextual usage of two concepts that are central to this study: security and sovereignty. In addition, it postulates the notion of "challenged sovereignty."

Understanding Vulnerability and Security

Distinguished Caribbean novelist and poet George Lamming, who passed to the Great Beyond in June 2022 at age ninety-four, once declared, "The architecture of our future is not only unfinished; the scaffolding has hardly gone up." Evidently from table 2.1, the region's scaffolding reflects intra-regional asymmetries. For instance, Cuba, the Dominican Republic, Haiti, and Jamaica are territorial and population "giants" compared to St. Kitts–Nevis, Grenada, Barbados, and other countries. As well, several countries lie outside the conventional population definition of a small state—one with a population of 1.5 million or less (see Commonwealth Advisory Group 1997, 9). Moreover, in his welcome address to the July 2012 CARICOM Summit held in St. Lucia, Prime Minister Kenney Anthony noted the following in relation to the fifteen-member (and five associate members) CARICOM group: "Ours is a peculiar region with great disparities in size and scale. One state, Haiti, represents 57 percent of our population; two states, Trinidad and Jamaica, 53 percent of our economy; Guyana and Suriname combined are 81 percent of our land mass; Saint Lucia, 50 percent of Nobel Prizes" (Anthony 2012). Nonetheless, overall, the characterization of the region as one comprising small states is more than justified. For these reasons and more, as Winston Dookeran (2022), scholar and erstwhile minister of finance and of foreign affairs of Trinidad and Tobago, aptly puts it, the Caribbean is a region "on the edge," with considerable stress in relation to its political stability, equality, and diplomacy. However, the region is more than just one of small states on the edge; it also is one of vulnerable states.

Vulnerability arises where geographic, political, economic, or other factors cause a nation's security to be compromised. Usually it is not a function of one factor but several, which combine to reduce or remove a state's influence or

TABLE 2.1 Some National Security Assets of Caribbean States

Country (Independence)	Size (km²)	Population	Armed Forces	Force Makeup	Police Force	GDP per Capita US$	Natural Resources
Anguilla (NA)	91	18,403 (2021 est.)	None	—	94 (2019)	12,200 (2017 est.)	None
Antigua-Barbuda (1981)	440	99,176 (2021 est.)	AF 180 RF 80 (2020)	G, CG	800 (2019)	18,000 (2020 est.)	None
Aruba (NA)	193	120,917 (2021 est.)	None[b]	—	481 (2020)	37,500 (2017 est.)	None
Bahamas (1973)	13,942	352,655 (2021 est.)	AF 1,500 (2020)	G, CG	2,749 (2019)	30,800 (2020 est.)	None
Barbados (1966)	430	301,865 (2021 est.)	AF 610+ RF 430 (2020)	G, CG	1,528+ (2019)	12,900 (2020 est.)	Oil, natural gas
Belize (1981)	22,960	505,633 (2021 est.)	AF 1,500 RF 700 (2020)	G, CG, AC	2,350 (2020)	6,100 (2020 est.)	Timber, oil
British Virgin Islands (NA)	150	37,891 (2021 est.)	None[a]	—	241 (2020)	34,200 (2017 est.)	None
Cayman Islands (NA)	264	63,131 (2021 est.)	None[a]	—	459 (2019)	73,600 (2019 est.)	None
Cuba (1902)	110,860	11,032,343 (2021 est.)	AF 38,000 YLA 70,000 (reservists) CDF 50,000 (reservists) Paramilitary 26,500 Territorial Militia 1,000,000 (reservists) (2020)	G, N, AC	Not Available	9,900 (2016 est.)	Oil, nickel, iron, cobalt
Dominica (1978)	750	74,584 (2021 est.)	None[1]	—	500+ (2019)	11,000 (2017 est.)	None
Dom. Republic (1844)	48,442	10,597,348 (2021 est.)	AF 56,050 RF 5,000 (2019)	G, N, AF	32,000 (2014)	17,000 (2020 est.)	Nickel, bauxite, gold, silver, copper

(continued)

TABLE 2.1 (continued)

Country (Independence)	Size (km²)	Population	Armed Forces	Force Makeup	Police Force	GDP per Capita US$	Natural Resources
French Guiana (NA)	90,909	290,691 (2020 est.)	None[c]	—	406 (2003)	18,313 (2017 est.)	Gold, kaolin, tantalum, oil
Grenada (1974)	345	113,570 (2021 est.)	None[2]	—	1,013+ (2020)	15,100 (2020 est.)	None
Guadeloupe (NA)	1,780	400,124 (2020 est.)	None[c]	—	660 (2003)	25,479 (2014 est.)	None
Guyana (1966)	214,970	787,971 (2021 est.)	AF 3,400 RF 670 (2019)	G, CG, AC	4,824 (2020)	18,700 (2020 est.)	Gold, diamonds, bauxite, timber, oil, gas, uranium
Haiti (1804)	27,750	11,198,240 (2021 est.)	None[3]	—	5,300 Interpol	2,800 (2020 est.)	Bauxite (no longer mined), gold
Jamaica (1962)	11,424	2,816,602 (2021 est.)	2,830 (2013)	G, CG, AC	11,500 (2020)	8,700 (2020 est.)	Bauxite, gypsum
Martinique (NA)	1,100	398,126 (2020 est.)	None[c]	—	603 (2003)	27,688 (2012 est.)	None
Montserrat (NA)	102	5,387 (2021 est.)	None[a]	—	89 (2019)	34,000 (2017 est.)	None
Puerto Rico (NA)	9,104	3,142,779 (July 2021 est.)	None[d]	—	11,600 (2020)	33,400 (2020 est.)	Nickel, copper
St. Kitts and Nevis (1983)	269	54,149 (July 2021 est.)	AF140+ RF 50 (2020)	G, CG	439+ (2019)	23,300 (2020 est.)	None
St. Lucia (1979)	616	166,637 (July 2020 est.)	None	—	1,200+ (2020)	12,300 (2020 est.)	None

TABLE 2.1 (continued)

Country (Independence)	Size (km²)	Population	Armed Forces	Force Makeup	Police Force	GDP per Capita US$	Natural Resources
St. Vincent and the Grenadines (1979)	388	101,145 (July 2021 est.)	None	—	1,000+ (2020)	12,100 (2020 est.)	None
Suriname (1975)	163,270	614,749 (July 2021 est.)	AF 1,840 (2019)	G, CG, AC	2,522 (2019)	16,100 (2020 est.)	Bauxite, timber, kaolin, gold, oil
Trinidad and Tobago (1962)	5,128	1,221,047 (July 2021 est.)	AF 4,050 (2019)	G, CG, AC	6,591 (2020)	23,700 (2020 est.)	Oil, LNG
Turks and Caicos (NA)	417	57,196 (July 2021 est.)	None[a]	—	301 (2019)	21,100 (2020 est.)	None
U.S. Virgin Islands (NA)	352	104,464 (July 2021 est.)	None[d]	—	581 (2019)	357,233 (2018 est.)	None

AC = Air Component (Air Force/Air Wing); AF = Active Forces; CDF = Civil Defense Force; CG = Coast Guard; G = Ground Forces; LNG = Liquified Natural Gas; N = Navy; NA = Not Applicable; RF = Reserve Forces; YLA = Youth Labor Army

+ = Member of the Regional Security System; a = Defense is the responsibility of the United Kingdom; b = Defense is the responsibility of the Kingdom of the Netherlands; c = Defense is the responsibility of France; d = Defense is the responsibility of the United States of America

Notes: (1) Dominica had an army from November 1975 to April 1981, when it was disbanded; (2) Grenada's People's Revolutionary Army was created in March 1979 and disbanded in October 1983, following the U.S. intervention; (3) The Haitian military was demobilized between November 1994 and April 1995, following Operation Restore Democracy in September 1994. However, in 2015 plans for re-establishment of a defense force were outlined in a white paper on security and defense, a plan was provided to ministers in September 2017, and in March 2018 an army high command was established. Ecuador and Brazil have pledged to assist with training the new army, which will have missions devoted to disaster relief and border security, with the initial five hundred troops having engineering and medical capabilities. However, as of February 2021 it was unclear whether the current budgetary provision was enough to fund the desired capability. (See International Institute for Strategic Studies 2021, 416.)

Sources: *The World Fact Book 2021* (for data on size, population, GDP, and natural resources), the World Factbook, CIA.gov, https://www.cia.gov/the-world-factbook/; Secretariat, Association of Caribbean Commissioners of Police (for data on police forces, except for Cuba, French Guiana, Guadeloupe, Martinique, Haiti, and the Dominican Republic); International Criminal Police Organization (INTERPOL) (for data on the police force of the Dominican Republic), https://www.interpol.int/Who-we-are/Member-countries/Americas/DOMINICAN-REPUBLIC/; International Institute for Strategic Studies, the Military Balance 2021, February 2021 (for data on armed forces and force makeup, except for St. Kitts and Nevis, which was provided by Major Gen. [Ret.] Stewart Saunders, National Advisor, St. Kitts and Nevis).

power, thereby opening it up to internal subversion or external incursion, among other things. Some writers argue that small states are "inherently vulnerable" because they can be perceived as potentially easy victims for external aggression (see, for example, Commonwealth Study Group 1985, 15). However, the perception of other states is merely part of the matter. Vulnerability also relates to objective geographic, economic, political, and organizational deficiencies, such as populations that are too small to meet security needs, have limited funds to acquire defense-related material, and have fragile economies.

It is easy to appreciate the reality of economic vulnerability. For instance, the region has some valuable natural resources, including oil, bauxite, silver, nickel, and gold. But these resources are spread very thinly across the region, as is evident from table 2.1. This limited resource base partly explains why Caribbean states have narrow economic bases of (a) agriculture (mainly sugar and bananas); (b) mining and manufacturing (notably bauxite, oil, gold, and nickel); and (c) services, mostly offshore finance, tourism, and call center business processing. It also explains the heavy reliance on remittances, notably from the diaspora in North America and Europe.

Caribbean vulnerability is not limited to the economic area, though. L. Erskine Sandiford, a former prime minister of Barbados, once eloquently described the structural and multidimensional nature of the region's vulnerability: "Our vulnerability is manifold. Physically, we are subject to hurricanes and earthquakes; economically, to market conditions taken elsewhere; socially, to cultural penetration; and now politically, to the machinations of terrorists, mercenaries, and criminals" (CARICOM Secretariat 1990, 6). Although more than three decades old, this description still resonates powerfully with the region's contemporary realities. More recently, Andy Knight probed the manifold vulnerabilities facing Caribbean states. In addition to placing the discussion in historical context of the slave trade, he examined the Cold War and post–Cold War threats, the globalization factor, and the vulnerabilities to natural disasters, the transiting of radioactive waste through the region, the drug trade, transnational crime, and homegrown violent extremism (Knight 2019). No doubt, vulnerability affects security.

Security in Context

The term "security" has long been a highly contested one, with a multiplicity of definitions and usages, most of which revolve around a few core concepts: international anarchy, survival, territorial integrity, and military power.[1] Moreover, the definitions mostly share a common theoretical foundation in traditional realism. Although there are different variants of realism, the common denominators are a focus on the state as the unit of analysis; stress on the competitive character of relations among states; and emphasis on military and, to a lesser extent, political aspects of security. The realist approach is oriented to the international arena, which sees states as national actors rationally pursuing their interests in that arena. It also considers military power capabilities as the most critical ones. Noteworthy too is that traditional realism pays attention mainly to "great powers" and views security as "high politics."

For most of the post–World War II period, there was wide consensus among political scientists and military theorists that traditional realist theory provided the appropriate conceptual architecture to examine questions of security. As might be expected, this paradigm was challenged but not concertedly. However, the dynamics of international politics since the end of the Cold War have led many scholars to pursue concerted journeys beyond the traditional realist paradigm in conceptualizing and probing security issues. Almost three decades ago, one scholar, himself an erstwhile proponent of realism, averred, "Realism, rooted in the experiences of World War II and the Cold War, is undergoing a crisis of confidence largely because the lessons adduced do not convincingly apply directly to the new realities. The broadened global agenda goes beyond what Realism can realistically be expected to address" (Kegley 1993, 141).

As might be expected, the tragedy of 9/11 has further undermined confidence in the utility of realism. The departure from sole reliance on traditional realism by Caribbean analysts predated the end of the Cold War, as works by Young and Phillips 1986; Bryan, Greene, and Shaw 1990; Griffith 1991; Griffith 1995a; and Rodríguez Beruff 2009 show. Understandably, then, analysis done since the end of the Cold War, such as Griffith 2004; Bowling 2010; McDavid 2011; and Chami et al. 2022, have made this even more obvious. Security in the Caribbean has never really been merely protection from military threats. It has not been just military hardware, although it has involved this; not just military force, although it has been concerned with it; and not simply conventional military activity, although it certainly has encompassed it.

For example, I have long defined security as "protection and preservation of a people's freedom from external military attack and coercion, from internal subversion, and from the erosion of cherished political, economic, and social values." As I explained in 1993 in *The Quest for Security in the Caribbean*, where the definition first was outlined, values include democratic choice and political stability in the political area, sustainable development and free enterprise in the economic domain, and social equality and respect for human rights in the social arena.

There is a plethora of literature on security—on theoretical, empirical, policy, and operational aspects. Consequently, there has been interchangeability of use and conflation of the terms "national security," "national defense," "public security," "human security," and "citizen security," by scholars, policy makers, and security practitioners. I support the approach by Douglas Kincaid and Eduardo Gamarra (1996, 12–13) that considers national defense as pertaining to the protection of the sovereignty and territorial integrity of the national state, largely from threats by foreign state and non-state actors; public security as pertaining to the maintenance of internal law and order; and citizen security as relating to the protection of the civil and political rights by people resident within the nation, both citizens and non-citizens. For me, national security encompasses all the other three—national defense, public security, and citizen security.

Thus, security is multidimensional, with military, political, economic, and other dimensions. But this approach is not merely academic prognostication; policy makers adopt it too. For example, one Eastern Caribbean national security minister contended:

> Security can no longer be achieved by merely building walls or forts. The very large and the very small states of this hemisphere have found that security, in an age of globalization, is rather complex. Security includes the traditional notions of yesteryear, but today, security must now be extended, in the case of small-island states, to encompass several non-traditional aspects. Natural disasters, for example, pose a greater threat to our security than does the loss of national territory to an enemy. (H. Simon 1998)

Moreover, as one Barbadian prime minister noted, and quite rightly, "It would be a fundamental error on our part to limit security concerns to any one area while the scourge of HIV/AIDS, illegal arms and drug trafficking, transnational crime, ecological disasters, and poverty continue to stare us in the face" (Arthur 2002, 3). Changing PWP dynamics also occasioned the need to further broaden the ambit of the concept. As Jamaican prime minister Andrew Holness remarked when he launched the Global Tourism Resilience and Crisis Management Centre in Montego Bay in January 2019, "Security no longer means protecting tourists against physical threats; it also means protecting people against cyber threats, including Internet frauds and identity thefts" (Davis 2019).

Over time, the multidimensional approach that long was embraced in the Caribbean has resonated with other parts of the Americas. Of significance in this respect is the October 2003 Organization of American States *Declaration on Security in the Americas*, which states: "The security threats, concerns, and other challenges in the hemispheric context are of diverse nature and multidimensional scope, and the traditional concept and approach must be expanded to encompass new and nontraditional threats, which include political, economic, social, health, and environmental aspects" (OAS 2003). The declaration was reinforced by the 2009 "Declaration of Commitment of Port-of-Spain," which was adopted at the Fifth Summit of the Americas, held in Trinidad and Tobago in April 2009. It reads in part: "We recognize the importance of addressing the threats, concerns and other challenges to security in the Hemisphere that are diverse, multidimensional in scope and impact on the well-being of our citizens. ... We therefore reaffirm our commitment to the Declaration on Security in the Americas" (U.S. Department of State 2009, 16).

The state is still the primary actor in the context of the international system, but the changing dynamics of international politics, the capability limitations of Caribbean states to adequately cope with those dynamics, and the matrix of issues and actors they face suggest the need to extend the actor matrix to include non-state actors. In this respect, Susan Strange's remark is quite apposite, and it extends beyond the area of international political economy where it was made: "Today it seems that the heads of governments may be the last to recognize that they and their ministers have lost the authority over national societies and economies they used to have" (Strange 1996, 1).

One influential security analyst has noted, "Only when one has a reasonable idea of both the nature of threats, and the vulnerabilities of the objects towards which they are directed, can one begin to make sense of national security as a policy problem" (Buzan 1991, 112). Of course, this raises a key question: What do we mean by "threat"? The two-decades-old definition by Richard Ullman has considerable explanatory utility and will be used for our purposes: "A threat to national security is an action or sequence of events that (i) threatens drastically and over a relatively brief span of time to degrade the quality of life for the inhabitants of a state, or (ii) threatens significantly to narrow the range of policy choices available to the government of a state or to private nongovernmental entities (persons, groups, corporations) within the state" (Ullman 1983, 133).

Given my earlier definition of security as having military, political, and other dimensions, it is understandable that I would view threats in commensurate terms. Thus, threats could be military, political, economic, or environmental. Because the use of military force against a state tends to present core threats by undermining national stability and sovereignty, military threats are generally viewed as the highest priority among threats in the various dimensions. Barry Buzan offers the sobering caution that since security has to be defined within a competitive environment, it is unwise to take the "easy route" of defining all threats as national security threats. I also agree with his suggestion that the difference between normal challenges and threats to national security necessarily occurs on a spectrum of threats that range from trivial and routine, through serious but routine, to drastic and unprecedented. And, he argues, where on the spectrum issues begin to get legitimately classified as national security problems is a matter of political choice rather than objective fact.

Threats are a function of subjective *and* objective factors. As Buzan observes, determination of when a threat becomes a national security matter depends on the kind of threat involved, how the state in question perceives it, and the intensity of the threat. He postulates that the key factors affecting the intensity of a threat are the specificity of its identity, its nearness in space and time, the weight of its consequences, and whether or not perceptions of the threat are enlarged by historical realities. Thus, "other things being equal, the more intense a threat, the more legitimate the invoking of national security as a response to it" (Buzan 1991, 134).

As with "security," the term "sovereignty" is highly contested. As such, it is necessary to contextualize its usage and highlight some relevant conceptual parameters. This is the task of the section that follows.

Understanding Sovereignty

Whether examined in theoretical, conceptual, or other terms, and irrespective of whether the context of use is philosophical, legal, or political, sovereignty has a multiplicity of descriptors and qualifiers, some of which are far from being terms of scholarly endearment. They include "the apparition of sovereignty," sovereignty as having "many faces," and sovereignty as akin to "organized hypocrisy." The late distinguished legal scholar Louis Henkin began a lecture at New York's Fordham Law School in 1999 with these words: "I don't like the 'S word.' Its birth is illegitimate, and it has not aged well. The meaning of 'sovereignty' is confused, and its uses are various, some of them unworthy, some even destructive of human values" (Henkin 1999, 1).

Key Elements

Whether or not one likes the "S word" is immaterial. Yet, Henkin is correct on some points; the literature on sovereignty is both voluminous and disputatious in relation to its historical and contemporary contexts and regarding its international legal or political aspects. Beyond this, I agree with Henkin that "in simpler days, state sovereignty implied several key elements. Primarily, it meant political interdependence. It also meant territorial integrity and virtually exclusive control and jurisdiction within that territory" (Henkin 1999, 2). In the context of things relevant to the Caribbean, several developments contributed to passage beyond "simpler days." One was decolonization, which gave rise to the birth of several independent states into a "brave new world" but with such small size and subordinate status in the international scheme of things that their sovereignty was compromised from "birth."

Globalization also has led to the end of "simpler days," impacting sovereignty in the Caribbean and elsewhere along the way. However, Raimo Väyrynen reminds us correctly that while "the recontextualization of sovereignty under conditions of globalization will gradually alter the rules of interstate behavior

. . . globalization is not an alternative to sovereignty, but it rather provides a new context in which it is embedded" (Väyrynen 2001, 234). But even before the advent of decolonization and the spread of globalization, discussions about sovereignty tended to focus on its international dimension: freedom from outside interference—in other words, that no authority is legally above a state except that which a state's leaders voluntarily confer on international bodies. Even so, many scholars and political elites accepted—and more so after decolonization—that a key aspect of sovereignty relates to a nation's internal dynamics. This aspect, called "positive sovereignty," pertains to state power holders not only being free from external interference but also having the ability to deliver "political goods" to citizens internally.

Positive sovereignty pertains to governance, and it entails having the economic, public security, psychological, and other capabilities to articulate and enforce public policy. As Robert Jackson argues, positive sovereignty enables states to take advantage of their independence. A government that is positively sovereign not only is able to enjoy rights of nonintervention but also has the ability to provide "political goods" for the society over which it exercises governance. Positive sovereignty includes having the economic, technical, military, psychological, and other capabilities to declare, implement, and enforce public policy, both domestic and foreign (Jackson 1990, 29).

Stephen Krasner, one of the scholars whose analysis has significantly advanced the contemporary discourse on sovereignty, has offered a four-dimensional categorization of sovereignty in his provocatively titled book *Sovereignty: Organized Hypocrisy*: (1) domestic sovereignty, referring to the organization of public authority within a state and to the level of effective control exercised by those holding authority; (2) interdependence sovereignty, referring to the ability of public authorities to control transborder movements; (3) international legal sovereignty, referring to the mutual recognition of states; and (4) Westphalian sovereignty, referring to the exclusion of external actors from domestic authority configurations (Krasner 1999). Moreover, elsewhere he has noted, "Conventional sovereignty assumes a world of autonomous, internationally recognized, and well governed states. Although frequently violated in practice, the fundamental rules of conventional sovereignty—recognition of juridically independent territorial entities and nonintervention in the internal affairs of other states—have rarely been challenged in principle" (Krasner 2001, 85). He then makes an assertion with considerable relevance to our unit of analysis: that these rules no longer work and that their inadequacies have had adverse consequences for both strong and weak states.

Writing in *Beyond Sovereignty*, Tom Farer offers the prescient observation that "while the practical necessities of interdependence eroded sovereignty from one side, the reality of power differentials hammered it from the other.

Yes, all sovereign units enjoyed an equal discretion to formulate, implement, and determine the circumference of public policy" (Farer 1996, 6). Moreover, we are reminded by Michael Fowler and Julie Bunck that "while sovereign states continue to coin and control currencies, oversee and regulate markets, and contribute funds to international institutions engaged in trade and finance, regional and global nonstate actors have taken on, and continue to take on, new and enterprising roles" (Fowler and Bunck 1995, 19).

Nevertheless, the scope of the authority and constraints are far more expansive than they suggest. The changing dynamics of the globalized environment, including the vicissitudes of the PWPs, make very attractive the prediction of Richard Haass: "Nation-states will not disappear, but they will share power with a larger number of powerful non-sovereign actors than ever before, including corporations, non-governmental organizations, terrorist groups, drug cartels, regional and global institutions, and banks and private equity funds" (Haass 2009, 1). Haas also argues that sovereignty will fall victim to the powerful and accelerating flow of people, ideas, drugs, viruses, emails, and weapons within and across borders, thereby challenging the ability of states to control what crosses their borders. Consequently, sovereign states will increasingly measure their vulnerability not to one another but to forces of globalization beyond their control.

Information technology and cyber innovation have taken the forces of globalization to new heights. Two Canadian scholars explained that after the revelations by Edward Snowden and WikiLeaks, many countries tried to protect their sovereignty and the sovereignty of their citizens by adopting laws and developing domestic technologies. For instance, Germany developed measures to counter U.S. surveillance of Angela Merkel's phone and email conversations, and Brazil and Canada worked toward creating more internet exchange points to redirect internet traffic outside of U.S. territory (see Couture and Toupin 2018, 5–6). As might be expected, states that are small and subordinate in the globalized world, like those in the Caribbean, are even more constrained by sovereignty.

And in a way that dramatizes how cyber challenges heighten the vulnerability of even the powerful United States, one military scholar observed:

> Imagine if 15 years ago a foreign analyst stated he could accomplish the following: (a) gain access to, and possibly alter, U.S. military plans; (b) monitor U.S. military operations and communications; (c) disable vital U.S. military command and control systems either immediately or at any chosen future moment; (d) target specific U.S. military personnel via their financial, medical, or family information; (e) seriously degrade, if not render wholly inoperable, some computer-dependent conventional weapons, thereby significantly negating the United States' conventional advantage; (f) strike at the United States'

critical infrastructure such as financial markets, power plants and grids, communication nodes, and transportation systems; and (g) achieve this all non-kinetically, without being physically present in the United States, leaving the United States unable to trace these activities back to the potential adversary's country generally, or its military specifically. Fifteen years ago, his superiors would probably have summarily dismissed this plan as too far-fetched. Yet today, due to the rapid maturity and expansion of cyberspace and the extent to which it increasingly permeates every aspect of society, potential enemies of the United States could possibly accomplish every one of the scenarios listed above. (Franzese 2009, 2)

Precisely because sovereignty is such a contested notion and is a central construct of this study, it is important to specify the working definition that will guide our analysis. Thus, sovereignty is used in this study to mean "the supreme authority of a state over itself, without any interference from foreign entities, unless expressly permitted by the state's authorized officials, that secures its territory and citizens and possesses the economic, technical, military, and other capabilities to promulgate and execute domestic and foreign policy."

Challenged Sovereignty

Mindful of the above working definition, I view challenged sovereignty as "a condition where the state's vulnerability is exacerbated by internal or external developments that compromise the ability of the supreme authority of the state to promulgate and execute domestic and foreign policy in its own deliberate judgment and on its own terms." It is a function of three conditions:

Condition 1 (C1): The authorized officials of a state can no longer effectively protect the territorial integrity of their state from intruders, whether such intruders are state or non-state actors and irrespective of whether the intruders aim to have a sustained presence in the jurisdiction in question or just transit it.

Condition 2 (C2): The authorized officials of a state face such capability constraints that they are compelled to rely on other states and on international agencies to underwrite public security equipment, training, and other resources and on a sustained basis, such that the absence of those resources jeopardizes the effective maintenance of public security or national defense.

Condition 3 (C3): The authorized officials of a state lack the requisite capabilities to exercise effective internal public order and external sovereign control, which necessitates reliance on external capabilities support that, in turn, risks further compromising the independence of their actions in promulgating and executing domestic and foreign policies and possibly aggravating the vulnerability of the state.

"Challenged sovereignty" might be captured as CS = Σ (C1 + C2 + C3), where CS is Challenged Sovereignty, C1 is Condition 1, C2 is Condition 2, and C3 is Condition 3. Although the conditions are numbered sequentially, there is no hierarchical relationship among them; the relationships are symbiotic. Moreover, all three conditions are required.

Understandably, challenged sovereignty is a circumstance that develops over time. Indeed, given the nature of state governance, the transnational dynamics of drugs, crime, terrorism, and cybercrime, the vicissitudes of bilateral and multilateral engagement to manage the PWPs, the stage setting for challenged sovereignty could take up to a decade to develop. Thus, challenged sovereignty is a structural condition, not just a functional one. As such, no single set of political and administrative elites by themselves is necessarily able to appreciably improve the situation. As this study will show, this is the reality of most Caribbean states. Undoubtedly, the Caribbean is not the only region where "challenged sovereignty" exists. Arguably, there are manifestations of it in Southeast Asia, Central America, the South Pacific, and the Persian Gulf. Importantly, too, "challenged sovereignty" lenses could be used to probe the circumstances of both regions and individual countries within a particular region.

In the context of the Caribbean, there is copious evidence to support the argument that "the experience of the Caribbean has been one in which the idea of sovereignty is conflated with a sense of self-determination, which in turn enjoys a relationship with that of nationalism" (L. Lewis 2013, 8). Linden Lewis is also quite persuasive in suggesting that "nationalism therefore is an important corollary of sovereignty in the Caribbean, and despite whatever crisis this phenomenon may be currently experiencing, it remains the last desperate shibboleth to hold onto for those who consider territory and belonging central to their identity and worldview" (8–9).

Long before scholar Linden Lewis, scholar-statesman Vaughan Lewis averred, "Sovereignty is an institutional fact; it is the right of self-determination that is expressed in this fact" (V. Lewis 1976, 229). Vaughan Lewis recognized the conditionalities involved given the global environment's tenuousness, though; he noted, "But the sovereign unit's relevant environment is constituted not simply of a set of institutional facts, but of processes which condition, determine, and change the content of these facts over time, and which are in turn changed by them" (229). As well, it is difficult to refute the contention that "the kind of state sovereignty for which the English-speaking Caribbean is wedded is, in fact, something of a chimera" (Bishop and Payne 2010, 13). Needless to say, this chimera ascription applies as well to the non-English-speaking Caribbean.[2]

Sociologist Anthony Maingot once remarked, "If it is a cliché that generals always fight the last war, it is equally true that civilian elites (including academics) tend to hold on to theories long after events have rendered them irrelevant" (Maingot 2000, 25). The statement often is true not only for theories but also for paradigms from which they spring and frameworks to which they give rise. Nonetheless, although revisiting theories and frameworks periodically is important, also crucial is the strategy for doing this. In this respect, it is important to ponder whether the strategy should be one of marginal adjustment or one of going back to the basics, as advocated by Rosenau (noted earlier).

This chapter has aimed at the latter, mindful of the proposition that scholars should have "the flexibility of mind to overturn old ways of looking at the world, to ask new questions, to revise designs appropriately, and then to collect more data of a different type than originally intended" (King, Keohane, and Verba 1994, 12). This chapter has been offered with flexibility in mind and with a view to posing new questions and sketching new designs in order to set the stage for data collection and analysis elsewhere. As will be seen later, the chapters that follow do ask new questions, sketch new designs, and present data in relation to some of the PWPs that affect the Caribbean and in relation to their security and sovereignty implications. The attention in the next chapter is on the first of the four PWPs of interest to us, the matter of drugs.

PART II

Problems Without Passports

3

The Drama of Drugs

Legalize it—don't criticize it
Legalize it and I will advertise it

Some call it tampee
Some call it the weed
Some call it Marijuana
Some of them call it Ganja

Singers smoke it
And players of instruments too
Legalize it, yeah, yeah
That's the best thing you can do

Doctors smoke it
Nurses smoke it
Judges smoke it
Even the lawyers too

It's good for the flu,
A good for asthma
Good for tuberculosis,
even umara composis[1]
—Peter Tosh, "Legalize It"[2]

As noted in chapter 1, Kofi Annan aptly characterized the illegal drug phenomenon as one of the world's "Problems Without Passports." These PWPs present multiple challenges that negatively impact citizens and states around the world. The *World Drug Report* for 2011 explained, "Despite increased attention to drug demand reduction in recent years, drug use continues to take a heavy toll. Globally, some 210 million people use illicit drugs each year, and almost 200,000 of them die from drugs. . . . Drug trafficking, the critical link between supply and demand, is fuelling a global criminal enterprise valued in the hundreds of billions of dollars that poses a growing challenge to stability and security" (U.N. Office on Drugs and Crime 2011b, 8). The assessment also notes that drug traffickers and organized criminals are forming transnational networks, sourcing drugs on one continent, trafficking them across another, and marketing them in a third. In some countries and regions, the value of the illicit drug trade far exceeds the size of the legitimate economy. Given the enormous amounts of money controlled by drug traffickers, they have the capacity to corrupt officials.

The situation had become worse by the time of the 2019 report: "In 2017, an estimated 271 million people, or 5.5 percent of the global population aged 15–64, had used drugs in the previous year, while 35 million people are estimated to be suffering from drug use disorders. Around 53 million people worldwide had used opioids in the previous year; these estimates are 56 percent higher than previously estimated. Among those people around 29 million had used opiates such as heroin and opium—these estimates are also 50 percent higher than previously estimated" (U.N. Office on Drugs and Crime 2019b, Booklet 1). The report also noted that in 2017, there were 585,000 deaths and 42 million years of "healthy" life lost as a result of the use of drugs. As if this was not enough, according to the *World Drug Report 2021*, the drug-related deaths in 2019 totaled 494,000. Moreover, there was a 17.5 percent increase in total deaths attributed to drugs during the decade (U.N. Office on Drugs and Crime 2021, 34).

Sadly, too many of the people and criminal networks cited in the international reports are in the Caribbean. As noted in chapter 1, the drug phenomenon is transnational and multidimensional. Yet, part of the drama of drugs is driven by a key logic of Peter Tosh's legalization plea: in most parts of the region, at least one of the substances deemed illegal by most of the authorities is not viewed as harmful by citizens. Acceptability is reinforced by a long history of use that is predicated on culture and religion and that has natural medicinal utility. Such is the case with marijuana in the Caribbean, which is similar to that of the coca leaf in parts of South America, where coping with the physical geography is also a factor and where the coca leaf has a long history of cultural- and religious-based usage.[3] I can attest to the value of coca to cope with heights, having had to drink coca tea while in La Paz, Bolivia, in May 2010 for a meeting in preparation for the Conference of Defense Ministers of the Americas later that year. La Paz is 11,942 feet above sea level.

As will be seen below, legalization and decriminalization options are also gaining increasing traction in the Caribbean. Noteworthy too is that the legalization of marijuana for medical and recreational use has been a reality in parts of Europe for a while now, and it has been rising in the United States as well. Indeed, in September 2010 the first television commercial promoting it within the United States was aired in California (see Sanchez 2010).[4] The geonarcotics milieu has become more complex as social acceptability and growing receptivity of legalization and decriminalization run up against legal proscription and pressures from powerful state and non-state actors outside the region. For instance, although as of June 2023 in the United States, forty-seven states and the District of Columbia had legalized the use of marijuana for medicinal and recreational purposes, federal law and policy still proscribe marijuana trafficking, which means the United States continues its international counternarcotics pursuits.

Interestingly, citing the March 2023 *International Narcotics Control Strategy Report*, on March 7, 2023, *InSight Crime* reported that marijuana legalization in the continental United States has led to a new phenomenon. While historically marijuana cultivated in the Caribbean (and Latin America) was smuggled to the United States, the reverse has begun, with the number of seizures of American and Canadian marijuana in the Caribbean beginning to rise in 2022; smugglers used both commercial carriers and express mail to deliver the drugs. In one case, Courtney Elizabeth Baker, a thirty-seven-year-old New York chef, was arrested on arrival in Jamaica on February 25, 2023, with twenty-one ounces of marijuana. She explained to customs officials that she was taking the product to show Jamaican friends that there is higher-quality ganja in the United States. According to the March 9, 2023, *Jamaica Observer*, at her appearance at the St. James Parish Court on March 8, 2023, Baker's possession charge was dismissed with an admonition from the magistrate in light of her explanation. However, she was ordered to pay a fine of J$30,000 (US$195) or spend thirty days in jail for importing the marijuana. Curiously, too, furor erupted in Jamaica in February 2023 when the country's Cannabis Licensing Authority authorized a Canadian company to ship 309 pounds of marijuana to Jamaica for research. The idea of Jamaica, which holds ganja production pride of place in the Caribbean, importing ganja from North America is anathema to many individuals within and outside Jamaica. This chapter examines some of these dynamics. It begins with an explanation of the geonarcotics framework and then discusses a factor that often is considered intuitive but often is not explained: the role of geography in drug trafficking in the Caribbean. The chapter then addresses legalization and decriminalization endeavors within the region.

Dynamics of Geonarcotics

Individuals unfamiliar with the Caribbean could easily conclude from some media headlines that the region's drug challenge is one- or two-dimensional in nature from headlines such as the following: the May 11, 2011, *Caricom News Network*: "Guyana: Drugs in Agri-Exports a Living Nightmare—Minister Persaud"; the September 30, 2011, Military.com *News*: "Second Interdiction of Western Caribbean Drug Sub"; the July 12, 2012, *InSight Crime*: "U.S. Deploys Drones to

Counter Caribbean Drug Trafficking"; or the February 20, 2013, *Stabroek News* (Guyana): "Nearly 700 Pounds of Cocaine Found in Lumber Container." Also worthy of mention is the April 9, 2013, Caribbean360.com: "Cruise Ship Granny Lands in Slammer for Drugs Stashed in Girdle";[5] the May 17, 2019, *Tribune* (Bahamas): "Bahamas and Turks and Caicos' Drug Seizures Already Surpass Those of 2018"; the December 3, 2021, DEA Press Release: "International Drug Trafficking Organization Member Sentenced for Trafficking over a Thousand Kilograms of Cocaine"; the February 3, 2022, *St. Lucia Times*: "680 Kilos of Cocaine Seized in Caribbean Sea"; and the February 21, 2022, *Demerarawaves*: "New York–Bound Man Held with Cocaine in Fried Rice—CANU."

However, keen regional observers know that the region's drug challenge goes beyond illicit production of marijuana and trafficking of a variety of substances; it also involves the consumption and abuse of illegal substances and the laundering of money derived from drug operations. Indeed, the October 2, 2011, *Jamaica Gleaner* reported on a nexus between drugs and prostitution in Jamaica, in which prostitutes are increasingly resorting to the use of ecstasy as a coping mechanism for their enterprise (Reid 2011). Ecstasy trafficking and use also has been a troubling reality in Guyana, Puerto Rico, the Dominican Republic, Cayman Islands, Trinidad and Tobago, and elsewhere in the region (see *Caymans Compass* 2019; Asmann 2019; George 2019; *Stabroek News* 2019a).[6] Moreover, the March 3, 2013, *Trinidad Express* carried a screaming headline about "Dirty Money" in a report that TT\$ 638,844,310 (US\$99,798,533) in alleged "dirty money" transactions passed through the country's financial institutions during 2012, according to the official report for that year by the country's Financial Intelligence Unit (see Medina 2013). Simply put, *the drug phenomenon is not one- or two- dimensional in nature; it is multidimensional.* Thus, it is understandable that conceptual constructs about it also would share this feature.

We observed in chapter 2 that the dominant twentieth-century conception of security was founded on realist propositions about the state as *the* central actor in an anarchic world, defense against external threats coming from other states, and the military as *the* instrument to safeguard sovereignty. These have given way to other approaches that do not completely repudiate thinking about the state, external threats, and the military's role, but they broaden the conceptual map to recognize contemporary realities, where states face serious threats from non-state actors, and where traditional military forces generally are ill-suited as protective instruments. But as also pointed out in the previous chapter, even before the end of the Cold War, which precipitated the theoretical reevaluation, realism did not circumscribe the thinking about security in the Caribbean. This is the context in which the concept of geonarcotics was originated in the early 1990s in *International Journal*, one of Canada's leading scholarly journals on international affairs (see Griffith 1993–1994).

Geonarcotics Framework

As indicated in that study, the geonarcotics framework is a heuristic device that can be applied in studying the drug phenomenon in different national or regional contexts. Thus, although the book *Drugs and Security in the Caribbean* offered an empirical application to the Caribbean, other scholars have found the concept useful in assessing illegal drug operations in other areas or as a point of departure for their own conceptual endeavors. Examples are Pablo Dreyfus (2002) in relation to South America, Svante Cornell and Niklas Swanström (2006) in relation to Eurasia, and Kyle Grayson (2008) in relation to Canada.

In their analysis, Cornell and Swanström observed, "Ivelaw Griffith, in 'From Cold War Geopolitics to Post–Cold War Geonarcotics,' has taken the theoretical discussion further than most academics, although his case studies are for the greater part focused on the Caribbean" (Cornell and Swanström 2006, 26). Writing in *Chasing Dragons*, Grayson observed, "Griffith saw his conceptualization of geonarcotics as a replacement for the policy certainties provided by Cold War geopolitical discourses. . . . In portraying the international illicit drug distribution system as a vast 'Underground Empire,' both aggressive and violent and with its own armed forces, diplomats, intelligence agencies, banks, and transportation services, Griffith was remapping the world in a way that re(territorialized) threats to (inter)national security as emanating mainly from the global South (Grayson 2008, 5). . . . Griffith's conceptualization of geonarcotics was intended to replace the policy guidance offered by Cold War geopolitics" (65, 267n3).

Beyond this, the book that applied the geonarcotics framework to the Caribbean was viewed as making an invaluable contribution to understanding the nexus between drugs and security in the region. For instance, one analyst remarked, "In my article 'Reading up on the Drug War,' *Parameters* (Fall 1995) I lamented the absence of serious strategic literature about the drug war. That complaint is now inoperative. Ivelaw Lloyd Griffith's *Drugs and Security in the Caribbean* is a meticulous description of the phenomenon, written in the precise idiom of national security calculus" (Ramsey 2003, 94). The point also was made that "Griffith's book has already been nominated for three awards: the Gordon K. Lewis Prize in Caribbean Politics, the Bryce Wood Award in Latin American Studies, and the Woodrow Wilson Foundation Award in Social Sciences Analysis. The book may win or lose as a literary endeavor, but the reader can only win, for this is the best regional treatment of the narcotics plague yet written" (95).

The geonarcotics framework, which is captured in figure 3.1, posits the dynamic interaction of four factors: narcotics, geography, power, and politics; that the narcotics phenomenon is multidimensional, with four main problem

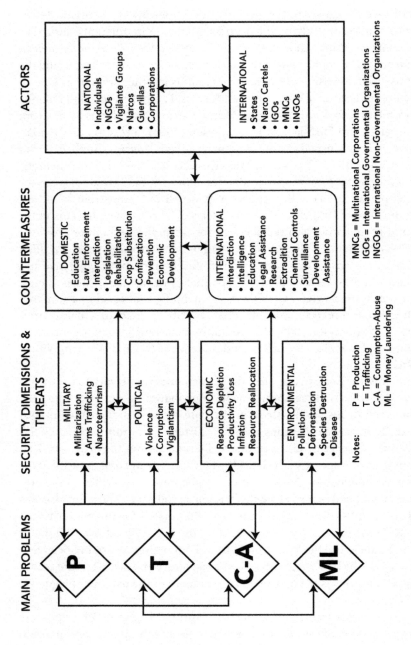

FIGURE 3.1 Geonarcotics Framework.

Source: Ivelaw Lloyd Griffith, "From Cold War Geopolitics to Post-Cold War Geonarcotics," *International Journal* 49 (Winter) 1993–1994, 32.

MAIN PROBLEMS

- P
- T
- C-A
- ML

SECURITY DIMENSIONS & THREATS

MILITARY
- Militarization
- Arms Trafficking
- Narcoterrorism

POLITICAL
- Violence
- Corruption
- Vigilantism

ECONOMIC
- Resource Depletion
- Productivity Loss
- Inflation
- Resource Reallocation

ENVIRONMENTAL
- Pollution
- Deforestation
- Species Destruction
- Disease

Notes:
P = Production
T = Trafficking
C-A = Consumption-Abuse
ML = Money Laundering

COUNTERMEASURES

DOMESTIC
- Education
- Law Enforcement
- Interdiction
- Legislation
- Rehabilitation
- Crop Substitution
- Confiscation
- Prevention
- Economic Development

INTERNATIONAL
- Interdiction
- Intelligence
- Education
- Legal Assistance
- Research
- Extradition
- Chemical Controls
- Surveillance
- Development Assistance

MNCs = Multinational Corporations
IGOs = International Governmental Organizations
INGOs = International Non-Governmental Organizations

ACTORS

NATIONAL
- Individuals
- NGOs
- Vigilante Groups
- Narcos
- Guerillas
- Corporations

INTERNATIONAL
- States
- Narco Cartels
- IGOs
- MNCs
- INGOs

areas (drug production, consumption-abuse, trafficking, and money launder-ing); that these problem areas give rise to actual and potential threats to the security of states; and that drug operations and the activities they spawn pre-cipitate both conflict and cooperation among various state and non-state actors. As well, the four problem areas give rise to other challenges, such as crime, corruption, and arms trafficking. Importantly, this approach does not view the "war on drugs" purely as a military matter.[7]

Geography is a factor in this schema because certain physical, social, and political geography features of countries facilitate drug operations. Power involves the ability of individuals and groups to secure compliant action. This power is both state and non-state in origin, and in some cases non-state power holders command relatively more power than state power holders. Politics entails the ability of power brokers to determine who gets what, how, and when through the allocation of resources. Since power in this milieu is not only state power, resource allocation is correspondingly not exclusively a function of state power holders. Moreover, politics becomes perverted, and even more perverted in situations where there are preexisting conditions that facilitate such. Indeed, the sagas over recent decades involving "Little Nut" in St. Kitts and Nevis, the "Guns for Antigua" in Antigua and Barbuda, then-colonel (later president) Desi Bouterse in Suriname, the Dole Chadee Gang in Trinidad and Tobago, Shaheed "Roger" Khan in Guyana, and the Christopher "Dudus" Coke saga in Jamaica—which is discussed in chapter 6—highlight some of the political perversions and security and sovereignty implications involved. The exploits of Suriname's Desi Bouterse are addressed in chapter 7.

There is no uniformity in drug operations or in their impact on individuals and societies in the Caribbean, or elsewhere for that matter. Some countries are affected by several or all operations; others by just a few. However, because the narcotics phenomenon is multidimensional, a meaningful understanding of any single drug operation or security implication requires an appreciation of the complete narcotics package. A comprehensive approach offers the best possible prospect for meaningful understanding of both the phenomenon as a whole and the dynamics of its individual parts, although comprehensive analysis is not always necessary.

The geonarcotics milieu involves a variety of actors, state as well as non-state, as figure 3.1 shows. The variety is understandable given the multidimensional and transnational character of the drug phenomenon. Actors vary in the way they are affected by the various problem areas, and their countermeasures also vary. Some initiate and maintain counternarcotics regimes; others strive to circumvent or eliminate them. Actors are proactive as well as reactive, and both proactive and reactive behaviors are possible from the same actor. For example, cartels are proactive in relation to production and trafficking but reactive when states, international nongovernmental organizations (INGOs), and nongovernmental organizations (NGOs) introduce countermeasures.

Conflict and Cooperation

Drug operations generate two basic kinds of interactions—conflict and cooperation—among different actors and at different levels. Relationships are bilateral and multilateral, symmetrical and asymmetrical, and involve both vertical and horizontal flows. Not all interactions involve force or military capabilities. Some involve nonmilitary pressures, such as the application of economic and political sanctions by the United States against countries that, in its estimation, are not proactive enough in fighting drugs. The range of sanctions includes loss of tariff benefits, a 50 percent withholding of bilateral aid, suspension of air services, cancellation of visas, and the denial of support for aid requested from multilateral funding institutions (see Perl 1989, 91–95).

For instance, in 1996 several of these sanctions were imposed by the United States against Afghanistan, Colombia, Iran, Myanmar, Nigeria, and Syria following their "decertification"—a declaration that they had failed to adopt effective narcotics countermeasures or to show good-faith efforts in that regard. For a variety of reasons, in recent years the United States has adopted a less belligerent approach in its geonarcotics engagement. In the 2013 *International Narcotics Control Strategy Report* (*INCSR*), for example, although Bolivia, Burma, and Venezuela were designated by the president as "having failed demonstrably during the previous 12 months to adhere to their obligations under international counternarcotics agreements and take the measures set forth in section 489(a)(1) of the FAA (Foreign Assistance Act)," no sanctions were imposed, as the counternarcotics and other engagement with them was deemed to be in the national interests of the United States.

Conflict interactions include protests, complaints, warnings, threats, seizures, blockades, and armed attacks. Many of these conflict types exist in the geonarcotics milieu. Some actors are engaged simultaneously in both cooperation and conflict. Over the years, the relationships between the United States and Colombia and between the United States and Afghanistan reveal this. In the Caribbean, the relationships between the United States and Cuba, especially since the 1980s, and between the United States and Jamaica during the 1990s, provide good evidence of this. As well, conflict interactions exist both nationally and internationally. With regard to non-state conflict, James Rosenau showed decades ago that NGOs and INGOs have emerged as prime movers on several interdependence issues—mobilizing constituencies, framing agendas, and monitoring compliance like a world police force. Since the NGO community is not united around a common core of beliefs, these issues constitute an arena for cooperation as well as conflict as different groups compete for scarce resources and access to states (see Rosenau 1995, 20).

The nature and source of drug threats could be external, internal, or both, depending on the actors and problem areas involved. For states, while some problems create threats within one area, the multidimensional and transnational nature of drug operations precludes strict internal-external distinctions between threats or implications. Whether the state faces one problem (say, production) or several (such as production, abuse, and trafficking), the security implications generally have both internal and external ramifications. As such, the real issue is not whether there are internal or external implications but the nature and extent of both sets of implications.

International countermeasures offer the best prospect for dealing with the transnational drug phenomenon, especially since all state and non-state actors battling the dilemma face resource limitations. Yet, collaboration among states also results in conflict, often because of domestic factors, including party rivalry, leadership changes, composition and control of the military, and budgetary and economic conditions. Some of these factors help explain a second reason for conflict: perceptual differences among ruling elites, which cause disparate definitions of the nature and severity of threats and, therefore, varied policies and measures to deal with them.

The multiple dynamics of the geonarcotics milieu presented above have considerable implications for the issue of sovereignty. As indicated in the previous chapter, no study dealing with sovereignty, especially when small states are involved, can afford to overlook its formal-legal aspect: freedom from outside interference—that no authority is legally above the state except that which the state voluntarily confers on international bodies it joins. This is a central principle of international law but also a sensitive issue for societies whose experience with colonization is still fresh in the national memory and for those that have been victims of intervention. But while looking at formal-legal sovereignty is necessary, it is not sufficient.

The dynamics of drugs, geography, power, and politics oblige us to consider the issue of sovereignty in all its aspects. As we saw in chapter 2, there are international legal, domestic, "positive," and other aspects of sovereignty. For instance, Robert Jackson views positive sovereignty as enabling states to take advantage of their independence. For him, a government that is positively sovereign not only is able to enjoy rights of nonintervention but also has the ability to provide "political goods" for the society over which it exercises governance. Positive sovereignty includes having the economic, technical, military, and other capabilities to declare, implement, and enforce public policy, both domestic and foreign (Jackson 1990, 29). This and later chapters show that both international legal and positive sovereignty are compromised in the Caribbean.

The challenge to Caribbean political elites has two main elements. One is the actual and potential challenge to governability presented by drug actors—in essence, a challenge to positive sovereignty. These actors do not seek to command the institutions of state power directly, but through corruption and other direct and indirect methods, they aim at altering the political and socioeconomic dynamics of society in ways that are conducive to their own pursuits and generally not conducive to national security and good governance. The other main sovereignty challenge is the international legal one. Often, the sovereign authority of the leaders of small states is challenged by other states. In pursuing their own agendas vis-à-vis drug trafficking or money laundering, some powerful states find the actions of others inimical to their interests.

Consequently, they adopt the kind of economic, political, and sometimes military measures that infringe on the sovereignty of small states. In the case of the Caribbean, the geonarcotics milieu is such that geography, power asymmetries, and the existence of the United States as the world's largest drug consumer all combine to heighten the region's vulnerability. This makes countries subject to sovereignty infringement, something that countries often have protested loudly. (For example, see West Indian Commission 1992, 348–49; Sanders 1993; and Office of the Prime Minister, Jamaica, 1996.)

Nevertheless, the challenge to sovereignty at the international level is not restricted to relationships among states. It is also a function of interaction between states and narcos, between states and international governmental organizations (IGOs), and between states and INGOs. Some IGOs are able to challenge and often subordinate small states to their interests because they possess relatively greater economic, political, military, or other resources than some small states around the world are able to mobilize. Further, the sovereignty challenge does not arise only from conflict relations; it also results from efforts at cooperation. An example of this is the controversy between the United States and Jamaica and Barbados that surfaced in 1996 in relation to the model "Shiprider Agreement" that had been signed by nine other Caribbean nations. The essence of the conflict was, on the one hand, the insistence by Barbados and Jamaica that maritime "hot pursuit" by the United States not be extended into their twelve-mile territorial waters and, on the other hand, the desire of the United States for the right to full "hot pursuit" to maximize the operational efficiency of that interdiction measure.[8] What, then, are some of the drug trafficking realities in the contemporary Caribbean?

The Geography of Drug Trafficking

The drugs that feature in the Caribbean are marijuana, cocaine, heroin, ecstasy, and their derivatives, such as crack, which comes from cocaine, and molly, which is derived from ecstasy. Insofar as production is concerned, only marijuana is produced in the region. The consumption-abuse situation is different, though, since all the drugs are involved. Of the four main problems identified in the geonarcotics framework—production, consumption-abuse, transshipment (also called trafficking), and money laundering—production and transshipment generate the greatest amount of conflict and cooperation interactions among both state and non-state actors in the geonarcotics milieu.

We saw above the conflict among state actors over the Shiprider Agreement. Plus, there has been disagreement over criminal deportation, arms trafficking, and other areas. On the cooperation side, there has been positive engagement in relation to the trafficking of drugs and arms and transnational crime, among other areas. Moreover, illegal transactions in relation to drugs, arms, and money have been the basis for conflict between state and non-state actors. Thus, it is important to offer a comment on the geography of drug trafficking. Although production, consumption abuse, trafficking, and money laundering are all present in the Caribbean, it is transshipment that dramatizes the importance of geography as a geonarcotics factor.

Physical and Social Geography

The Caribbean Sea is the most dominant geographical feature of the region. It is 1,049,500 square miles in area, and its north-south width ranges from 380 to about 700 miles. The greatest depth of passage connecting the Eastern Caribbean with the Atlantic Ocean is the Anegada Passage, a sea-lane of 48 nautical miles between the Anegada and Sombrero islands. The name "Caribbean" was introduced in 1773 by Thomas Jeffreys, author of *The West Indies Atlas*. He named the sea after the Carib people, who are native to many of the islands in the area. The islands in the Caribbean Sea form a chain almost 2,500 miles long but never more than 160 miles wide, creating a bridge between North and South America (see Griffith 1993, 51).

Both the physical and social geography of the Caribbean make it conducive to drug trafficking. Aspects of the former are more important than the latter, and in the physical geography area the key elements are island character and location. Except for mainland Belize, French Guiana, Guyana, and Suriname, Caribbean countries are all island territories. Some are plural-island territories, such as the Virgin Islands, consisting of about one hundred islands and cays. Indeed, one—the Bahamas—is an archipelago of seven hundred islands and two thousand cays. This island character permits entry into and use of Caribbean territories from scores, sometimes hundreds, of different places from the surrounding sea. For the mainland states, access is from various places in the Atlantic Ocean in the case of Guyana, Suriname, and French Guiana, and from the Caribbean coast in the case of Belize. And when one adds to the matrix the inability of Caribbean countries to provide adequate territorial policing, their vulnerability to trafficking is more readily appreciated.

The most important location feature of the region's physical geography is proximity. This proximity has two aspects: to South America, a major drug supply source, and to North America, a major drug consumer. On the supply side, the *World Drug Report* for 2012 shows that the world's cocaine is produced in South America, coming notably from Colombia, Peru, and Bolivia, with coca leaf cultivated in those states as well as elsewhere in South America, especially in Ecuador and Venezuela (see U.N. Office on Drugs and Crime 2012, 35–43). Colombia's cocaine production has declined over the past decade, but that nation continues to be the world's leading cocaine producer, and the United States continues to be the single largest market. A significant proportion of global heroin and marijuana production also comes from South and Central America, especially Colombia, Mexico, Peru, Paraguay, Brazil, and Guatemala. On the demand side, the United States has the dubious distinction of being the world's single largest drug-consuming nation.

There is not much distance between the Caribbean and South America, or between the Caribbean and the United States, especially the southern and northeastern parts of the United States. Some countries, like the Bahamas, Cuba, Haiti, Jamaica, and the Cayman Islands, are practically just "a stone's throw" away from Miami. Except for French Guiana and Suriname, all Caribbean countries are less than two thousand miles from Miami. And only seven of them—Barbados, French Guiana, Grenada, Guyana, St. Vincent and the Grenadines, Suriname, and Trinidad and Tobago—are more than two thousand miles from Atlanta and Washington, D.C. As for distances between the Caribbean and some main South American drug centers, twenty-four Caribbean territories are less than one thousand miles from Caracas, and all except Belize (in relation to Caracas), French Guiana (in relation to Cali and Medellín), and Suriname (in relation to Medellín) are less than fifteen hundred miles away from Bogotá, Cali, Caracas, and Medellín.[9]

These distances are calculated using air distances from Caribbean capitals and from international airport locations where non-capital cities are involved. Thus, what is masked is the reality that for some trafficking purposes the distances are often shorter, given the fact that there are places in some Caribbean territories, outside of the capitals, that are closer to U.S. or Latin American territory, and traffickers use this greater proximity. For example, Nassau is only 183 miles away from Miami, but Bimini is even closer—40 miles from the Florida Keys. A mere 90 miles separate Cuba from the United States. The distance between Port-of-Spain and Caracas is 371 miles. However, it is merely 7 miles between La Brea in southwestern Trinidad and Pedernales in northeastern Venezuela, a point called Serpent's Mouth. Moreover, the town of Lethem in southwest Guyana is a mere 75 miles away from the city of Boa Vista in northeast Brazil; and Eteringbang, Guyana, is only 28 miles from El Dorado, Venezuela.

Europe is also a huge drug-consuming area, with methamphetamines, cocaine, heroin, and marijuana imports coming through and from the Caribbean. However, despite the relatively great distance between that continent and the Caribbean region, the Caribbean is a major transit area for drugs bound for Europe. Several reasons explain this. One is the proximity between the Caribbean and South America. A second relates to commercial, communications, and other linkages between Europe and the Caribbean, which provide the institutional and other infrastructure for trafficking.

In addition, because French Guiana, Guadeloupe, and Martinique are Départements Outré Mer of France; Anguilla, Bermuda, the British Virgin Islands, the Cayman Islands, Montserrat, and the Turks and Caicos are British dependencies; and Bonaire and Saba are integral parts of the Kingdom of the Netherlands, there are certain customs, immigration, and transportation connections between these territories and their respective European "owners" that are exploited by traffickers. Although Aruba, Curaçao, and Sint Maarten acquired a semi-autonomous status within the Kingdom of the Netherlands in 2010, the immigration, transportation, and other connections with Holland were not altered. Some of the arrangements are similar to those involving the United States and Puerto Rico and the U.S. Virgin Islands, which also facilitate traffickers aiming for destinations in the continental United States.

Each of the two physical geography elements—island character and location—can by itself be conducive to trafficking. However, the region's vulnerability to trafficking and the prospects for continued trafficking can be better appreciated when it is recognized that these factors are often mutually supporting and reinforcing. Moreover, they interact with aspects of social geography such as the fact that (a) for most of the plural-island states, such as the Bahamas and St. Vincent and the Grenadines, the majority of the islands are uninhabited—and therefore are unpoliced—and (b) in both Guyana and Suriname, which are mainland territories, most of the population lives along the Atlantic coast, which leaves most of the territory underpopulated and under-policed.

Interdiction and surveillance show that a variety of private go-fast speedboats, pleasure craft, and fishing vessels are used in transshipment operations. Semi-submersibles and aircraft have been used, and drugs are also hidden in legitimate, containerized cargo. Understandably, trafficking patterns vary over time. One report commissioned by the United States Senate (U.S. Senate 2012, 11–14) found three maritime pathways for trafficking mainly cocaine, heroin, and synthetic drugs from South America to North America. They are reflected in figure 3.2 and are:

- The "Central Corridor," used mostly for cocaine leaving South America and flowing through Jamaica, Haiti, the Dominican Republic, and the Bahamas into the United States.

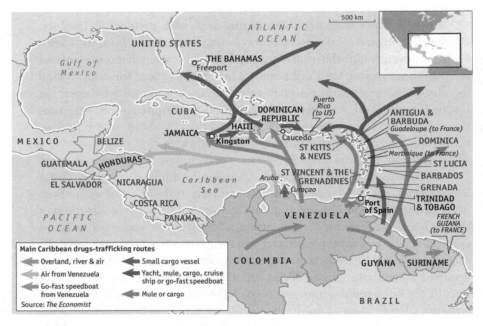

FIGURE 3.2 Main Caribbean Maritime Trafficking Corridors.

Source: *The Economist*, "Drug Trafficking in the Caribbean: Full Circle," May 24, 2014. https://www.economist.com/the-americas/2014/05/24/full-circle/.

- The "Eastern Corridor," comprising the Eastern Caribbean and Trinidad and Tobago. Often the cocaine and heroin make their way to Puerto Rico for onward passage to the United States.
- The "ABC Corridor" of Aruba, Bonaire, and Curaçao, which is used for cocaine shipment and, to a lesser extent, for synthetic drugs.

Geonarcotics Milieu

Aspects of the region's drug challenges are captured in the *World Drug Report*, which initially was prepared as a periodic report by the U.N. Office on Drugs and Crime and is now produced almost annually. In 2010 the Inter-American Drug Abuse Control Commission also released the findings of research on drug use among students ranging in ages between fourteen and seventeen in a dozen countries: The study was conducted during 2005 and 2007 in Antigua and Barbuda, Barbados, Dominica, Grenada, Guyana, Haiti, Jamaica, St. Kitts and Nevis, St. Lucia, St. Vincent and the Grenadines, Trinidad and Tobago, and Suriname. It included alcohol, cigarettes, and inhalants and found that alcohol and marijuana are the main drugs used by students in most of the countries.

Prevalence is relatively high among students, although there is considerable variability among countries. Tobacco is also used throughout the region but to a lesser extent than alcohol and marijuana. There is significant experimentation with cigarettes, but in relation to the use of cigarettes versus marijuana, the latter has overtaken the former in most countries by a factor of two to three times in some instances.

Drug Use Plus

According to the study, the age of first use of substances in general was typically around eleven to twelve years of age. Haiti and Suriname were notable exceptions, with a slightly later age of first use. The reported found: "A very important finding relates to students' perception of how easy it is to access drugs. Perception of availability of marijuana was very high—four to five of every ten students indicated that they could access marijuana easily. Also noteworthy is that relatively high proportions of students also felt that cocaine/crack cocaine was easily available—on average, 14% of students" (OAS Inter-American Drug Abuse Control Commission 2010, 66). Marijuana was the drug most likely and most often offered to students for consumption of purchase. Thankfully, the study found only negligible proportions of students reporting that they were offered cocaine, crack, or ecstasy. The Organization of American States's inaugural report on citizen security in the Americas also provides trend analyses of many aspects of the drug phenomenon, although the way the hemispheric analysis is undertaken prevents readers from discerning appreciably the dynamics of the various regions (see OAS Secretariat for Multidimensional Security 2011).

The subjects of drugs and crime also are addressed in the periodic *Human Development Report*, which is published by the U.N. Development Program. However, the most consistent reporting on drug operations is to be found in the *INCSR*, which is produced annually by the U.S. Department of State for reporting to Congress as mandated by the U.S. Foreign Assistance Act. As had been the case with previous reports, the 2021 *INCSR* named five Caribbean countries—the Bahamas, Belize, the Dominican Republic, Haiti, and Jamaica—among the world's top twenty-two drug-producing or -transit countries.[10] In an earlier report the point was made that "without factoring in illegal maritime and air drug smuggling believed to be destined for Europe and beyond, approximately 5 percent of all drugs destined for United States are estimated to pass through the Bahamas, Dominican Republic, Haiti and Jamaica" (U.S. Department of State 2013, 6).

This figure represents a decline from earlier decades, providing evidence of some payoff for the counternarcotics efforts by the United States, Caribbean,

European, and other stakeholders over the previous two decades. Indeed, one September 2012 report issued by the U.S. Senate noted: "The Caribbean region has come a long way since it served as the primary transit route for South American drugs entering the United States in the 1980s. Current estimates show that no more than five percent of the cocaine destined for the United States flows through the Caribbean. This is down from ten percent in 2006 and 26 percent in 2001. Increased interdiction efforts by both the U.S. and partner nations in the region have largely forced traffickers to abandon the Caribbean for Mexico and Central America" (U.S. Senate 2012, 9). However, quite troublingly—but understandably—in spring 2013 the U.S. assistant secretary of state for International Narcotics and Law Enforcement Affairs warned that the Caribbean should brace for a massive resumption of trafficking. He forecast that successful counternarcotics measures in Mexico and Central America soon will witness another manifestation of "the balloon effect," with traffickers looking for alternative routes to evade military and law enforcement authorities in Mexico and Central America (Tatone 2013; Pachico 2011a).

Thankfully, no Caribbean country is listed among the top precursor chemical source countries in the 2021 *INCSR*, although the report cites Belize for the seizure of significant quantities of chemicals in 2020. However, the 2021 *INCSR* deemed the following nineteen nations among the major money laundering jurisdictions worldwide: Antigua and Barbuda, Aruba, Bahamas, Barbados, Belize, British Virgin Islands, Cayman Islands, Cuba, Dominica, Dominican Republic, Guyana, Haiti, Jamaica, St. Kitts and Nevis, St. Lucia, St. Vincent and the Grenadines, Sint Maarten, Suriname, and Trinidad and Tobago. The official U.S. definition of a "major money laundering country" is guided by the Foreign Assistance Act of 1961, which views a major money laundering country as one "whose financial institutions engage in currency transactions involving significant amounts of proceeds from international narcotics trafficking" (U.S. Department of State 2021, 13).

Yet, the *INCSR* concedes that "the complex nature of money laundering transactions today makes it difficult in many cases to distinguish the proceeds of narcotics trafficking from the proceeds of other serious crime. Moreover, financial institutions engaging in transactions involving significant amounts of proceeds of other serious crime are vulnerable to narcotics-related money laundering" (U.S. Department of State 2013). Moreover, the *INCSR* for 2019 accepts that a country's presence on the United States lists does not reflect adversely of its government's anti-drug efforts or level of cooperation with the United States. As a matter of fact, it acknowledges that one of the reasons major drug-producing or -transit countries are placed on the list is the combination of geographic, commercial, and economic factors that allow drugs to be produced or transshipped despite the relevant government's conscientious counternarcotics measures.

A full appreciation of the region's geonarcotics milieu requires understanding the dynamics of individual countries. However, as that topic is beyond the scope of this chapter, readers interested in that aspect may consult the assessments captured in the annual *INCSRs*. Still, it is also important to offer some general conclusions about the contemporary regional narcotics scene. Overall, the following observations can be made about the region's contemporary geonarcotics milieu:

- Despite the valiant efforts employed and considerable resources deployed by Caribbean countries, the United States, European nations, entities of the OAS, and other sources, the regional situation is not improving *appreciably and consistently*. In most places there have been both gains and losses.
- Compared to a decade ago, there is increased marijuana production in Guyana, Barbados, St. Vincent and the Grenadines, and other places. There has also been amelioration of consumption in many places, albeit increases in Cuba, the Dominican Republic, parts of the Eastern Caribbean, and Puerto Rico. Plus, there are active anti–money laundering efforts in most places but lackluster ones in a few, despite legislation and the extensive work of the Caribbean Financial Action Task Force.
- There have been major trafficking arrests in the Bahamas, Jamaica, Puerto Rico, and other places but increased trafficking in Guyana, the Dominican Republic, and in the Eastern and Southern Caribbean, partly as a balloon effect of the Mérida Initiative in Mexico and Central America. Indeed, the trials and tribulations facing Belize in this respect are becoming increasingly problematic for both that country and the Central American region as a whole.[11]
- Two "g" words—"guns" and "gangs"—have combined to present troubling new norms, creating climates of fear in both urban centers and rural communities. Further, they highlight two crucial dimensions of the phenomenon: it is transnational and multidimensional, and it necessitates commensurate countermeasures.
- Deficits by state security forces and high crime have led, among other things, to the rapid expansion of private security companies. In some places, private security is regulated; in others it is not. Elsewhere, the combined sizes and capabilities of private security rival—and often exceed—the security establishments of the state.
- The power exercised by drug lords and other criminals in several societies and the state security deficits have increased the vulnerability of those states. Moreover, some countries, including Haiti, Jamaica, the Bahamas, Suriname, Puerto Rico, St. Lucia, Antigua and Barbuda, Guyana, and Trinidad and Tobago, have been pushed by drugs and crime to the edge of the governance precipice at various times over the last few decades.

As noted earlier and indicated in figure 3.1, the region's geonarcotics milieu involves drug production, trafficking, consumption-abuse, and money laundering. The drugs involved are mainly cocaine, marijuana, heroin, and ecstasy and their derivatives. I also remarked in the introduction to this chapter that the milieu becomes more complicated as social acceptability and growing receptivity of marijuana legalization and decriminalization run up against legal proscription and pressures from powerful state and non-state actors outside the Caribbean. Thus, it is important to understand some of the region's contemporary marijuana reform dynamics.

Bold Marijuana Reforms

The decades-long advocacy by Peter Tosh, Bob Marley, and other Rastafarians and non-Rastafarians for a different approach to the legal and social status of marijuana received a major fillip in March 2014 when the CARICOM leaders agreed to establish a commission on the matter. In an effort to ensure inclusiveness, individuals from the scientific, medical, legal, and social science arenas, as well as representatives from the youth, Christian, and Rastafarian religious communities were selected as commissioners, with distinguished legal scholar and then–University of the West Indies (St. Augustine) Law School dean Rose-Marie Belle Antoine appointed as chair.

Regional Marijuana Commission

The ten-member commission was mandated to (a) conduct a rigorous inquiry into the social, economic, health, and legal issues surrounding marijuana use in the Caribbean and to determine whether there should be a change in the current drug classification of marijuana, thereby making the drug more accessible for all types of usage (religious, recreational, medical, and research); and (b) recommend, if there is to be a reclassification, the legal and administrative conditions that should apply. It also was authorized to "engage in an extensive consultation process with members of the Community and other key stakeholders at the national level to elicit the population's view about current usage and re-classification" (CARICOM Regional Commission on Marijuana 2018, x).

The team convened in 2016 and held the first national consultation in June of that year. Regrettably, the absence of funding caused a suspension of its work until financial underwriting was secured from the Foundation to Promote Open Society. The consultations resumed in June 2017, with the final report tendered in June 2018. The commission felt that CARICOM should aim to totally dismantle marijuana prohibition and replace it with a strictly regulated framework similar to that for alcohol and tobacco, which are harmful substances that are not criminalized. It acknowledged that law reform could take many forms and should be mindful of realities; it also recommended that "law reform should not adopt a laissez-faire, liberalized approach, but proceed within a responsible, controlled regime that will depend on focused and adequate institutional resources to achieve the desirable objectives" (CARICOM Regional Commission on Marijuana 2018, 5). The commission agreed unanimously that the current classification for cannabis/marijuana as a "'dangerous drug' with 'no value,'" or a narcotic, should be altered to one that views it as a "controlled substance."

The team was unanimous in thinking that legal policy toward marijuana should not be informed by punitive approaches but by public health rationales, within a human rights, social justice, and developmental ambit. It advocated the removal of all criminal penalties from marijuana laws, noting that if only decriminalization is envisaged, reasonable fines and compulsory rehabilitative treatment should be substituted. As well, the commission espoused the view that children and young persons should be protected from possible adverse effects of the drug, which suggests the need for prohibition for children and young persons within an appropriate age limit except for medical reasons. Further, the commission recommended unanimously that drug-driving laws and mechanisms should be introduced to prevent persons from driving under the influence.

The CARICOM body felt that possession and use in private households and for personal use only should be decriminalized, and it agreed with the view held by many law enforcement experts that effectively enforcing prohibitionist laws in private households is nearly impossible. Moreover, it said, "It is an opinion reinforced by recent judicial precedents on the rights to health as demonstrated by the upholding of the freedom to grow and use cannabis for personal medical use and on the right to privacy. Given these precedents, limited home-growing for a small number of plants should be permitted. A number of legislated models permitting home-growing already exist, including Uruguay, Colorado, and Washington and in the Caribbean, Jamaica, and Antigua and Barbuda" (CARICOM Regional Commission on Marijuana 2018, 6).

A section of the findings of the commission is worth replicating fully:

Marijuana is a plant substance with historical, cultural and religious significance to the Commonwealth Caribbean, which existed benignly as a beneficial plant without condemnation or legal intervention for centuries. Legislative history illustrates that cannabis/marijuana acquired an illegal status and classification as a "dangerous drug" with "no value," without scientific or moral rationales to support the radical change in the law, both internationally and domestically. Further, there is considerable evidence to suggest that this transformation was due to cynical motives to quash competition with the merging alcohol industry, itself emerging from prohibition and even racial policy. This resulted in the draconian legal regime existing today for cannabis/marijuana which by virtue of its now illegal classification, acquired a demonized social status.

The Commission acknowledges that there are documented health risks associated with cannabis/marijuana. However, modern scientific data demonstrates that there is conclusive evidence that cannabis/marijuana has considerable value as a medicinal substance and as liberalization in the law occurs, scientific studies are proving more medicinal uses for the plant. At the same time, medical science has disproved some of the most important myths or propaganda about the supposed negative physiological impact of cannabis/marijuana, including a causative link to psychosis and its status as a gateway drug. It has also proved that cannabis/marijuana is no more harmful than alcohol and other substances that are no longer prohibited and, in many respects, less so.

Science has also proven some important adverse impacts of cannabis/marijuana. These relate mainly to specific, high risk groups, among the most important being the young (adolescents) and its negative impact on psychomotor functions. . . . The argument for law reform is premised on the finding that the identified risks are more effectively managed and minimized within a responsibly regulated public health/ rights framework and market, than a punitive criminal justice led response and unregulated criminal market. (CARICOM Regional Commission on Marijuana 2018, 63)

The marijuana study team proposed some far-reaching reforms:

- Cannabis/marijuana should be declassified as a "dangerous drug" or narcotic, in all legislation and reclassified as a controlled substance.
- CARICOM states should act to remove "Prohibition" status from cannabis/marijuana, substituting the current prohibitive, criminal sanctioned regime with legal and social policy that emphasises public health, education and human rights; CARICOM states should have a margin of appreciation as to how to achieve this ultimate goal, either:
  —complete and immediate removal of all prohibitive legal provisions, thereby rendering cannabis/marijuana a legal substance, which is regulated only in strictly defined circumstances; or
  —as a preparatory step, the decriminalization of cannabis/marijuana for personal use in private premises and medical purposes.
- Full prohibition for children and adolescents with an appropriate age limit should be maintained except for medical reasons; however, young people who use marijuana will be directed to treatment and diversion programs rather than being prosecuted or criminalized.
- The law should enact legal definitions of hemp based on low THC levels and make clear distinctions between hemp and other varieties of cannabis and ensuring that all legal sanctions be removed from hemp and hemp production.

- Legislation should provide for the protection of seeds, strains of cannabis, through intellectual property mechanisms.
- Customs Law should be amended to make provision for the import and export of cannabis and cannabis products, as appropriate.
- To avoid the implications of Anti-money laundering and Proceeds of Crime legislation which currently prohibit legitimate banking and other financial transactions for illegal cannabis, commercial cannabis activities will need to be legalised.
- Small farmers and small business persons should be included in production and supply arrangements with appropriate controls limiting large enterprise and foreign involvement.
- An equitable land use policy for marijuana cultivation should be formulated.
- Distribution points for cannabis and its products should be limited.
- Special provision should be made to protect religious rights in the new regime.
- Retroactivity should be used as a tool to correct past injustices, such as expungement of criminal records and CSME rules.
- Restrictions that support no public smoking and vaping of cannabis in alignment with tobacco smoking and vaping restrictions should be adopted. Cannabis/marijuana use should be banned in public spaces with appropriate exceptions for Rastafarians on religious grounds. Such restrictions should include prohibiting use in workplaces, enclosed public spaces, on health authority and school board property, transit shelters, common areas of apartment building[s] and community care facilities.
- States should regulate the locations of marijuana retail establishments, by ensuring an appropriate distance from playgrounds and schools and also prohibiting stores that sell other products to minors from selling marijuana.
- Regulations should be aimed at reducing the likelihood of children accidentally ingesting marijuana. States with legal marijuana can regulate the appearance, packaging, and labeling of products likely to be appealing to youth, such as marijuana-infused candy and baked goods.
- Limit marijuana's appeal by implementing restrictions on marketing through traditional media such as billboards, television, radio, newspapers.
- Retail availability of marijuana should be tightly regulated. States should develop licensing policies applying to all actors in the recreational marijuana supply chain, including retailers.
- Apply limits of allowable THC in products.
- Drugged driving regulations should be created.
- Ensure appropriate and reasonable pricing to deter consumers from purchasing cannabis through illegal means.
- Moderate taxes should be imposed taking care that the black market is not reinvigorated.

- Availability of cannabis should be limited by placing caps on retail density and hours of sale.
- Environmental conservation and preservation must guide commercial marijuana activities.
- Public Education programs should be prioritized.
- A data collection system to track processes and outcomes should be established.
- Regular performance evaluations should be conducted to guide policy refinements.

(CARICOM Regional Commission on Marijuana 2018, 65–67)[12]

Country Legalization Efforts

Although Peter Tosh, Bob Marley, and other dead and living longtime advocates of drug reform would have celebrated or are celebrating—some, perhaps, from the Great Beyond—the bold recommendations by the CARICOM Commission and the subsequent actions by several Caribbean states, they likely would have been or are ecstatic about the audacious leadership by officials in Jamaica even before the commission began its work.

As Vicki Hanson (2016) recounted, 2015 was a banner year in Jamaica's marijuana reform pursuits. In January of that year, Jamaica hosted the inaugural "International Cannabis Investors Conference," and the following month the Parliament enacted legislation to amend the Dangerous Drugs Act to provide for, among other things, the modification of penalties for the possession of ganja in specified circumstances and for a scheme of licenses, permits, and other authorizations for medical, therapeutic, or scientific purposes. Although the new legislation did not legalize marijuana, it decriminalized the possession of two ounces or less and recognized the sacramental use of the plant by the Rastafarian community. The amendment also made way for the medicinal, therapeutic, and scientific use of the plant, thereby recognizing a provision that was always available under the U.N. Convention on Narcotic Drugs. The new law took effect on April 15, 2015.

In April, the University of the West Indies (UWI), Mona, was granted a ministerial order by the minister of science, technology, energy, and mining, under the new legislation, to cultivate cannabis and engage independent growers of the plant for research purposes. This led to the historic signing of a memorandum of understanding between the UWI Mona and the Ganja (Future) Growers and Producers Association later that month. As well, the cabinet approved the establishment of a sixteen-member Cannabis Licensing Authority, with the mandate to regulate the hoped-for hemp and medicinal ganja industry. The following month Justice Minister Mark Golding participated in the U.N. High-Level Thematic Debate on International Drug Policy in preparation for the U.N. General Assembly Special Session on the World Drug Problem, scheduled for April 2016.

In July the minister of justice signed the Criminal Records (Rehabilitation of Offenders) (Automatic Expungement of Convictions) Order 2015 to allow for the expungement of the records of persons with previous convictions for smoking marijuana and its possession where the sentence imposed was a fine not exceeding J$1,000 (US$7.46) and the possession of pipes or other paraphernalia used for the smoking of ganja. The order took effect on July 9, 2015.

August of that year saw the minister of industry, investment, and commerce announcing that the work on the ganja regulations for the industry was proceeding as planned and that consultants from the U.S.-based research company BOTEC Analysis were engaged to assist with the development of recommendations for the country's regulatory framework. The First National Congress of the Ganja Growers and Producers Association was held in September. Among other things, the congress called for the government to establish two new pieces of legislation—namely, the Cannabis Industry Development Act and the Rastafarian Sacramental Rights Act—to govern the new approach to the ganja industry. Also, that month the Cannabis Licensing Authority outlined its eight guiding principles for the sector, intended to provide assurance, transparency, and structure for individuals who seek to operate in the official marijuana industry (Hanson 2016).

Among other things, the Ministry of Justice Fact Sheet on the matter explained that possession of two ounces or less of ganja is no longer an arrestable offense, and it will not result in a criminal record. However, the police may issue a ticket to a person in possession of two ounces or less of the drug, and the person has thirty days to pay the sum of J$500 (US$3.73) at any tax office. Someone found to possess two ounces or less and who is under the age of eighteen years, or who is eighteen years or older and appears to the police to be dependent on ganja, will also be referred to the National Council on Drug Abuse for counseling, in addition to having to pay the ticket. Under the new law it remains a criminal offense to possess over two ounces of marijuana, and offenders can be arrested, charged, tried in court, and, if found guilty, sentenced to a fine, imprisonment, or both. The conviction will also be recorded on that person's criminal record.

The rules against possession do not apply to possession for religious purposes as a sacrament in adherence to the Rastafarian faith; or possession for medical or therapeutic purposes as recommended or prescribed by a registered medical doctor or other health practitioner or class of approved practitioners; or possession for purposes of scientific research that is conducted by an accredited tertiary institution or is approved by the Scientific Research Council; or possession pursuant to a license, authorization or permit issued under the new legislation. Smoking of marijuana in a public place or within five meters of a public place is prohibited in a manner similar to cigarettes. A person who smokes in public cannot be arrested or detained, but the police can issue a ticket to that person, who will have thirty days to pay J$500 (US$3.73) at any tax office.

Smoking of marijuana at privately occupied residences that are not used for commercial purposes is not an offense. Moreover, smoking of marijuana is legally permitted in places that are licensed for smoking of the drug for medical or therapeutic purposes. Adherents of the Rastafarian faith also are permitted to smoke the herb for sacramental purposes in locations registered as places of Rastafarian worship (Government of Jamaica 2015; Charles 2019). History was made in September 2018 when Jamaica announced approval of the first shipment of marijuana oil to Canada. The consignment, which was requested by Health Canada, the Canadian government's agency that oversees the nation's health care programs, was fulfilled by Jamaican-based licensed producer Timeless Herbal Care (see *Jamaica Gleaner* 2018b).[13]

text continues on page 66

Status of Marijuana Reforms in the Caribbean, October 2019

ANTIGUA & BARBUDA

Status: Medicinal + Decriminalized. Cannabis has been decriminalized in Antigua and Barbuda and they now have a Medicinal Cannabis Authority in place which is responsible for regulating and controlling the licensing of the cultivation, manufacture, processing, extraction, import, export, testing, research, distribution, and sale of medicinal cannabis and cannabis for sacramental purposes. The rules for decriminalization are that—Anyone older than 18 is allowed to possess a maximum of 15 grams of cannabis. It is lawful to cultivate up to four plants per household. Cannabis sales remain illegal. Smoking Cannabis is prohibited in public places, including bars, restaurants and tourist establishments. Tourist establishments are allowed to set aside "open areas" where guests can smoke Cannabis.

ANGUILLA

Status: Medicinal + Decriminalization Being Debated. Anguilla has proposed new Cannabis decriminalization laws. It will allow for regulated, supervised and limited access for sick citizens, especially those with cancer, HIV/AIDS, glaucoma, and epilepsy. The new laws when enacted will allow for up to 10 grams and seek to expunge the records of those previously charged for possession of small amounts of Cannabis. More details of the laws will be made public soon.

ARUBA

Status: Medicinal + Decriminalisation by Year-End 2019. Aruba will approve Medical Cannabis by the end of 2019. Aruba makes a big step towards legalizing and decriminalizing medical cannabis (CBD Oil). Soon adults will be free to buy and use cannabis products with a low THC, such as CBD oil, without a prescription. Drugs with a higher THC content will be available through medical doctors and specialists, with a prescription. It continues to ban the recreational use of cannabis for the time being.

BARBADOS

Status: Medicinal + Decriminalization Being Debated. Cannabis in Barbados is in the process of being decriminalized as the Government announced plans to establish a medical Cannabis industry project implementation unit, that is mandated to establish an administrative framework for a medical Cannabis program and bring it to fruition. Parliamentarians are expected to debate Marshall's bill in August 30. The government said that decriminalization of Cannabis for recreational use will have to be decided by a referendum. In the meantime, while laws are being changed, the ministry of health and wellness has approved five medicinal Cannabis drugs submitted by the drug formulary committee to be placed on the National Drug Formulary. The drugs will be imported by the Barbados Drug Service.

BAHAMAS

Status: Medicinal + Decriminalization Being Debated. Cannabis in the Bahamas is currently in the process of being decriminalized. The Bahamas National Commission on Cannabis (BNCM) has been formed and after a series of town halls and other consultations, they are to submit a report by the end of summer 2019. The commission's report will cover five aspects: the medical use of cannabis; the economic and industrial use of cannabis, for example for paper, alternative plastics, concrete, biofuels, etc.; the religious and ceremonial use of cannabis, for the Rastafarian community or other communities that may use it as part of their ceremonies; the recreational use of cannabis, regarding potency edibles, tourism and any other aspects in that area; finally, regulatory issues related to cannabis regarding age restrictions, legislative framework and other issues. Unfortunately, the Government has started to crack down on the advertisement, import and sales of CBD oils and products as Cannabis-derived products are still Illegal. Up until the call for the ban, there were no restrictions on CBD products.

BELIZE

Status: Medicinal + Decriminalized. Cannabis in Belize was decriminalized in 2016. The amended Misuse of Drugs Act was passed, and it decriminalizes possession and use of small amounts of Cannabis. Adults can have up to 10 grams of Cannabis in their possession and smoke it on their premises or somebody else's private premises, once the owner gives permission.

BERMUDA

Status: Pointlessly Decriminalized. Cannabis in Bermuda has been decriminalized with the changes to the country's Misuse of Drugs [Decriminalization of Cannabis] Amendment Act 2017. What the amended Act has done, is to remove criminal offences for the simple possession by any person of 7 grams or less of cannabis. The Amendment does NOT make it legal for a person to consume, cultivate, traffic or import cannabis in any quantity. The changes in the law do not provide any guarantee that a person will not be stopped when attempting to travel to the United States of America for any reason, including if that person already has a prior conviction for simple possession of cannabis. The government of Bermuda is currently on a public education campaign.

BONAIRE

Status: Illegal. Not Like their Mother Country. The big question has always been, does the same tolerance and decriminalization laws in the Netherlands also apply in Bonaire, its territory in the Caribbean, as it's legal to buy and consume cannabis in Amsterdam? The Bonaire Tourism office answers say it all. "Bonaire does NOT support the same Dutch tolerance laws towards pot and other narcotics as the Netherlands in Europe. If someone is caught with it, that person could face serious charges and jail time. I would advise it not be included in a vacation on Bonaire." The status of Cannabis in Bonaire is NOT like that of its mother country.

BRITISH VIRGIN ISLANDS

Status: Decriminalization Being Debated. Currently, possession and distribution of Cannabis of any quantity are illegal in the territory. That said, there is a fast-rising expressed openness to reconsidering the laws concerning Cannabis. Politicians are listening closely to the public discussions and consultations being raised at Cannabis educational events about how to move forward. It has been said that consultations are the first step in what has been called "a long journey to decriminalization and legalisation of Cannabis in the British Virgin Islands."

CAYMAN ISLANDS

Status: Medicinal. In the Cayman Islands, the Misuse of Drugs (Amendment) Law was amended. It states that "the use of cannabis extracts and tinctures of cannabis for medical or therapeutic purposes, where prescribed by a medical doctor licensed under the Health Practice Law as part of a course of treatment for a person under that medical doctor's care, is lawful." This step by the government legalised the medical use of Cannabis in the form of an oil or tinctures to treat cancer, epilepsy, or as a pain reliever for osteoarthritis and rheumatoid arthritis, among a list of other conditions. The oils can be legally imported.

CUBA

Status: Illegal. Cannabis is illegal in Cuba, and so is any related action.

CURACAO

Status: CBD Oil Prevalent. Decriminalization Pending. Already, hundreds of patients in Curaçao use Cannabidiol (CBD) oil. The CBD oils are available through the pharmacy and are largely imported from Spain currently. There is a very strong and vibrant Cannabis community, non-profit movement and online petitions behind the Curacao Cannabis Act of 2018/2019. Among other things, the Cannabis Community is calling for the creation of a Cannabis Commission; for the laws to change to allow the personal, medicinal, and commercial use of Cannabis in Curaçao provided that such activity occurs pursuant to this chapter; To permit persons licensed, controlled, and regulated by Curaçao to legally manufacture and sell Cannabis to persons 18 years of age and older and To create Hemp Industries for Curaçao and more. They have since put out a 12-point proposal.

DOMINICA

Status: Medicinal + Decriminalization Pending. After rounds of Cannabis Consultations with various stakeholders, the Government announced in July 2019, that they will bring to the Parliament for consideration, legislation that would allow for the regulated and controlled use of Cannabis for medicinal, scientific, religious and recreational purposes. The Government will, therefore, propose that the possession of not more than 28.35 grams (1 ounce) of Cannabis, be decriminalized. The government will go further and make the necessary amendments to have struck off from the record of those convicted for Cannabis possession, any conviction in respect of the possession of 28.35 grams (one ounce) or less.

DOMINICAN REPUBLIC

Status: Decriminalization Being Discussed. Neurosurgeon José Joaquín Puello, opened the debate with different sectors to discuss the possibility of decriminalizing Cannabis for medicinal and recreational use.

GUADELOUPE

Status: Medicinal Decriminalization. From 2018, the Guadalupe City Council voted to ban everything but medicinal deliveries of Cannabis to city residents, setting the stage for a wide-ranging moratorium on storefronts, commercial cultivation and other adjacent or associated businesses.

GRENADA

Status: Decriminalization Being Discussed. This Caribbean Nation is eyeing Cannabis Tourism by decriminalizing Cannabis. The country is still in study and discussion mode, but no position has been taken on it as yet. So it is still illegal there. In November 2017, Grenada enforced the rehabilitation offenses legislation which provides for persons with convictions for possession of Cannabis joints to have their records removed after four years. There was a recent call by Cannabis advocates focused on Cannabis Tourism, for the government to take immediate steps to accommodate Canadian visitors who need to use cannabis for medicinal purposes.

GUYANA

Status: Piecemeal Decriminalization Pending. In January 2019, the Guyanese Government announced that Cannabis, hemp decriminalization is on Guyana's election agenda. In July 2019 Cabinet approved a bill intended to amend the Narcotic Drugs and Psychotropic Substance Control Act to prevent persons from being incarcerated if found with up to 30 grams of Cannabis. Though the bill, when passed into law, will not decriminalize the use of Cannabis, Trotman said it will prevent hundreds of persons, particularly young people, from being imprisoned for possession of small quantities of cannabis. He explained that persons found with up to 30 grams of cannabis will either pay a fine or do community service. The Act is not intended to decriminalize the use of Cannabis but rather prevent persons from being jailed for having up to 30 grams of cannabis in their possession. The overall intention is to reduce the prison population.

HAITI

Status: Illegal. No Decriminalization Process in Near Sight. Cannabis is illegal in Haiti, and so is any related action.

JAMAICA

Status: Medicinal, Sacramental, Decriminalization. A self-described leader in the Caribbean Cannabis Market, Jamaica passed the "Ganja Law" in 2015, which decriminalized the growing, consuming, selling and researching of Cannabis for medical, therapeutic and sacrament purposes. You can possess 2 ounces / 56 grams or less of cannabis and personally cultivate up to 5 plants maximum per household. Cannabis Legal for Rastafarians for Sacramental Use. As of the end of August 2019, 54 licensees had been issued by the Cannabis Licensing Authority (CLA). Additionally, the CLA has issued just over 600 applications to date that includes 190 applications at the conditional approval stage and another 367 at desk review and verification stage. The CLA will complete the export regulations shortly to facilitate the legal export of Cannabis Raw Materials such as buds and oil extracts.

MARTINIQUE

Status: Illegal. Cannabis in Martinique, the French Overseas Territory in the Caribbean, is illegal under French law.

MONTSERRAT

Status: Illegal. Cannabis in Montserrat, the British Overseas Territory in the Caribbean Leeward Islands, is illegal under British law.

PUERTO RICO

Status: Medicinal. Legal for medicinal purposes but illegal for recreational purposes. Although the medical use of Cannabis is permitted, smoking the substance is not legal. Puerto Rico has legalized medical Cannabis, setting up several dispensaries on the island and the number of patients registered in Puerto Rico has surpassed 20,000, signaling that the industry is gaining momentum.

SABA

Status: Illegal. Not Like Their Mother Country. Cannabis in Saba, a Caribbean Island in the Lesser Antilles chain and a special municipality of the Netherlands, is illegal.

ST. BARTHELEMY

Status: Limited Medicinal. Cannabis is illegal in Saint Barthélemy for personal use. Limited types of cannabis-derived products are permitted for medical uses. As an overseas collectivity of France, Saint Barthélemy is subject to French law and all international conventions signed by France.

ST. MARTIN

Status: Illegal. Not Like Their Mother Country. While a Cannabis Culture thrives there, even the Dutch Territory still marks Cannabis as illegal.

ST. KITTS & NEVIS

Status: Medicinal, Scientific, Religious and Recreational Purposes. In July 2019, the government of St. Kitts and Nevis filed a Cannabis Bill, the landmark legislative amendments to the Drugs (Prevention and Abatement of the Misuse and Abuse of Drugs) (Amendment) Bill, 2019. This is a follow-up from the report of its National Cannabis Commission and its recommendation that the country's Drugs Act of 1986 be amended to take into consideration the latest research on the benefits of cannabis. Among its proposals, the Commission supported legalizing the use of Cannabis and its derivatives for medicinal and scientific purposes, decriminalizing possession of 15 grams of cannabis or less and the expungement of criminal records for people convicted for similar amounts.

ST. LUCIA

Status: Decriminalization Pending. The St. Lucia government has given the nod to the re-establishment of a Cannabis commission that has been given the mandate to consult and provide advice on the design of a legislative and regulatory framework for cannabis. Public Consultations have begun, and it is expected that Saint Lucia will be decriminalizing Cannabis before end of 2019 and focused on medical Cannabis.

ST. VINCENT & THE GRENADINES

Status: Medicinal. Saint Vincent & the Grenadines became the first member of the Organization of Eastern Caribbean States (OECS), the community of Lesser Antilles nations, to decriminalize cannabis and establish a medical Cannabis program in December 2018 by passing a Medicinal Cannabis Bill. The Medicinal Cannabis Authority which regulates the cultivation, supply, possession, production and use of cannabis for medicinal purposes in the country have so far given 25 licenses so far. The president of Saint Vincent and the Grenadines would rather export cannabis than grow bananas.

SURINAME

Status: Medicinal Pending. Cannabis will soon be permitted within the health care system of Suriname. To this end, the Advisory and Monitoring Body for Scientific Research on Hemp Cultivation has been installed. Cannabis will only be permitted by law for medicinal and not for recreational use.

TRINIDAD AND TOBAGO

Status: Decriminalization Pending. Imported CBD Oil is readily available in Smoke Accessories stores and pharmacies and used in the private practice healthcare system. What is coming next is the legislation for the decriminalization of Cannabis. The draft legislation was completed in June 2019 and will be tabled in Parliament in September 2019. The new legislation is expected to cover regulations that govern medicinal, manufacturing, production and sale aspects of Cannabis, in addition to the expungement of the records of individuals in jail.

TURKS & CAICOS ISLANDS

Status: Medicinal. In January 21, 2019 the Medical Cannabis Patient Care Act (MCPCA) was signed into law, to create a new medical cannabis tourism industry by allowing patients from states and countries with regulated markets to access Virgin Islands medical cannabis for a fee and to "allow non-cannabis patients worldwide to visit the Virgin Islands and receive cannabis therapy as part of an in-patient program." Additionally, three classes of cultivation will also be allowed: 1) Patients and caregivers will be permitted to grow a small quantity for personal use; 2) "Family farms" will be allowed to cultivate up to 100 plants; 3) Larger commercial grow operations will be allowed to grow up to 1,000 plants.

Source: Ingrid Riley, *Sun, Sea, and Sensi—Guide to Current Caribbean Cannabis Laws*, IngridRiley.com /2019/08/27/sun-sea-and-sensi-guide-to-current-caribbean-cannabis-laws/, August 27, 2019.

Still, as the sidebar, "Status of Marijuana Reforms in the Caribbean," indicates (thanks to Riley 2019), Jamaica is not the only state where bold reforms have been pursued. Notable are the pursuits in Antigua and Barbuda, Barbados, Belize, St. Kitts and Nevis, Trinidad and Tobago, Grenada, and St. Vincent and the Grenadines. For instance, not only did the authorities in St. Vincent and the Grenadines promote cannabis production for medicinal and tourism purposes, but on January 5, 2022, they also approved the first export certificate. The license was to export 110 pounds of medicinal marijuana to Germany's Federal Institute for Drugs and Medical Devices. It was the first Eastern Caribbean country to do so (see Searchlight 2022).

In November 2019, authorities in Barbados passed the Medical Cannabis Industry Bill, 2019, to cover activities related to marijuana cultivation, processing, dispensing, and export. It also empowers the Medicinal Cannabis Licensing Authority to develop policies and guidelines for a newly regulated medicinal marijuana industry. Also adopted was the Sacramental Cannabis Bill, 2019, which permits adherents of the Rastafarian religion to consume and cultivate marijuana as a sacrament in worship. Barbados has adopted a three-tiered approach to cultivation and processor permits: Tier 1 licenses are limited to less than one acre; Tier 2 permits are for one to five acres; and Tier 3 licenses are for more than five acres of medical cannabis.

License holders are required to be citizens, permanent residents, hold immigrant status (which can be gained through investing), or be citizens of a CARICOM member state. The new legislation allows medical cannabis to be prescribed by a practitioner to Barbadians or visitors to the island. As with other Caribbean countries, Barbados has established a Medicinal Cannabis Licensing Authority to issue licenses; establish a database for the electronic tracking of cannabis; and establish a register of practitioners, patients, and caregivers. The new approach contemplates the issuance of business licenses for the cultivation of cannabis for medical purposes. It also envisages the transport and manufacturing of medical cannabis products, their dispensing at therapeutic facilities, the sale of medicinal cannabis, research and development for medical or scientific purposes, laboratory testing, and the import and export of medical cannabis (Lamers 2019).

In the case of St. Kitts and Nevis, the cabinet accepted the final report of their National Marijuana Commission following a meeting with members of the commission on February 18, 2019. The commission could not agree that cannabis should be legalized for religious or recreational purposes, and the cabinet decided on a phased adoption of the recommendations, anticipating further consultation on creating a framework for the use of cannabis for medicinal purposes and for the development of the medical cannabis industry. However, authorities there imagined a situation where individuals found with under fifteen grams of cannabis or growing fewer than five plants would receive only tickets for their offenses and would have no criminal record. Individuals in prison on convictions for small amounts of fifteen grams or less would have their sentences reviewed, and individuals convicted for such small amounts would have their conviction quashed.

The commission unanimously recommended that:

- The blanket criminalization of cannabis had been overtaken by passage of time and regional and international developments and should be amended.
- The definitions in the Drugs Act relating to cannabis should be amended, considering the scientific developments that had occurred since its passage in 1986.
- The use of cannabis and its derivatives for medicinal and scientific purposes should be permitted under license.
- The regime for the use of cannabis for medicinal purposes should include:
  —the establishment of a medicinal licensing authority to regulate importation, local cultivation, and production;
  —a requirement that two tiers of practitioners must complete a requisite amount of continuous medical education hours on cannabis: (1) medical practitioners for prescriptible marijuana products; and (2) herbalists for non-prescriptible marijuana products;
  —and a requirement that prescriptible marijuana products must meet international labeling standards.

Moreover, it suggested that production and trade be permitted under license and a strict legislated regime of hemp and hemp products; the penalty for possession of less than fifteen grams of cannabis should become a ticketable offense without a criminal record; the penalty for the growth of fewer than five plants per household should be reduced to a ticketable offense without a criminal record; the current regime for rehabilitation should be amended to permit the court to expunge the criminal records of persons previously convicted for possession of cannabis in quantities below fifteen grams; a massive public messaging program should be created prior to any changes in the law and continuing thereafter to inform the public of the benefits and risks and the potential harm to young persons of the use of cannabis; the program should be adapted for use in the school curriculum; the smoking and use of cannabis in public places should remain a criminal offense and attract substantial penalties; and that offenses and penalties of driving under the influence of cannabis should be introduced (*WIC News Reporter* 2019).

Prime Minister Timothy Harris used the occasion of his August 5, 2019, Emancipation Day message to announce the initiation of legislation to amend the Drugs (Prevention and Abatement of the Misuse and Abuse of Drugs) Act in order to decriminalize marijuana. The government later established a Cannabis Core Committee to provide guidance on legalization and the creation of a domestic cannabis industry. Dr. Wycliffe Baird, who had worked in Africa and the Caribbean with their cannabis legislation and industry, was named to head the committee, which included representatives from youth, the Christian and Rastafarian communities, the Chamber of Industry and Commerce, and the Office of the Attorney General (Herrington 2019). Reform measures were advanced on February 12, 2020, with the unanimous passage in the legislature of the Cannabis Bill, 2020; of the Drugs (Prevention and Abatement of the Misuse and Abuse of Drugs) (Amendment) Bill, 2020; and the Criminal Records (Rehabilitation of Offenders) (Amendment) Bill, 2020 (*Caribbean National Weekly* 2020b).

In Trinidad and Tobago, the Dangerous Drugs (Amendment) Act took effect beginning December 23, 2019. Under the legislation, anyone with more than thirty grams, but not more than sixty grams, of cannabis, or more than five grams, but not more than ten grams, of cannabis resin, commits an offense and is liable on summary conviction to a fine of TT$50,000 (US$7,315). The law also allows individuals to cultivate or have in their possession up to four growing female cannabis plants. The act leaves intact the prohibition against trafficking within a school zone. While an adult is allowed the thirty grams of marijuana, if caught within five hundred meters of a school, they can be punished with as little as a TT$50,000 (US$7,315) fine on summary conviction and to as much as TT$150,000 (US$21,945) or thirty-five years to life in prison on indictment. The law also prohibits the consumption of marijuana in any public space.

According to Attorney General Faris Al-Rawi, eighty-seven adults and fourteen children then in the prison system, some there for as little as a half a gram of marijuana, would benefit from the drug decriminalization. He also noted the absurdity of having someone who could not pay a TT$1,000 (US$146) fine to be jailed for three months at a cost of TT$75,000 (US$10,972) to the state. In addition, Al-Rawi revealed that the new measures would remove eighty-five hundred cases from the system. He also gave the age breakdown of the people charged for cannabis possession during the years 2015–2018:

under 15:	38
15–19:	902
20–25:	2,848
25–29:	2,783
30–34:	2,466
35–39:	1,639[14]

Clearly, the geonarcotics milieu is a complex one, with the drug PWP presenting myriad security and sovereignty challenges to the citizens and states of the Caribbean. Sadly, the alarm bells that were sounded some three decades ago by the West Indian Commission still toll loudly: "Nothing poses greater threats to civil society in CARICOM countries than the drug problem and nothing exemplifies the powerlessness of regional governments more. That is the magnitude of the damage that drug abuse and trafficking hold for our Community. It is a many-layered danger. At base is the human destruction in drug addiction; but, implicit also, is corruption of individuals and systems by the sheer enormity of the inducements of the illegal drug trade in relatively poor societies" (West Indian Commission 1992, 343–44). The commission cited the critical security-sovereignty dynamic: "On top of all this lie the implications for governance itself—at the hands of both external agencies engaged in international interdiction, and drug barons themselves—the 'dons' of the modern Caribbean—who threaten governance from within" (343–44).

Needless to say, the threat never was restricted to the fifteen CARICOM countries; the entire Caribbean is implicated. But there are reasons for guarded optimism that some of the reforms introduced will lead progressively to amelioration of the situation in three to five years, especially in relation to the illegal drug cultivation and trafficking and some of the activities deemed criminal. In all likelihood, the reform movement will grow to include other countries. Still, unless demands in North America and Europe for cocaine, heroin, and other substances are reduced dramatically, the marijuana reforms will not alter the use of the region for the transshipment of cocaine and other hard drugs.

Keep in mind that the region's geographic realities of proximity both to South American source countries and North American demand mainstays are fairly fixed. Thus, the marijuana initiatives by themselves will not end the PWP challenges related to drugs. Evidently—and as purported in the geonarcotics framework—some of the threats spawned by the drama of drugs and the crucible of crime are interconnected. Thus, having probed the drama of drugs in this chapter, it is now important to consider the crucible of crime, the subject of the next chapter.

The Crucible of Crime

It pains my heart that many of our brothers and sisters, and our children were deprived of seeing 2020 due to violence. This is a social epidemic and requires national consensus around the use of emergency powers to bring the disease under control. Unfortunately, there are those among us that appear to accept the high level of crime and violence as normal. Political disunity and gamesmanship over crime fighting and national security policy have real effects on our lives.
—Prime Minister of Jamaica, Andrew Holness, New Year Message 2020

Intentional homicide is the ultimate crime and has ripple effects that go far beyond the original loss of human life. For homicide also blights the lives of the victim's family and community, who may therefore be described as "secondary victims." It creates a violent environment that has a negative impact on society, the economy and government institutions. Homicide is not limited to people living on the margins of society; rather, it can affect all people, irrespective of their age, sex, ethnicity and socioeconomic background.
—U.N. Office on Drugs and Crime, *Global Study on Homicide*, 2019a, 7.

The sad portrait of the trauma and drama facing Jamaica painted by Prime Minister Holness in his 2020 New Year's message only partially depicts the clear and present dangers that the crime Problems Without Passports present to Jamaica. The many brothers, sisters, and children who were "deprived of seeing 2020 due to violence" actually numbered 1,339: the number of individuals who were murdered in 2019. This gave Jamaica a homicide rate of 47.4 per 100,000 inhabitants, the second-highest rate in the entire Latin America and Caribbean region for 2019, after Venezuela. The number dropped slightly in 2020, to 1,323 (46.5 per 100,000 inhabitants) and reached 1,463 in 2021, an increase of some

10 percent. This new homicide rate reached almost 50 per 100,000 people in 2021: 49.4 per 100,000 individuals, actually. Jamaica's crime rate was worse than Venezuela's in both 2020 and 2021.[1] The bloodbath continued in 2022. Indeed, more than 70 people were murdered in just fifteen days in January, and by the time the year ended, the country had recorded 1,498 murders (*InSight Crime* 2022; *Jamaica Gleaner* 2023).

Yet, as will be seen later in this chapter, Jamaica is not singular in experiencing the pain to which Prime Minister Holness referred. Trinidad and Tobago, for instance, experienced 536 homicides in 2019, giving the country a homicide rate of 37.4 per 100,000 inhabitants. Thankfully, the number dropped to 393 in 2020. Still, it bounced back to 448 in 2021 and leaped forward to 601 in 2022, over 22 percent more than in 2021, making that year the deadliest in the nation's history (*InSight Crime* 2023). However horrific the images conjured up by the numbers, they tell only part of the story. Prime Minister Holness and, more so, the U.N. report (in the second epigraph to this chapter) point to the ripple effects on individuals, families, and communities on the social, economic, and other dimensions affected and on the fact that political and national security ramifications are involved.

The nature, scope, and connectivity of the criminality highlight the multidimensionality of the PWP under scrutiny. They also reflect an element of another feature of PWPs that was discussed in the three earlier chapters—transnationality. This feature is obvious when one considers the criminality linkages to the production, sale, and trafficking of drugs; the prosecution of the crime in some places by gangs with cross-national connections; and the inordinate use of guns that originate outside the Caribbean. Furthermore, civilizational implications both flow from and are part of the criminality landscape. This chapter examines some of these aspects, first by surveying the crime landscape. A discussion of States of Emergency, which dramatize the gravity of the situations and provide public security coping mechanisms, allows us to appreciate some of the sobering extant realities. We then probe some of the economic and social costs involved and some civilizational implications.

Sobering Situations

At an international criminal justice meeting in Port-of-Spain at the turn of the twenty-first century, then–Trinidad and Tobago attorney general Ramesh Maharaj made the following declaration on behalf of the Caribbean: "There is a direct nexus between illegal drugs and crimes of violence, sex crimes, domestic violence, maltreatment of children by parents and other evils. Our citizens suffer from drug addiction, drug-related violence, and drug-related corruption of law enforcement and public officials. Aside from the very visible decimation of our societies caused by drug addiction and drug-related violence, there is another insidious evil: money laundering" (Maharaj 2000). Quite rightly, the attorney general highlighted the essence of the danger to governance in noting that it changes democratic institutions, erodes the rule of law, and destroys civic order with impunity. Maharaj's statement, which highlighted the link between drugs and crime, remains largely true today. Moreover, there is local-global connectivity reflected in the fact that the crime is not all ad hoc and local; some of it is transnational and organized, extending beyond the region to North America, Europe, and elsewhere.[2]

Quotidian Experiences

In too many places violent crime defines the quotidian experiences of individual and corporate citizens, reaching almost pandemic proportions at times. Indeed, a U.N.–World Bank study once cited the murder rates in the Caribbean—at 30 per 100,000 population annually, using data for the 2000s—as being higher than for any other region of the world. The study provided credible evidence of the wide-ranging economic, social, and other negative impact crime is having on Caribbean nations (U.N. Office on Drugs and Crime–World Bank 2007). Thankfully, the U.N. global crime report for 2011 revealed that the region had moved from first to fourth place, after Southern Africa, Central America, and South America. However, still troubling was the high gun usage; the region ranked second after South America and ahead of Central America in the percentage of homicides by firearms (see U.N. Office on Drugs and Crime 2011a, especially chapters 1, 3).

Several things are noteworthy about the regional crime realities over recent decades. First, murder, fraud, theft, and assault are precisely the crimes associated with drugs. Moreover, the countries with high and progressive crime reports in the theft, homicide, and serious assault categories are the same ones that have featured prominently over the last two decades as centers of drug activity. These countries include the Bahamas, the Dominican Republic, Puerto Rico, Jamaica, St. Kitts and Nevis, Trinidad and Tobago, the U.S. Virgin Islands, and Guyana. As well, the last decade has witnessed crime sprees in some places, sometimes with dramatic temerity, including attacks on police stations, kidnappings, and vicious murders of police officers.

The crime crucible is dramatized by the high murder rates. Incidentally, the terms "murder" and "homicide" are used interchangeably. As well, because of the multiplicity of usages of the term "homicide," it is important to identify our definitional parameters. This study adopts the U.N. definition of "intentional homicide": "unlawful death purposefully inflicted on one person by another." It has three key qualifying elements: the killing of a person by another person (objective element); the intent of the perpetrator to kill or seriously injure the victim (subjective element), and the unlawfulness of the killing (legal element) (U.N. Office on Drugs and Crime 2019a, 7).

The focus on homicides is not to suggest that assault, rape, domestic violence, and other crimes are unimportant or have not increased in some places.[3] As a matter of fact, there has been troubling growth in domestic violence in Guyana, Puerto Rico, Jamaica, and elsewhere. Murders command attention here because they constitute the "ultimate crimes," with human finality and powerful economic, social, public security, and other consequences. Indeed, the 2019 U.N. report captured in the epigraph reminds us that, among other things, homicides have ripple effects that extend beyond the loss of life by individuals and negatively impact the families and communities of the victims and affect the governance institutions and economies of the societies involved. Moreover, although as suggested in the 2019 U.N. report, they are not limited to individuals who live on the margins of societies; in the Caribbean these are the people who are most significantly impacted.

The point also was made in the 2011 *Global Study on Homicide* that "homicides also represent a reasonable proxy for violent crime in general, and due to the 'invisible' nature of much violent crime in terms of the failure to record it, homicide can be considered the tip of the violence 'iceberg.' Thus, homicide data can also provide valuable insights into the nature and extent of this wider concern" (U.N. Office on Drugs and Crime 2011a, 15). Besides, murders provide indicators about anomie and, perhaps more troubling, about distressing civilizational implications, as will be seen below. The civilizational impact relates not just to the crimes but also to the responses to them, including police impunity in some places.

The 2019 global crime survey explained that organized crime groups and gangs are largely responsible for the high homicide rates in the Americas. Yet the relationship is not a straightforward one, because high murder rates caused by organized crime groups can rise even higher when such groups lose control. Such was the case in Mexico, where there was a crackdown against the drug cartels that began in 2007. By 2011 the murder rate had tripled. Then it stabilized until 2015, when the cartels began to fragment and diversify, following which murders started to increase again, resulting in an all-time high of more than thirty thousand killings in 2017. The *Global Study on Homicide* reported that "Jamaica suffered a similar turn of events during the first decade of the twenty-first century, when drug routes shifted from the Caribbean to Mexico, causing a spike in the homicide rate as organized crime groups imploded" (U.N. Office on Drugs and Crime 2019a, 33).

Figures 4.1 through 4.7 provide troubling snapshots of the region's crime crucible and allow for some grasp of the pain to which Prime Minister Holness

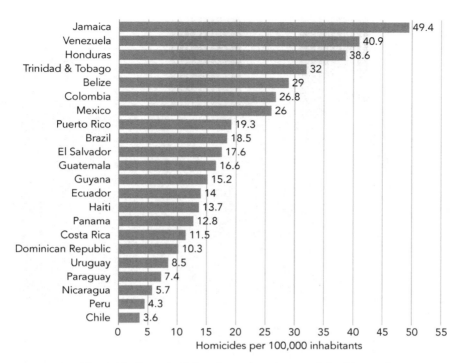

FIGURE 4.1 Homicide Rates in Select Latin American and Caribbean Countries 2021.

Source: "2021 Homicide Round-Up." *InSight Crime*, February 1, 2022.

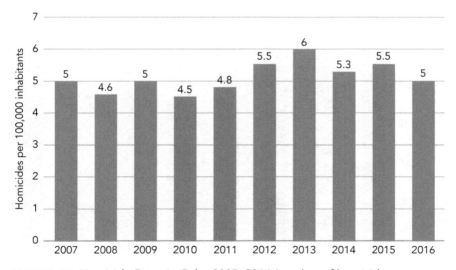

FIGURE 4.2 Homicide Rates in Cuba 2007–2016 (number of homicides per 100,000 inhabitants).

Source: *Statista*, Homicide in Latin America and the Caribbean—Statistics and Facts, September 2019. https://www.statista.com/statistics/1002695/homicide-rate-cuba/.

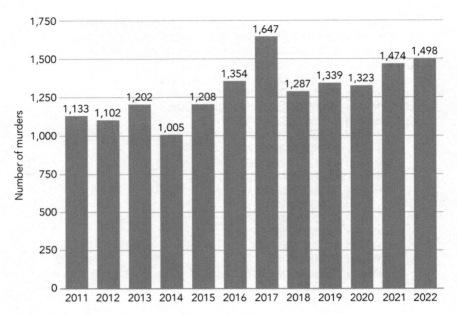

FIGURE 4.3 Homicides in Jamaica 2011–2022.

Source: *Statista*, Homicide in Latin America and the Caribbean—Statistics and Facts. https://www.statista.com/statistics/312483/number-of-homicides-in-jamaica/.

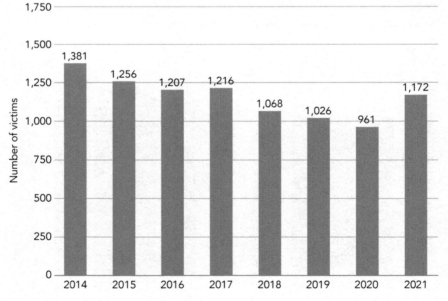

FIGURE 4.4 Homicides in the Dominican Republic 2014–2021.

Source: *Statista*, Homicide in Latin America and the Caribbean—Statistics and Facts. https://www.statista.com/statistics/312508/number-of-homicides-in-the-dominican-republic/.

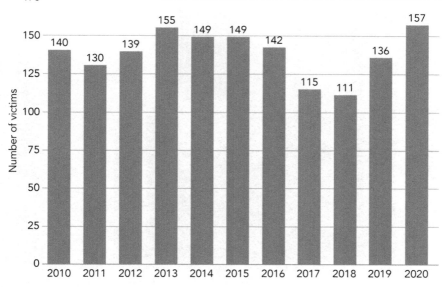

FIGURE 4.5 Homicides in Guyana 2010–2020.

Source: *Statista*, Homicide in Latin America and the Caribbean—Statistics and Facts. https://www.statista.com /statistics/312475/number-of-homicides-in-guyana/.

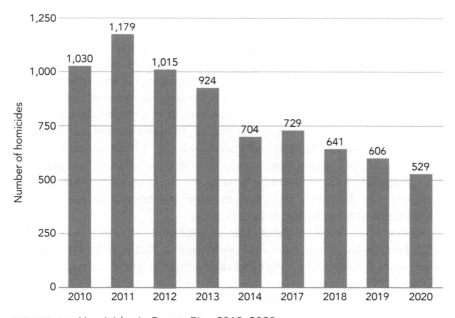

FIGURE 4.6 Homicides in Puerto Rico 2010–2020.

Source: *Statista*, Homicide in Latin America and the Caribbean—Statistics and Facts. https://www.statista.com /statistics/1040771/number-homicides-puerto-rico/.

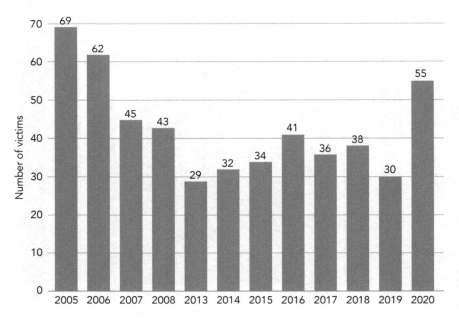

FIGURE 4.7 Homicides in Suriname 2005–2020.

Source: *Statista*, Homicide in Latin America and the Caribbean—Statistics and Facts. https://www.statista.com /statistics/312511/number-of-homicides-in-suriname/.

referred in the first epigraph. It is disconcerting to have seven Caribbean countries—Jamaica, Trinidad and Tobago, Belize, Puerto Rico, Guyana, Haiti, and the Dominican Republic—featured in figure 4.1. Moreover, it is worrisome to see the upward trend for Jamaica and Puerto Rico. Suriname has a mixed portrait. Also noteworthy is the relatively low rate of homicides in Cuba, as shown in figure 4.2, and the steady, albeit marginal, reductions in the number of murders in the Dominican Republic (fig. 4.4) and Puerto Rico (fig. 4.6) for most of the time frame reported on. Jamaica continues to have the dubious distinction of leading the "criminality pack," not just by heading the top twenty Latin America and Caribbean murder list for 2022, as figure 4.1 shows, but also because murders there increased dramatically, as noted earlier.

Moreover, as Prime Minister Holness reminded the nation in November 2021, Jamaica has another dubious distinction: a 2021 murder rate that was three times the regional average and eight times the global average (*Jamaica Observer* 2022). In his message to the nation on New Year's Day 2022, the prime minister explained that all serious crimes except murders declined by 8 percent in 2021. But he also reported that "85 percent of the country's homicides are committed using an illegal firearm, meaning a gun that was brought into the country illegally, never registered in the national firearm database, and the owner was never put through a process to determine whether they are fit and proper" (Holness 2022). The prime minister was confident that legal firearms do not pose a criminal threat.

Although Jamaica, Trinidad and Tobago, Puerto Rico, Haiti, and Belize tend to dominate the headlines about crime and violence in the Caribbean, the pain exists just as powerfully in some of the smaller states. For instance, St. Kitts and Nevis, and St. Vincent and the Grenadines featured, along with Jamaica, Belize, and Trinidad and Tobago, among the ten countries with the highest murder rate in the world in 2017. Indeed, the dramatic increase in murders in the Eastern Caribbean in 2022 prompted *InSight Crime* (2023) to pay special attention to that subregion. The editors explained they had expanded their "homicide round-up to include smaller Caribbean nations and territories, many of which saw a sharp rise in murders in 2022." They explained that while the subregion had comparatively small populations and homicide numbers, "we include them in the ranking below to show how patterns of violence are affecting the entire region."

The problem is not entirely new. For instance, while Latin America and the Caribbean made up just 8 percent of the world's population in 2017, they accounted for almost 40 percent of the murders committed worldwide that year. The average murder rate in the region was 24 per 100,000—almost five times the global average. Jamaica ranked third in the world at 60 per 100,000, and the U.S. Virgin Islands placed fourth, at 47 per 100,000. Of the ten countries with the highest murder rate in the world that year, nine were from the region, five of which are CARICOM states. Of the fifty cities with the highest murder rates, forty-three are to be found in the region (*South Florida Caribbean News* 2019).

In 2018, Jamaica, Trinidad and Tobago, Puerto Rico, and the Dominican Republic registered some of the highest homicide rates in the entire Latin American and Caribbean region. It was estimated that more than 43 people for every 100,000 inhabitants were murdered in the Puerto Rican capital every year, whereas Port-au-Prince, the capital of Haiti, was among the Caribbean cities with the highest number of murder victims. In the Dominican Republic, the most unsafe regions, based on number of homicides in 2018, were the province of Santo Domingo, followed by the province of Santiago and the country's capital, Santo Domingo City. Randy Seepersad's analysis reveals that for the period 2000–2010, "of the 12 countries for which data were available, murders increased in 11 and decreased in only one. The countries with the highest murder rates were Jamaica, Belize, St. Kitts and Nevis, and Trinidad and Tobago" (Seepersad 2018, 49).

Even though the actual numbers are high, they represent only part of the reality—the crimes reported by victims. The U.N.–World Bank study cited above makes the following pertinent observation regarding official data: "Reported rates are highly sensitive to the level of trust in the local police in general and the willingness to report domestic violence, in particular" (U.N. Office on Drugs and Crime–World Bank 2007, iii). Moreover, it is reasonable to posit that in some countries, low citizen confidence in the effectiveness of basic law enforcement leads them to underreport crimes. Sometimes citizens see few arrests that lead to arraignments and timely trials and convictions with the kind of punishment that serves as a deterrent. Thus, they perceive an absence of justice, and this undermines their confidence in the criminal justice system—not just in the police but in the courts and other parts of the system as well.

As is evident from Jamaica's experience, places where tourism is a key industry also have been vulnerable to high crime. In the case of the Bahamas, for example, Bahamian national security minister Tommy Turnquest presented the startling situation to his country's parliament in October 19, 2011. Murder, attempted murder, rape, attempted rape, armed robbery, robbery, and attempted robbery had all increased. In offering comparative data for January 1–October 1, 2011, with the same period in 2010, he reported that murders increased by 44 percent from 72 in 2010 to 104 in 2011, while rapes increased by 38 percent— from 58 in 2010 to 80 in 2011. Armed robberies increased by 10 percent—704 cases in 2011, compared to 639 in 2010; robberies increased by 16 percent: from 237 to 274; and house break-ins rose by 9 percent, stealing from vehicles by 58 percent, and theft of vehicles by 7 percent (Rolle 2011).

Still, while the portrait in the Bahamas and most other places reflects increases, there also have been decreases in recent history, as figures 4.4 and 4.7 indicate. For example, there was a notable reduction in Antigua and Barbuda between 2009 and 2010, and Jamaica witnessed a 15 percent downturn for the same period. Indeed, milestones were created in Jamaica in 2010, when for several months there were fewer than 80 murders in any single month after July 2010. Murders for the month of September 2010 numbered 72, which was 42 percent lower than for the same period in 2009. Plus, there were reductions in reported rapes, carnal abuse, and robbery.

There once was reason for hope that Jamaica's downward crime trend would persist. In his May 2011 budget speech, Prime Minister Bruce Golding was able to declare, "The number of murders committed over the past 12 months is the lowest since 2003. Crime statistics for this year show a significant reduction in most major crimes: Murder 44 percent reduction; Shootings 36 percent reduction; Break-ins 13 percent reduction. The number of persons arrested by the Police is up by 50 percent. Of significance, the number of fatal shootings by the Police is down by 37 percent" (Golding 2011a). Quite rightly, the prime minister attributed that outcome to the leadership of Commissioner Owen Ellington, better intelligence and investigations, and "a reinvigorated determination to put criminals where they belong—behind bars."

Undoubtedly, the Dudus affair, which is discussed extensively in chapter 6, also aided the crime reduction in several ways. First, the combined army-police operation amounted to shock therapy that sent powerful "line in the sand" messages to criminals in Tivoli Gardens and other garrisons. Second, the messages were received in places outside the garrisons, in the general society, leading criminals to rethink proposed criminality. Finally, in my estimation, the violence and the political subterfuge in the Dudus affair so outraged Jamaicans that it precipitated powerful civil society outcries against all kinds of crime, contributing to the development of a "zero tolerance for crime" climate. Indeed, in September 2011 Commissioner Ellington stated, "You will observe the dramatic change in the crime and security environment when certain criminal actors meet their demise or are removed from the streets. Matthews Lane is a changed place without Donald 'Zekes' Phipps" (Reid 2011a).[4]

Daring and Dastardly Acts

Still, it has not been just the high, and in some cases increasing, homicide numbers that have been worrying people within and outside the Caribbean. Also worrisome have been the very high use of weapons in murders and the daring and dastardly nature of some of the criminal acts. A few instances will suffice to make the point:

- Who would have thought that St. Lucia would be the location of an attempted assassination of a judicial officer? The intended victim was Jamaican-born magistrate Ann Marie Smith, known to be tough on drug dealers. The incident occurred in the capital, Castries, in broad daylight on April 8, 2010, as Smith was heading to work with her four-year-old daughter. Two masked gunmen emerged from hiding in the bushes near her house and opened fire. Luckily, they were amateurs and neither Smith nor her daughter was injured (Dominica News Online 2010). Regrettably, the gunmen were never found. Incidentally, Smith left St. Lucia and became chief magistrate in Belize in September of the following year.
- St. Lucia also was the place where a gang member murdered a rival right in the constituency office of then–prime minister Stephenson King while he was in his office meeting constituents. This happened on September 17, 2010. During the incident, the prime minister himself had to be hidden under a desk by his lone security detail, the other member of his detail having gone for lunch. In a statement on the incident later, Prime Minister King lamented, "None of us is safe!" (*St. Lucia Star* 2010; King 2010). The murderer was never caught.
- In August 2011, authorities in the Dominican Republic arrested four people, including a prominent hotel owner, for the August 2, 2011, assassination of Jose Silvestre, publisher of the weekly newspaper *Voice of Truth* and host of a radio program; Silvestre had been reporting stories of alleged criminal links of the businessman and his associates. Six weeks later, on September 19, there was the murder of Col. Cesar Ubri, top aide to Dominican Republic's drug czar, Rolando Rosario. Initially, it was thought that Ubri's murder was a response to and a warning by Domini-

can drug barons to drug countermeasures by Dominican authorities. It turned out, though, that Ubri was killed in order to steal his car, which was a model in high demand for its parts. The murder was committed by an organized crime ring specializing in car theft (*Los Angeles Times* 2011; *Washington Post* 2011; *Dominican Today* 2011).

- Trinidad and Tobago and the rest of the Caribbean were shocked at the assassination of a prominent prosecutor, Senior Counsel Dana Seetahal, on May 4, 2014. The fifty-nine-year-old former university law lecturer, and author of the book *Commonwealth Caribbean Criminal Practice and Procedure*, was heading home from a social event shortly after midnight when a van and a white station wagon sandwiched her Volkswagen SUV and opened fire, shooting her multiple times in the head and chest and killing her instantly. Police indicated that Seetahal appeared to have been trying to reach for her licensed firearm, which was later recovered from her purse. Nothing was taken from the SUV. Seetahal had served as an Independent senator, a state prosecutor, assistant solicitor general, and a magistrate. At the time of her murder, she was lead prosecutor in a prominent murder trial. Eleven individuals later were charged with the murder, which was deemed by local and international intelligence agencies as a hit orchestrated by organized crime. The trial of ten of the accused began on July 23, 2020, and up to March 2023 it was still working its way through the judicial labyrinth (see Seelal 2014; Mejia 2014; Ramdass 2020; and *Saturday Express* 2023).

- On January 12, 2022, forty-five-year-old noted Westmoreland, Jamaica, businesswoman Sophia Brown and her fifty-eight-year-old domestic helper, Bernie Lewis, were murdered at the grocery and wholesale business operated by Brown. The murder was committed by two men wearing hoodies who entered the shop pretending to be customers and opened a hail of gunfire that wounded Brown in the upper body and Lewis in the head. Police authorities believe the incident was a targeted assassination, as the two women were the only individuals in the grocery store who were attacked (J. Smith 2022).

- On October 16, 2021, a group of sixteen U.S. citizens and one Canadian citizen, comprising five men, seven women, and five children, was kidnapped by the four-hundred-member Mawozo gang in Haiti. The gang demanded US$1 million ransom per person. The group of missionaries were from the Ohio-based Christian Aid Ministries. Although law enforcement and missionary authorities did not disclose whether any ransom was paid, the hostages were eventually released in batches by December 2021. This kidnapping placed a spotlight on the long-standing kidnapping challenge in Haiti, where there were some 628 reported abductions in 2021 alone (see Treisman 2021; Daniels 2021).

- The resort city of Montego Bay, Jamaica, was the scene of a bizarre incident on October 17, 2021, when 2 members of Pathways International Kingdom Restoration Ministries were murdered in an alleged sacrificial murder and 42 members of the community, including the leader, were detained for questioning. Earlier that day, Kevin Smith, self-styled "Prophet to the Nations" summoned the church's 144 men, women, and children, with instructions for them to be robed in white. Smith, an anti-vaxxer, had told congregants that only "pure blood"—that is, unvaccinated—members would be allowed to enter the "ark," to survive a flood that was imminent. This allegedly prompted the slashing of the throats of two members who had been vaccinated, reputedly by "pure blood" church members. Another vaccinated congregant called the police. Smith later died in a mysterious car cash on October 25, 2021, while being transferred to the capital, Kingston, to be charged with the two murders (Pickering 2021; E. Lewis 2021).

- Two elderly sisters from the Spring Village community in St. Catherine, Jamaica—seventy-two-year-old disabled Lola Lewis and sixty-nine-year-old Christine Lewis, a retired teacher and a justice of the peace—were victims of a murder-burglary on November 2, 2021. They were found in their home with their throats slashed, one victim in the front room of the ransacked house, and the other in the back room (*Jamaica Observer* 2021).

The nature of the criminality in parts of the region has a particular psychosocial dimension. Jamaica's prime minister was candid about that dimension in relation to his nation when he noted the following in November 2021: "Every Jamaican would have recognized that *the nature and frequency of the violence have evolved to a level of barbarity and a level of savagery; it is almost a competition for cruelty; the worst of the worst. It appears to be designed and properly calculated to drive fear into the citizenry of the country and panic in communities*" (*Jamaica Observer* 2022; emphasis added). What a sobering observation!

Truth be told, though, the region's crime crucible does not derive just from the significant criminality but also from the limited capability to deal adequately with it. Some of this limitation results in the poor performance in the clearance rates of homicides and other crimes. Although treatment of this aspect is beyond my purview, some of the conclusions of an excellent study about Trinidad and Tobago have relevance beyond the twin-island republic and are worthy of replication:

Our findings suggest that as the number of homicides increased precipitously, the response to homicides in Trinidad and Tobago became increasingly disjointed and poorly coordinated, much as one would expect when any organisation manages to perform adequately in a "normal" environment but lacks the capacity to respond to a rapidly emerging crisis. Before the rise in homicides, the nation's infrastructure for investigating homicides was sufficient, routinely generating homicide clearance rates on par with developed nations like the USA, Britain, Japan, Canada and Australia. However, once the number of homicides began to increase sharply, the existing organizational structures and processes became overwhelmed. This appears to be attributable ultimately to a lack of management capacity. Because there was no clear division of labor or system of accountability for investigating homicides, the police service itself lacked the capacity to plan, organize, staff and coordinate an effective response to the growing problem. This generalized lack of capacity was made even more difficult because the police did not have a contingent of officers trained to process crime scenes, and preserve and collect physical evidence necessary to solve cases. (Maguire et al. 2010, 395)

It must be acknowledged, however, that police and police performance are only two elements in the larger crime-control matrix. Randy Seepersad reminds us, quite rightly, that while media reporting tends to blame the police for crime, assuming that the police alone are responsible for crime control, many other factors, such as socialization and poverty, have an impact on crime; the police represent only one piece in a larger puzzle. Thus, police performance will affect only a limited proportion of the variance in crime rates (Seepersad 2018, 45).

States of Emergency dramatize the seriousness of the crime situations in the region and provide public security coping mechanisms to deal with them. Chapter 6 offers case analysis of the Dudus affair in Jamaica, which triggered a SoE there, and of the historic 2011 SoE in Trinidad and Tobago. However, it would be useful here to mention a few other SoEs.

States of Emergency

A SoE is a suspension by a state's rulers of the normal rights of citizens and a modification of the customary functioning of the state, especially in terms of security and judicial procedures and practices. Generally, the head of state or the head of government issues a declaration to that effect. The declaration can suspend or restrict the following freedoms: of movement, through instituting curfews; of assembly, by curtailing or prohibiting street rallies and marches; of speech, by banning certain media or the kind of material they issue; and of due process, by removing probable cause as the basis for arrest, modifying the presumption of innocence in judicial proceedings, and modifying customary arrest, trial, and appeal procedures.

Moreover, with an emergency the security forces usually acquire enhanced powers, and sometimes lawmaking and other parliamentary business is also suspended or limited. In some cases, especially in authoritarian governmental arrangements, the SoE is accompanied by the declaration of martial law. Especially in democracies, but also in some authoritarian contexts, the declaration of a SoE has a basis in law—sometimes a special legislation and not just an executive order for the contemplated SoE—and is done under provisions of the country's supreme law, generally the constitution. A SoE is an extreme governance measure and is reserved for situations where the political and national security leaders perceive a threat to the conduct of normal governance because of civil unrest, high and persistent crime, armed conflict—whether civil war or war with another state—or natural disaster.[5]

Looking back historically, several Caribbean nations other than Jamaica and Trinidad and Tobago have experienced SoEs. For instance, one was declared in Dominica in 1980 over an attempted coup. Guyana also has experienced a few, the first in the decolonization era being the one declared in 1953 by the British colonial government, which perceived the electoral victory of the People's Progressive Party, led by Marxist doctor Cheddie Jagan, as a national security threat. The British also suspended the constitution for four years and sent troops from London to occupy then-British Guiana. Guyana also saw declarations between 1962 and 1964 because of political unrest and racially motivated strikes and violence and, in 1998, because of political disturbances in the aftermath of the 1997 elections. In Suriname a growing rebellion prompted a SoE in the eastern and southern parts of the country in 1986. St. Kitts and Nevis also had a SoE in 1994 due to disturbances following the November 1993 elections.[6]

Haiti has had several SoEs over the years, including in June 1994 and March 2004 over political unrest and violence, in January 2010 following the devastating earthquake, in February 2019 over unrest driven by deteriorating economic conditions, and in 2022 and 2023 as gang rule traumatized the society and brought normal governance to a halt. Furthermore, in 2009 devastating hurricanes forced the declaration of emergencies in both Puerto Rico and the Dominican Republic and again in Puerto Rico in 2017 and 2019. Additionally, following the terrorist bombing in Paris in November 2015 that left 129 individuals dead and more than 350 injured, French president François Hollande, declared a SoE, which was extended to the territories in the Caribbean: Guadeloupe, French Guiana, Martinique, Mayotte, Reunion Island, and St. Martin and St. Barths. Interestingly, the French SoE was extended six times, into the presidency of President Emmanuel Macron, and lasted for almost two years, ending on November 1, 2017.[7]

Jamaica has the dubious distinction of being the Caribbean nation with the most and the most dramatic SoEs. Apart from those associated with the Tivoli and other garrison confrontations, the most extraordinary one was in 1976, in the throes of electoral politics, which witnessed both ideological polarization and political violence. Overall, between independence in 1962 and early 2022, Jamaica has had to declare more than a dozen SoEs, the longest of which was in 1976, lasting for a full year; three of them were in 2019 alone, and several occurred in 2020 and 2021. Two of the SoEs were prompted by natural disasters, and the rest of them were because of crime and political violence, as follows:

October 1966: From October 3 to November 2, a State of Emergency was enforced in West Kingston, triggered by political violence in a constituency held by cabinet minister Edward Seaga. The prime minister at the time was Alexander Bustamante.

June 1976: With political violence at an all-time high and elections looming, Prime Minister Michael Manley advised the governor-general to declare a SoE that lasted an entire year—until June 1977. The action was allegedly taken because of reports of attempts to overthrow the government. This was disputed by members of the opposition, who claimed the SoE was more of a "smokescreen" move to secure electoral victory.

September 2004: Ahead of category 4 Hurricane Ivan, and with evacuation orders issued to almost five hundred thousand people in the fourteen parishes of Jamaica, a SoE was declared by Prime Minister P. J. Patterson. The national electricity grid was also shut down, leading to a blackout across the island and security troops being deployed to enforce the SoE restrictions.

August 2007: A day after Hurricane Dean ravaged sections of the island, leaving much destruction in its wake, Prime Minister Portia Simpson-Miller declared a two-day SoE.

May 2010: In advance of the attempt to arrest Christopher "Dudus" Coke on an extradition warrant, an emergency was declared by Prime Minister Bruce Golding for the parishes of Kingston, St. Andrew, and St. Catherine. During this time there was a stand-off between security forces and members of the "Shower Posse" gang that left sixty-nine civilians and thirty-nine security personnel dead.

January 2018: On January 18, Prime Minister Andrew Holness declared a State of Emergency in St. James because of increasing crime and violence in the parish. Holness said, "The level of criminal activity experienced [in St. James] is of such a nature and so extensive in scale as to endanger public safety." In 2017, St. James recorded 335 murders, almost twice more than the parish with the second-highest number of murders for the same period.

March 2018: On March 18, Prime Minister Andrew Holness declared an emergency in the St. Catherine North Police Division (especially Spanish Town, Linstead, and Bog Walk). It was prompted by a spike in murders and increased gang activity.

April 2019: Declared by Prime Minister Holness on April 30 because of high crime and violence in Westmoreland, Hanover, and St. James.

July 2019: Declared by Prime Minister Holness on July 7 because of high crime and violence in the Corporate St. Andrew.

September 2019: Declared by Prime Minister Holness on September 9 because of high crime and violence in Clarendon and St. Catherine.

(Jamaica Gleaner 2018a; News Caribbean Jamaica 2019)

In speaking at the April 30, 2019, press conference where the prime minister announced the SoE, Commissioner of Police Antony Anderson provided some of the evidence for the declaration, explaining that between January 1 and April 28, 2019, twenty-nine persons were murdered in Westmoreland; twenty-seven persons in St. James, and eighteen persons in Hanover, and that in 2018, some ninety-seven persons had been killed in Westmoreland; eighty-four persons in Hanover, and fifty-five persons in St. James. Indeed, he explained that in 2018, the parish of Westmoreland was the most murder-dense place in the country, followed by the parish of Hanover (A. Morris 2019). In July 2019, Anderson painted the sobering portrait in the part of the country in which the SoE had been declared: "There are some 25 gangs engaging in inter and intra-gang warfare in the division. There have been 94 murders and 98 shootings—the highest among police divisions in Jamaica (so far this year). St Andrew South is 33 per cent above the next highest police division, Clarendon. . . . Murders in this division (St Andrew South) have increased by 19 per cent, and the gang warfare has caused the disruption of the lives of citizens" (Jamaica Loop News 2019).

The SoE declared in September 2019 was extended to October 28 of that year and expanded to the popular tourist destination of Montego Bay in St. James Parish. A separate SoE issued for St. Andrew Parish, which includes areas of the capital, Kingston, remained in effect until October 5. More than a dozen areas in Greater Kingston and half a dozen areas of Montego Bay were listed as having a substantial gang population with a significant level of violent crime, though petty crime, credit card, and ATM fraud were also common. A SoE was first declared for St. James in January 2018 and was extended several times (Ho 2019).

In addition, the authorities felt compelled to declare a SoE during January 2020, this time in Eastern Kingston. At the January 26, 2020, press conference where the prime minister made the announcement, the commissioner indicated that the Eastern Kingston Division had been experiencing a high incidence of violent crimes from the latter part of 2019 and since the start of this year. According to him, Eastern Kingston had become one of the country's crime hot spots, with several gangs engaged in deadly inter- and intra-gang conflicts or other criminal enterprises. Official estimates placed the number of gangs there at thirty-two along with thirty-four violence influencers within the division (*Caribbean National Weekly* 2020a). As well, he noted that murders in the division increased by 16 percent in 2019 compared to 2018, while shootings increased by 49 percent; that 67 percent of these incidents were gang-related; that in 2019, police recovered 36 firearms and 622 rounds of ammunition in East Kingston alone; and that since the start of 2020, the Eastern Kingston Division had recorded eleven murders compared to three murders during the same time in 2019.

As might be expected, there have been mixed results with the SoEs. In offering a reflection toward the end of February 2020, Prime Minister Holness welcomed the slight decrease in crime resulting from the SoEs, but he acknowledged that in almost half the country's police divisions, murders soared some 10 percent since the start of 2020 when compared with the corresponding period in 2019. Regretfully, the crime reduction in six of the eight police divisions under SoEs "had not applied cumulative shock to the criminal underworld. Instead, murders have ballooned in most other non-emergency zones, with St Andrew North recording almost 270 per cent more killings this year than in 2019" (E. Campbell 2020). Up to February 22, 2020, there were twenty-two murders in St. Andrew North, and murders were occurring at a rate of about four per day nationally.[8] Needless to say, SoEs were also declared in 2021; on November 14, 2021, SoEs were declared across seven police divisions; in the rural police divisions of St. James, Westmoreland, and Hanover; and in the urban ones in St. Andrew South, Kingston Western, Kingston Central, and Kingston East (Jamaica Loop News 2021).

Criminality Contextualized

Prime Minister Holness provided sobering contextualization of the criminality in his 2020 New Year message to the nation, in noting:

> Jamaica's high homicide rate did not happen overnight. In the decade of the '80s, 4,870 murders were committed in Jamaica; by the decade of the '90s this increased to 7,621 murders; and by [the] decade of the 2000s, even with the formation of various special squads and units, murders skyrocketed to 13,418. This past decade, 2010 to 2019[,] has seen a reduction in murders to 12,698. The level of crime we are now experiencing is over and above the capacity of our existing security apparatus to manage. While the crime and murder numbers have grown over the past 4 decades, successive governments have not increased the national security budget apace; or kept abreast with technology; or increased the number of investigators and other critical capabilities commensurately; or effectively controlled corrupt activity in the force. (Holness 2020)

As part of continuing efforts to cope with the crime crucible in Jamaica, the authorities there introduced some innovations with the passage of "The Law Reform (Zones of Special Operations) (Special Security and Community Development Measures) Act" in July 2017.[9] The country's crime spike compelled the government to consider a different approach to battling the crime. One local newspaper considered the crux of the matter as being violent rivalries among Jamaica's lottery scam rings that helped to drive the island's homicide rate to the highest level in five years. The Jamaica Constabulary Force said the country had at least 1,192 slayings in 2015, a roughly 20 percent increase from the previous year. There were 1,005 killings in 2014, the lowest annual total since 2003. Jamaica recorded about 45 slayings per 100,000 people in 2015, keeping it ranked among the most violent countries in the world (*Jamaica Observer* 2016). As a matter of fact, the World Bank placed Jamaica in the world's top five most violent nations in 2013 and noted that the city of Chicago in the United States, which had a population similar to Jamaica—about 2.7 million—had suffered 468 killings in 2015, whereas Jamaica endured 1,192.

Prime Minister Holness presented the context and intent of the new approach in his March 21, 2017, budget speech, noting that areas with high crime and violence "map closely with high unemployment, low incomes, poor infrastructure, unplanned settlements, and generally a lack of access to state amenities and services. Criminals operate freely in these communities, taking life, taking property, taking your daughters and extorting tax to protect you from them" (Holness 2017). The prime minister then tendered a proposition that applies to other nations and their efforts as well: "The history of intervention by the state shows that an overreliance on strong policing measures may attenuate the situation in the short-term but does not bring long term stability and normalization. Any strategy to address these areas must be comprehensive, sustained, inclusive and respectful of human rights and the dignity of the people" (Holness 2017).

The law regarding the Zones of Special Operations (ZOSOs) "provides for special measures for upholding and preserving the Rule of Law, public order, citizen security and public safety within certain geographically-defined areas of Jamaica, or, in short, zones of special operations," allowing the prime minister, on the advice of the National Security Council, to declare any high-crime area of Jamaica a zone for special security operations and community development measures (Jamaica Information Service 2017; Dig Jamaica 2017).[10] A key provision is for a Social Intervention Committee to be formed in each zone in order to assess conditions there, including physical infrastructure, health conditions, housing, and other social amenities.

The new measure purports to "strike a balance between policing and respect for human rights and fundamental freedoms," as part of Jamaica's "Clear, Hold, Build" public security strategy, the components of which are:

- Clear: Law Enforcement goes into selected community and saturate[s] community with their presence and displaces the criminal element and removes their space to operate while at the same time reassuring law-abiding citizens.
- Hold: Law Enforcement maintains a sustainable level of presence and control over the area, creating the space and support for a multi-sectoral intervention into the community to address outstanding and critical human needs and basic infrastructure.
- Build: Psycho-cultural, social capital, and leadership and organization building and support.

(Holness 2017)

Nevertheless, it should be stressed that the crime and violence in the Caribbean are not all driven by drugs; some derive from poverty and general social anomie. Plus, the inability of governments to solve crimes swiftly; to provide functional equipment and training to law enforcement agencies; to fill vacancies in police forces, the courts, and elsewhere; and to secure more timely judicial proceedings serve to embolden the criminals and undermine the confidence of citizens in the state. Complicating matters is the prominence of gangs and guns.

There is abundant evidence of the nexus between homicides and the use of guns and the connectivity between criminality and gang activity in the region.[11] Thus, Sheridon Hill's 2013 statement still is even more valid a decade later: "There are compelling data which demonstrate that murders are at epidemic levels in a number of Caribbean countries and that gang violence is an important contributory factor in the countries with the highest murder rates" (Hill 2013, 72). Jamaica's deputy prime minister and minister of national security acknowledged the futility of using social intervention to cope with gunmen. He told Parliament on June 1, 2022, during the budget sectoral debate that "'shottas' [people who use guns] cannot be dealt with by social investment. Many of them, especially in Area One, are earning huge sums of money, either as advance fee scammers or big traders, who buy the weapons to kill our people. These are persons who are empowered by the possession of a gun. They cannot be empowered by counselling and JM$5,000 per week" (Chang 2022). He touted the necessity for specialized police teams, with the army mobilized as necessary, and stressed the need for body cameras, body armor, adequate weapons, and credible intelligence about criminals and criminal gangs. Understandably, there is variability among countries both of the number of gangs and the nature and scope of gang involvement in crime.[12]

Clearly, the dramatic link between guns and violent crime is not unique to Jamaica, or Haiti, or Trinidad and Tobago; it is a region-wide reality. A crucial question regarding the nexus between guns and crime is: what is the source of most of the weapons available in the region? Although small arms have been smuggled to the Caribbean from Europe, Latin America, and Asia, most of the weapons originate in the United States. One award-winning Caribbean journalist cited the Bureau of Industry and Security of the U.S. Department of Commerce: "Since 2020 about half of all firearms-export investigations have been concentrated in the Caribbean region—a top smuggling destination fueled by the demand of drug traffickers and huge black-market markups on U.S.-made guns. The other 50% are scattered throughout the world" (Charles 2023). The weapons and appropriate ammunition are smuggled in large and small quantities in a variety of ways—in foodstuff, toys, used clothing, preowned cars, and cargo containers, among other products. The guns, which often cost hundreds of dollars each in the United States, often are resold for thousands of dollars each in the region. According to U.S. government officials, products with name-brand popularity, such as "9mm Glock pistols, can sell for $400 to $500 each at a federally licensed firearms store or private gun show in South Florida, but can be resold for $2,000 to $5,000 in St. Thomas, the U.S. Virgin Islands, and then fetch as much as $10,000 in Jamaica, Trinidad or Haiti" (Charles 2023).

One *InSight Crime* analysis also found that in 2020, almost three-quarters of all guns traced by the U.S. Bureau of Alcohol, Tobacco, Firearms and Explosives (ATF) to the Dominican Republic originated in the United States (den Held 2022) And this was true not only in relation to the Dominican Republic, as Tim Padgett and other close observers of the region have shown (see Padgett 2022; Charles 2023; U.S. Congress 2023). Thankfully, there have been notable successes in the efforts to combat the smuggling. For example, during the period September 24–30, 2022, INTERPOL and the CARICOM Implementation Agency for Crime and Security (IMPACS) conducted a joint operation that produced considerable results, as figure 4.8 shows. Dubbed Operation Trigger VII, it led to the seizure of 350 weapons, 3,300 rounds of ammunition, 10.1 tons of cocaine, and 2.5 tons of marijuana. A total of 510 arrests also were made. The operation involved officials from nineteen countries who coordinated measures at airports, seaports, land borders, and inland locations. They acted on human and virtual intelligence about organized crime groups and individuals involved in weapons

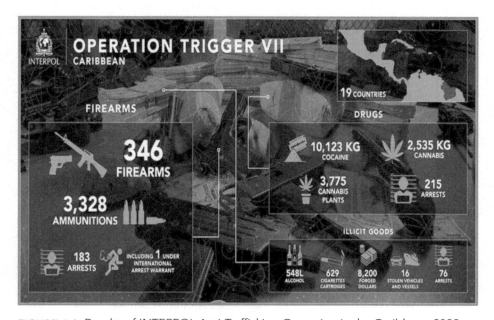

FIGURE 4.8 Results of INTERPOL Anti-Trafficking Operation in the Caribbean 2022.

Source: INTERPOL, "Hundreds of Firearms and 12.6 Tonnes of Drugs Seized in Caribbean Operation," October 13, 2022. https://www.interpol.int/en/News-and-Events/News/2022/Hundreds-of-firearms-and-12.6-tonnes-of-drugs-seized-in-Caribbean-operation.

and drug trafficking, searched warehouses, inspected packages, and executed targeted checks at firearms dealerships, shooting ranges, and private security outfits (INTERPOL 2022).[13]

Concern and consternation about U.S.-sourced weapons fueling crime and violence have been voiced not only by political and law enforcement officials in the Caribbean but also by U.S. lawmakers. In April 2023, for instance, Senator Richard Durbin of Illinois, Congressman Joaquin Castro of Texas, and Congressman Gregory Weeks of New York highlighted the increased arms trafficking, its deadly trend, and "the tremendous impact on the people of the region." They also mandated the U.S. Government Accountability Office (GAO) to undertake a comprehensive assessment of the phenomenon (U.S. Congress 2023). Specifically, they asked for the study to include an examination of:

1. The latest country-by-country information on the number and types of U.S. arms being trafficked to Caribbean countries (excluding Cuba) and whether this number is growing annually;
2. Information on where and how illicit weapons are being obtained in the United States as well as how they are being smuggled into their final destinations;
3. A country-by-country breakdown on the legal export of American firearms to the Caribbean region;
4. Information on whether arms are being diverted to illicit actors from legally exported purchases by private or government entities in the region;
5. The measures being taken by U.S. and Caribbean law enforcement to share information, make arrests, and prosecute individuals or groups involved in the arms trafficking as well as what gaps exist in the efforts being taken by U.S. agencies and their regional counterparts;
6. What legislation might assist the efforts being taken by U.S. authorities to combat trafficking or diversion of U.S. origin firearms; and
7. What additional, enhanced, or modified foreign assistance would be helpful to regional efforts to curtail the arms trafficking. (U.S. Congress 2023)

The arms trafficking unease has led to an unprecedented action in the region. In March 2023, Antigua and Barbuda, Belize, the Bahamas, Jamaica, St. Vincent and the Grenadines, and Trinidad and Tobago joined an *amicus curiae* (friend of the court) brief filed by Mexico appealing a U.S. judicial decision to hold gun manufacturers responsible for enabling the trafficking of weapons used to prosecute crimes outside the United States. Mexico's lawsuit, for US$10 billion, named several defendants, including major gun manufacturers Smith and Wesson Brands Inc.; Sturm, Ruger and Co.; Barrett Firearms Manufacturing Inc.; Beretta USA Corp.; Colt's Manufacturing Co.; Century International Arms Inc.; Witmer Public Safety Group Inc.; and Glock Inc. Mexico was appealing a decision rendered in September 2022 in the federal District Court of Massachusetts that had dismissed its lawsuit, citing the Protection of Lawful Commerce in Arms Act, which protects arms manufacturers from being held liable for crimes committed with their products (Caribbean Council 2023).

CARICOM leaders raised their level of official anxiety about the matter both at their regular summit, held in the Bahamas in February 2023, and at a special meeting on the subject involving a variety of experts, convened in April 2023 by Prime Minister Keith Rowley of Trinidad and Tobago, who holds the portfolio for security within the CARICOM quasi cabinet. Quite importantly, the conference framed the crime and violence issue as one of public health (see CARICOM 2023). The then-chairman of CARICOM, Prime Minister Phillip Davis of the Bahamas, explained that 98.6 percent of all recovered illegal firearms in the Bahamas is traced directly to the United States, and in Haiti the figure is 87.7 percent. The figure for Jamaica is 67 percent, while for Trinidad and Tobago the requisite number is 52 percent (Munnings 2023). Moreover, he said, "We do not manufacture guns in the Caribbean. Every gun used to commit a crime in the Caribbean is smuggled into our countries."

The Caribbean leaders declared a "war on guns to combat the illegal trade which provides the weapons that contribute significantly to crime and violence in our region causing death, disabilities and compromising the safety of our citizens," and implored the United States to actively aid their efforts to halt the illegal weapons trafficking. They also lamented the disproportionate portions of their national budgets they are obligated to allocate to national security, especially to combat crime and violence and grapple with mental health and other health-related challenges spurred by the arms trafficking business (Ramdass 2023).

They also issued a fifteen-point action plan, including the following:

1. Undertake comprehensive overhaul of the criminal justice system to address criminal terrorists with a focus on proactive management of prosecutions, sentencing and the diversion of young people at risk, and strengthen regional forensic capabilities and collaboration among national forensic agencies with a view to improving the quality of evidence and speed the conduct of trials.
2. Prepare regional model legislation to bring greater harmonization and efficiency to the development and revision of national laws, augment the jurisdiction of magistrates, the consideration of defendants' options to judge-only trials, and the intra-regional rotation of judges and magistrates to admit or foster their greater exposure, and strengthen the capacity of the Regional Intelligence Fusion Centre (RIFC) to deliver its mandate through development of agreed protocols for data sharing amongst Member States.
3. Ban assault weapons in the region, except for security forces and sporting competitions, stand with Mexico on its legal action against U.S. gun

manufacturers and retailers, and establish an entity under IMPACS to assist in the containment of corruption and financial crimes, including money laundering and cybercrimes, through greater collaboration to harmonize related legislation and operational processes.

4. Empower and engage young people as positive content developers to offset the negative impact of social media and engage with the creative industries to re-engineer culturally acceptable norms and promote public awareness and education campaigns in our communities, that challenge harmful beliefs, attitudes and behaviors that contribute to crime and violence.

5. Develop and implement targeted programmes and strategies to address young vulnerable youth at risk of becoming perpetrators and victims of crime and appoint an eminent person to lead and advise heads and the secretariat on further strategies and reforms and on effectively operationalizing the decisions of heads.

(CARICOM 2023; Ramdass 2023)

Small Arms Survey

The results of a study on gun violence and arms trafficking in the Caribbean conducted by Small Arms Survey and CARICOM IMPACS released on April 26, 2023, left no doubt that the unease about the issue is more than justified. Among other things, the study found that:

- The rate of violent deaths in CARICOM member states is almost three times the global average. Firearms are used in more than half of all homicides in the entire Caribbean region, and in some countries this proportion reaches 90 percent.
- Case study research in the Bahamas, Barbados, and Jamaica reveals that firearm-related violence imposes significant public health and economic burdens on Caribbean communities and societies, where the average medical expense for treating a single gunshot exceeds the annual health spending per capita by ratios ranging from 2:1 to 11:1.
- Based on seizure and trace data, the vast majority of illicit firearms circulating in the Caribbean are handguns. While illicit rifles and rifle ammunition are emerging concerns for law enforcement officials, their use by criminals in the region remains limited.
- The U.S. domestic market is a major source of illicit arms and ammunition in the Caribbean and is likely the largest source in some states and territories, although weapons are also sourced from other countries. Arms and ammunition are smuggled to the region via commercial airliners, postal and fast parcel services, and maritime shipping companies. Although the primary transport mode varies from country to country, trafficking by maritime cargo shipments is particularly common.[14]

Moreover, the study found that:

- According to seizure and trace data, the vast majority of illicit firearms circulating in the region are handguns, which account for as much as 88 percent of the firearms in the data sets of seized weapons, with little apparent geographic difference in the availability of the top brands of firearms, including pistols.
- Although illicit rifles and rifle ammunition are emerging concerns for law enforcement officials, their acquisition by criminals in the Caribbean generally remains marginal. This contrasts sharply with the situation in parts of Central and North America, where up to 47 percent of seized firearms are rifles.
- Most trafficking schemes are notable for their simplicity. The modus operandi of most U.S.-based traffickers is straightforward and requires minimal funding, infrastructure, or knowledge. The trafficker simply needs to camouflage arms and ammunition well enough to blend in with the thousands of shipments of other goods departing and arriving from international ports daily.
- Caribbean authorities often lack the personnel and equipment to adequately monitor their coasts, land borders, and air and sea ports. In some of the smaller jurisdictions, officials need to patrol hundreds of beaches and bays with only a small police force and little or no coast guard or customs support. In some places port officials lack even basic scanning technology, making it difficult to identify and interdict illicit shipments of weapons and other contraband.
- The ready accessibility of arms and ammunition in some neighboring countries including the United States, combined with inadequate screening of outbound mail and cargo shipments, undermines the often-robust controls on firearms and ammunition required by many Caribbean nations when they signed on to international agreements.

The Small Arms Survey assessment also found that handguns account for some 88 percent of the seizures, and pistols make up most of the seized handguns. The five most commonly seized brands were Glock, Taurus, Beretta, Smith & Wesson, and Ruger. With the exception of Haiti and the British Virgin Islands, rifles comprise less than 10 percent of firearms seized, which is considerably lower than in places such as Mexico, with more than 29 percent of seized firearms submitted for tracing annually are rifles, and in Canada, where the number is 41 percent. Yet, the proliferation of military-style rifles in some Caribbean countries is a significant concern for local and regional law enforcement officials.

In August 2022, for instance, U.S. officials warned of a notable increase in the trafficking of large-caliber rifles and other firearms to Haiti and elsewhere in the Caribbean. The alarm about ghost guns was sounded in the discussion about Privately Made Firearms (PMFs), with the report noting: "The growing popularity of ghost guns in the United States has potentially significant implications for the Caribbean given the role of U.S.-sourced crime guns in the region. Since 2020, U.S. customs and law enforcement officials have seized possible PMFs, components often used to assemble PMFs, and production equipment bound for Caribbean states on multiple occasions."[15] It also was noted that U.S. Customs and Border Protection experienced a notable increase in seizures of receivers and frames bound for the Caribbean, possibly intended for use in the assembly of PMFs.

The matter of 3D printing was also flagged. It was noted that 3D printing of firearms poses a major threat to key aspects of national and international arms control protocols, including the CARICOM Firearms Roadmap, especially because the refinement of user-friendly designs and production techniques for 3D-printed firearms, plus the increasing availability and decreasing costs, all make such weapons accessible to more individuals, including criminals. The report cautioned that "the threat from 3D-printed firearms in the Caribbean is currently minimal, but that could change quickly and without warning. Authorities in the region would be well-advised to ensure that their laws and regulations allow for the seizure of unlicensed 3D-printed weapons and the prosecution of illicit producers before these weapons gain a foothold in criminal circles."[16] In relation to economic aspects, the report reveals that direct medical costs and productivity losses due to gun-related violence amount to at least US$49 million in the Bahamas, US$12 million in Barbados, and US$135 million in Jamaica for 2019. On average, medical expenditures for treating a single gunshot wound exceed health spending per capita, and firearm wounds tend to result in higher medical costs than wounds caused by sharp objects. Notable, too, homicides using guns account for the largest portion of the total estimated productivity losses due to violence-related wounds. Besides, while significant, medical costs and productivity losses represent only a small portion of the total costs of gun-related violence.

Thus, the Caribbean is facing some clear and present dangers with crime and violence. Here is how the symposium's host prime minister conveyed the gravity of the situation for his nation: "Violence in the Caribbean is a public health emergency which threatens our lives, our economies, our national security and by extension every aspect of our well-being. In Trinidad and Tobago, in the years 2011 to 2022 we have lost and had to grieve for 5,439 lives to violent murder, largely through the use of imported firearms and ammunition. In 2011 we lost 352 lives and by 2022 the annual count was over 600, a new record, already being challenged by the murder rate for 2023. Except for Covid, in a pandemic, none of the listed dangerous diseases have taken lives like this in our population."[17]

Prime Minster Keith Rowley also explained:

For the thousands of wounded, victims and perpetrators alike, a surgical intervention to the head costs approximately TT$170,000, a surgical intervention for a chest wound would cost about TT$135,000. A shot to the leg requiring surgical intervention would cost just under TT$100,000 and a leg shot without surgical intervention would cost about TT$40,000 in medical care and attention. All of these frequent daily incurred costs are to be borne by the taxpayers at every level from scarce revenues diverted from other more deserving productive priorities.

Our current laws acknowledge a suite of afflictions, yellow fever, Smallpox, Plague, Cholera, Ebola, Novel Corona virus as notifiable, warranting emergency responses if even only a few cases are known to appear. Violent behavior, violent crime, violent crime involving the use of firearms, the associated individual and group mental health trauma accompanying violent behavior, so ever present amongst us now, pose a far greater destructive threat than these diseases and on that basis alone qualifies violence as a public health emergency.

During the last 15 years, using the Trinidad and Tobago example, in the growing quest for safety and security we have seen a significant increase in the allocation in the national budget for National Security. In 2008 policing alone represented 32 per cent of the TT$4 billion National Security budget. By 2017 this rose to 38 per cent. Even in the tighter budgetary environment of 2023 policing still accounted for 43 per cent of the National Security allocation. . . .

Our presence here is admission that Crime and Violence are now a major part of the Caribbean's overall plethora of problems, ranging from petty theft to school violence, home invasions, domestic violence, sexual abuse, human trafficking, drive-by shootings, drug-gang warfare, mindless daily revenge murders, etc.[18]

Haiti is, undoubtedly, the region's most dramatic case of "challenged sovereignty" because of the combined effects of political instability, economic destitution, out-of-control crime and violence, feuding gangs, and kidnappings. Indeed, as respected Haiti expert Georges Fauriol observed gloomily in May 2023, "Haiti is headed toward a catastrophic humanitarian and political crash. With an estimated 90 percent of the Port-au-Prince region under the chaotic control of gangs, kidnappings remain a lucrative trade (389 recorded incidents in the first quarter of 2023). Societal life—including the operation of schools—is essentially shut down. Haiti is halfway off the cliff."[19] Thus, a special comment on the contemporary circumstances of the world's first Black Republic is warranted.

Perhaps the United Nations Office on Drugs and Crime presented the best encapsulation of Haiti's sad contemporary realities in its report released in March 2023. The report explains that the country's persistent security crisis took a terrifying turn for the worse in 2021, even before the assassination of president Jovenel Moïse by local and foreign mercenaries in July of that year, because of the worsening economic situation, rising social unrest, and the increasing boldness of armed gangs. This has resulted in the physical displacement of an estimated

100,000 Haitians in Port-au-Prince alone. Moreover, the protracted instability has contributed to rising food prices, increasing hunger, and a cholera outbreak, all of which precipitated increased legitimate and illegitimate emigration from the country (UNODC, 2023:3). Table 4.1 provides a portrait of the results of the criminality over the last few years.

In response to the deteriorating situation, in late 2022 the country's Council of Ministers authorized the prime minister to take the unusual step of requesting the international community to deploy a "specialized armed force." The United Nations Security Council then issued a sanctions regime freezing assets, establishing travel bans and embargoing arms flows to individuals and groups considered to be responsible for or contributing to the threats to the nation's peace and security. Interestingly, while Haitians previously balked at the mention of foreign intervention, a survey conducted by Reuters in January 2023 claimed that as much as 70 percent of the population, especially people living in gang-controlled areas, supported international security assistance.[20]

The lawlessness persisted, with U.S. law enforcement authorities detecting a sharp increase in arms shipment in 2022, and Haitian law enforcement and international and domestic human rights groups reporting increased levels of murders, rapes, and kidnappings between 2020 and 2023, some of which are captured in table 4.1. As well, the U.S. Coast Guard registered a fourfold increase in intercepted Haitian migrants between 2021 and 2022. In addition, 43,900 Haitians, including 1,800 children, were reportedly deported from the Dominican Republic between July and October 2022 alone (UNODC, 2023:4). Incidentally, up to May 2023, myriad difficulties prevented the desired international peace-keeping force from being assembled and deployed.

According to the United Nations report, the intensified activities of the estimated 150 to 200 gangs are particularly disconcerting. Jimmy Cherizier, said to be one of the country's most influential gang leaders, reportedly leads an alliance known as the "G9 Family and Allies." Gangs have been expanding their

TABLE 4.1 The Haitian Crime Scene 2019–2022

	2019	2020	2021	2022
Homicides	1,141	1,380	1,615	2,183
Kidnappings	78	234	664	1,359
Police killed	42	30	49	54
Haitian migrants detained by U.S.	932	418	1,527	7,175

Source: United Nations Office on Drugs and Crime, "Haiti's Criminal Markets: Mapping Trends in Firearms and Drug Trafficking," 2023, https://www.unodc.org/documents/data-and-analysis/toc/Haiti_assessment _UNODC.pdf, 3.

influence over urban neighborhoods, targeting critical infrastructure—including access to seaports, fuel terminals, airports, and key roads in and out of major cities—and controlling access to fuel reserves. Several gangs and gang alliances, notably the G9, G-Pep, 400 Mawozo, Baz Galil, Vilaj de Dye, Vitelhomme, and Ti Mkak, reputedly have targeted public and private institutions. Many of them also are said to have engaged in predatory behavior in areas under their control, contributing to rising levels of extortion, sexual violence, kidnappings, and murders. Not unexpectedly, the mounting crime and violence has precipitated an expansion of the private security industry, which provides protection services for the nation's political and economic elite and for public facilities, critical infrastructure, and businesses. Many private security companies recruit directly from the Haitian National Police (HNP), either on a moonlighting basis or permanently, with better pay (UNODC, 2023:5–6).

Irrespective of the variability of the crime and the source of the weapons used to fuel the violence in the region, crime and violence have economic and social costs, and the crime and the response to it raise serious civilizational concerns, as is seen below.

Socioeconomic Costs

Economic and Social Costs

As always is the case, and evident from one Inter-American Development Bank (IDB) study (Jaitman 2017), a broader contextual portrait allows for a better appreciation of the economic costs than a focus just on countries in the region, and gross domestic product (GDP) representation is one recognized way to offer the portrait. In this respect, figure 4.9 provides a sobering comparative portrait involving seventeen countries, in which all four of the Caribbean countries studied bore crime-related costs higher than 2 percent of their 2014 GDP, and three of them bore costs representing upward of 3 percent: Trinidad and Tobago, 3.52 percent; Jamaica, 3.99 percent, and the Bahamas, 4.79 percent. Figure 4.10 captures crime-related costs in U.S. dollars in per capita terms, with the dollar adjusting for the purchasing power parity of each country. It shows that each of the Caribbean countries had 2014 costs upward of US$350 and that Trinidad and Tobago and the Bahamas had the highest costs of almost US$1,200 per capita each, surpassing Argentina, Chile, and Brazil.

The IDB study shows that the social costs of crime include the costs of victimization in terms of quality-of-life loss due to homicides and other violent crimes and the foregone income of prisoners. Also part of the calculus are private sector costs, which include spending on crime prevention, especially on security services, and costs incurred by the government, which include spending on law enforcement agencies, the courts, and prisons (Jaitman 2017, 20).[21]

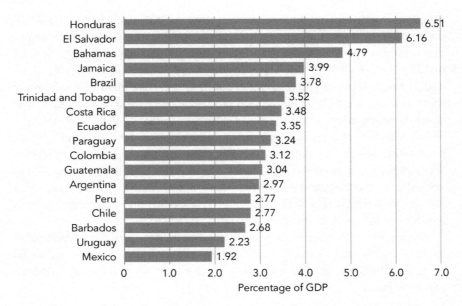

FIGURE 4.9 Crime-Related Costs as a Percentage of GDP in Latin America and the Caribbean.

Source: Laura Jaitman, ed., *The Costs of Crime and Violence: New Evidence and Insights in Latin America and the Caribbean.* Washington, D.C.: Inter-American Development Bank, 2017, 27.

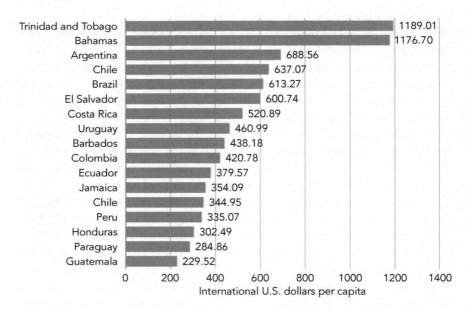

FIGURE 4.10 Crime-Related Costs in International U.S. Dollars per Capita in Latin America and the Caribbean 2014.

Source: Laura Jaitman, ed., *The Costs of Crime and Violence: New Evidence and Insights in Latin America and the Caribbean.* Washington, D.C.: Inter-American Development Bank, 2017, 28.

In what clearly is a manifestation of the resource constraints of states, on the one hand, and a misalignment of existing resources, on the other, Caribbean countries have responded to the problem of high crime with some of the lowest expenditure on administration of justice and some of the highest spending on police, compared to the average for seventeen countries in Latin American and Caribbean. For example, according to Heather Sutton, the Bahamas, Barbados, and Jamaica are among countries that spend the least on justice administration—about 0.06 percent of GDP. Conversely, Jamaica has the highest percentage of crime-related police expenditures—2.04 percent of GDP—and is followed by the Bahamas, with police costs of just under 2 percent of GDP (Sutton 2017, 83). Curiously, the study found that overreliance on the police has resulted in relatively high police-to-population ratios compared to the average for Latin America and around the world.

Quite disconcertingly, though, the study noted:

> However, high police density has not necessarily resulted in rapid police response or higher police effectiveness in solving and investigating crime. Of those polled in the Caribbean Crime Victimization Survey (CCVS) in capital metropolitan areas for the five Caribbean countries previously noted, an average of 56 percent said that if they called the police because someone was entering their home, it would take the police more than thirty minutes to arrive. It would take more than three hours, according to 9 percent of respondents, and 2.5 percent said there are no police in their area at all. Additionally, police detection rates for the most violent crimes (i.e., homicides) are generally low. (Sutton 2017, 85)

The study also revealed that in 2013, just 50 percent of all homicides were resolved in the Bahamas. The detection rate in Jamaica was 41 percent, and in Trinidad and Tobago it was a paltry 13 percent.

One gets a sobering sense of some of the socioeconomic impact involved in recognizing that victims of homicide in the Caribbean are disproportionately young males between the ages of 18 and 35, although in the Bahamas and Barbados the rates are higher for individuals in the 18–25 age range than for young people between ages 25 to 35 (Sutton 2017, 80–81). Quite troublingly, the research revealed that 24.8 percent of Caribbean adults have lost someone close to them as a result of violence. This indirect victimization is highest in Jamaica, where half the population reported having lost someone to violence, followed by the Bahamas, with 37.1 percent. The figure for Barbados was 28.6 percent, that for Trinidad and Tobago was 18.9 percent, while that for Suriname was 8.9 percent.

Yet, as noted above, the ripple effects of crime are not limited to citizens and state entities; the private sector also is affected. Heather Sutton's study revealed that crime takes a heavy toll on the private sector in terms of the costs, in that some 23 percent of the businesses reported experiencing losses due to theft, robbery, vandalism, or arson during the preceding fiscal year, according to the 2013/2014 Productivity, Technology, and Innovation (PROTEqIN) Survey. This was higher than the world average of 19.4 percent, according to the World Bank Enterprise Survey. The percentage of businesses victimized ranged from 8 percent in Belize to 33 percent in Guyana. Beyond this, 70 percent of firms reported spending money in 2013/2014 on security, including equipment, insurance, personnel, and professional security services, which was substantially higher than the world average of 55.6 percent (Sutton 2017, 83).

The portion of firms paying for security in the Caribbean ranged from 44 percent in St. Lucia to 85 percent in Trinidad and Tobago. Sixty-three percent of the firms reported their highest spending on alarm systems, security cameras, and gates, and Suriname, Guyana, and the Bahamas showed the highest levels of expenditure among Caribbean countries (5.9, 5.0, and 3.8 percent of annual sales, respectively), with Barbados's spending being 1.5 percent of annual sales. The IDB study reminds us that this expenditure takes funds away from other activities that could potentially enhance productivity, such as research and development, which is lower than the amount spent on crime.

The theft of electricity is one of the areas of nonviolent criminality with economic costs to the private sector in terms of profit and to the state in terms of tax revenue. For instance, one 2013 report for the Dominican Republic stated that taxpayers footed a RD$51.0 billion (US$1.24 billion) bill for losses incurred by electricity distributors with subsidy and energy theft in 2012. It noted that while the electric bill subsidy to avert an increase to customers reached RD$21 billion (US$394 million) in 2012, electricity distributors lost some RD$20 billion (US$375 million) annually on energy theft by irregular users. The losses amounted to 36.6 percent of energy supplied and not charged, 23.6 percent from theft alone, with the remainder due to grid and equipment overload, inadequate voltage levels, and the poor state of the network. Moreover, up to August 31, 2013, the electricity subsidy was RD$32.23 billion (US$750 million), which was 96 percent of the RD$33.3 billion (US$624 million) that the government had budgeted for the electricity sector (*Dominican Today* 2013b).

In the case of Guyana, in 2018 the Public Utilities Commission expressed concern about the billions of dollars in losses suffered by Guyana Power and Light due to electricity theft and network issues. The commission noted that the electricity company had lost close to US$450 million since 1999, the year the commission was inaugurated, and it called these losses "the bane of the company," remarking that the theft had been a continuous practice for a quarter century (Wilburg 2018). When it comes to Jamaica, their public service entity estimates that 20 percent of the electricity generated is stolen, involving some two hundred thousand households (Mahfood 2020). Writer John Mahfood observed, "If, for argument [*sic*] sake, we assume that there are three persons per household, that means that 600,000 persons are associated with the theft of electricity every day. That represents one in five persons in Jamaica that is either committing a criminal offence every day or is associated with persons in their household that are" (Mahfood 2020).

Quite rightly, Mahfood notes that the theft of electricity has been occurring for many years—decades, actually—and "is ingrained in our psyche and is a fact of life that we have to live with. If JPS [Jamaica Public Service] turned off the electricity to an inner-city community because the vast majority of the households were stealing electricity, then all hell would break lo[o]se. In particular, the member of parliament that represents the community would raise hell and would not allow it to happen!" (Mahfood 2020). According to one report, "In Jamaica roughly 12% of electricity is stolen via illegal connections, whereas in Haiti a whopping 65% of supply is lost to illegal connections and an outdated energy grid." In 2018 "Jamaicans paid about US$0.42/kWh for electricity, 3.5-times higher than that paid by the average US household" (Bnamericas 2019).

Whether for violent crimes, such as intentional homicides, or nonviolent ones, such as the theft of electricity, some of the costs to states relate to the prison aspect. Table 4.2 presents IDB study estimates of incarceration for the seventeen countries examined that aggregates public expenditure on prison administration and the losses caused by the deprivation of liberty of inmates. It shows that on average between 2010 and 2014, the overall cost of imprisonment was more than US$13,800 million, or 0.39 percent of GDP. As might be expected, costs vary among countries, with the cost of prison administration in Argentina, Barbados, Chile, Jamaica, Trinidad and Tobago, and Uruguay being higher than the losses incurred due to incarceration, while in Brazil, Ecuador, Honduras, Paraguay, Peru, and El Salvador, income losses are greater than public expenditure on the prison system. It is quite revealing that Barbados incurred the highest costs, representing 0.71 percent of its GDP. Yet, prisons have more than economic and social cost implications; they also have civilizational ones.

Civilizational Concerns

The Problems of Prisons

Fyodor Dostoevsky, author of *Crime and Punishment, House of the Dead,* and other classics, is credited with saying, "The degree of civilization in a society can be judged by entering its prisons." If one accepts that proposition and applies it to the Caribbean, the conclusion must be drawn that Caribbean civilization is developing some dubious and degenerative aspects.[22] As table 4.3 and figure

TABLE 4.2 Incarceration Cost, Average for 2010–2014 (percent of GDP)

	Expenditure on Prison Administration	Losses Due to Incarceration	Global Cost
Argentina	0.25	0.11	0.36
Bahamas	0.30	0.35	0.65
Barbados	0.47	0.24	0.71
Brazil	0.06	0.14	0.20
Chile	0.33	0.24	0.57
Colombia	0.16	0.16	0.32
Costa Rica	0.27	0.28	0.55
Ecuador	0.09	0.12	0.21
El Salvador	0.20	0.41	0.61
Guatemala	0.08	0.05	0.13
Honduras	0.10	0.27	0.37
Jamaica	0.34	0.10	0.44
Mexico	0.12	0.10	0.22
Paraguay	0.09	0.18	0.27
Peru	0.09	0.17	0.26
Trinidad & Tobago	0.33	0.14	0.47
Uruguay	0.25	0.18	0.43
Average for Latin America and the Caribbean	0.20	0.19	0.39
Total cost (in millions of U.S. dollars)	6,504.8	7,336.6	13,841.4

Source: Laura Jaitman, ed., *The Costs of Crime and Violence: New Evidence and Insights in Latin America and the Caribbean*. Washington, D.C.: Inter-American Development Bank, 2017, 43.

4.11 show, the profile of prisons in the region is one of significant overcrowding. Importantly, too, figure 4.11 reveals the dangerous and desperate situations in which smaller jurisdictions, such as Grenada, Antigua and Barbuda, St. Lucia, and St. Vincent and the Grenadines, find themselves. As might be expected, overcrowding (and poor conditions) in some prisons and pretrial facilities derives from several factors, including the high volume of crime and violence; legislation about marijuana cultivation, possession and use, and the harsh sentencing that attaches to some infractions; the backlog of cases in some jurisdictions; inefficiencies in some courts; and budget constraints. (Some of the marijuana reforms discussed in chapter 3 ameliorate the situation in some jurisdictions.)

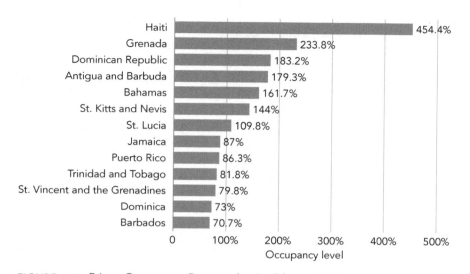

FIGURE 4.11 Prison Occupancy Rates in the Caribbean 2022.

Source: *Statista*, Crime and Law Enforcement. https://www.statista.com/statistics/1297433/prison -occupancy-rates-caribbean-country/.

One IDB case study of Jamaica covering the period 2016–2019 provides some valuable information about the region. It notes that the region's correctional systems face significant challenges, notably high prison population rates that range between 145 and 379 per 100,000 inhabitants, the world average being 140 per 100,000 inhabitants; overcrowding, in some cases exceeding the official capacity by 70 percent; and overuse of pretrial detention (Satchell 2020, 14). Thus, rehabilitation is a rarity. This situation is aggravated by ineffective criminal justice systems characterized by case processing delays and backlogs, insufficient alternatives to prison, excessive use of punitive approaches, and inadequate staffing. Beyond this, correctional services suffer from insufficient investment. Recidivism is also a major contributor to overcrowding and an indicator of the ineffectiveness of the criminal justice system. In Jamaica's case it was 42.5 percent in 2017 (Satchell 2020, 41). (Recidivists are individuals who reenter the criminal justice system after being detainees of the system in the past.)

Both small and large jurisdictions face the civilizational challenges. For instance, Antigua and Barbuda, which has one prison with an official capacity of 150, had an occupancy of 371 in 2016. Consider the case of the Bahamas, with its official capacity of 1,000 and a 2016 prison population of 1,746, which represents an occupancy level of 174.6 percent. In the case of the Dominican Republic, there are 41 penal institutions, with a total official capacity of 14,219. Yet in 2016 they were reported to have housed 25,129 individuals, 10,910 more than should be accommodated. In 2018 there were 26,078 inmates, 11,859 more

TABLE 4.3 Prison Occupancy Profile of Caribbean Countries

Country	Total Capacity	Total Prison Population/Rate (per 100,000 of population)											
		2005	2006	2007	2008	2009	2010	2011	2012	2013	2014	2015	2016
Antigua-Barbuda	150	NA	193/233	NA	229/268	NA	295/339	NA	361/403	NA	331/363	NA	371/398
Aruba	310	231/232	NA	277/272	NA	NA	NA	246/241	NA	240/233	NA	NA	NA
Bahamas	1,000	NA	1,500/446	NA	1,400/402	NA	1,322/367	NA	1,600/428	NA	1,396/36	NA	1,746/438
Barbados	1,250	997/365	NA	1,010/365	1,046/376	NA	910/324	NA	1,045/368	NA	853/298	NA	913/315
Br. Virgin Islands	150	105/457	NA	NA	117/450	NA	117/433	NA	138/493	NA	NA	NA	NA
Cayman Islands	233	NA	210/404	NA	203/363	NA	212/382	NA	NA	NA	NA	NA	NA
Curaçao	590	NA	549/431	NA	NA	NA	541/365	NA	440/288	NA	348/221	NA	NA
Dominica	300	NA	301/424	NA	235/331	NA	295/415	NA	275/382	NA	NA	NA	NA
Dom. Republic	14,219	NA	13,800/145	NA	16,718/170	20,743/208	NA	NA	24,044/235	NA	25,203/241	NA	25,129/235
Grenada	198	NA	334/324	NA	386/371	432/411	NA	NA	441/420	NA	484/457	NA	465/435
Guadeloupe	632	743/169	NA	790/177	NA	NA	NA	784/174	NA	871/193	NA	907/202	NA
Guyana	1,505	NA	1,861/248	NA	2,117/281	NA	2,160/286	NA	2,032/268	NA	1,967/257	NA	2,113/274
Haiti	2,431	NA	4,663/49	NA	8,204/83	NA	5,331/53	NA	8,722/84	NA	10,461/98	NA	10,538/97

TABLE 4.3 (continued)

Country	Total Capacity	Total Prison Population/Rate (per 100,000 of population)											
		2005	2006	2007	2008	2009	2010	2011	2012	2013	2014	2015	2016
Jamaica	4,352	4,825/180	NA	4,709/174	NA	5,163/188	NA	4,457/161	NA	4,112/148	NA	3,860/138	NA
Martinique	738	631/159	NA	763/192	NA	920/233	NA	885/225	NA	918/236	NA	940/244	NA
Puerto Rico	14,240	NA	13,788/351	NA	12,130/306	NA	10,878/294	NA	12,244/338	NA	12,327/351	NA	NA
St. Kitts and Nevis	232	NA	237/474	NA	271/531	NA	256/488	NA	366/678	NA	334/607	NA	NA
St. Lucia	500	503/303	NA	NA	518/299	NA	526/296	NA	568/313	NA	634/345	NA	559/301
St. Vincent and the Grenadines	588	364/334	NA	NA	410/376	NA	413/379	NA	460/422	NA	412/378	NA	460/418
Trinidad-Tobago	4,886	NA	3,514	NA	3,732/283	NA	3,766	NA	3,800/284	NA	3,481/258	NA	NA
U.S. Virgin Islands	355	NA	586/548	NA	612/572	NA	577/544	NA	577/542	NA	NA	NA	NA

NA=Not Available

Notes: Rate is calculated on the basis of 100,000 adult residents ages 18 and older. Although the data for Cuba were limited, it is useful to note what was provided: total official capacity: 57,337; total population and rate for 2003: 55,000/487; total population and rate for 2006: 60,000/531; total population and rate for 2012: 57,337/510. Guadeloupe also had the following in 2017: prison population of 956, and rate of 213. Martinique also had the following in 2017: prison population of 870 and rate of 226.

Source: Institute for Crime and Justice Policy Research, World Prison Brief 2019. https://prisonstudies.org/map/caribbean/.

people than should be there. Grenada also has a troubling case, with an official capacity of 198 and a 2016 population of 465; and Guyana, which has 8 institutions, with a total capacity of 1,505, recorded 2,113 prisoners in 2016, exceeding the official capacity by more than 1,900. However, as has been the case in other nations, it was not just the overcrowding that was a problem but also the deplorable conditions under which inmates had to live. Thus, it was unsurprising that prisoners in Georgetown and Lusignan would riot on several occasions between 2002 and 2020, the most serious incident being in March 2016 in Georgetown, which resulted in the complete destruction of the prison and the death of 17 inmates (see *Kaieteur News* 2016).

One report on the incident raised some broader issues: "That highly public tragedy is the consequence of a hidden one. Of the 50 countries with the highest incarceration rates, 15 are, like Guyana, former British Caribbean colonies or current ones. High levels of violence are partly to blame. So are the criminalization of cannabis use and harsh sentencing laws" (*Economist* 2016). Also, the important point was made that in most of the English-speaking Caribbean, at least a third of prisoners are merely suspects awaiting trial. One inmate who died in the Camp Street prison had been waiting eight years for his murder trial to begin. Evidence also suggests that suspects sometimes exploit pretrial delays in order to have witnesses silenced.

The conditions of many of the region's prisons are not only unbelievably appalling but also harmful to both prisoners and prison officers.[23] As a matter of fact, over the years, in addition to the cases in Guyana mentioned earlier, prisoners in Puerto Rico, Barbados, Haiti, the Dominican Republic, Trinidad and Tobago, and Jamaica have rioted over the conditions under which they were incarcerated. In addressing conditions in Jamaica, one medical practitioner there made the following plea:

> Prisons, like the GP [General Penitentiary], obviously serve as deterrents, but the harsh conditions dehumanise inmates and harden them; many of whom have already been dehumanised and hardened by society. We need more alternatives to custodial sentencing for certain crimes. Some prisons are in dire need of upgrading. Twenty hours of lockdown, three to four persons to a tiny cell with no bunks is unacceptable; the bathroom and eating conditions are degrading. We must reform prisoners, not make them brutish. (Rattray 2010)

Overcrowding and unsavory conditions exist not only in prisons but in many of the holding cells at police stations as well. Indeed, one newspaper headline in January 2020 in Jamaica—"Rats Chase Inmates out Spanish Town Lock-Up; Jail Ordered Closed as Rodents 'Big Like Puss' Bite Detainees"—graphically captured the reality in parts of the country; detainees at the Spanish Town Police Station lockup in St. Catherine had to be relocated because of rodent infestation and overcrowding. The parish's chief health inspector reported that the facility was beset by rat infestation, inadequate ventilation, and sewage overflow. Several prisoners are known to have been hospitalized after being bitten by rats at the facility, which was built to house forty-five detainees but sometimes is packed with up to one hundred individuals. The facility was closed on January 29, 2020, and detainees were sent to the Linstead lockup, the Horizon Remand Centre, and the Tamarind Farm Correctional Centre (Turner 2020).

The situation in Trinidad and Tobago provides another illustration of the challenge. According to the *Country Reports for Human Rights Practices* for 2018, most prisons suffered from extreme overcrowding, although the maximum-security prison was not at full capacity. The poor conditions and the overcrowding were notable particularly in the Port-of-Spain Prison, the remand prison, and the immigration detention center, which had as many as 9 prisoners in cells of eighty square feet. Indeed, according to the U.S. Department of State, in 2016 the Port-of-Spain Prison, which was designed to hold 250 inmates, held 595, and the remand prison, designed to hold 655 inmates, held 1,049 (U.S. Department of State 2019b, 2).

In what amounted to a civilizational indictment and resonates beyond Trinidad and Tobago, then–opposition senator Verna St. Rose–Greaves, who later became minister of gender, youth, and child development, delivered the following remarks during a March 2010 parliamentary debate:

Our prisons are overrun by illicit, illegal, underground activity, inclusive of sex, cell phones, drugs and other contraband. . . . This place [the central Port-of-Spain Prison] is not fit for animals, let alone human beings. Men sleeping head-to-toe in a cell, packed in like sardines, some without mattresses and without proper bedding layered from ceilings in hammocks straight down to the floor on cardboard. The stench of human and cat urine soaked into a hundred-year old concrete floor. . . . In the evening, they must stuff their ears and their nostrils. They must put bread in a corner to deflect the cockroaches from crawling into their unguarded orifices. . . . It is in the evening that men must press their backs against the wall, afraid to sleep. Their cries and protestations can be heard as they grow faint and change with time. How does a man admit in a hostile environment, that he was raped in prison, that he has had sex with other men or that he was forced to put on a sex show for some perverted senior official? . . .

By the clock, I see it is 2.47 pm. At this precise time, the prisoners would be now moving to empty their slop buckets left to bubble overnight. This stench, while it may be unbearable to you and to I, but so accustomed to them. You would probably see young men put their hands into a plastic salt beef bucket to scrub and dislodge fecal matter. You would see prisons [sic] officers with pain on their faces, because this has also become their life. Imagine, grown men and women held in cells without sanitary facilities, forced to defecate and urinate in the presence of their fellow prisoners without privacy, in bottles, plastic bags and on paper, to be poured into plastic buckets provided for the purpose. And we talk about human rights! (*Trinidad and Tobago Newsday* 2010)

Haiti represents the most appalling case and the sharpest reflection of the validity of civilizational concerns in the region. With 17 institutions and an official capacity of 2,431, the records showed an occupancy of 10,538 in 2016, which is 8,107 beyond the official capacity. *InSight Crime* reported that Haiti has the highest overcrowding rate in the world, at 454 percent. Some 80 percent of the 11,000 total inmates are in pretrial detention, meaning they have never been convicted of a crime. Indeed, it was common for prisoners to be held for three years before their trial (Clavel 2017). In 2014, 300 inmates escaped. Two years later there was another prison break, in which more than 170 inmates escaped, killing one guard and stealing firearms in the process. Both incidents pointed to the significant shortcomings of the prison system.

In its report for 2018, the *Country Report on Human Rights Practices* provided a sobering portrait of the harsh realities facing society and civilization in Haiti:

Prison and detention center overcrowding was severe, especially in the National Penitentiary and the prison in Cap Haitien [Cap-Haïtien], where each prisoner had 4.2 square feet of space. In many prisons detainees slept in shifts due to lack of space. Some prisons had no beds for detainees, and some cells had no access to natural light. In other prisons the cells often were open to the elements or lacked adequate ventilation. Many prison facilities lacked basic services such as plumbing, sanitation, waste disposal, medical services, potable water, electricity, adequate ventilation, lighting, and isolation units for contagious patients. Some prison officials used chlorine to sanitize drinking water, but in general prisoners in older prisons did not have access to treated drinking water. Most prisons had insufficient sewage facilities for their populations. (U.S. Department of State, Haiti 2019a, 3)

The discussion above supports the assertion by one scholar-practitioner that many of the prisons in the region have not been prepared for prison life in the twenty-first century. Quite rightly, Karen Lancaster-Ellis also highlights the extant contradictions between platitudes and practices, where human rights guarantees that are enshrined in constitutions are honored in the breach by the manner in which states conduct their prison affairs and in their noncompliance with several international human rights conventions. Lancaster-Ellis also makes the supportable argument that long has been purported by both academics and policy makers: "If Caribbean governments are to deal with the issues of prison overcrowding, it is vital that they look at the type of matters for which prisoners are incarcerated. It therefore may be an option to reconceptualize the categories of the offenses/matters for which inmates are incarcerated and seek alternative methods of punishment, retribution, or rehabilitation instead of an over-emphasis on custodial sentences" (Lancaster-Ellis 2018, 111).

Clearly, rehabilitation is an unrealistic expectation with the prevailing conditions in prisons, although it may appear on the list of institutional objectives of prisons and government ministries. Retribution is the default, not the design. Consequently, dehumanization results. Nevertheless, civilizational concerns extend legitimately beyond the how and why factors of the prisons issue to the who factor, to demographics. An examination of the age distribution of inmate populations of most Caribbean jurisdictions would reveal that large proportions are of inmates who are in the most productive period of their lives, between eighteen and forty-five years of age.

Incarceration is not merely an economic and social loss to the Caribbean societies, but values such as respect (for self and for rules) and integrity, which are essential for healthy societal development, are both devalued and repudiated. Moreover, males constitute significant proportions of prison populations, which undermines the social-sexual and socioeconomic sustainability of societies. As if all this were not enough, the impunity and corrupt acts of commission and omission by state officials further complicate the civilizational landscape.

Corruption and Impunity

The proposition was made elsewhere (Griffith 1997, 195) that, as in other places, drug-related corruption in the Caribbean violates both laws and norms. It involves acts of commission and omission that breach laws and deviate from accepted social, political, and other norms and values. Such acts by public officials are especially problematic, as those officials pledge to uphold the societies' laws and norms and are expected to serve as models of their societies' high ideals.

Ethan Nadelmann's approach is particularly attractive in differentiating among three types of corruption: sporadic, systemic, and institutionalized. The first type involves the absence of broad patterns of corruption, where individuals or small groups take bribes without sharing their takings or knowledge of their activities with others. Systemic corruption has two variants. In the first, corruption is pervasive but poorly organized: although corruption may be rampant, not everyone in the hierarchy is corrupt. The second is distinguished by a hierarchical payoff arrangement in which lower-level officials hand over most of their takings to their superiors; the flow may also be in the reverse order. And in institutionalized corruption, all lesser "payoff cones" fall within a centralized national "payoff cone," or only one "payoff cone" exists for the entire nation (Nadelmann 1993).

Although evidence from across the Caribbean points to sporadic and systemic corruption following the Nadelmann typology—except, perhaps, for Haiti at one stage of its history—no contemporary Caribbean society fits Nadelmann's definition of institutionalized corruption. However, if one adopts the approach to the matter by Peter Andreas, institutionalized corruption surely has been a feature of the Caribbean reality. For Andreas, "Corruption becomes institutionalized when individuals within an institution are complicit in the [drug] trade and the institution acts as a shield against accountability" (Andreas 1993, 24). Of course, corruption features not just in the drug PWP, with its production, trafficking, consumption, and money-laundering dimensions, but also in relation to the PWPs related to terrorism and cybersecurity, which are examined in chapter 5. But whether related to drugs alone, crime alone, or all the PWPs, corruption undermines societal values and destabilizes civilizational propriety.

According to Transparency International, the gold standard of international NGOs that deal with corruption, the concern about the Caribbean is still justified. This is evident from figures 4.12 and 4.13, which place the Caribbean in

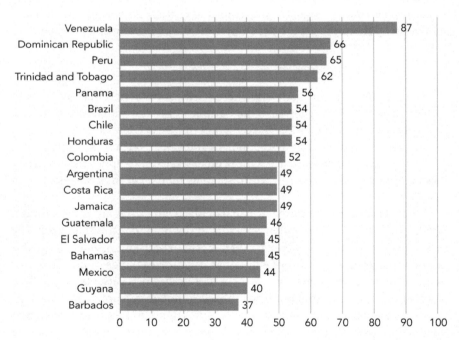

FIGURE 4.12 Percentage of People Who Think Corruption Increased in Past 12 Months, Select Latin American and Caribbean Countries 2019.

Source: Transparency International, *Global Corruption Barometer Latin America and the Caribbean 2019 Citizens' Views and Experiences of Corruption*, 2019, 8. https://www.transparency.org/files/content/pages/2019_GCB_LatinAmerica_Caribbean_Full_Report.pdf/.

broader comparative terms. Transparency International's Corruption Perceptions Index annually ranks countries by their perceived levels of public sector corruption, judged by experts and businesspeople. A score of 100 represents the most corrupt and zero represents no corruption (Paynter 2020). Figures 4.12 and 4.13 show that perceptions at the popular level are not as laudable. Figure 4.12 indicates that in both the Dominican Republic and Trinidad and Tobago, more than 60 percent of the people surveyed considered corruption to have increased over the previous twelve months, while in Jamaica and the Bahamas, the figure was 45 percent and above. With regard to the perception of citizens about government corruption, figure 4.13 reveals troubling numbers, the worst being 85 percent in Trinidad and Tobago and 93 percent in the Dominican Republic.

Aspects of crime and punishment in the region often evoke musical musings. Peter Tosh, for example, who was invoked in chapter 3, comes to mind again. Take his "Equal Rights" song, where he declares, "Everyone is talking about crime. / Tell me, who are the criminals?"[24] In too many cases, the brazen

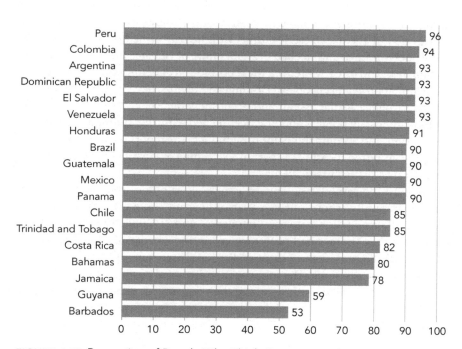

FIGURE 4.13 Perception of People Who Think Government Corruption Is a Problem, Select Latin American and Caribbean Countries 2019.

Source: Transparency International, *Global Corruption Barometer Latin America and the Caribbean 2019 Citizens' Views and Experiences of Corruption*, 2019, 10. https://www.transparency.org/files/content /pages/2019_GCB_LatinAmerica_Caribbean_Full_Report.pdf/.

criminality of police officers is unbelievable. For instance, in February 2020 in Trinidad and Tobago, forty-seven-year-old acting inspector Rajesh Gookool and forty-three-year-old acting sergeant Richard Lalbeharry from the Central Police Division were among three individuals charged with trafficking children for the purpose of exploitation. They also were charged with receiving a benefit knowing that it resulted from trafficking in children, supporting a gang in the commission of gang-related activity, and misbehavior in public office. Inspector Gookool also was charged with sexual assault of a child (*Trinidad Express* 2020). Peter Tosh raises relevant issues about corruption, ineptitude, and desperation to solve crimes that often lead some protectors against crime to become perpetrators of crime.

In Puerto Rico, for instance, the corruption exposé resulted from investigation of that country's police department by the U.S. Department of Justice over a three-year period beginning in July 2008. The 133-page report, which was released in September 2011, was scathing, with evidence of "profound" and "long-standing" civil rights violations. It indicated that rather than helping to solve the island's crime wave, the police were part of the problem, and it highlights "rampant" and "unnecessary or gratuitous use of force." This was aggravated by the use of tactical units with heavily armed police officers who were poorly trained and steeped in a subculture of violence that relies on intimidation, fear, and force. Moreover, the report found endemic corruption, routine discrimination against people of Dominican Republic descent, consistent failure to report police sexual assault and domestic violence, and significant infractions in almost all policies and practices related to hiring, training, assignment, promotion, and accountability for misconduct. The report recommended more than one hundred measures as part of a sweeping overhaul of the force (Savage and Alvarez 2011; Alvarez 2011).

Around the same time, Guyana experienced one of the most egregious cases of impunity, where fourteen-year-old Twyon Thomas was tortured at the Leonora Police Station between October 27 and 31, 2009. The police officers suspected that Thomas had been involved in the murder of a local politician, Raminauth Bisram, deputy chair of Region Three, one of the country's ten administrative divisions. The interrogation involved covering his head with a T-shirt, tying his hands with wire, and then dousing his genitals with mentholated spirits and setting him alight. This case, which involved the complicity of a medical doctor, outraged civil society sectors in Guyana and elsewhere. The two policemen involved, Sergeant Narine Lall and Constable Mohanram Dolai, were charged, but the cases against them were dismissed after neither Thomas nor his mother appeared for the trial, allegedly having received payment from the attorneys representing the police officers.[25] Still, the Guyana Police Force was sued successfully.

Justice Roxanne George heard the case, and in her June 2011 decision, she ordered a total payment of G$6.5 million (US$32,000), about half being for torture and degrading punishment. In her thirty-six-page judgment she affirmed, "The torture and cruel and inhuman treatment meted out to Thomas has demonstrated and established an absolute and flagrant disregard for his constitutional rights." The judge also declared unlawful the teenager's detention and denial of a hospital visit, despite his injuries and the intervention of his mother and attorney. "How it was that the police hoped to keep such a horrendous occurrence under wraps was a mystery," she wrote, adding that his fundamental rights were violated not only by acts and omissions by the police officers directly involved but also by others in the police force, including police surgeon Dr. Mahendra K. Chand. The ruling by Justice George, who later, in March 2017, was appointed acting chief justice, also noted that "by failing to provide him with any medical examination for over a day after he was burnt, the unprofessional medical attention he received, and by failing to permit him to go to hospital for further medical attention for another two days, they displayed a callous indifference, lack of care, and an absence of concern for Thomas as a detainee and as a child." The attorney general later appealed the decision on behalf of the Guyana Police Force (see *Kaieteur News* 2009; Chabrol 2011).

With regard to judicial proceedings, Jamaican justice minister Delroy Chuck offered some sobering statistics in his address at the October 8, 2011, Norman Manley Law School graduation: thousands of cases lingered in the court system. He shared that in 2010 there were almost 460,000 cases before the courts, more than half of which were due to a massive backlog. The minister offered a troubling, but frank, appraisal in noting the corruption within the court and the justice system, where the police have been paid to say they cannot find a witness or where persons have been paid to have documents destroyed. Minister Chuck also lamented cases that languished for years with very little progress and clients who became frustrated and could not move on with their lives (Hall and Thuffe 2011). Years later, still holding the same portfolio, Delroy Chuck was able to identify improvements in this area. In making his contribution to the 2020 Budget Sectoral Debate on May 21, 2019, he noted that on December 31, 2016, there was a backlog of 30,667 criminal cases in the parish courts. As at the end of fiscal year 2018/2019, some 12,399 of these cases had been cleared, representing a 40 percent reduction in the backlog (Linton 2019). However, Minister Chuck lamented the reality of too many matters in the courts dragging on for five years or more, some in excess of ten years.

Impunity and corruption have been costly to Jamaica. In one case, according to Minister Chuck, between 2006 and 2011, court judgments and out-of-court settlements forced consecutive administrations to pay out some J$365 million (US$4.26 million) in thirty-seven civil suits against government employees.

The minister also revealed that the government still owed almost J$400 million in civil suit judgments and that most of the outstanding money was for cases involving police abuse, although medical negligence and other infractions were involved. He indicated that the J$400 million in arrears did include the J$1.85 billion (US$21.57 million) owed to the National Transport Co-operative Society for breach of contract, a case that dates to the mid-1990s. The settlement was expected to top J$2 billion (US$23.32 million) when interest is added. Jamaican authorities generally settle judgments in monthly half-a-million-dollar tranches. However, there were cases of single multimillion-dollar payouts. Between 2010 and October 2011, for example, they paid out J$178.2 million (US$2.08 million) of the J$365 million (US$4.3 million) ordered by the court or agreed on in out-of-court settlements. The cash-strapped government still had to find J$129.4 million ($US843,688) to settle the remaining ten of the thirty-seven cases (Reid and Scarlett 2011).

Needless to say, corruption by government officials exists elsewhere in the region. For instance, on May 17, 2021, fifty-eight-year-old Miguel Andrés Gutiérrez Díaz, a deputy in the Dominican Republic's ruling Modern Revolutionary Party, was arrested in Miami on drug trafficking charges. Gutierrez was elected to the chamber of deputies in 2020 to represent the city of Santiago. Along with brothers Miguel Emilio Gutiérrez and Endy and Danny Núñez, the legislator was alleged to be part of a transnational cocaine smuggling ring from 2014 to 2017 that operated between the Dominican Republic, Colombia, and the United States. Earlier in the year, on March 11, he was indicted by a federal grand jury on charges of conspiracy to import, possess, and distribute cocaine in the States. If convicted, he faces up to life in prison. The trial was initially scheduled to begin early September 2021, but the prosecutors sought a postponement until April 2022 to allow for adequate preparation of their case The deputy was later placed on suicide watch and subsequently declared medically incompetent to stand trial (Wyss 2021; Memesita 2021; Weaver 2022).

In addition, in June 2022, Jeremias Jimenez Cruz, former consul general of the Dominican Republic to Jamaica, was sentenced to 179 months in prison for using his position and contacts in the government of the Dominican Republic to import cocaine into the United States. Jimenez Cruz, who also had a diplomatic posting to Germany earlier, pled guilty to conspiring to import more than five kilograms of cocaine into the United States. Interestingly, he also had served as president of the National Christian Movement. Evidence showed that he had used his position, connections, and planes to traffic large quantities of cocaine and to launder drug proceeds. He was caught on tape admitting that with his government connections, he was able to move up to six hundred kilograms of cocaine by airplane and up to one ton of cocaine by boat (U.S. Secret Service 2022).

Clearly, then, crime in the region presents some clear and present dangers. Lamentably, the assertion by former corrections commissioner of Jamaica Dudley Allen about his nation in 1976 is true about the entire Caribbean in 2023: "It is no longer possible to think of crime as a simple or minor social problem. . . . Mounting crime and violence have been declared leading national problems, and the issue of law and order has assumed high priority in national planning and policymaking. Fear of crime is destroying freedom of movement, freedom from harm, and freedom from fear itself" (Allen 1980, 29). Evidently, the crucible of crime in the region is complex. This complexity coexists with the complexity of other PWPs. Because of the complexity and the interconnectivity involved, Caribbean leaders and citizens do not have the luxury of compartmentalized or sequential attention to the challenges; holistic, multidimensional, local-global engagements are necessary. As well, part of the frustration—to statesmen and citizens—is that crime and the other PWPs are not amenable to quick fixes. As if the herculean challenges presented by drugs and crime were not enough, there are the threats and apprehensions related to terror and cyber, the subject of the next chapter.

The Trauma of Terror and Cyber Threats

Prior to September 11, 2001 (9/11), in the United States of America (USA) terrorism was not a major security issue of the governments of the Caribbean as it had been for much of the rest of the world. . . . The realization that individuals will employ extreme violence, in ways yet to be imagined, in an attempt to change a way of life when the accepted political processes do not comport with their ends, is now a phenomenon that we all have to live with. The means to execute violent acts are no longer largely the preserve of state actors. In contemporary times, no country or region of the world is exempt from what has been described as "the primary security threat of the 21st century."

—Dion E. Phillips, "Terrorism and Security in the Caribbean before and after 9/11"

There is a view in parts of the region that the Caribbean is somehow immune or unlikely to be of interest to cybercriminals. However, one only has to consider the enormous sums of money transferred regularly through the region's offshore financial centres, the commercially sensitive documents held in registries and lawyers' offices, matters of national security and criminality that all governments regularly engage with, the expansion of citizenship programmes, and the millions of daily commercial banking transactions, to immediately see the dangers cybercrime poses to small nations.

—David Jessop, "Action Needed to Address Caribbean Cyber Security: The View from Europe"

Terrorism and cyber threats, the Problems Without Passports examined in this chapter, share some commonalities with the drug and crime PWPs that were examined earlier. The commonalities are transnationality and multidimensionality, both of which are a function of their global interdependence character. As well, in the context of the post-realist paradigm in which security is defined as having traditional and nontraditional facets, terrorism and cyber threats highlight the salience of the nontraditional facet. Yet, there are some differences. Although there had been terrorist incidents in the region prior to 2001, as Dion Phillips rightly asserts in the first epigraph to this chapter, terrorism was not viewed as a security concern by and for the region until September 11, 2001. As well, cyber threats came into vogue long after terrorism. In contrast, drugs and crime had been defined as clear and present dangers for the region dating back to the 1970s. Attention to cybersecurity underscores the reality that economic and political security features are critical desiderata. This is a key aspect of Jessop's proposition in the second epigraph, which also highlights the multiple areas of cybersecurity vulnerability, a feature also shared by terrorism.

In probing the threats and vulnerabilities associated with terrorism and cyber threats, I focus initially on terrorism. First, the chapter places the region in global context and recalls important experiences prior to September 11, 2001. Geopolitical and geoeconomic considerations related to strategic materials and strategic waterways, tourism, and terrorist financing then command our attention. Special consideration also is paid to the circumstances of Trinidad and Tobago, once viewed as the epicenter of terrorism concerns in the region. As to cyber matters, the chapter provides global and regional portraits and highlights some specific cyberattacks in the region over recent years. Among other things, it concludes that although there is good reason to be anxious about the profile of Trinidad and Tobago in ISIS recruitment, there is little regional susceptibility to a spread of religious or religiously driven political upheaval within Trinidad and Tobago by jihadists who return from the Middle East, much less to the wider Caribbean.

The Terrorism Trauma

Earlier chapters pointed out that the concepts "security" and "sovereignty" are highly contested and that this necessitated clarification of the respective definitional parameters used in this study. The same is true for the use of "terrorism" in this chapter. As explained in *Global Terrorism Index 2019*, "Defining terrorism is not a straightforward matter. There is no single internationally accepted definition of what constitutes terrorism and the terrorism literature abounds with competing definitions and typologies" (Institute for Economics and Peace 2019, 6). One scholar who used the opportunity of the tenth anniversary of the September 11 episode in New York to comprehensively examine the subject notes, "The quest to establish a universal definition of terrorism is entangled in questions of law, history, philosophy, morality, and religion" (Setty 2011, 6). Thus, the matter is pregnant with complexity, which is all the more reason for us to "define our terms," as French philosopher Voltaire was famous for advising.

Violence for Effect and Violent Experiences

In light of the above, we are adopting as our working definition the one articulated by the Institute for Economics and Peace, which defines terrorism as "the threatened or actual use of illegal force and violence by a non-state actor to attain a political, economic, religious, or social goal through fear, coercion, or intimidation" (Institute for Economics and Peace 2019, 6). Brian Jenkins calls terrorism "violence for effect," sometimes "not only, and sometimes not at all, for the effect on the actual victims of the terrorists" (Jenkins 1975,1). This approach recognizes that terrorism involves not just the physical act of an attack; it also involves the psychological impact it has on a community or a society, giving new meaning to the notions of power and of powerlessness.

As might be expected, not only is there a multiplicity of definitions of the concept, but there also is an array of paradigms and typologies. One typology identifies four basic types of terrorists—leftists, rightists, ethnonationalists/separatists, and religious or "sacred" terrorists—and recognizes that there is some overlap among the categories, as many groups have a mix of motivating ideologies (Cronin 2000). All four types are said to have enjoyed relative prominence in modern times; the first was intertwined with communist movements, the second drew its inspiration from fascism, and the bulk of the third type accompanied the wave of decolonization, particularly immediately after World War II. As well, it is contended that the fourth type—religious or "sacred" terrorism—has been the most significant of the four recently.

An appreciation of the violence for effect at the global level is important before turning our attention to the realities of the Caribbean. In reflecting on the period since 2001, the *Global Terrorism Index 2019* indicates that since that fateful September 11, 2001, event, the world has experienced four distinct trends in global terrorism. Between 2002 and 2007, attacks increased steadily, correlating with an increase in violent conflicts in Iraq. That trend crested in 2007, coinciding with the U.S. troop surge, after which terrorist incidents declined steadily, with deaths falling by 35 percent between 2007 and 2011. The third trend, from 2011 to 2014, witnessed another surge, with deaths increasing by more than 350 percent in a mere three years. This wave itself coincided with the rise of ISIL (Islamic State in Iraq and the Levant), the start of the Syrian civil war, and the reemergence of Boko Haram in Nigeria (see Institute for Economics and Peace 2019, 35–36).

With regard to the fourth and current trend, which began in 2014, there has been a substantial decrease in the number of deaths from terrorism, with the most dramatic reductions occurring in Iraq, Nigeria, Pakistan, and Syria. The winding down of the Syrian civil war, the collapse of ISIL, and increased international counterterrorism coordination are said to have contributed to reduction of the violence for effect. The premier terrorism monitoring international nongovernmental organization reported that in 2001 fifty-one countries experienced at least one death from terrorism. The number of countries implicated declined to thirty-nine in 2004, but it increased steadily since then, with sixty or more countries experiencing at least one fatal attack each year since 2012, and peaked in 2016, when seventy-nine countries had at least one death from terrorism. Between 1998 and 2006, there was never more than one country in a year that recorded more than a thousand deaths from terrorism. Nevertheless, since 2012 there have been at least four countries every year, until 2018, when the number dropped to three (Institute for Economics and Peace 2019, 35–36).

According to the 2020 global terrorism assessment, the world witnessed an end of the surge in terrorism, with a 59 percent drop between 2014 and 2020, the largest decreases happening in Iraq and Syria, with deaths in Nigeria fluctuating over the years. The winding down of the Syrian civil war, the collapse of ISIL, and increased counterterrorism coordination at both the state and international levels all played significant roles in the reduction. The terrorism saga continued abated in Afghanistan, though. Indeed, the *Global Terrorism Index 2020* contended that although terrorism declined in most countries between 2014 and 2020, there was a steady increase in Afghanistan. As a matter of fact, deaths increased by 439 percent from 2009 to 2019 (Institute for Economics and Peace 2020,40).

In terms of regional terrorism experiences, seven of the nine world regions witnessed a decline of terrorism in 2018.[1] This was consonant with the global trend, which saw a significant reduction in both deaths from terrorism and the number of terrorist attacks. The largest improvement occurred in the Middle East and North America (MENA), while South America had the largest deterioration, followed by Central America and the Caribbean. South Asia has recorded the highest regional score on the Global Terrorism Index (GTI) between 2002 and 2018, and Central America and the Caribbean logged the lowest score for the same period.[2]

A total of 212 deaths from terrorism have been recorded in Central America and the Caribbean between 2002 and 2018, with 28 deaths occurring in 2018. Between 2002 and 2018, South Asia, MENA, and sub-Saharan Africa accounted for 93 percent of all deaths from terrorism, with MENA having the largest number—more than 93,700 fatalities. South Asia had some 67,500 deaths over the same period, with 45,000 occurring in sub-Saharan Africa. MENA, South Asia, and sub-Saharan Africa also had the most lethal terrorist attacks, averaging 2.67, 1.95, and 4.11 people killed per attack, respectively. Conversely, in Asia-Pacific, Europe, South America, and North America, there were more terrorist attacks than total deaths from terrorism.

In relation to Central America and the Caribbean, although only four of the twelve countries there deteriorated in 2018, the size of the deteriorations was enough to cause a decline in the overall score for the region. Significant score reductions occurred in Nicaragua, Guatemala, Mexico, and Haiti. Costa Rica, Cuba, and El Salvador recorded no terrorist activity over the study period, although El Salvador regularly registered one of the highest homicide rates in the world. As well, Honduras, Jamaica, Dominican Republic, Panama, and Trinidad and Tobago improved from 2017 to 2018. Nicaragua has recorded nine terrorist attacks since 2002, with seven occurring in 2018. The *Global Terrorism Index 2019* reveals that terrorism in Nicaragua in 2018 was driven by political instability, civil unrest, and criminal violence and may have included right-wing extremist elements. None of the 2018 perpetrators were known terrorist organizations.

Mexico recorded a 58 percent increase in terrorism in 2018, with a noticeable uptake in attacks on politicians. There were 22 more terrorist attacks in 2018 than in 2017, with a total of 19 fatalities. Attacks on politicians there historically have been rare; only 3 occurred in the 15 years before 2018. However, the 2018 elections in Mexico were particularly violent, with at least 850 acts of political violence recorded during the campaign period. Terrorists in Mexico are known to target the media significantly, with such attacks making up 25 percent of the 122 attacks recorded since 2002. Guatemala and Haiti also recorded deteriorations in their scores due to a resurgence of terrorism in 2018, although neither country has experienced more than 20 incidents since 2002. Both also were free of terrorism in 2017, but in 2018 Guatemala suffered 5 attacks and Haiti 2. Thankfully, there were no fatalities in either country. (See Institute for Economics and Peace 2019, 37–44, for data and a narrative assessment of regional trends.)

The *Global Terrorism Index 2020* reports that the situation in five of twelve Central American and Caribbean countries deteriorated in 2019, which led to an overall regional deterioration. The countries involved were Costa Rica, Honduras, Mexico, Haiti, and Trinidad and Tobago. It was a point of pride that Cuba and El Salvador remained unaffected by terrorism, although El Salvador regularly registered one of the highest homicide rates in the world. Moreover, Guatemala, Nicaragua, Jamaica, the Dominican Republic, and Panama all improved their scores from 2018 to 2019. Also noteworthy is that Guatemala showed the biggest improvement in the region, with zero terrorist incidents documented in 2019. Nicaragua followed with the second-largest improvement in the region, with incidents dropping from seven in 2018 to three in 2019. Plus there were no deaths during that period (Institute for Economics and Peace 2020, 30).

Terrorism's economic impact also has been significant. Calculations by the Institute for Economics and Peace are that the global economic impact of terrorism in 2018 amounted to US$33 billion, a decline of 38 percent from 2017, and the fourth consecutive year that the economic impact declined from the 2014 peak of US$111 billion.[3] The institute acknowledges that the "estimates are considered conservative, as there are many items that are not included in the methodology due to the difficulty in costing them. These include the longer-term economic implications of terrorism such as reduced tourism, business activity, production and investment" (Institute for Economics and Peace 2019, 29). Understandably, the reduced economic impact reflects the decreasing incidence of violence.

The improvement between 2014 and 2018 is said to be driven largely by the reduced terrorism-related violence in Iraq, Nigeria, and Pakistan. Indeed, since 2014 terrorism's economic impact declined by 62 percent in Nigeria, 82 percent in Iraq, and 90 percent in Pakistan. Understandably, countries enduring armed conflict experienced higher economic impacts. In 2018, Afghanistan was the country most impacted in terms of economic cost, amounting to 19.4 percent of its gross domestic product, an increase of 7 percentage points over 2017. Afghanistan has experienced a consistent increase in the level of terrorist violence and their ongoing conflict. No other country experienced a cost of terrorism greater than 5 percent of its GDP. The country that experienced the second-highest impact, Iraq, suffered 3.9 percent of its GDP in 2018. (See Institute for Economics and Peace 2019, 29–33, for a discussion on impact.)

The institute explains that terrorist violence and the fear of it creates significant economic disruptions. The fear changes economic behavior, especially by altering investment and consumption patterns and diverting public and private resources away from productive activities and toward protective measures. Terrorism and the fear of it also cause productivity shortfalls, foregone earnings, and distorted expenditure, all of which influence the price of goods and services. As stated earlier, the institute's cost-of-terrorism model focuses on the direct costs of terrorism that stem from deaths, injuries, property damage, and GDP losses in relevant countries experiencing conflict. However, the institute also acknowledges that terrorism also results in indirect costs related to economic growth, financial markets, trade, and tourism. According to the institute, terrorism's global economic impact was estimated to be US$26.4 billion in 2019, which was 25 percent less than in 2018 and the fifth consecutive year that it has declined. This reportedly was driven by the reduced terrorism in Iraq, Nigeria, Pakistan, and Syria. As well, it is noteworthy that since its peak in 2014 of

US$116 billion, the economic impact has fallen by 77 percent, reflecting the reduced number of terrorism deaths, injuries, and attacks globally (Institute for Economics and Peace 2020, 30).

With regard to tourism, which, as will be seen below, is an area of special interest and vulnerability in the Caribbean, the area is especially vulnerable to terrorism, as terrorism increases the anxiety of travel, and terrorist attacks reduce tourism revenue by reducing tourist arrivals. In fact, reports indicate that tourism to Israel from 1991 to 2001 was hindered more by the frequency of attacks rather than the severity of the terrorism. Estimates quantifying the dollar value of terrorism on a selection of European countries from 1974 to 1988 found collectively, the countries lost US$16.145 billion due to terrorism (Institute for Economics and Peace 2019, 33). Moreover, terrorism effects spill over into neighboring countries and reduce the level of tourism in those countries.

Violence and Vulnerability in the Caribbean

As sociologist Dion Phillips noted in the first epigraph to this chapter, prior to the September 2001 terrorist attack against the United States, terrorism did not command attention in the Caribbean or in relation to it. Not that there had been no "violence for effect," to use Brian Jenkins's term, before September 11, 2001. Indeed, Leslie Manigat once remarked, "If the transition from colonial rule to independence in the English-speaking [world] was largely peaceful and nonviolent, the mid- and late 1970s saw a veritable outburst of terrorism. Ideologically inspired terrorism that was suspected of having international links accounts for the 'party bombings' in Jamaica, 'independentista bombing' in Puerto Rico, and nationalist bombings in Guadeloupe" (Manigat 1988, 35).

Table 5.1 captures the most notable intra-Caribbean terrorist incidents between 1967 and 1995. It reveals fewer than twenty incidents over the almost three decades covered, with a recurrence of incidents in Dominica, Barbados, Jamaica, Grenada, and Trinidad and Tobago. Entries in the list cover all the categories of the Cronin terrorism typology: leftists, rightists, ethnonationalists/separatists, and religious or "sacred" terrorists. For instance, the Cubana bombing falls into the rightists category, while the actions of the Macheteros fit the leftists one. The June 1967 efforts in Anguilla and those in Union Island in December 1979 manifest intent aligned with separation, while those by the Jamaat-al-Muslimeen in Trinidad and Tobago were driven by religious motives. Although even a single life lost is one too many, thankfully, the overall fatality count was low: less than 150. The most devastating experience, with more than half of the entire fatality count, was the bombing off Barbados in 1976. Incidentally, this was the first occasion in the Americas in which an airplane was the instrument used to deliver "violence for effect."

TABLE 5.1 Terrorist Incidents in the Caribbean before September 11, 2001

Date(s) of Event	Jurisdiction Affected	Actors Involved	Actions Involved
1967 (May 29)	Anguilla	Anguillan nationals open fire on police and civilians	Expulsion of St. Kitts police and attempted overthrow of government
1967 (June 10)	Anguilla	Five Anguillans	Attempted secession of Nevis from Anguilla
1970 (April 21)	Trinidad and Tobago	85 Trinidad and Tobago Defense Force soldiers	Attempted overthrow of government; 24/31 civilians were killed
1970 (May 1)	Jamaica	Two Afro-American freedom fighters	Hijacking of BWIA aircraft from Kingston, JA, to Cuba
1976 (June 19)	Jamaica	Jamaica Labor Party official Pernel Charles and ex-Jamaica Defense Force officer Peter Whittingham	Attempted overthrow of governmentof Prime Minister Michael Manley
1976 (Oct. 1)	Barbados	Sydney Burnett Alleyne intercepted off Martinique	Attempted overthrow of government of Prime Minister Tom Adams
1976 (Oct. 6)	Barbados	Anti-Castro activists Freddy Lugo, Luis Posada Carriles, Orlando Bosch, and Hernan Ricardo Lozano	Bombing of a Cubana de Aviación plane off Barbados on the way to Cuba, killing 73 people: 5 North Koreans, 11 Guyanese, and 57 Cubans
1978 (Nov. 18)	Grenada	Mongoose gang	Members of New Jewel Movement beaten and jailed
1979 (March)	Grenada	40 armed cadres of the New Jewel Movement	Overthrow of government of Prime Minister Eric Gairy; several people killed
1979 (May 29)	Dominica	Elements of Dominica Defense Force	Protest against govt.; 1 killed, 9 injured
1979 (Dec. 7)	Union Island	50 Rastafarians, led by Lennox Charles	Attempted secession from St. Vincent and the Grenadines; 1 fatality
1980 (June 13)	Guyana	Sergeant Gregory Smith of Guyana Defense Force	Car bombing of scholar-politician Dr. Walter Rodney, co-leader of WPA
1980 (June 19)	Grenada	2 unidentified suspects	Attempted assassination of Prime Minister Maurice Bishop et al.; 3 killed, 1 injured

(continued)

TABLE 5.1 (continued)

Date(s) of Event	Jurisdiction Affected	Actors Involved	Actions Involved
1981 (Jan. 1)	Puerto Rico	Puerto Rican Nationalist group Macheteros (cane cutters)	Destruction of 11 planes belonging to the Puerto Rican National Guard, worth US$45 million
1981 (March 7)	Dominica	9 ex-Dominica Defense Force members and ex-Prime Minister Patrick John	Attempted overthrow of government of Prime Minister Eugenia Charles
1981 (Sept. 9)	Dominica	7 members of the Dominica Defense Force, incl. Major Frederick Newton	Attempted overthrow of Eugenia Charles government and freeing of Malcom Reid
1983 (Oct.)	Grenada	Revolutionary Military Council headed by General Hudson Austin	Assassination of Prime Minister Maurice Bishop, cabinet members et al.
1990 (July 22)	Trinidad and Tobago	114 members of Jamaat-al-Muslimeen Muslim religious-political group	Attempted overthrow of Prime Minister A.N.R. Robinson; murder of 31 people
1995 (June 20)	Trinidad and Tobago	2 unidentified individuals	Assassination of Selwyn Richardson, former attorney general and minister of National Security

Sources: Leslie Manigat, "The Setting: Crisis, Ideology, and Geopolitics," in *The Caribbean and World Politics: Cross Currents and Cleavages*, ed. Jorge Heine and Leslie Manigat, 35. New York: Holmes and Meier, 1988; and Dion E. Phillips, "Terrorism and Security in the Caribbean before and after 9/11," *Armed Forces and Conflict Resolution: Sociological Perspectives*, vol. 7, 2008: 103–105.

It is well known that the September 11, 2011, terrorist attack was a defining moment. One month after the attack, CARICOM leaders held an emergency summit in the Bahamas, at the end of which they issued *The Nassau Declaration on International Terrorism*, in which they declared:

> We are concerned that the attacks and subsequent developments have been especially devastating to our tourism, aviation, financial services, and agricultural sectors, which are the major contributors to our Gross Domestic Product (GDP), foreign exchange earnings, and to employment in our Region. We are particularly conscious that our ongoing efforts to combat money laundering must now take specific account of the potential for abuse of financial services industries by terrorists, their agents, and supporters in all jurisdictions. (CARICOM 2001, 1)

Analysis of several of the impact areas and implications raised by the Caribbean leaders that was provided by scholars and security practitioners in *Caribbean Security in the Age of Terror* highlighted the seriousness of the region's circumstances. It was revealed that in Jamaica, for instance, where tourism at the time earned about US$1.2 billion annually and employed some thirty thousand people, the impact was very dramatic, with the national airline at the time, Air Jamaica, losing US$11 million within the week following the incident. In Barbados, where tourism contributed about US$1 billion to the economy, they anticipated a US$30.3 million decline in receipts, a 30–35 percent reduction in the cruise industry, US$857,000 less from the head tax, and a drop in tourist spending of US$9.2 million (Griffith 2004, 39).

Thus, September 11, 2001, compelled leaders and citizens within the Caribbean and state and non-state policy actors outside the region with interests in it to adopt a new approach to and heightened interest in terrorism as a PWP. Since then, the increased apprehension has been predicated on a broad combination of the national interests of Caribbean states and interests shared with state and non-state actors elsewhere. As the *CARICOM Counter-Terrorism Strategy* puts it:

> The main regional concerns relate to the phenomenon of FTFs (Foreign Terrorist Fighters), including their return and relocation to the Region, the increasing influence of extremist religious leaders and radicalized terrorist sympathizers in CARICOM States, violent extremists who could be inspired or directed to carry out an attack, the growing volume and accessibility of terrorists, group propaganda, online and via pe[e]r-to-peer networks, and the potential exploitation of the banking system to fund terror networks." (CARICOM 2018, 5)

Raymond Izarali (2018, 250) cautions against naivety about terrorism and the potential vulnerability of the region, either through direct attacks on Caribbean citizens and infrastructures or by using Caribbean countries as platforms to launch attacks on assets of the United States and other Western nations. What, then, are some of the realities of the contemporary Caribbean that contribute to its vulnerability to terrorism? Those realities revolve essentially around geopolitical and geoeconomic factors.

Geopolitical Vulnerability Factor

Geopolitics is the relationship between physical and political geography, on the one hand, and national power, on the other. It provides the context in which national power can be enhanced directly or indirectly or threats and vulnerabilities may develop or be heightened. In relation to the Caribbean, the region's geopolitical value revolves mainly around its strategic materials, such as oil, bauxite, and nickel; strategic waterways like the Panama Canal and the Mona Passage; and military installations operated by the United States.[4]

THE STRATEGIC MATERIALS COMPONENT   Although most Caribbean countries lack mineral wealth, overall the region has a significant endowment of strategic materials, notably bauxite (Dominican Republic, Guyana, Jamaica, Suriname, and Venezuela), nickel (Cuba, the Dominican Republic, and Venezuela), diamonds (French Guiana, Guyana, and Venezuela), manganese (Guyana and Venezuela), silver (Cuba and the Dominican Republic), cobalt (Cuba), gold (Cuba, the Dominican Republic, Guyana, Haiti, French Guiana, Suriname, and Venezuela), and uranium (Guyana and Venezuela).

Energy—especially oil and liquified natural gas (LNG)—is a key variable in the geopolitical matrix. Oil is produced in Barbados, Belize, Cuba, Suriname, Trinidad and Tobago, and Venezuela, which has the distinction of having the world's largest oil reserves. Oil exploration is under way in Grenada, the Bahamas, and Jamaica, while expanded operations are planned for Barbados (see Wilkinson 2019).

China also has been aiding Cuba in its expansion efforts. For instance, in April 2019, China's Great Wall Drilling Company, part of China National Petroleum Corporation, began work on an offshore joint venture with the Cuba Petroleum Company, the state oil company. Great Wall Drilling, which began operating in Cuba in 2005, was commissioned to drill most of Cuba's oil wells, using high-tech equipment capable of accessing shallow offshore oil deposits from land. The operations were conducted off the coastal town of Boca de Camarioca, about 120 kilometers east of Havana (Xinhuanet 2019). Moreover, according to one geosciences report, "The Caribbean currently offers an unprecedented number of hydrocarbon exploration opportunities, with promising potential in Cuba, the Dominican Republic, Jamaica, Honduras, Nicaragua, and the Bahamas" (GEOExPro 2019).

The region's energy geopolitical value-added increased dramatically with the entrance of Guyana on the world crude oil stage and with the expansion in Suriname from onshore production to offshore discovery. May 2015 was a milestone for Guyana with the discovery of massive oil deposits by a three-member consortium of ExxonMobil, Hess Corporation, and China's National Offshore Oil Corporation. There were forty oil discoveries between that fateful May in 2015 and February 2023. Total oil reserves are now estimated at close to 11 billion barrels equivalent. Production began in December 2019 and stood at about 120,000 barrels per day until February 24, 2023, which marked a milestone with production of 400,000 barrels of oil that day. Production is projected to hit 800,000 barrels per day by 2025 and 1 million barrels per day two years afterward.

ExxonMobil senior vice president of Upstream, Neil Chapman, told investors in March 2021 that the company's acreage in the Guyana-Suriname Basin is the largest of all the international oil companies (OilNOW 2020; A. Bryan 2021). Moreover, companies from Britain, Canada, France, Israel, and Spain also are pursuing Guyana's oil bounty. As for Suriname, which had an onshore production of some 16,000 barrels in 2020, January 2020 was the petro power month to remember; it was then that American-owned Apache Corp and French-owned Total SA announced a major offshore discovery.[5] Since then, Apache and its partner Total have announced four discoveries, with others declared by ExxonMobil and its Malaysian partner, Petronas. Apache owns lease rights to nearly 2.3 million acres, and Exxon and Petronas have a similar-size lease (Krauss 2021). Offshore production is expected to begin in 2027.

Thus, Guyana and Suriname are the world's newest petro-powers-in-making. The Guyana-Suriname Basin is abuzz with exploration and extraction activity. Indeed, one respected expert has declared that "the Guyana Suriname Basin (GSB) is the Holy Grail of new oil province discoveries. Oil energy experts predict that during 2021 there will be a major increase in offshore drilling activity in the Southern Caribbean and northern South America led by Guyana" (A. Bryan 2021). Two factors will drive this, he argues: the increased price of crude oil worldwide and the pursuit by companies of opportunities for quick financial returns. Moreover, the petroleum pursuits in Guyana and Suriname have been sending geopolitical ripples beyond the region. As one *New York Times* report noted, "Suriname, Guyana, and Brazil are now attracting more new investment than the Gulf of Mexico and other more established oil fields. And they are helping to keep global oil prices relatively low, undermining efforts by Russia and its allies in the Organization of the Petroleum Exporting Countries, like Saudi Arabia, to manage global supply and push up prices" (Krauss 2021).

Oil refining operations in Aruba, Curaçao, Cuba, Trinidad and Tobago, Suriname, Puerto Rico, and Jamaica also are an important part of the energy factor. Not to be forgotten as an energy factor is the production of liquified natural gas, which occurs in Trinidad and Tobago. The twin-island republic exports its LNG to many markets, but the United States is its most important client, although U.S. imports have declined recently: 84,190 Mcf (millions of cubic feet) in 2016; 70,450 Mcf in 2017; 65,819 Mcf in 2018; 46,872 Mcf in 2019; and 39,233 Mcf in 2020 (U.S. Energy Information Administration 2021).

THE STRATEGIC WATERWAYS AND INSTALLATIONS COMPONENT The Caribbean is endowed with two of the world's major strategic waterways: the Caribbean Sea and the Panama Canal. The former occupies 1,063,000 square miles and is larger than the Mediterranean Sea, which comprises 965,255 square miles. It is smaller than the South China Sea, which is 1,400,000 square miles and has been described as being to China what the Caribbean Sea is to the United States (see Patel 2021). The 80-kilometer-long Panama Canal connects the Atlantic and Pacific oceans and saves 8,000 miles and up to thirty days of steaming time. It opened for business in August 1914 and has military and civilian value to the United States and strategic partners such as Canada, Chile, Ecuador, Japan, and South Korea. Between 2007 and 2016, the canal underwent a US$5.25 billion expansion project that doubled its capacity, and it now facilitates passage of vessels with three times the cargo, significantly impacting global trade into the future. Once ships enter the Atlantic from the Panama Canal, they must transit one or more of the fourteen strategic waterways en route to ports of call in the United States, Europe, and Africa. The Florida Strait, Mona Passage, Windward Passage, and Yucatan Channel are the main strategic waterways.

Panama Canal Authority data indicate that the United States, China, Japan, Chile, the Korean Republic, Mexico, Colombia, Peru, Ecuador, Canada, Guatemala, and Trinidad and Tobago were among the top fifteen users of the canal in 2020. The canal facilitates 144 maritime routes that link more than 1,700 ports in 160 countries and territories globally, around 6.3 percent of the world's maritime trade of grains, 3.4 percent of its trade of chemical products, and 3.1 percent of containers (Sáenz 2020). During much of the twentieth century, until the late 1990s the United States maintained a considerable military presence in the Caribbean Basin, mainly in Puerto Rico at the Atlantic threshold, in Panama at the southern rim, and in Cuba at Guantánamo on the northern perimeter. In 1990, for instance, there were 4,743 military and civilian personnel in Puerto Rico, 20,709 in Panama, and 3,401 in Cuba. Much has changed since 1990, requiring strategic redesign and force redeployment. For example, the Pentagon relocated the U.S. Southern Command's headquarters from Panama to Florida in September 1997, leaving behind only small components. Puerto Rico too is now home to fewer military forces.

Between the time of the collapse of the Soviet Union in 1989 and the September 11, 2001, terrorist attack, the forty-five-square mile Guantánamo Bay base was considered to have little strategic value, serving essentially as a political outpost in the hemisphere's last remaining communist bastion. However, the view by the United States about Guantánamo, in existence since 1903, was altered dramatically with 9/11 and the housing there of individuals accused of terrorism. For a variety of reasons, President Barack Obama was unable to keep a key promise of his first presidential campaign—to close the Guantánamo Bay prison.

Other Caribbean territories also are vital to the United States in terms of basing operations. These include the Bahamas, with the Atlantic Underwater Testing and Evaluation Center on Andros Island, which is used to test new types of weaponry and reputedly is the U.S. Navy's premier East Coast in-water test facility. It is affiliated with the NATO Naval Forces Sensor and Weapon Accuracy Check Site program. In addition, as part of United States counternarcotics efforts, Aruba and Curaçao host Cooperative Security Locations (CSL), formerly known as Forward Operating Locations. The U.S. Southern Command explains that "the CSLs are strategic, cost-effective locations in Comalapa, El Salvador and Aruba-Curaçao, formerly part of the Netherlands Antilles, which allow U.S. and partner nation aircraft the use of existing airfields to support the region's multinational efforts to Combat Transnational Organized Crime. The CSLs are the result of cooperative, long-term agreements between the United States and host nations" (U.S. Southern Command 2020).

Antigua and Barbuda hosted a key facility until recently. July 7, 2015, witnessed the deactivation of the Antigua Air Station after more than fifty years of operations. The deactivation ceremony was presided over by Brigadier General Nina Armagno, commander of the United States 45th Space Wing, and was attended by Governor-General Sir Rodney Williams, Prime Minister Gaston Browne, and United States Ambassador to Barbados and the Organization of Eastern Caribbean States Larry Palmer. The base originally was established under a revision of a World War II–era lend-lease agreement between the United States and the United Kingdom, which also made available bases in the Bahamas, Guyana, Jamaica, St. Lucia, Trinidad and Tobago, and Newfoundland, Canada.

The mission of Detachment 1 of the 45th Operations Group, which included the Antigua operations, was to support the space-lift mission of the United States Air Force Eastern Range by providing high data rate telemetry. During the ceremony, Brigadier General Armagno observed that "Antigua Air Station has been an extremely valuable asset to the success of the 45th Space Wing. It served as one of the primary Range and Control instrumentation sites for space and launch vehicle tracking support" (A. Wallace 2015). Overall, geopolitical factors long have been central to the thinking about and engagement in the Caribbean by the United States and erstwhile colonial powers France, the United Kingdom, and the Netherlands. However, over the last few decades, China, Russia, and Iran have been flexing their geopolitical muscles in the area. Geoeconomic factors are important complementary considerations and deserve some attention.[6]

Geoeconomic Vulnerability Factor

In speaking at the launch of the Global Tourism Resilience and Crisis Management Centre in tourism hot spot Montego Bay in January 2019, Jamaican prime minister Andrew Holness averred:

> While Caribbean destinations were never traditionally considered to be at risk for terrorist activities, recent terror attacks in tourist destinations, such as Barcelona, Paris, Nice, Tunisia, Egypt, Bohol in the Philippines, Turkey, Las Vegas, Florida, Bali in Indonesia and also in Algeria have shown that we can no longer take the terrorist threat for granted as radical elements are becoming increasingly globalized, with an effective powerful recruiting platform via the World Wide Web. (Davis 2019)

THE TOURISM COMPONENT   The observation above by Prime Minister Holness placed concisely in global context the vulnerability of Caribbean tourism. My earlier discussion on the economic impact of terrorism provided an important appreciation of the effect on tourism globally, and I provided a few vignettes about the Caribbean in noting the impact on the region in the aftermath of 9/11. However, an understanding of tourism as a geoeconomic vulnerability factor in the Caribbean requires a few insights into the nature and importance of the industry to the region.[7]

Brenda and James Lutz remind us that "tourists have come to be a group under attack, sometimes as symbols of their country, as symbols of unwanted foreign values, or as a means of weakening the government that domestic terrorists oppose" (Lutz and Lutz 2018, 2). Attacks on tourists could result in reduced income for tourism operators and governments, with the latter limiting the government's ability to underwrite security operations to deal with the dissidents or to fund projects that would undermine the appeal of opponents. Moreover, reduced tourist visits can lead to unemployment in the tourism sector, which would trigger increased discontent with the government among individuals and groups whose livelihood is affected, which, in turn, could aid dissident recruitment efforts. A downturn in tourism in countries that rely heavily on the industry could trigger a decline in both foreign and domestic investment (3). As will be seen below, this is precisely what resulted from the advent of the COVID-19 pandemic.

Contrary to the likely popular impression that Caribbean tourism revolves around just stay-over visits and cruises, the industry is rather diversified. As the Caribbean Development Bank's study titled *Tourism Industry Reform: Strategies for Enhanced Economic Impact* explains, the tourism industry has components that relate to ecotourism, heritage and culture, sports, education, cuisine, and yachting. As the study does not cover Cuba, the Dominican Republic, and Puerto Rico, it is important to note that those three countries also have robust and diversified tourism sectors. Were the study to include those three areas, it surely would have listed them under at least ecotourism, heritage and culture, sports, and yachting. Also notable is that medical tourism and health and wellness tourism are coming into their own. Cuba, Jamaica, the Cayman Islands, and Barbados are the leading locations that offer medical tourism (Caribbean Development Bank 2017, 29–30).

One Caribbean Development Bank (CDB) study on the industry indicates that "in 2015, the 19 BMCs [borrowing member countries] recorded a total of 22.7 million visitors, 64 percent of whom were cruise visitors and 36 percent of whom were long-stay visitors" (Caribbean Development Bank 2017, 6).[8] Ten of the nineteen countries accounted for 91 percent of cruise arrivals and 86 percent of long-stay arrivals, with the Bahamas, the Cayman Islands, and Jamaica leading the way with passenger arrivals. Jamaica, the Bahamas, and Barbados are the top three countries for long-stay tourism. In its regional analysis for 2018, the Jamaica Tourist Board cited Caribbean Tourism Organization (CTO) data that showed an estimated 29.9 million visitors that year, which was 700,000 fewer tourists (2.3 percent) than the 2017 figure of 30.6 million (Jamaica Tourist Board 2019, 6).

Although some destinations, particularly Puerto Rico, St. Maarten, and the British Virgin Islands, struggled in the aftermath of a very active hurricane season, the Dominican Republic, Cuba, Jamaica, and the Bahamas showed continued growth from their main source markets in the Americas and Europe. As table 5.2 shows, the United States remained the most important supplier of tourists to the region, even with a 6.3 percent decrease in arrivals. Over 13.9 million Americans visited the region, mostly to the Dominican Republic, Jamaica, and the Bahamas. Arrivals from Canada increased by 5.7 percent, and those from European countries grew modestly by 1.3 percent, while intra-regional travel increased by 5.3 percent. The cruise sector is estimated to have increased by an estimated 6.7 percent during 2018 to over 28.9 million, with eighteen of

TABLE 5.2 Caribbean Tourism Performance by Main Market

Main Market Areas						
Major Market	2016	2017	2018	2019	2020	% change
USA	14,638.0	14,735.1	14,404.8	15,666.9	5,502.0	−64.9%
Canada	3,309.0	3,321.9	3,372.0	3,424.2	1,310.2	−61.7%
Europe	5,732.3	5,965.9	6,010.0	5,925.5	1,950.3	−67.1%
Other	6,027.8	6,548.8	6,889.0	6,998.9	2,288.2	−67.3%
Total Tourist Arrivals (000)	29,707.1	30,571.7	30,675.8	32,015.5	11,050.7	−65.5%

Tourist Arrivals by Subregion						
Subregion	2019	2020	% change			
Commonwealth Caribbean	9,240.0	2,706.3	−70.7%			
Dutch Caribbean	2,079.4	734.2	−64.7%			
French Caribbean	1,289.5	625.6	−51.5%			
U.S. Territories	3,942.7	1,806.3	−54.2%			
Other Caribbean	15,463.9	5,178.3	−66.5%			
Total Tourist Arrivals (000)	32,015.5	11,050.7	−65.5%			

Source: Jamaica Tourist Board, *Annual Travel Statistics 2020*, 7. https://www.jtbonline.org/wp-content/uploads/Annual-Travel-Statistics-2020.pdf/.

TABLE 5.3 Cruise Passenger Arrivals 2017 to 2020

Destination	2017	2018	2019	2020	% Change
Bahamas	4,626.3	4,877.6	5,429.5	1,327.1	−75.6%
Cozumel (Mexico)	4,103.8	4,265.5	4,569.5	1,131.6	−75.2%
Cayman Islands	1,728.4	1,921.1	1,831.0	535.7	−70.7%
Puerto Rico	1,229.1	1,658.8	1,784.9	465.4	−73.9%
Jamaica	1,923.3	1,845.9	1,552.3	449.3	−71.1%
U.S. Virgin Islands	1,317.2	1,430.7	1,433.1	440.4	−69.3%
St. Maarten	1,237.8	1,597.1	1,631.5	435.5	−73.3%
Dominican Republic	1,108.0	982.3	1,103.9	344.5	−68.8%
Belize	1,014.2	1,208.1	1,170.6	343.1	−70.7%
St. Lucia	668.0	760.3	786.7	297.9	−62.1%
Aruba	792.4	815.2	832.0	259.4	−68.8%
Antigua and Barbuda	792.9	794.6	733.5	259.4	−64.6%
Curaçao	634.4	757.3	809.9	256.0	−68.4%
Barbados	681.2	675.8	686.8	250.5	−63.5%
British Virgin Islands	409.7	200.6	575.1	219.4	−61.8%
Turks & Caicos Islands	827.4	1,021.7	1,111.8	205.9	−81.5%
Martinique	405.6	392.6	257.8	170.4	−33.9%
Grenada	299.4	342.8	337.9	162.5	−51.9%
Dominica	157.0	134.5	229.7	118.0	−48.6%
St. Vincent & the Grenadines	174.2	217.9	191.8	101.6	−47.0%
Bermuda	418.0	484.3	535.5	6.5	−98.8%

Source: Jamaica Tourist Board, *Annual Travel Statistics 2020.*

the twenty-four destinations recording increased cruise activity over 2017. The Bahamas, Cozumel (Mexico), the Cayman Islands, Jamaica, and Puerto Rico were the top five most popular destinations (Jamaica Tourist Board 2019, 6).

According to the CDB, quantifying the economic impact of tourism is a complex exercise, as several different mechanisms drive its impact, and some are connected to or dependent on each other. In addition, the impact of tourism expenditure can occur over several years, plus displacement effects may offset some of the impact. However, "despite these challenges, there is growing empirical literature on the relationship between tourism and economic growth. Much of this literature is based around the tourism-led growth hypothesis, which views tourism as an alternative form of exports and applies econometric techniques to isolate the economic impact of tourism, typically using GDP per capita or

GDP growth as the relevant variable of interest" (Caribbean Development Bank 2017, 14).

Figure 5.2, which provides a summary of the economic impact of tourism, reveals that the impact is direct and indirect. As the CDB study explains:

The goods and services purchased by tourists generate demand for local businesses and support the employment of local individuals. There are also benefits along the tourism value chain as tourism-related businesses need to source inputs to meet the higher demand, and this create[s] opportunities for other sectors of the economy. In addition, there are spin-off benefits that come from developing the specialized infrastructure and human capital needed to support the industry. A range of factors influences the overall magnitude of these economic impacts. The number of tourists; how long they stay; how much they spend; and where they spend all influence the distribution of the demand injection into the local economy. (Caribbean Development Bank 2017, 13)

The CDB study calculated economic impact using an econometric model of the relationship between tourism activity and GDP growth in the BMCs. The model accepted that as many factors other than tourism that help determine GDP growth, it needed to control for, among other things, business investments, government spending, and openness to trade in order to isolate the effect that tourism specifically has on GDP. The analysis for the nineteen BMCs showed that "with the annual growth of visitor spending in the BMCs averaging 2.7 percent

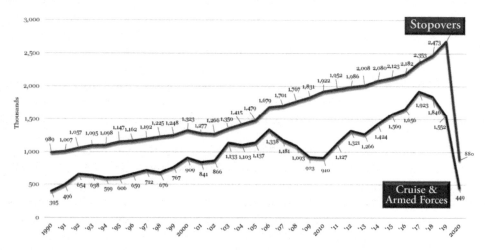

FIGURE 5.1 Visitor Arrivals to Jamaica 1990–2020.

Source: Jamaica Tourist Board, *Annual Travel Statistics 2020*, 12. https://www.jtbonline.org/wp-content/uploads/Annual-Travel-Statistics-2020.pdf/.

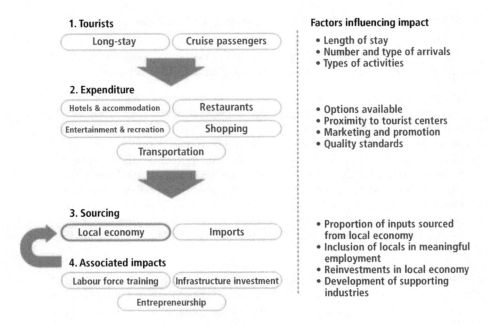

1. Tourists

| Long-stay | Cruise passengers |

2. Expenditure

| Hotels & accommodation | Restaurants |
| Entertainment & recreation | Shopping |
| Transportation |

3. Sourcing

| Local economy | Imports |

4. Associated impacts

| Labour force training | Infrastructure investment |
| Entrepreneurship |

Factors influencing impact

- Length of stay
- Number and type of arrivals
- Types of activities

- Options available
- Proximity to tourist centers
- Marketing and promotion
- Quality standards

- Proportion of inputs sourced from local economy
- Inclusion of locals in meaningful employment
- Reinvestments in local economy
- Development of supporting industries

FIGURE 5.2 Overview of How Tourism Generates Economic Impact in the Caribbean.

Source: Caribbean Development Bank, *Tourism Industry Reform: Strategies for Enhanced Economic Impact,* 2017, 14.

between 1989 and 2014, it is estimated that each year the contemporaneous impact of tourism on GDP growth was between 0.16 percent and 0.24 percent. In the long-term, this impact is estimated to be much greater. A 10 percent increase in tourism spending is associated with a cumulative increase in GDP per capita of approximately 2.6 percent after the first 5 years" (Caribbean Development Bank 2017, 16). Total GDP growth for the BMCs averaged 3.5 percent for the period between 1989 and 2014. The impact of tourism also is expected to continue to yield returns for many years after the original increase in tourist spending.

Quite importantly, the CDB study explains that the average GDP impact of an additional US$100 of tourism expenditure is estimated to be US$35–US$54 in the short term, and between US$155 and US$160 in the long term. In the short term, between 30 percent and 50 percent of tourist spending translates to GDP, and in the long term, it generates between 1.5 and 1.6 times its value in terms of GDP in the BMCs (Caribbean Development Bank 2017, 16). The CDB study also noted that in 2014 the total tourism expenditure in the BMC was US$13.1 billion and that tourism supports nearly US$40.3 billion of GDP across the region.

COVID-19 has had a deleterious impact on the tourist industry, as CTO data captured in tables 5.2 and 5.3 indicate. The 11.1 million tourists who visited in 2020 represented a decrease of 65.5 percent from the previous year; some 21.0 million fewer tourists. The CTO reported that at the end of the first quarter, international tourist arrivals declined by 21.8 percent. The decline was even more dramatic during the second quarter, amounting to 97.3 percent. Things began to turn around in the third quarter, and continued to do so during the fourth quarter, with 2.2 million arrivals (Jamaica Tourist Board 2021, 7). Understandably, the reduction was not uniform across the region. Figure 5.1 shows the dramatic impact on Jamaica, for example.

Jamaica's finance minister, Nigel Clarke, painted the picture vividly in opening Jamaica's 2021–2022 parliamentary budget debate on March 9, 2021. He reminded fellow legislators that tourism and remittances are the country's two largest sources of foreign exchange. He reported, "COVID-19 has decimated Jamaica's foreign exchange inflows from tourism. . . . During the 9–11 terrorist attacks tourism earnings declined by 14 percent. In the global financial crisis, tourism earnings declined by 5 percent" (Clarke 2021). Then came a sobering factoid: "*Madam Speaker, as a result of the COVID-19 pandemic, Jamaica's foreign exchange inflows from tourism are projected to fall by 74 percent or US$2.5 billion in 2020/21. In 2019/20 we earned US$3.4 billion from tourism but in 2020/21 we are expected to earn only US$874 million or approximately one quarter of 2019/20 earnings*" (Clarke 2021; emphasis added). Thankfully, the situation has been improving. For instance, Tourism Minister Edmund Bartlett reported to the Caribbean Hotel and Tourism Association's 41st Caribbean Travel Marketplace held in May 2023 in Barbados that Jamaica recorded one million visitor arrivals year-to-date for 2023. The milestone was reached about one month earlier than in 2022. He noted proudly that from January to December 2022 the country secured 2,478,386 stopover arrivals, a 69.2 percent increase over 2021, and nearly a full recovery to 2019 levels. Moreover, he projected sustained growth, surpassing 5 million tourists in 2025.[9]

THE FINANCING COMPONENT   This factor revolves around three realities: the significance of banking and financial services to the economies of many Caribbean countries; the utilization of banking and non-banking services globally to facilitate terrorist financing; and the potential for the Caribbean to be used to launder money and otherwise wittingly or unwittingly facilitate the financing pursuits of terrorists.

One study on the subject of terrorist financing argues that financing, preferably with a secure financing network, is crucial for terror organizations and that establishing al-Qaeda's financing network was one of Osama bin Laden's earliest and most important accomplishments because it provided millions in "steady and secure" income to the organization (Baradaran et al. 2014, 480). Moreover, it was argued, "Because terrorists can accomplish enormously destructive attacks with very little money, a successful war on terror must reach deep into the financial heart of terrorism" (480–81). Terrorist entrepreneurs use money laundering to avoid detection, as drug traffickers have done for decades.

As has been posited elsewhere, "money laundering is the conversion of profits from illegal activities, in this case drug operations, into financial assets that appear to have legitimate origins and uses. Generally, three stages are involved: placement, lawyering, and integration" (Griffith 1997, 94). This three-phase process is captured in figure 5.3. One World Bank reference guide explains that the initial stage of the process involves placement of illegally sourced funds into the financial system, usually through a financial entity. This can be done by depositing cash into a bank account. Large amounts of cash are broken into smaller, less conspicuous amounts and deposited over time in different offices of a single financial institution or in multiple financial entities. The exchange of one currency into another, and the conversion of smaller notes into larger denominations, may occur at this stage. Also, illegal funds may be converted into financial instruments, such as money orders or checks, and mixed with legal funds to divert suspicion.

Layering occurs after the ill-gotten gains have entered the financial system, at which time the funds, securities, or insurance contracts are converted or moved to other institutions, further separating them from their criminal source. Such funds could then be used to purchase other securities, insurance policies, or other easily transferable instruments and then sold through another institution. The funds could also be transferred by any form of negotiable instrument, such as a check or money order, or they may be transferred electronically to other accounts in various jurisdictions. The launderer may also disguise the transfer as a payment for goods or services or transfer the funds to a shell corporation. The third stage involves the integration of funds into the legitimate economy. This is accomplished through the purchase of assets, such as real estate, securities, or other financial assets or luxury goods. These three stages are also seen in terrorist financing schemes, except that stage three integration involves the distribution of funds to terrorists and their supporting organizations, while money laundering, as discussed previously, goes in the opposite direction—integrating criminal funds into the legitimate economy (Schott 2006, 1-7–1-9).

Evidence suggests that although terrorists frequently launder money through financial institutions, terrorism is also financed through legitimate means, such as charities and trusts. In this respect, terrorists are said to exploit the principle of *zakat*, or charity—one of the five pillars of Islam. Moreover, they shift money through trusts in order to take advantage of privacy laws that conceal trust formation data. The anonymity and privacy afforded by trusts are attractive qualities, since the true or "beneficial" owners, as well as the recipients of the funds

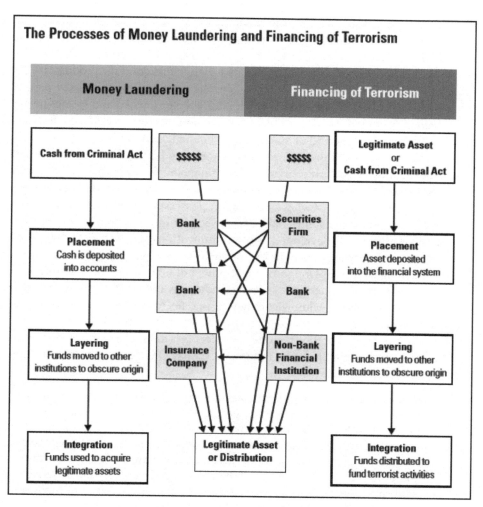

FIGURE 5.3 Money Laundering and Financing of Terrorism Processes.

Source: Paul Allan Schott, *Reference Guide to Anti–Money Laundering and Combating the Financing of Terrorism*. Washington, D.C.: World Bank, 2006, 1–8.

(including terrorist organizations), can be hidden beneath layers of corporate identities. Shell companies also are used to conceal and transfer money through bank accounts around the world. As with trusts, shell companies provide the desired identity protection, which can shield actual ownership of the enterprise (see Baradaran et al. 2014, 490–92).

One harsh reality is that some Caribbean countries have little, and some no, natural resources and therefore rely heavily on tourism and financial services for their economic survival. Anguilla, Aruba, Barbados, the Bahamas, the Cayman Islands, St. Lucia, and the British Virgin Islands are among these countries. Indeed, banking and financial services are important economically even to some countries with agriculture and manufacturing, such as Jamaica and the Dominican Republic. In fact, one IDB study maintains that "on the whole, the financial sector is large relative to the gross domestic products (GDP) of Caribbean economies. Total assets of the sector amounted to 124 percent of regional GDP at the end of March 2012. Foreign-owned and locally-owned banks accounted for 45 percent and 20 percent, respectively, of total financial system assets at the end of March 2012" (Grenade and Wright 2018, 2).

Yet, banking—both onshore and offshore—and other financial services are not the only important elements in our financing factor matrix. What is true for money laundering for drug operators also holds true for terrorist operators. As described elsewhere, the region possesses other conducing factors, including political stability, bank secrecy, low or little taxation in some places, and relatively well-developed telecommunications (Griffith 1997, 98). Thus, concerns about money laundering for terrorist ends are credible because of the conducing factors and longtime involvement of financial entities in the region in drug money laundering, as several studies have shown.[10] Caribbean leaders have been candid in acknowledging this, as reflected in the October 2001 *Nassau Declaration on International Terrorism*, which was noted above.

As with drug operations, money laundering is not the only mechanism used to facilitate terrorist financing. Indeed, the CARICOM Counter-Terrorism Strategy notes:

> Nationals of the Region have been cited in respective national Financial Intelligence Unit (FIU) Reports as suspects involved in terrorism financing. A variety of both legal and illicit activities are utilized to finance terrorist acts. A growing trend has been the increased use of wire-transfers. The potential exploitation of the banking system to fund terror networks and the abuse of non-governmental, non-profit and charitable organizations by and for terrorist purposes are key threats to the Region. An increasing source of funding is the exploitation of the Internet and social media to attract donations from individuals and legal entities, by misleading users about the true recipients of the funds. (CARICOM 2018, 8)

One fascinating study of three islands in the Dutch Antilles is illustrative of larger regional realities and reinforces the validity of the concerns. In their study of Bonaire, Sint Eustatius, and Saba, Henk van der Veen and Lars Franciscus Heuts identified several geographic, demographic, economic, sociocultural, and criminological context factors that impact the prevalence of money laundering in that part of the Caribbean. These factors are captured in figure 5.4. They offer the supportable proposition that "the risks of money laundering are a function of three factors (threats, vulnerabilities and consequences). This results in the following risk equation: $r=f(t,v,c)$" (van der Veen and Heuts 2018, 21).

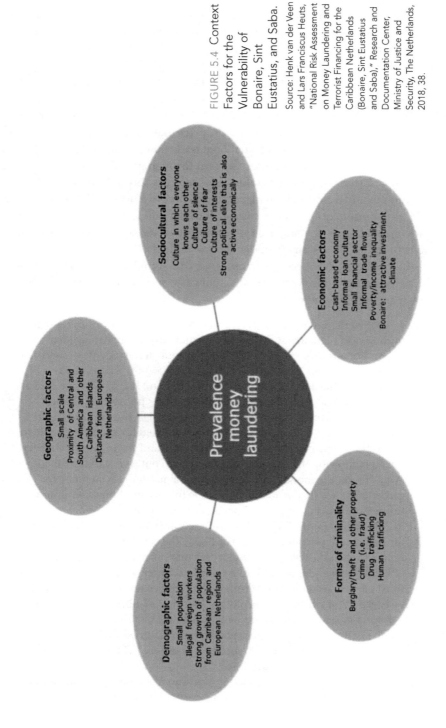

FIGURE 5.4 Context Factors for the Vulnerability of Bonaire, Sint Eustatius, and Saba.

Source: Henk van der Veen and Lars Franciscus Heuts, "National Risk Assessment on Money Laundering and Terrorist Financing for the Caribbean Netherlands (Bonaire, Sint Eustatius and Saba)," Research and Documentation Center, Ministry of Justice and Security, The Netherlands, 2018, 38.

The study also found that the landscape of criminal activities related to revenue generation, including property crimes and drug-related crimes, may be predicate offenses for money laundering and that risks revolve around the purchase of private homes; the purchase of resorts/holiday parks; real estate project development; the purchase of business premises; new construction; abuse of notary services; money transactions/deposits through licensed credit institutions; money transactions/deposits through licensed money or value transfer services; turnover manipulation, price manipulation, and/or over- and underbilling in national and international trade flows; funds obtained through crime introduced into the financial system through gambling (casinos, online gambling, lotteries); money transactions/deposits through unlicensed credit institutions/underground banking; exchange of cash from small denominations to large denominations (and vice versa) through unlicensed credit institutions/underground banking; and physical movement of large amounts of cash (money from/to island via sea/air) (van der Veen and Heuts 2018, 11).

The concerns about money laundering and apprehensions about terrorist financing come to life with several actual cases recalled in the study, a few of which are provided here:

- In 2014 Netherlands Customs and law enforcement authorities reported finding cash regularly at the airport, particularly for flights originating on Bonaire. For the 2013–2014 period some ten incidents occurred, involving amounts varying from €10,000 to €56,000 [US$11,446 to US$64,109]. Most of the cash was carried in hand luggage; in one case, it was stuffed inside the suspect's underwear, pants pockets, and shoes.
- FIU (Financial Intelligence Unit)–Netherlands describes on its website a European-Dutch case in which someone arranged for multiple people to spend the whole day going from shop to shop and buying lottery tickets. Receipts showing the winnings that were paid out were carefully filed away. It took the money launderer around a quarter of his money to gather evidence that he had obtained the funds from lottery winnings; in this way he tried to launder 75 percent of his criminal money.
- In 2016, a civil law notary on Bonaire was convicted under criminal law for failing to report unusual transactions. The civil law notary did not report to the unusual transactions reporting office that an amount of US$100,000 was deposited into a so-called *derdengeldenrekening*, literally third parties' account. Furthermore, the civil law notary allowed deeds to be executed in which various plots of land and a building were given by a suspect of money laundering to his underage daughter. The court contended that the civil law notary should have assumed that this transaction was "potentially linked to money laundering." The notary was fined US$5,000 in a suspended sentence.
- In 2017, searches were conducted in Curaçao of dwellings, minimarkets, and business premises owned by Chinese businesspeople. According to

the Public Prosecution Service in Curaçao, the searches were part of an investigation into money laundering and underground banking. One man was arrested and 1 million Antillean guilders (almost half a million euros) [(US$572,500] were seized, as well as a number of cars and buildings valued at approximately 10 million Antillean guilders (nearly 5 million euros) [US$5,725,000].

(van der Veen and Heuts 2018, 40–46)

Elsewhere, on January 16, 2020, a federal jury in the U.S. District Court for the Eastern District of New York found Donville Inniss, a former minister of industry, international business, commerce, and small business of Barbados, guilty of two counts of money laundering and one count of conspiracy to commit money laundering. In 2015 and 2016, while serving as a minister, Inniss partook in a scheme to launder US$36,000 in bribes received from top executives of the Insurance Corporation of Barbados Limited (ICBL) into the United States. In exchange for the bribes, Inniss used his ministerial position to enable ICBL to obtain two insurance contracts from the Barbados government to insure over $100 million worth of government property, and to hide the bribes, he arranged to receive them through a U.S. bank account in the name of his friend's dental company in New York (Zagaris 2020). Beyond the financing factor at the regional level, attention must be paid at the individual level to the country that generates the most terrorism anxiety, both within and outside the region.

Trinidad and Tobago as TNT

Trinidad and Tobago is known popularly as TNT. Still, in the context of concerns about terrorism in the Caribbean, the letters TNT might well conjure up "trinitrotoluene," which is explosive material that is considered the standard measure of bombs and the power of explosives, as Trinidad and Tobago once became the epicenter of concerns about terrorism in the region. As mentioned above, the preponderant contemporary terrorist pursuits are associated with Islamic religious terrorists. Interestingly, according to the Washington, D.C.–based Pew Research Center, in 2020 only three Caribbean countries had populations where adherents to Islam amounted to 5 percent or more of the religious affiliation: Guyana, with 6.1 percent; Suriname, with 14.3 percent; and Trinidad and Tobago, with 5.8 percent.[11] With Trinidad and Tobago having the lowest figure, what, then, explains their once epicenter status?

The answer to this question has three elements. As we saw above, the country's oil and liquified natural gas, not to mention its petrochemical industry, certifies its geopolitical importance, especially vis-à-vis the United States, which is the main protagonist of many of the religious terrorists worldwide. This is one of the three elements. A second element is the country's enabling environment, significant to which was their own religiously motivated terrorism experience:

the coup in 1990 that was attempted by the Jamaat-al-Muslimeen, as cited in table 5.1.[12] The third element is the role that Trinidad and Tobago has been playing in the recruitment of fighters for the terrorist causes of the Islamic State in Iraq and Syria (ISIS), although individuals from Suriname, Jamaica, and Venezuela also have joined the causes. Incidentally, no one from Guyana, which, as we saw above, has a greater proportion of Muslim adherents than does Trinidad and Tobago, is known to have traveled east for the jihadist cause.

Calypso Recruitment for Caliphate

Outstanding analysis of the recruitment dynamics has been provided by John McCoy and Andy Knight (2017), Simon Cottee (2019), Sanjay Badri-Maharaj (2017), Efraim Benmelech and Esteban Klor (2016), Amandla Thomas-Johnson, 2018; and Leah de Haan (2019), among other scholars (and journalists). This, plus the fact that extensive assessment of the matter is beyond our purview, obviates the need for more than a few observations on the subject. In this respect, one striking aspect is the high profile of the twin-island republic on the global recruitment landscape. Analysis by Benmelech and Klor, some of which is evidenced by table 5.4, shows Trinidad and Tobago ranking sixth globally in the number of ISIS foreign fighters relative to the Muslim population of countries.

McCoy and Knight adduced evidence that suggested a range of between 75 and 125 extremist travelers, and they indicated that "in November 2015, the Minister of National Security publicly affirmed that at least 89 Trinidad and Tobago nationals had traveled to the MENA region. There have also been at least 25 Trinidad and Tobago nationals intercepted by Turkish officials while attempting to gain entry into Syria and Iraq" (McCoy and Knight 2017, 279). For Simon Cottee, "The official number of Trinidadian nationals who journeyed to Syria and Iraq between 2013 and 2016 is around 130. This may well be a conservative estimate, although it seems unlikely to be as high as 400, as one opposition Member of Parliament claimed in April 2016" (Cottee 2019, 303). For its part, CARICOM estimated that more than 200 individuals from CARICOM countries had made the trek between 2013 and 2017. Evidence also indicates that countless individuals failed in their efforts to travel east for the Holy War. Notable here are the 12 individuals who were interdicted in Turkey in July 2016 while trying to cross the border into Syria and were returned to Trinidad and Tobago the following April.

The numbers have been troubling, especially when put in comparative global context, as table 5.4 does. McCoy and Knight capture this thusly:

> On the surface the identified range may seem relatively small; however, when one considers that T & T's population is roughly 1.3 million, the total is strik-

TABLE 5.4 Ranking of Countries Based on ISIS Foreign Fighters to Muslim Population

Country	Fighters/Muslims	Country	Fighters/Muslims
1. Finland	1,590.9	34. Japan	70.8
2. Ireland	724.64	35. Moldova	69.4
3. Belgium	699.4	36. United States	58.8
4. Sweden	631.2	37. Italy	54.6
5. Austria	619.2	38. Tajikistan	47.0
6. Trinidad and Tobago	615.8	39. Albania	37.8
7. Tunisia	546.6	40. Morocco	35.4
8. Denmark	544.4	41. Israel	34.5
9. Norway	529.4	42. Kazakhstan	30.8
10. Maldives	508.1	43. Turkey	28.1
11. France	342.4	44. Argentina	21.4
12. Lebanon	335.0	45. Kuwait	21.3
13. Jordan	306.7	46. Philippines	19.8
14. Montenegro	270.3	47. Romania	16.8
15. Australia	268.8	48. Brazil	14.6
16. United Kingdom	256.2	49. China	12.2
17. Netherlands	236.7	50. Madagascar	11.6
18. Serbia	228.4	51. Azerbaijan	11.1
19. Bosnia	208.8	52. Egypt	7.1
20. Macedonia	199.2	53. Somalia	6.8
21. Portugal	192.3	54. Qatar	5.9
22. Germany	187.9	55. Malaysia	5.5
23. New Zealand	172.8	56. Algeria	4.5
24. Russia	142.7	57. Cambodia	4.1
25. Kosovo	140.6	58. Indonesia	3.1
26. Canada	130.8	59. Sudan	2.5
27. Spain	124.6	60. Singapore	2.4
28. Switzerland	122.0	61. United Arab Emirates	2.2
29. Georgia	105.8	62. Afghanistan	1.6
30. Libya	98.6	63. South Africa	1.2
31. Kyrgyzstan	97.1	64. Pakistan	0.4
32. Saudi Arabia	83.3	65. India	0.1
33. Turkmenistan	72.8		

Source: Efraim Benmelech and Esteban F. Klor, "What Explains the Flow of Foreign Fighters to ISIS," National Bureau of Economic Research Working Paper No. 22190, April 2016, https://www.nber.org /system/files/working_papers/w22190/w22190.pdf.

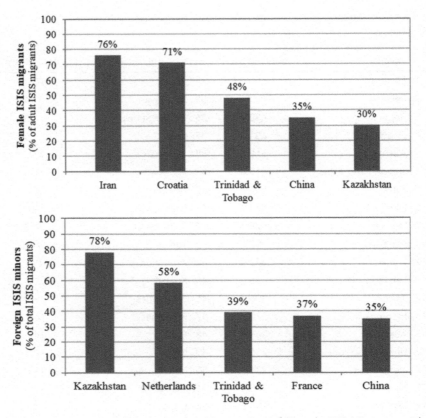

FIGURE 5.5 Countries with the Highest Proportion of Female ISIS Migrants and ISIS Minors.

Source: Simon Cottee, "The Calypso Caliphate: How Trinidad Became a Recruiting Ground for ISIS," *International Affairs* 95, no. 2 (2019): 305.

ing. If the high end of the estimate (125) is accurate, this would equate into a rate of 96 individuals (per million)—a rate that is roughly double that of Belgium, which, according to data collected from the International Centre for the Study of Radicalization (ICSR), experiences the highest per capita rate of "foreign fighters" in the Western world. The total would also exceed per capita rates seen in Saudi Arabia and some of the MENA region with the exception of Tunisia and Jordan that display the highest rates in the world, again according to ICSR numbers." (McCoy and Knight 2017, 279–80)

Who and Why?

In undertaking a demographic analysis of the list of 102 individuals in a leaked Trinidad and Tobago Police Service file, Simon Cottee found the list to comprise 31.4 percent males between 30 and 50 years of age and 29.4 percent females between 30 and 40 years of age. He also found that 39.2 percent of the migrants were children between ages of 2 and 16. Also disconcerting, the analysis showed Trinidad and Tobago to have the dubious distinction of being among the top five countries globally when it came to the proportion of women and children involved, as figure 5.5 indicates. Incredibly, the twin-island republic was ahead of China and Kazakhstan when it came to the proportion of female migrants and led France and China in terms of the proportion of child migrants.

In terms of places of origin within Trinidad and Tobago, the genesis of the 2013–2016 migrations was traced to a social network of around 350 like-minded individuals located in three parts of Trinidad and Tobago: Chaguanas in west-central Trinidad, Diego Martin in the northwest, and Rio Claro in the southeast, with the Umar Ibn Khattab mosque in Rio Claro being a key operational location (Cottee 2019, 298). Although 55 percent of the adults who migrated were unskilled and mostly female homemakers, 20 percent of them were skilled; 15 percent semiskilled; and 10 percent were professionals, including a teacher, a truck driver, an agricultural worker, an auto mechanic, an offshore welder, a marine safety technician, a taxi driver, a building contractor, a cell-phone store owner, a professional football player, a debt collector, a car salesman, a seaman, and a farm owner (Cottee 2019, 307).

With regard to motivation, two sets of reflections are noteworthy. As the McCoy and Knight study revealed, the presence of Trinidad and Tobago citizens in the Syria–Iraq War attracted the national spotlight with the release of an Islamic State (IS) propaganda video titled "Those Who Believe and Make the Hijra" in November 2015, which featured several individuals and their families. Analysis of the video suggested it had three main themes: the supposed religious freedom offered to Trinidadians and Tobagonians in the IS; the "family friendly" nature of the IS; and religious obligations to engage in the *hijra* (McCoy and Knight 2017, 281).[13] For his part, Cottee offered the following: "What drove these individuals to join ISIS? Often, the answer is framed in terms of 'push' and 'pull' factors, making a distinction between what is attractive or felt to be attractive about ISIS that 'pulls' people to join it and what is prohibitive or felt to be prohibitive about the joiners' own society that 'pushes' them to search for radical alternatives (Cottee 2019, 301–302).

It is worth mentioning that even with my reference to trinitrotoluene and Trinidad and Tobago once considered the epicenter of terrorism concerns in the region, their profile is not indicative of region-wide realities; the rest of the Caribbean lacks the historical and political vulnerability preconditions to make homegrown terrorism a serious concern as in Trinidad and Tobago. Indeed, a review of any number of the *Country Reports on Terrorism*, produced annually by the U.S. Department of State, would reveal that besides Cuba, Trinidad and Tobago is the only country in the Caribbean that commands attention. Cuba once was in the terrorism crosshairs of the United States because of communism and alleged support of leftist terrorist pursuits globally and had been designated a state sponsor of terrorism. Interestingly, that designation was rescinded on May 29, 2015, during the presidency of Barack Obama but was restored on January 11, 2021, by President Donald Trump just before he left office. As of March 2023, the Biden administration had decided to retain the designation.

Beyond the attention to Trinidad and Tobago, we saw earlier that the misgivings about terrorism are credible, both from the vantage point of Caribbean states and from that of state and non-state actors outside of it that have economic and other interests there. For instance, the vulnerability of tourism is real, as is that of the oil and LNG tankers that convey high-value strategic materials from the region. Just imagine the loss of life and the environmental and economic damage that would occur from oil tankers from one of the oil-producing states or an LNG tanker from Trinidad detonated in any port or along one of the region's strategic waterways. But as we saw above, 9/11 showed clearly that the region does not have to be the intended target of terrorist actions to suffer serious consequences. Overall, the region's geopolitical landscape and the extensive United States and other Western links and interests there conduce to the vulnerability to terrorism by forces hostile to the United States and its strategic partners. As if this were not enough, the region also has to cope with the cyber PWP, the subject of the section that follows.

The Cybersecurity Conundrum

Chapter 2 observed that information technology and cyber innovation have taken the forces of globalization to new heights, and that in relation to "security" and "sovereignty" that conceptual contestation necessitated definitional specificity. Similarly, and as was done with "terrorism" above, the multiplicity of usages of "cybersecurity" obliges us to specify our definitional parameters. In this respect, I have adopted as my working definition the one articulated by *Digital Guardian's* Nate Lord, who views cybersecurity as "the body of technologies, processes, and practices designed to protect networks, devices, programs, and data from attack, damage, or unauthorized access. Cyber security may also be referred to as information technology security" (Lord 2019).

There is broad consensus around Lord's proposition that the importance of cybersecurity revolves around the fact that government, military, corporate, educational, and health organizations collect and store huge quantities of data on computers and other electronic devices. Considerable amounts of the data are sensitive, being intellectual property, financial data, personal information, or other types of data for which unlawful access or use could have damaging outcomes. Insofar as cyberspace and cybercrime are concerned, I embrace the approach to the former, which views it as "a global domain within the information environment consisting of the independent network of information technology infrastructures and resident data, including the Internet, telecommunications networks, computer systems, and embedded processors and controllers" (Jasper and Wirtz 2017, 158). As to cybercrime, Corlane Barclay observes that "'cybercrime' or 'computer crime' relates to any criminal act that affects the confidentiality, integrity and availability of a computer or network, or privacy and security of a person online" (Barclay 2017, 84).

Importantly, Barclay, who is both an information technology specialist and an attorney, contends that cybercrime can be broadly classified into the use of the computer as a tool or target in the commission of a crime (with or without intent to cause harm). Crimes that use the computer as a tool or as a means to commit a crime include fraud, identity theft, phishing, spamming, and other malicious acts, such as cyberbullying and cyberwarfare. On the other hand, crimes where the computer is a target include viruses, worms, Trojan horses, and other malware. Denial-of-service attacks are ones where the computer is used both as a tool and a target.

Respected information technology specialist Deepak Rout contends that the term "cyber" has Greek roots, generally meaning "one who guides a boat," such as a pilot or rudder operator. The philosopher Plato is said to have adapted the word to mean something along the lines of governance and associated it with government control, as governments steer society. In the twentieth century, American mathematician and philosopher Norbert Wiener foresaw the rise of sophisticated robots that would need artificial intelligence for their functionality. He coined the word "cybernetics," adapting the Greek roots to refer to intelligent controllers, and he retained the connection between technological control and governance. Novelist William Gibson, who envisaged virtual interactions in his 1984 novel *Neuromancer*, coined the term "cyberspace," borrowing the prefix "cyber" from Wiener (Rout 2015, 1).

Rout contends that cyberspace became a standard name for the place where people visit the internet. But Gibson disregarded the governance context, given that the internet is inherently not amenable to central control. Meanwhile, security experts had already settled on the term "information security" to mean securing of information and digital systems, and it was viewed as synonymous with "computer security" and "network security." Moreover, as digital technology became vital for citizens, businesses, and governments, the military began to make it a top priority. Rout also posits that "because conventional military thinking is based on the defense and attack of some kind of space (e.g., terrain, aerospace), cyberspace became a useful reference to the digital domain. Hence, securing cyberspace became cybersecurity" (2015, 1).

Evidence suggests that for effective cybersecurity, an organization needs to coordinate its efforts throughout its entire information system. Elements of cyber encompass all of the following: network security, application security, endpoint security, data security, identity management, database and infrastructure security, cloud security, mobile security, disaster recovery/business continuity planning, and end-user education (Lord 2019).

Jeff Melnick, director of Global Solutions Engineering at data security firm Netwrix, holds the view that "a cyber attack is any type of offensive action that targets computer information systems, infrastructures, computer networks or personal computer devices, using various methods to steal, alter or destroy data or information systems" (Melnick 2018). Using this approach, Melnick identifies the following as the most common cyberattacks: denial-of-service and distributed denial-of-service (DDoS); man-in-the-middle; phishing and spear phishing; drive-by; password attacks; Structured Query Language injection; cross-site scripting; eavesdropping; birthday; and malware.[14] Clarification of our definitional context and appreciation of modes and methods enables us to acknowledge a few significant aspects of the global threat landscape before we turn our attention to the Caribbean.

According to the *Global Cybersecurity Index 2018*, more than half of the world population currently has online access. It was estimated that by the end of 2018, almost 3.9 billion people, about 51.2 percent of the world's population, were using the internet and that internet penetration will have skyrocketed to 70 percent by 2023 (ITU 2019, 6). Clearly, this will dramatically increase global cybersecurity needs. Also noteworthy is that 73 percent of all hostile activity in 2018 fell into four categories: web attacks, reconnaissance, service-specific attacks, and brute-force attacks (Nippon Telegraph and Telephone 2019, 7).[15] Brute-force password attacks entail randomly trying different passwords and hoping that one of them works. Sometimes a bit of logic is applied by trying passwords related to someone's name, job title, or hobbies.

For its part, the *Global Threat Intelligence Report 2021* revealed that in 2020, of the five main enterprise sectors, finance remained the most attacked sector, as had been the case for seven of the previous eight years; manufacturing came in second (Nippon Telegraph and Telephone 2021). As table 5.5 shows, application-specific and web-application attacks accounted for nearly 75 percent of all hostile traffic. Moreover, in health care a whopping 97 percent of the attacks were via web applications and application-specific invasions. It also is notable that although education represented the smallest of the five industry areas, more than 60 percent of the strikes there came from web-application and application-specific sources.

The same report not only indicated that finance was the most attacked industry, with a 50 percent increase in attack volume, but manufacturing leapt from fifth place in 2019 to second in 2020. In addition, whereas health care was the sixth most attacked sector in 2019, it grew to third place in 2020. The rates for application-specific and web-application attacks saw a remarkable increase, accounting in 2020 for 67 percent of all attacks, up from 55 percent in 2019 and 32 percent in 2018. As to the reason, reputable analysts suggest that "the biggest contributor is likely the increased use of web applications and infrastructures as organizations accelerated cloud adoption. Simply put, hostile threat actors are attacking the technology and functionality of newly deployed by organizations. This accelerated during COVID-19 as organizations raced to become digital, increasing their use of client portals and cloud technologies, as well as mobile and web-enabled applications" (Nippon Telegraph and Telephone 2021, 13).

The United States and China were cited as the most common sources of attack in every region of the world in 2018, with ten countries comprising all of the top five attack sources. The business and professional services sector remained a popular target, with attackers leveraging vendor trust relationships to access shared data. The education and government sectors were new to the global top five list due to continued long-term activity against those sectors. The *Global Threat Intelligence Report* notes that the top five attacked sectors accounted for

TABLE 5.5 Global Cyberattack Types and Sources in 2020

Industry	Percent of Global Attack	Percent of Attack Types for Industry
Finance	23%	Application-specific: 42% Web application: 31% Reconnaissance: 12%
Manufacturing	22%	Application-specific: 49% Reconnaissance: 24% Web application: 20%
Healthcare	17%	Web application: 59% Application-specific: 38% Known bad source: 1%
Business and professional services	10%	Reconnaissance: 53% Web application: 13% Brute force: 12%
Education	6%	Web application: 24% Application-specific: 22% Reconnaissance: 21%

Source: Nippon Telegraph and Telephone, *Global Threat Intelligence Report 2021*, 13. https://services.global .ntt/en-us/insights/2021-global-threat-intelligence-report/.

66 percent of all attacks, supporting trends that imply attackers continue to focus on specific sectors. Although most countries on the list of the most common attack sources remain consistent over the years, 2018 did experience some small changes. According to *Statista*, between august 2021 and December 2022, the following countries were the top six sources of Internet of Things (IoT) attacks: United States, with 48.3 percent of the attacks; Vietnam, with 17.8 percent of them; Russia, 14.6 percent; The Netherlands, 7.4 percent; France, 6.4 percent; and Germany, 2.3 percent.[16]

Undoubtedly, the pandemic impacted the cybersecurity landscape. As two systems engineers explained, COVID-19 generated new challenges in cybersecurity. Work and study at home due to COVID-19 caused increased internet use, enticed more people to spend time online, and provided more opportunities for cybercrime. Deadly cybersecurity threats included malware, spam email, malicious websites, ransomware, malicious domains, DDoS attacks, business email compromises, malicious social media messaging, and so on (Wang and Alexander 2021). The telework, telemedicine, and distance learning that the pandemic necessitated increased the vulnerability of individual, governmental, and corporate operators in cyberspace.

In addressing the matter, the authors of the 2021 global threat report noted that cybercriminals exploited the pandemic to spread malware for financial gain. As well, they distributed malicious PDF (portable document format), RTF (rich text format), and Word documents; circulated spyware, keyloggers, and other malware; used specific COVID-19-related phishing lures; and targeted education or health-care institutions involved in COVID-19 patient care and vaccine research, production, and distribution (see Nippon Telegraph and Telephone 2021, 7; Nabe 2020). In one of the many health-care cases, from mid-2019 intelligence and law enforcement agencies in several jurisdictions began monitoring electronic communications between two members of a Nigerian criminal group called the Ozie Team who were planning an operation against a manufacturer of N95 masks. The operation led to the discovery of a transaction for over US$550,000 in an account controlled by the Ozie Team. The group's modus operandi involved distributing malware via malspam. With malspam, once the victim opens the malicious attachment, FormBook injects itself into its desired running process or Windows Explorer. Then, once FormBook is uploaded, Ozie Team operators can see details of the user's activity from the FormBook web interface, including keystrokes and web forms (Nippon Telegraph and Telephone 2021, 8).

There is copious evidence to support the contention by Scott Jasper and James Wirtz that "today cyber security issues threaten national security and economic prosperity. . . . Cyber security has emerged as a major political, military, technical, and economic issue that affects every user of the Internet, which will soon be just about everyone on the planet" (Jasper and Wirtz 2017, 158). Actually, according to the International Telecommunication Union (ITU), the global average cost of a data breach grew by 6.4 percent in 2018, and due to increased use of information and communication technology, the projected cybercrime cost for 2019 was projected to stand at US$2 trillion (ITU 2019, 6). Additionally, the *Global Cybersecurity Index 2020* estimates that global losses due to cybercrime range between US$1 trillion in 2020 at the low end to as high as US$6 trillion in 2021 at the high end (ITU 2021, 3). Noteworthy, too, is that in his foreword to the IDB study on the subject, IDB president Luis Alberto Moreno pegged the cost of cybercrime worldwide at US$575 billion a year, which amounts to almost four times the annual donation for international development. He calculated the cost of cybercrime to Latin America and the Caribbean as being US$90 billion a year (IDB 2016, ix).[17] Looking ahead, analysts at *Statista* project a dramatic increase in costs globally between 2023 and 2027: from US$11.5 trillion in 2023 to US$14.67 trillion in 2024, then to US$17.65 trillion the following year, followed by US$20.74 trillion in 2026, and US$23.84 trillion in 2027.[18]

Recognition of the scope and cost and the impact implications prompted the ITU in 2013 to launch the annual Global Cybersecurity Index, which is a composite that aggregates twenty-five indicators into one benchmark, to monitor and compare the level of the cybersecurity commitment of countries with regard to the five pillars of the Global Cybersecurity Agenda, which were launched by the ITU in 2007:

1. Legal: Measures based on the existence of legal institutions and frameworks dealing with cybersecurity and cybercrime.
2. Technical: Measures based on the existence of technical institutions and framework dealing with cybersecurity.
3. Organizational: Measures based on the existence of national policy coordination institutions and strategies for cybersecurity development at the national level.
4. Capacity building: Measures based on the existence of research and development, education and training programmes, certified professionals and public sector agencies fostering capacity building.
5. Cooperation: Measures based on the existence of partnerships, cooperative frameworks and information sharing networks. (See ITU 2019, 7–8.)

Countries are ranked in one of three commitment categories: high, medium, and low.

The Regional Landscape

One cybersecurity assessment for 2018 placed eighty-seven countries in the low category (see ITU 2019, esp. 13–51). Quite disappointingly, all Caribbean countries fell into that category. This is all the more troubling considering the substantial internet penetration in the Caribbean, as tables 5.6 and 5.7 reveal. Table 5.6 shows that almost 48 percent of the region's population of nearly 45 million, although under 5 percent of the population of the Americas, were internet users at the end of December 2020. Moreover, some 17 million people were on Facebook. Figure 5.6 shows the internet penetration rate of the Caribbean is 47.5 percent, less than 10 percent below the world average and less than 15 percent below that for Central America. Understandably, as shown in table 5.7, internet and Facebook usage varies among countries; there is internet penetration of more than 80 percent in eleven countries, with Aruba, Curaçao, and French St. Barthélemy having more than 90 percent penetration. On the low side, Haiti stands out with just 2 million of its 11 million population (17.8 percent) having internet connectivity.

Needless to say, internet and other telecommunications connectivity extends across the popular, business, social, and business sectors, albeit not uniformly within countries and sectors. Mindful of this and the portraits reflected above, one can appreciate the vulnerability to attacks that exists from sources mentioned in the global portrait described earlier and from other sources. As Hopeton Dunn and Indianna Minto-Coy remarked, and quite rightly, "The growth of the Internet economy brings not only new opportunities, but also challenges in the form of the conduct of illicit activities, or 'cybercrime,' particularly for countries with an already limited law enforcement capacity" (Dunn and Minto-Coy 2010, 15).

TABLE 5.6 Internet Profile of the Caribbean and the Rest of the Americas in 2022

Regions	Population (2022)	% Pop. Americas	Internet Users July 31, 2022	% Pop. (Penetration)	% Users (Table)	Facebook July 31, 2022
North America	374,226,282	36.0	349,572,583	93.4	39.1	306,853,600
South America	437,156,844	42.1	369,970,548	84.6	41.4	362,236,599
Central America	183,082,224	17.6	144,007,500	78.7	16.1	143,999,200
The Caribbean	43,860,773	4.2	29,418,573	67.1	3.3	18,632,515
Total: The Americas	1,038,326,323	100.0	892,969,204	86.0	100.0	831,721,815

Source: Internet World Stats: Usage and Population Statistics, https://www.internetworldstats.com/stats2.htm.

TABLE 5.7 Internet Profile of Caribbean Countries

Caribbean	Population (2019 est.)	% Pop. Carib.	Internet Usage, 31 Mar. 2019	% Pop. (Penetration)	Users % Region	Facebook 31 Dec. 2017
Anguilla	15,174	0.0%	12,377	81.6%	0.1%	9,000
Antigua & Barbuda	104,909	0.2%	79,731	76.0%	0.4%	62,000
Aruba	106,053	0.2%	103,052	97.2%	0.5%	91,000
Bahamas	403,095	0.9%	342,631	85.0%	1.5%	220,000
Barbados	287,010	0.6%	234,659	81.8%	1.0%	160,000
Bonaire, St. Eustatius, Saba	25,971	0.1%	20,956	80.7%	0.1%	15,000
British Virgin Islands	32,206	0.1%	14,620	45.4%	0.1%	12,000
Cayman Islands	63,129	0.1%	54,630	86.5%	0.2%	48,000
Cuba	11,492,046	25.8%	5,642,595	49.1%	25.0%	4,180,000
Curaçao	162,547	0.4%	151,274	93.1%	0.7%	120,000
Dominica	74,679	0.2%	51,992	69.6%	0.2%	39,000
Dominican Republic	10,996,774	24.7%	7,146,803	65.0%	31.7%	5,100,000
Grenada	108,825	0.2%	69,245	63.6%	0.3%	62,000
Guadeloupe	448,798	1.0%	240,000	53.5%	1.1%	220,000
Haiti	11,242,856	25.3%	2,000,000	17.8%	8.9%	1,800,000
Jamaica	2,906,339	6.5%	1,581,100	54.4%	7.0%	1,100,000
Martinique	385,320	0.9%	303,302	78.7%	1.3%	170,000
Montserrat	5,220	0.0%	3,000	57.5%	0.0%	2,600
Puerto Rico	3,654,978	8.2%	3,047,311	83.4%	13.5%	2,100,000
St. Barthélemy (FR)	7,160	0.0%	7,240	101.1%	0.0%	6,400
St. Kitts & Nevis	56,345	0.1%	45,476	80.7%	0.2%	35,000
Saint Lucia	180,454	0.4%	142,970	79.2%	0.6%	92,000
St. Martin (FR)	32,284	0.1%	16,100	49.9%	0.1%	15,000
St. Vincent & Grenadines	110,488	0.2%	76,984	69.7%	0.3%	61,000
Sint Maarten (NL)	40,939	0.1%	33,000	80.6%	0.1%	31,000
Trinidad & Tobago	1,375,443	3.1%	1,063,630	77.3%	4.7%	700,000
Turks & Caicos	36,461	0.1%	28,000	76.8%	0.1%	25,000
U.S. Virgin Islands	104,909	0.2%	67,540	64.4%	0.3%	22,000
Total Caribbean	44,460,412	100.0%	22,580,218	50.8%	100.0%	16,498,000

Source: Internet World Stats: Usage and Population Statistics, https://www.internetworldstats.com/stats2.htm/.

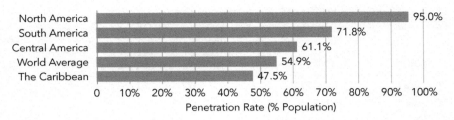

FIGURE 5.6 Internet Penetration Rates in the Americas by Geographic Regions, June 30, 2018.

Source: Internet World Stats: Usage and Population Statistics. www.internetworldstats.com/stats2.htm/.

CARICOM called attention to the matter, noting the significant growth in cybercrime in the region, reflected in the number of government websites hacked, online child exploitation that infiltrated schools, and the growing use of cryptocurrencies to fund criminal activities, among other developments. Indeed, "According to the Commonwealth secretariat, 'Major cybercrimes reported in the region to date include the theft of $150 million from an international bank in 2014; individuals claiming to be local ISIS supporters hacking government websites in 2015; and, in the same year, hackers infecting tax authorities with ransomware, which blocks users from accessing their systems and demands money'" (CARICOM 2016, 4). CARICOM also called attention to the existence of significant cybersecurity vulnerabilities and raised the alarm about cybercrime's devastating impact on national security and socioeconomic development.

Cyber Cases

In this respect, it will suffice to call attention to a few cybercrime cases:

- The Jamaican government is said to have reported a 14 percent increase in the number of cybercrime incidents in 2012, which mostly targeted public institutions and critical infrastructure. A major service provider was also the object of high-profile hacking incidents in 2014 (C. Bryan 2015). Indeed, in May 2022 Jamaica's minister for science, energy, and technology told Parliament that the country experiences a cyberattack every thirty-nine seconds, with most of the attacks being ransomware, targeted attacks, malicious spam emails, malicious URLs, and scams. Interestingly too, as we saw earlier with many other jurisdictions, the COVID-19 pandemic occasioned a spike in cyberattacks, as private and public sector agencies adjusted their operations, including work-at-home protocols that increased the vulnerability of computers and technology systems (Vaz 2022).

- On May 4, 2015, the government website of St. Vincent and the Grenadines was attacked by a self-identified Islamic State hacker. The Information Technology Unit of the Royal St. Vincent and the Grenadines Police Force, which is responsible for responding to and investigating cyberattacks and cybercrime, received technical assistance from the United States to deal with the matter (IDB 2016, 102).[19] In April 2018, St. Maarten was the victim of an attack that caused a total public shutdown for an entire day (Erez 2018).
- At the annual end-of-year press conference in December 2019, the Guyana Lands and Surveys Commission commissioner, Trevor Benn, revealed that the commission had been enduring many cyberattacks throughout the year, forcing it to involve the Guyana Police Force. Reportedly, the attackers were unable to compromise the commission's data but were able to access the PBX telephone system and attempted to take control of it. The commissioner reported that other cyber-related attacks were done by spoofing and phishing and that he found it necessary to have the Information Systems Division inspect and clean his account weekly because of the quantity of "mischief" email received. As part of its protection, the commission began to benefit from the cybersecurity expertise of the National Data Management Authority, had begun to digitize its paper records, and planned to implement an Electronic Document Management System to manage correspondence received by commission staff (K. King 2019).
- In August 2018, Puerto Rico's then–General Services Administration chief, Ottmar Chávez Piñero, reported that the agency's Single Registry of Bidders online platform had suffered a cyberattack, and in March of the same year the government admitted to being the victim of two cyberattacks in less than twenty-four hours that blocked public officials' access to the information systems of both the Electric Power Authority and the Environmental Quality Board. Moreover, in March 2017, Puerto Rico's Treasury Department was compromised for several days and the government coffers ceased receiving millions of dollars in tax revenue. At the time, then–chief information officer Luis Arocho confirmed to the Center for Investigative Journalism that a lack of an adequate cybersecurity policy was responsible for the cyberattacks of these systems (Hernández Cabiya 2020).
- In January 2017, a payment of US$2,609,495.67 was made to a fraudulent account outside of Puerto Rico. The payment reportedly was supposed to be made to the Commonwealth Retirement System as part of the monthly pay-as-you-go remittances.
- In January 2020, hackers stole US$63,000 from the Puerto Rico's Employees Retirement System, and in February of the same year the Puerto Rican government announced that several agencies had been victims of five cyberattacks over the previous four years.

Most of the attacks occurred during the first months of the year and cost millions of dollars in public funds. The most recent attack occurred on February 13, 2020, and involved a US$1.5 million transaction by the Puerto Rico Tourism Corporation. As well, the Puerto Rico Industrial Development Company revealed that a US$2.61 million transaction had been made after receiving an email from an alleged hacker (Hernández Cabiya 2020).

On January 26, 2022, the president of Puerto Rico's senate, José Luis Dalmau, announced that the senate was the target of a cyberattack that disabled its internet provider, phone system, and official online page. Although the matter was being investigated, the senate president indicated that there was no evidence that the hackers accessed sensitive information belonging to employees, contractors, or consultants (Associated Press 2022). Incidentally, Puerto Rico is reputedly the target of the largest number of cyberattacks in the Caribbean. FortiGuard Labs's *Global Threat Landscape Report* revealed that more than 152 million cyberattacks were registered in Puerto Rico during 2020 (*Caribbean Business* 2021).

In March 2020 the Jamaica National Group (JNG) reported that one of its systems suffered a ransomware attack that led to the theft of data belonging to some members and customers, although customer accounts were unaffected. JNG information technology and cybersecurity teams immediately contained the effects of the malware and sought to identify the source of the sophisticated attack. The Jamaica Constabulary Force's Major Organized Crime and Anti-Corruption Agency was notified, and they launched an investigation (*Jamaica Gleaner* 2020). JNG, which comprises a dozen companies with banking, insurance, real estate, money transfer, and other operations, is one of Jamaica's leading companies, with operations elsewhere in the Caribbean. According to their 2019 *Director's Report and Financial Statement*, the deposit-taking parts of the group accounted for some J$16.6 billion (US$122.5 million) in new funds associated with some sixty-nine thousand new accounts, which increased the overall savings portfolio to J$129.5 billion (US$955.7 million) by the end of the financial year, up from J$118 billion (US$870.8 million). The lending institutions in the group—JN Bank Limited, JN Small Business Loans Limited, JN Fund Managers Limited, and JN Cayman—approved more than forty-one thousand loans valued at just over J$30 billion (US$221.4 million), mostly for housing, small and micro enterprise, personal loans, and premium financing (Jamaica National Group 2019, 29).

In their study of the Dominican Republic, Maurice Dawson and Pedro Manuel Taveras Nuñez found a wide range of internal and external attacks there. The internal threats were mostly from individuals who target banks, with the three most significant attacks taking the form of phishing, card cloning, and hacking, although there also is CD/DVD cloning, unauthorized access, theft of email, cloning of modem boxes, data manipulation, and software piracy. As elsewhere in the Caribbean, many people in the Dominican Republic use mobile devices but rarely inspect the links to ensure that they originate from legitimate sources, not to mention that a significant number of Android users carry no virus protection (Dawson and Taveras Nuñez 2018, 177). The *Statista* database indicates that in one month—June, 2019—five Caribbean nations suffered the largest number of web application attacks on their energy and utilities sector: the Dominican Republic (3,210), Trinidad and Tobago (1,072), Jamaica (638), Puerto Rico (234), and the Bahamas (152).[20]

The connection between cybercrime and other criminal pursuits was on full display in March 2022, when law enforcement authorities from the Dominican Republic and the United States dismantled a transnational cybercrime network believed to have defrauded hundreds of American citizens of some US$200 million. Named Operation Discovery, the yearlong law enforcement effort revealed the existence of a criminal network that allegedly defrauded its victims via financial shakedown, sexual extortion, and identity theft. Operation Discovery led to the arrest of seventy individuals in New York City, Santiago, Santo Domingo, La Vega, and Puerto Plata. During the raids, officials seized US$400,000, more than 19 million Dominican pesos in cash (almost US$350,000), thirty luxury vehicles, as well as hundreds of pieces of electronic equipment, such as computers and cell phones, and several firearms. An allied criminal network, called the Trinitarios, which operated in the Dominican Republic, the United States, and Spain, allegedly used cryptocurrencies, deposits through remittance companies, and fraudulent money transfers (Shuldiner 2022).

As with Jamaica and other countries noted above, cybercrime in the Dominican Republic increased dramatically with the advent of the COVID-19 pandemic. Indeed, local media reported that cybercrime had become more lucrative than drug trafficking during the early stages of the pandemic, presumably due to the difficulty of transporting drug shipments internationally during initial lockdowns. Moreover, sexual extortion, called "sextortion," reportedly also skyrocketed during the early stages of the pandemic as businesses and schools ended in-person operations and conducted their business online. Evidence suggests that during the first year of the pandemic, numerous Ponzi and pyramid schemes materialized in Guyana, Trinidad and Tobago, Barbados, Antigua and Barbuda, and elsewhere in the region. The schemes purportedly involved victims recruited online and asked to invest small sums of money, sometimes as little as five dollars, in exchange for massive returns (Shuldiner 2022).

In a case with clear national security implications, the day after the International Court of Justice (ICJ) April 6, 2023, decision rejecting Venezuela's preliminary objections to Guyana's case before it, Guyana's Minister of Natural Resources Vickram Bharrat confirmed that the government's petroleum website was hacked. This was reputedly by Venezuelan operatives as the attackers littered the portal with "EL ESEQUIBO ES VENEZUELA" graphics, proclaiming Venezuela's position on the border controversy, and maps depicting the Essequibo region as part of Venezuela. The compromised website carried essential information about the Production Sharing Agreement with Exxon Mobil and Guyana's inaugural bid round for 14 offshore oil blocs, among other things. It took fully one week for the web portal to be restored.[21]

The discussion above of the dynamics and implications of the terrorism PWP should make it easy to endorse the sentiment expressed by the envoy of Antigua and Barbuda to Washington and the Organization of American States:

> If it turns out that, despite its greater experience of terrorism, Egyptian airport security could not stop a bomb being placed on the Russian Civilian plane whose explosion killed hundreds of tourists, how much more vulnerable are Caribbean airports and seaports? And the answer to this growing problem cannot be simply to bolster security. That is only part of the answer, and a very expensive one for small countries with limited resources. (Sanders 2016)

We saw, of course, that although the externally driven September 11, 2001, incident catapulted terrorism to the top of the clear and present dangers list for the Caribbean, the region had its own terrorism experiences earlier.

Clearly, though, the contemporary reality is that the terrorism vulnerability derives less, if at all, from intra-regional political or religious discontent and more from geopolitical and geoeconomic factors connected to relationships with the United States and its European strategic partners that are the nemeses of Islamic terrorist forces. The worry, then, as was seen with the 9/11 attack, is that Caribbean countries do not have to be the intended targets of Islamic terrorist actions to suffer their harmful consequences; collateral damage can render significant damage and disrupt lives and livelihoods. Moreover, as small and subordinate states, Caribbean countries have to adopt counterterrorism measures that sometimes conduce to front-end vulnerability but also create rearguard exposure. Such is the situation with banking and financial services—a key sector of many economies—where de-risking pursuits by the United States and Europe to combat terrorist financing are hurting the banking sector. De-risking pertains to the restriction of correspondent banking relationships or business services from major international banks to certain jurisdictions due to concerns over money laundering or potential involvement in terrorist financing (see MacDonald 2019a; Marczak and Mowla 2022).

Although there once was justifiable anxiety over the profile of Trinidad and Tobago in the global terrorist constellation, there appears to be little regional susceptibility to a spread of religious fervor and associated military action, or even of religiously driven political instability within Trinidad and Tobago by jihadists who return from the east. Cyber challenges also present clear and present dangers to the region. Jamaica's minister of science, energy, and technology, Daryl Vaz, was prescient in his October 1, 2021, speech when he launched Cybersecurity Awareness Month: "We live in an era where we are not only protecting our geographic boundaries but our virtual borders as well. Cybersecurity is both a collective and individual responsibility. In an age where technology is evolving at an unprecedented pace, we need all hands on deck to fight the unseen enemy" (Dawkins 2021).

Hopefully, this chapter has shown the nature, impact, and implications of the terrorism and cybercrime PWPs for the Caribbean. The global and multidimensional dynamics are quite evident, and the region's multiple vulnerabilities are obvious, although there is no parity in scope and salience between terrorism and cybersecurity matters. This chapter ends the second part of this book, where the four PWPs—drugs, crime, terrorism, and cybersecurity—were examined. Part III moves from the regional-level unit of analysis to the state-level unit of analysis, with case studies that have region-wide value. The next chapter probes two controversial cases, the Dudus affair in Jamaica in 2010, which was a political and public security volcano, and the less volcanic but equally contentious State of Emergency in Trinidad and Tobago in 2011.

Controversial Cases

6

Security and Sovereignty Under Siege

Our murder rate is equivalent to that of a country experiencing
two civil wars at the same time. . . . The gangs and organized
crime actors are the ones responsible for the fear gripping
the population and the decline in citizen and investor
confidence in broad sections of the society. The turnaround in
social and economic fortunes which we need to put Jamaica
in the reach of Vision 2030 cannot be achieved without
dramatic and sustained improvement in our public security.
—Owen Ellington, Commissioner of Police of Jamaica, "Dealing Effectively
with Guns and Drugs for Improved Public Safety"

In simpler days, state sovereignty implied several key
elements. Primarily, it meant political interdependence.
It also meant territorial integrity and virtually exclusive
control and jurisdiction within that territory.
—Louis Henkin, "That 'S' Word: Sovereignty, and
Globalization, and Human Rights, Et Cetera"

A central premise of this book is that while some Caribbean countries face
traditional security issues, for most of them the greatest dangers relate to Problems Without Passports. In the first epigraph to this chapter, Commissioner
Ellington highlights some of the dangers that Jamaica faced in relation to two
of the four PWPs under consideration in this study. He also made the following
sobering statement:

Over 2,000 Jamaicans are victims of gun attacks each year. Just over a half of
those die and the remainder are scarred for life. The Jamaican police have to
endure an average [of] 500 gun attacks from criminals each year. This same
police force removes from the streets over 600 illegal firearms and thousands
of live ammunitions each year, while arresting thousands of gun offenders,

most of whom return to the streets in short order on bail or on suspended sentences after conviction, even as many are acquitted due to weak prosecution cases. (Ellington 2013)

Thankfully, all Caribbean countries do not share Jamaica's profile. Nevertheless, the situation across the region truly is serious, with security, economic, and other consequences, as Ellington pinpoints in relation to Jamaica. Thus, for the Caribbean as a region, drugs and crime present core, high-intensity threats with regional salience; they are threats of the first order. As Louis Henkin infers in the second epigraph, generally the present-day essentials of sovereignty have undergone change over time. For the Caribbean, these are hardly "simpler days," as drugs and crime have disrupted the lives and livelihoods of citizens of the region in incredible ways.

The two cases studies examined here—the 2010 Dudus affair in Jamaica and the 2011 State of Emergency in Trinidad and Tobago—clearly show this. Several reasons explain their selection. First, they represent threats spawned by crime and drugs that have pushed two of the leading Caribbean nations to the edge of their security and sovereignty precipices. Moreover, they featured the dangerous combination of gangs and guns that not only traumatized the citizens of their nations but also sent shock waves throughout the region, portending incalculable dangers because of the transnational criminal linkages involved and the relatively greater security deficits in other parts of the region. As one Eastern Caribbean law enforcement officer asked me rhetorically in Miami in spring 2012, if Jamaica and Trinidad and Tobago couldn't handle their situations, what chance do we have? Finally, the two cases were selected because they highlight the complexity and gravity of the challenges facing the region as a whole. Challenged sovereignty was in full international view in both of these cases.

The 2010 Dudus Affair in Jamaica

The Man in the Middle

The Dudus affair has had both domestic and international dimensions. Central to it are Christopher "Dudus" Coke, criminal entrepreneur and leader of the Shower Posse, and Tivoli Gardens (hereafter, TG), a geographic/criminal/political zone where Dudus was the don, the boss. There are differing explanations of the origin of the name "Shower." One is that it derived from the reputation of the gang for spraying—showering—opponents with bullets. Another is that it came from the promises of politicians associated with it to "shower" supporters with gifts. Dudus's birth name is Michael Christopher Coke. Dudus as a nickname—"DUD-us"—reputedly stuck to Coke because growing up he wore dashikis (African-style shirts), which were a favorite of one of his idols, Jamaican World War II hero Dudley ("Dud") Thompson (Hamilton and Burke

2010).[1] Michael Coke had aliases other than Dudus, including "Omar Clark," "Paul Christopher Scott," "Presi," "President," "General," and "Shortman."

Christopher Coke was born on March 13, 1969, in TG to Patricia "Miss Patsy" Halliburton and Lester Lloyd Coke, also known as Jim Brown.[2] Lester Coke, who once led the Shower Posse, died in 1992 in a mysterious fire in a Jamaican prison where he was being held pending hearing for extradition to the United States for trial for murder and other crimes. Just 5 feet 4 inches in height, Dudus has several brothers, including Omar Coke; Everton Jones, otherwise called "Corn Pipe"; and Andrew Coke, also known as "Liviti." Two other brothers, Omar and Mark Anthony, had been killed earlier in gang shootouts, as had been a sister. A surviving sister, Sandra "Sandi" Coke, surrendered to police on June 4, 2010. Officially, Christopher Coke was an entrepreneur; he was the director of a construction company called Incomparable Enterprises Limited, which received state construction contracts, and he was the owner of a company called Presidential Click, which handled the promotion of sporting, music, and cultural events.

Father of four children, Coke assumed control of the Shower Posse at age twenty-two following the death of his father and elder brother. Coke was known for his modesty and for avoiding the media spotlight (*Jamaica Gleaner* 2010; Hamilton and Burke 2010). In Jamaican political vernacular, TG is known as a garrison, defined by respected political scientist Rupert Lewis as "essentially a constituency in which the core of its political capacity among the grass-roots is based on the power of the area leader or don who controls the use of violence and scarce benefits and keeps the constituency aligned to the party with a huge plurality of the votes so the member of parliament is guaranteed a safe seat" (R. Lewis 2010, 16–17). As figure 6.1 shows, TG is but one of Jamaica's many inner-city enclaves of urban poverty. Of course, Coke also was just one of the country's several dons (see Allen 1980; Leslie 2010; Gunst 1996; Harriott and Katz 2015; den Held and Voss 2023).

The Saga, The Siege

A study by the Economic Commission for Latin America and the Caribbean (ECLAC), conducted at the request of the Jamaican government, explains that the areas affected by the confrontation were in the parishes of Kingston and St. Andrew, known collectively as the Western Kingston Area. It comprises Denham Town, Central Downtown, Tivoli Gardens, Fletchers Land, Hannah Town, and West Downtown, and it had a combined estimated population of 39,332, of which 41 percent is in TG. The study found that the primary population affected was just about 2 percent of the country's total populace but that a secondary population also was impacted. It defined the secondary population as the individuals in the employed labor force working in Kingston and St. Andrew. That secondary

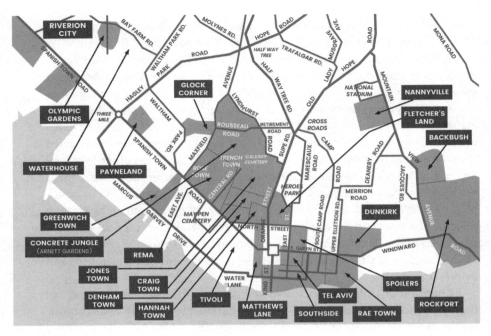

FIGURE 6.1 Map of Kingston Inner City.

Source: Imani Duncan Waite and Michael Woolcook, *Arrested Development: The Political Origins and Socio-Economic Foundations of Common Violence in Jamaica*, Brooks World Poverty Institute Working Paper 46, June 2008, 15. https://hummedia.manchester.ac.uk/institutes/gdi/publications/workingpapers/bwpi/bwpi-wp-4608.pdf/.

group accounted for 11 percent of the island's population. Thus, ECLAC found that about 349,674 individuals, representing about 13 percent of the island's population, may have been directly affected by the events (ECLAC 2010, v).

It is useful to note some of the saga's key milestones:

August 2009: An indictment was unsealed in New York against Coke for conspiracy to distribute guns and illegal drugs. That same month the United States requested extradition.

August 2009–April 2010: A combination of government and Jamaica Labor Party (JLP) efforts was made to forestall Coke's extradition.

September 2009: Although no formal contract was yet signed with the United States lobbying firm Manatt, Phelps, and Phillips, a retainer of US$49,892.62 was paid to them.

March 2010: People's National Party (PNP) parliamentarian Peter Phillips raised the matter in Parliament. Thus began a political saga. Prime Minister Golding eventually reversed himself and ordered the arrest and extradition of Coke in May 2010.

May–July 2010: A State of Emergency was declared under Section 26 of the constitution for Kingston and St. Andrew on May 23, extended on June 22 for a month and expanded to St. Catherine, and lifted on July 22.

June 2010: Coke finally was detained in St. Catherine on June 22, in the company of the Rev. Dr. Merrick "Al" Miller, reputedly on the way to the United States embassy to surrender to United States authorities.[3] The search for Coke was eventful, as his TG defenders and dons and comrades from other garrisons battled the security forces.

June 24: At a special extradition hearing at the Mobile Reserve in Kingston, Coke waived his right to an extradition trial and issued a statement through attorney Tom Tavares-Finson indicating his decision to forego the extradition trial: "I take this decision for I now believe it to be in the best interest of my family, the community of West Kingston and in particular the people of Tivoli and, above all, Jamaica. I leave Jamaica and my family, in particular Patsy, with a heavy heart, but fully confident that in due course I will be vindicated and returned to them." Coke, who was penitent over the death and destruction in TG, was flown to New York on June 24 and later arraigned there.

October 2010: A Commission of Inquiry (COI) was formed to probe the extradition and allied matters. It comprised Queen's Counsel Emil George, as chair, along with Anthony Irons and Queen's Counsel Donald Scharshmidt. After some delay caused by political wrangling, the commission undertook its work and presented its report to the governor-general in June 2011. (Aspects of the report are discussed below.)

August–September 2011: On August 31, Coke pleaded guilty, declaring, "I am pleading guilty because I am." Sentencing was set for December 8, 2011. On September 7, 2011, he sent a seven-page, handwritten leniency letter to Judge Robert Patterson offering thirteen reasons as the basis for a request for a sentence below the possible twenty-three years to which he could be sentenced.[4]

June 2012: The judge imposed the maximum sentence on Dudus: twenty-three years. Coke first was housed at the high-security Metropolitan Detention Center in Brooklyn, New York, after being extradited, and he remained there until 2013, when he was transferred to the Edgefield Federal Corrections Institution, located near the border of South Carolina and Georgia (see *New York Post* 2012; Henry and Bailey 2012).

February 2014: Appointment of the Western Kingston Commission of Enquiry, headed by Barbadian jurist Sir David Simmons. The commission report, which is discussed below, was submitted in June 2016.

May 2017: Coke was transferred to the Fort Dix Federal Correctional Institution, in New Jersey. Interestingly, the Fort Dix facility is a low-security prison with no bars, towers, or locks, where prisoners are expected to demonstrate a high degree of responsibility. Coke is scheduled to be released on July 4, 2030 (see *Caribbean Times NYC* 2017).

Costs and Consequences

The May–June 2010 TG confrontation was history-defining in terms of the scope of the violence, the extent of the deaths and destruction of property, and the political fallout, as will be seen below. But it was not the first time security forces and TG residents had engaged in battle. Among the previous confrontations were those related to the arrest of drug don Wayne "Sandokhan" Smith from West Central St. Andrew in 1988 and the arrest of Donald Phipps, better known as "Zekes," in downtown Kingston in September 1998. The arrest of Zekes resulted in three days of rioting and confrontation with the security forces, resulting in five deaths and several civilians and policemen shot and wounded (ECLAC 2010, 52).

The saga had some notable outcomes. Prime Minister Golding survived a no-confidence motion on June 1, 2010, by a 30–28 vote. On June 6, 2011, the George COI tendered its report, which was startling in its no-culpability-by-anyone conclusion and offered only four recommendations, the most notable being to separate the roles of attorney general and minister of justice, as elaboration below will show. There was substantial civil society disenchantment with the inquiry and its outcome. Notable too, the George COI proceedings amounted to a political soap opera that allowed Jamaicans and other people around the world to witness some unflattering aspects of Jamaican politics and society, as it was live-streamed.

In terms of political fallout, Golding reshuffled his cabinet on June 29, 2011, firing Attorney General and Minister of Justice Dorothy Lightbourne. He also separated the Ministry of Justice from the attorney general's chambers, as urged by the COI. Speaker Delroy Chuck was named the new minister of justice, and a few weeks later attorney Ransford Braham was appointed attorney general. Ultimately, the party lost the elections called in December 2011. During the political drama it was revealed that former PNP national security minister Peter Phillips had signed secret extradition memoranda of understanding with the United States but had not shared that fact with then–prime minister P. J. Patterson or the cabinet. However, the initial plan by the ruling JLP to bring a censure motion against Phillips was abandoned.[5]

The ECLAC study captured some of the economic and social costs of the confrontation:

> The total cost of the fall-out from the civil unrest was determined by, among other factors, the severity and duration of losses to affected sectors and activities, the cost of physical assets damaged[,] and the extent of contingency spending occasioned by its impact. Influenced by these factors, the total effect of the unrest on the economy of Jamaica was estimated at J$22,515.8 million, equivalent to US$258.8 million. The total impact represented some 2.1 percent of 2009 GDP and 50 percent of tourism GDP.

The sectoral composition of the impact indicate[s] that the productive sectors suffered the bulk of the impact (93 percent), with tourism suffering most of the losses due largely to loss of business and the outlay on marketing and advertising to encourage visitors to return. The distribution sector suffered 3.5 percent of impact nevertheless; the social fall-out in the sector would have been considerable, as a number of independent vendors were badly affected. The infrastructure sector suffered 4.8 percent of the total impact, with the bulk of the fall-out in transportation, reflecting in part the disruption of operators on the route from Kingston to a number of areas.

Productivity losses represented 0.9 percent of the total and stemmed from morbidity and loss of life, social distancing resulting in lost labor productivity. Costs to the health sector were also contained (US$1 million), while the fall-out in communication services amounted to US$2.6 million. The initial estimate for the cost of security operations was US$2.7 million, made up of US$1.5 million for the Jamaica Constabulary Force and over US$1 million for the Jamaica Defense Force and US$0.16 million for Office of the Public Defender. (ECLAC 2010, v, vi)

The political fallout also manifested itself in the September 25, 2011, announcement by Golding that he would not seek reelection as JLP leader at the party's annual general conference in November 2011. Understandably, there was speculation within and outside Jamaica about a possible direct link between Coke's plea agreement and Golding's departure; that perhaps Coke had given United States authorities information that so compromised Golding that his continued leadership became untenable; that perhaps "singing" by Dudus led to "croaking" by Golding, even though Coke's attorneys insisted there was no "singing" (Henry 2011; Cooper 2011).

In a national broadcast on October 2, 2011, Golding contextualized his announcement in relation to the then-recent death of his mother, JLP governance requirements, and the impending general elections. He also explained:

Questions about the role I played in the Coke/Manatt matter have remained a source of concern in the minds of many people. It was never about Coke's guilt or innocence. It was about a breach of our Constitution and had it been a person other than Coke it perhaps would never have become the *cause célèbre* that it turned out to be. We have since amended the Interception of Communications Act to permit in the future, the action that was taken in Coke's case but which, at that time, was in violation of our Constitution. (Golding 2011b)

The prime minister added, "However, the entire episode has affected me deeply and the perceptions that are held by some people have not been dispelled, notwithstanding the exhaustive deliberations of a Commission of Enquiry. I cannot allow the challenges we face and the issues that we as a people must confront to be smothered or overpowered by this saga and the emotions that they ignite. It would not be fair to my country; it would not be fair to my party" (Golding 2011b).

Unexpectedly, Golding raised another sobering reality: "There are other considerations that led to my decision. It is time for my generation to make way for younger people whose time has come, who are more in sync with 21st century realities, whose vision can have a longer scope and who can bring new energy to the enormous tasks that confront us" (Golding 2011b). Some in the JLP "old guard" initially rebuked Golding for what might be called his next-gen approach, but the party leadership quickly rallied around Andrew Holness, the thirty-nine-year-old education minister, who was first elected to Parliament in 1997 to represent the West Central St. Andrew constituency. On October 23, 2011, Holness became Jamaica's youngest-ever prime minister, which is another history-defining aspect of the fallout from the Dudus affair.[6]

The next general elections were due constitutionally by October 2012. Golding practiced expediency politics: he made a personal sacrifice in hopes that the leadership change would avert political disaster for his party at the polls. His survival of the no-confidence vote by a razor-thin majority in June 2010, mentioned earlier, mirrored a broad loss of confidence in his leadership within Jamaica. Additionally, TG was his constituency (since 2005). But citizens there considered him a traitor for ordering Coke's arrest and extradition. Therefore, representing that constituency no longer was tenable.

Golding's political troubles were aggravated by the economic pain Jamaicans were experiencing, although the pains derived largely from PNP pursuits when it ruled and from contemporary international economic realities beyond Golding's control. Indeed, the October 1, 2011, *Economist* lauded him, saying, "Sometimes almost despite himself, he has been Jamaica's most successful leader in decades." It credited him with restructuring Jamaica's debt, reaching an agreement with the International Monetary Fund as part of that effort, and with buttressing Jamaica's economy amid the global financial crisis. It noted also that Jamaica was the only Anglophone Caribbean nation with tourism growth and that Golding's ratings in the polls had improved from 25 percent in June 2010 to 32 percent a year later (*Economist* 2011).

Elsewhere I have posited that the Dudus affair was a manifestation of the compromising of Jamaica's internal sovereignty (Griffith 2010). As demonstrated in previous chapters, sovereignty has both internal and international dimensions; the Dudus affair compromised the former and exposed the vulnerability of the latter. Paradoxically, while the constituents of TG and other garrisons have been instrumental to electing key political elites, for several decades formal state power holders were precluded from exercising sovereign power over garrison territory the way they do over places such as Montego Bay or Ocho Rios, unless the garrison dons sanctioned this. Keep in mind that, as was observed earlier, TG is not Jamaica's only garrison. Thus, under normal circumstances, the security services are persona non grata in garrison areas. The posses (gangs) provided their own law enforcement. So in terms of law enforcement and public policy related to crime, justice, and national security, which are essential to governance and positive sovereignty, there was only a limited exercise of sovereignty by the Jamaican state over the entire national territorial and political space.

Rupert Lewis observed that "the Tivoli garrison was a mini-state within the Jamaican state system with its own system of punishment and rewards" (R. Lewis 2010, 17). And there is some credence to John Rapley's proposition: "Not all cases in which private actors have assumed state-like functions, however, involve chaos or failure. The gang-controlled communities in Jamaica, for instance, are often among the safest in the country" (Rapley 2006, 96). Complicating things were the disrespect, acts of impunity, and corruption by a number of individuals within some security and criminal justice agencies. Yet, the sovereignty impact of the Dudus affair involves more than the political vicissitudes discussed above; important too is a crucial political economy aspect. What is true for many societies is patent in Jamaica: economic inequalities are structural, and poor communities often cope with relative economic and social deprivation by being complicit with or turning a blind eye to actions by criminal gangs or individuals that provide economic and social goods not offered by the state power holders.

Surely, not that all residents in garrison communities were—or are—criminals. But in the context of survival realities, they recognized the locus of the political and economic power, and their loyalties shifted from the power holders of the official state to those within "their state." This is especially when their power brokers are able to secure contracts from the state to help meet their economic and social needs, as has been the case in Tivoli Gardens and other garrisons.[7] Indeed, TG residents affectionately called Coke their president, and some garrison residents were willing to die for him. To this point, during the siege the world saw on television signs that screamed, "After God, Dudus," and "Jesus died for us and we will die for Dudus."

In sum, then, the Dudus affair dramatized the fact that the state in Jamaica did not have a monopoly of force within the country's sovereign land territory of 10,991 km². (I say "land territory" because Jamaica's sovereign territory includes archipelagic waters of 22,000 km², a territorial sea of 17,995 km², and a contiguous zone of 21,055 km²; see R. Smith 2004). Dudus and other garrison bosses did not attempt to exercise authority over the maritime jurisdiction. Moreover, the confrontation in 2010 both repudiated the state's legal authority polemically and challenged it with the use of force. Remember too that "comrades" from other garrisons went to TG to provide reinforcement and show solidarity. This suggests that they also repudiated the official state and were prepared to confront it militarily. Thus, it is more than reasonable to view the

Dudus affair as spectacular evidence of a situation that had existed for decades: the compromising of Jamaica's security and sovereignty.

Before leaving this section, a cord of concern should be struck about another area in which the dons exercised power. As with the exercise of power in the political sphere, this arena raises serious questions about both state tolerance and capacity. An April 2013 *Jamaica Gleaner* editorial—called "Tyranny in the Ghetto"—captured an aspect of the matter thus:

> A police superintendent has this week confirmed what was often rumored about girls who have been reported missing from inner-city communities. According to Deputy Superintendent Steven Moodie, some teenage girls living in such neighborhoods are sent away by their mothers to the country, or to relatives elsewhere, to get them out of harm's way. These girls are then reported missing. By sending their daughters away, parents are trying to prevent their daughters' sexual exploitation by inner-city dons who are known to summon these girls, explained the deputy superintendent. Presumably, there are some parents who have nowhere to send their daughters, which means they have no alternative but to expose them to sexual abuse.
>
> This revelation by DSP Moodie raises serious questions about the national effort to protect our children. First, there is genuine puzzlement that the police would expose the fact that these parents have developed their own survival strategy as they fight for existence in tough, lawless, inner-city communities. And second, if the police have all this knowledge, when was the last time a so-called don was brought before the court and tried and punished for child abuse? (*Jamaica Gleaner* 2013)

Commissions of Inquiry

As noted earlier, a three-member Commission of Inquiry headed by distinguished attorney Emil George was empaneled by Governor General Sir Patrick Allen on October 19, 2010. Among other things, it was mandated to inquire into how the extradition request by the United States of America was handled by Jamaican authorities and the role and conduct of the various public officials who handled the extradition request; the circumstances surrounding the engagement of the lobbying firm Manatt, Phelps, and Phillips; and whether there was any misconduct by anyone in the matter. The panel also was asked to make recommendations for the referral of such individuals to the relevant authority or disciplinary body for appropriate action (George Commission of Inquiry 2011, 1–2).

Among other things, the George panel recommended that the positions of minister of justice and attorney general be separated, as noted earlier; that the cabinet be informed of any amendments or memoranda affecting constitutional rights of citizens; and that commissioners of inquiry be accorded the powers of a Supreme Court judge to be able to cite individuals for contempt.[8] They also proposed that the Inquiries Act should be amended to provide that commissioners are able to seek the opinion of the Jamaican Supreme Court on matters of law. They also found that the provision of Coke's telephone records to the U.S. government agencies was a breach of his constitutional rights. On the question as to whether the minister of justice should have signed the Authority to Proceed with the extradition, they found the minister acted properly, noting that the Extradition Act is the sole exception to the constitutional right to immunity from expulsion from Jamaica under Section 16 of the country's constitution.

With regard to who engaged the services of the United States lobbying firm of Manatt, Phelps, and Phillips and why this was done, they found that the order came from the JLP, the ultimate purpose being to forestall the extradition. The commission repudiated this conduct, noting that "it was imprudent for the Prime Minister to have instructed his party to deal with diplomatic matters involving US/Jamaica relations, when the party is obviously not accountable to Parliament, unlike the Minister of Foreign Affairs. It was also imprudent for any such initiative not to have been led and managed by our ambassador in Washington. Surely, that would have been the appropriate diplomatic channel, accountable through the Ministry of Foreign Affairs, to Parliament" (George Commission of Inquiry 2011, 42).

As well, the George Commission held that the prime minister's involvement with Coke's extradition was inappropriate and that the JLP should not have been involved in the matter. In the end, no one was considered guilty of any malfeasance; the commission stated:

> We have considered the question as to whether any person may be guilty of misconduct in the matters we have enquired into. By "misconduct" we accept it to be unacceptable or deliberate, dishonest, and mischievous conduct on the part of these persons engaged in the matters concerning the request for the extradition of Mr. Christopher Coke. We have found no misconduct on the part of persons we enquired into. Mistakes and errors of judgement were made, but no one in our view was guilty of misconduct in the part he or she played in the matter of the extradition of Mr. Coke. It is regrettable that the memories of some of these witnesses failed them at the Enquiry. (George Commission of Inquiry 2011, 53)

On February 21, 2014, the governor-general appointed a second Commission of Inquiry, for a more comprehensive probe. It was headed by distinguished Barbadian jurist Sir David Simmons, with the other members being Justice Hazel Harris and criminologist Professor Anthony Harriott of the University of the West Indies. The Terms of Reference were extensive, running three pages (see Simmons Commission of Inquiry 2016, 1–3). The team began its work in December 2014 and held nine sessions over a one-year period, during which evidence was heard from ninety-four individuals. Their report, which was submitted in June 2016, amounted to some nine hundred pages, including appendixes. It offered wide-ranging recommendations, all of which are captured in the sidebar presented here. Among other things, the following remarkable details were provided:

No. of security personnel killed:	39
No. of civilians killed:	69
No. of individuals detained:	4,614
No. of Detention Orders issued:	129
No. of cases that appeared before the Emergency Review Tribunal:	24
No. of rifles, shotguns, and handguns seized:	115
No. of rounds of assorted ammunition seized:	15,550

(Simmons Commission of Inquiry 2016, appendix F)

text continues on page 184

Recommendations of the Western Kingston Commission of Enquiry, 2016

PART 1—REDRESS DOING JUSTICE AND RESTORING TRUST AND CONFIDENCE IN THE STATE

1. APOLOGY

15.5. It is undoubted that the events of May 2010 have left enduring physical, psychological and emotional scars on the people of West Kingston and, in particular, the residents of Tivoli Gardens and Denham Town.

15.6. Although the operation of the security forces was justified, the manner of its execution by some members of the security forces was disproportionate, unjustified and unjustifiable. We have indicated in this Report, our disquiet and dissatisfaction about the deaths and injuries of several persons.

15.7. With a view to assuaging the hurt feelings, bitterness and resentment of the people of West Kingston and, with a view to promoting restorative justice and bringing closure to this sorry chapter in Jamaica's history, we recommend that the Government of Jamaica (GoJ) apologize in Parliament to the people of West Kingston and Jamaica as a whole for the excesses of the security forces during the operation. The Government is, in the last resort, responsible for the conduct of its security forces.

2. COUNSELLING FOR TRAUMATISED PERSONS

15.8. During the public hearings, it was evident that some witnesses are still traumatized by their experiences of May 2010. The Ministry of Justice sensitively provided counselling assistance to these persons. Nevertheless, we are satisfied that there needs to be a programme of continuing counselling for some of the residents including children. The United Nations ECLAC estimated in its report to the Government that approximately 2,500 children were witness to and affected by the events of 24 May.

15.9. We therefore recommend that this matter be pursued by the appropriate Ministry.

3. COMPENSATION FOR VICTIMS

15.10. Term of Reference (Q) which requires us to determine the adequacy of compensation to victims of the events of May 2010, implies a willingness on the part of the GoJ to adequately compensate the victims who suffered personal injuries and property damage. We find this predisposition of the Government to be admirable. It is the right thing to do. And it should be done fairly and promptly.

Establishment of a Compensation Committee

15.11. While we recognize that there is a pressing need to bring closure to this matter and, while we are conscious of the Independent Commission of Investigations (INDECOM) continuing investigations which must not be constricted, we are of the opinion that redress by way of compensation should proceed without delay. An apology alone will not meet the justice of the legitimate claims of the people of West Kingston and related areas.

15.12. Accordingly, we recommend the establishment of a Compensation Committee with two broad mandates:

(i) To investigate and determine claims for compensation for loss and damage to property and business. Since there already exists in the possession of the Ministry of Labor and Social Security (MoLSS) and the Office of the Public Defender (OPD) a substantial body of relevant and useful documentation relating to loss and damage of property, we do not envisage that this recommendation will involve a protracted exercise.

(ii) On completion of this exercise, the Compensation Committee should investigate and determine the quantum of compensation payable to injured persons and to the personal representatives of deceased persons without prejudice to the investigations of INDECOM.

15.13. We have been assured by the Public Defender, Mrs. Arlene Harrison-Henry, that the OPD is ready, willing and able to assist in the swift dispatch of (i) and (ii) above. We respectfully further recommend that the Compensation Committee be chaired by a retired judge or senior attorney-at-law, expert and experienced in the assessment of compensation for personal injuries and death, and the Committee should be directed to complete its work within 9 months.

4. WAIVER OF LIMITATION PERIOD

15.14. It has been represented to us that formal legal claims against the State for compensation in matters of the kind referred to at para.15.12 above, will be barred after 3 years in some cases of death and 6 years in all other cases. As a result, it will be too late for persons to institute litigation against the State for compensation for personal injuries, death and loss and damage to property.

15.15. We therefore recommend that the State waive its strict legal rights to all claims and agree to settle compensation on an ex gratia basis in respect of claims brought by aggrieved persons, personal representatives and/or near relations and/or dependents of deceased persons. In this regard, we again have the assurance of the OPD that it is ready, willing and able to assist in the facilitation of the procedural requirements to obtain grants of representation. We wish to make it clear that our recommendation for a waiver also applies to claims for loss and damage to property and personal injuries.

PART 2—PREVENTION

15.16. We think that the prevention of similar events turns on the following (non-exhaustive) set of measures:

i. How the responsible officers who were in various ways negligent or derelict in their duties are dealt with administratively by their respective services, that is, rewarded or punished. If they are rewarded with promotions, then others may be expected to engage in similar reward-seeking behavior. If their careers are negatively affected, then similar behavior may be discouraged. We know that human motivations are more complicated than simply responding to rewards and punishment but these things matter.

ii. Policies and doctrine[s] that better control the use of weapons systems by the security forces.

iii. Improvement in the systems of internal control within the security forces with emphasis on the special operations units that are typically deployed in cases where violent confrontations involving large numbers of gunmen are expected.

iv. Improved external, independent civilian oversight of the security forces.

v. Dismantling garrison communities.

1. ADMINISTRATIVE REVIEWS

15.17 Consistent with our findings with regard to the conduct of certain officers and other ranks of the Jamaica Constabulary Force (JCF) and the Jamaica Defence Force (JDF), we recommend that both forces undertake administrative reviews of the conduct of the named officers. It is not too late for the security forces to further examine these matters administratively as issues of internal accountability and thereby signal to their members that such matters will be treated seriously. We note that since May 2010, some of these officers have been promoted—in some cases to very senior ranks.

15.18. We recommend that the serving police officers against whom adverse findings have been made be relieved of any operational commands that they may hold and that they be prohibited from serving in any special operations units. This measure is not recommended as punishment but as a protective measure against similar abuses of power in future operations.

The Mobile Reserve

15.19. Most of the accusations of extra-judicial killings were levelled at members of the JCF who entered Tivoli Gardens on the afternoon of May 24, 2010. We have identified the units to which they belonged as elements of the Mobile Reserve.

15.20. Where the accusations of extra-judicial killings on the part of the security forces were found by this Commission to be credible, and where persons were identified as being in dereliction of duty or were administratively or operationally incompetent, we recommend that these persons should never again be allowed to lead or otherwise participate in internal security operations. The persons to whom we refer are SSP Graham, SSP Budhoo, DSP Tabannah, Sgt. Waugh and Sgt. Pratt. This point similarly applies to the commander of the JDF's Mortar Unit, Maj. Dixon. CDS Saunders, CoP Ellington, ACP Gause and DSP Turner are not included in our recommendation because they are no longer serving members of the JDF and JCF.

15.21. We further recommend that the Mobile Reserve be subjected to special external oversight arrangements. The Police Citizen Oversight Authority (PCOA) should be tasked to develop a proposal on how best to configure such oversight. Mobile Reserve's systems of internal accountability should also be reviewed—perhaps by the Inspectorate of the Police and the PCOA either in partnership or as separate and independent reviews.

2. USE OF WEAPONS SYSTEMS

15.22. Both Forces have use of force policies that set high standards of conduct which their members are required to meet. We find these policies to be appropriate. The experience of May 2010, however, suggests that there is a gap in policies that guide the selection of weapons systems that may be used in internal security operations. This issue is not and should not be narrowly regarded as an operational issue and therefore beyond the reach of the civil authorities. Innocent citizens lost their lives because of the use of inappropriate weapons systems. The citizenry must be protected by sound public policy and doctrines that should not be the preserve of the security forces only. We strongly recommend that a group of competent persons be tasked to draft such a policy.

Future Use of Mortars and Other Indirect Fire Weapons

15.23. We support the principle of the operational independence of the Chief of Defence Staff of the JDF as enshrined in the Defence Act. Thus, we are reluctant to suggest the imposition of a fetter on the independence of the Chief of Defence Staff in operational matters. However, we think that the case against the use of mortars in built-up areas is unanswerable. Contemporary international best practice and international humanitarian law do not advocate the use of such weapons in built-up areas.

15.24. We therefore recommend that, in future, the leadership of the JDF pay careful regard to contemporary best practice and learning in relation to the use of weapons of indirect fire. Consistent with international humanitarian law, the use of these weapons in built-up areas should be prohibited.

15.25. And, where their use in other settings may be contemplated, the Chief of Defence Staff (CDS) should utilize the procedure for consultation with the Prime Minister as provided for in section 9 of the Defence Act before resorting to the use of mortars or similar weapons. There should be a strict application of the relevant doctrine.

15.26. Incendiary devices should not be used.

3. IMPROVING LEGAL AND ADMINISTRATIVE ACCOUNTABILITY FOR USE OF FORCE

15.27 The evidence that was presented to the Commission revealed a pressing need to improve the administrative systems that were designed to ensure individual accountability for the use of force. In this regard, we recommend the following firearm related systems and procedures for favorable consideration by the GoJ:

a. Evidence given before the Commission of Enquiry suggested that the weapons used by the JCF are not given to ready ballistic traces. We therefore recommend that the JCF progressively change its weapons systems to developing an armory of weapons that are more traceable. In making this recommendation we recognize that we are simply endorsing a recommendation that was made by a number of earlier reports (for other stated reasons).

b. We also recommend that while the JCF should phase out from general use weapons whose use is not easily traceable, we recognize that some units of the JCF will necessarily be obliged to continue their use. But in order to promote greater accountability by these units, new and better administrative systems should be put in place for the purpose of after-action identification of the users of these types of weapons.

c. We recommend that the JCF, like the JDF, adopt the "same person same weapon" policy. That is to say, that for the service life of a weapon, it is assigned to the same person. We strongly recommend that this policy be immediately implemented in respect of the Mobile Reserve and other special operational units.

d. Specifically, we recommend that:

(i) The issuing officer and the supervisor be made accountable for the state of the records (the Firearms Register).

(ii) The PCOA be adequately resourced to be able to inspect the Firearms Register of all divisions and special operations units at least once per year.

(iii) There must be formal written responses by the responsible commanders to the inspection reports of the PCOA.

(iv) All firearm related violations and the related disciplinary actions or inactions be noted on the personal files of the offenders.

e. We recommend that the JCF institute a method of tracking and making readily available to all operational commanders the use of force records of all members of their respective units who have been the subject of accusations of the unlawful use of force against citizens.

Use of Masks or Other Concealment Gear

15.28. We accept that in some circumstances there may be justification for members of the security forces to use masks. However, we recommend that the use of masks and/or other concealment gear be limited to special cases when the identities of particular officers and units are best protected by these means. We also recommend that where masks and other concealment gear are used by entire units or groups, this be done only with the approval of the CDS and CoP for the JDF and JCF respectively. And in the case of their use by individuals who are accompanied by unmasked and uniformed or otherwise easily identifiable officers and units, approval may be granted by senior officers (superintendent of police and higher). Moreover, we recommend that in all cases, there be reliable and verifiable means of internally identifying all individuals for whom approval is given to wear masks and or other concealment gear. There must be a record of all persons for whom such approval was granted and the units to which they were assigned. It should be the responsibility of the supervising officer(s) to ensure that the conditions for accountable conduct are met.

Body-Worn Cameras

15.29. For decades there have been allegations of extra-judicial killings levelled against the security forces and, in particular, the JCF. There also seems to be a pervasive distrust of the JCF among many citizens.

15.30. The most significant and worrying feature of our Enquiry was the fact that the JCF did not acknowledge responsibility for any civilian deaths whatsoever. The JDF, for its part, gave evidence of only one such death—a sniper on the Blood Bank building. The time has surely come to usher in a radical new culture in the operations of the security forces: a culture that provides for greater transparency and accountability.

15.31. Since 2005, police forces in many countries have introduced body-worn video cameras to assist in capturing evidence in real time, to improve the quality of evidence and to provide a mechanism for greater accountability by members of police forces. The technology has been tried and tested. Rigorous evaluations have found that body-worn cameras are effective in reducing violence by police and complaints against the police. They protect both citizens and police.

15.32. This recommendation should also apply to soldiers who participate in special policing operations. Most of all, they should be routinely used in house clearing operations.

15.33. We fully appreciate that the provision of such technology will be costly but the use of the technology can be phased in according to the resources available to the GoJ. We also appreciate that amendments to legislation will necessarily be required. Nevertheless, we believe that the introduction of body-worn cameras must occur without undue delay. We therefore recommend the introduction of this type of technology.

4. ACCOUNTABILITY IN JOINT OPERATIONS—A TRANSITION COMMAND PROTOCOL

15.34. We recommend that the JDF and JCF fashion a transition command protocol that would be applied in instances of large-scale joint internal security operations. This protocol would formalise the transition of command and would include but not necessarily be limited to:

a) The names of the commander or commanders from and to whom responsibility is transferred as well as the names of the units involved;
b) The time of the transition;
c) An accounting for all detainees;
d) A preliminary accounting for the dead that would include the number of persons killed, the places where they were killed and the circumstances under which they met their deaths.
e) These matters should be reduced to writing at the earliest opportunity.

5. STRENGTHEN OVERSIGHT OF THE JCF

15.35. The structures that are responsible for the oversight of the police include the INDECOM, the PCOA and the Police Service Commission (PSC). These structures are responsible for different aspects of the oversight of the

JCF. We recommend that they be strengthened in terms of their capacities to fulfill their functions effectively.

6. OVERSIGHT OF THE JDF's INVOLVEMENT IN POLICING OPERATIONS

15.36. If there is a structural gap in the system of oversight, it is related to the JDF. Armies are treated differently from police forces. They are accountable in different ways. However, to the extent that the JDF has become routinely involved in policing and is required to play a major role in internal security operations, it is our view that this aspect of their work, that is, their policing work, should be subjected to a greater measure of external civilian oversight. In this report we limit ourselves to proposing that the principle be accepted or at least be examined by the Government and the leadership of the JDF.

7. TACKLING THE GARRISON PHENOMENON

15.37. Much focused and scholarly writing has been given to the "garrison phenomenon." Beyond our observations in Chapter 2, we shall eschew the temptation to add yet another layer of scholarship to the issue. Rather, we shall make a series of recommendations which we hope will provide a basis for meaningful action.

15.38. By way of prefatory remarks, however, we accept that in parliamentary democracies there are certain constituencies which are considered electorally safe seats for one political party or another. There is nothing unique or unsavory in that reality.

15.39. The nature of the garrison phenomenon in Jamaica is rooted in the fact that, over time, these constituencies have been allowed to become, in the popular vocabulary, "states within the State." They have their own credo and ethos. They give the appearance of living outside the mainstream of society. Promotion of a political party's interests is paramount. All else is secondary, including the rule of law. Political patronage and violence are two of the hallmarks of a garrison constituency. Criminals are highly organized and challenge the conventional societal order in order to establish and magnify their own. Fear of reprisals leads inexorably to adherence to a code of silence among law-abiding citizens who are forced, by necessity, to allow criminality to reign within the garrison constituency.

15.40. Tivoli Gardens is an example of an advanced stage garrison community. But it has been represented to us that, six years after the events of 24 May 2010, the situation in that community has ameliorated. One member of the public who submitted recommendations wrote: "Today, people are able to move freely from Arnett Gardens to Tivoli Gardens, two communities that belong to opposing political parties. There is friendly rivalry between opposing football teams. . . . This was not always so." We were also told that the influence of "Dons" is on the wane. However realistic those portents may be, we are still concerned about the concentration of illegal firearms and the emotion of pecuniary greed that exist among criminal organizations that have their headquarters within garrison communities.

15.41. The establishment of a police post within Tivoli Gardens after 24 May 2010 was and is a positive development. We recommend that this approach be replicated in those garrison constituencies where none presently exists. Such institutional strengthening is vital to the development of community policing and problem-oriented policing strategies and engendering respect for the rule of law. No democratic nation can have, within its own borders, communities that cannot be effectively and efficiently policed by the legitimate civil power. It is crucial that garrison communities be brought into mainstream existence and benefit from the services and protection provided by the State.

15.42. In addition, since "de-garrisonisation" ultimately requires consensus among political parties, we recommend

a. A bi-partisan approach leading to agreement towards the dismantling of garrison communities facilitated by an independent third party.

b. A road map for "de-garrisonisation" should be handed over to an independent body similarly structured in composition to the Electoral Commission, to develop the details of the process.

Integration of Garrison Communities

15.43. In addition to our process recommendations under the previous heading, we recommend the following (i) to (iii) infra, for urgent consideration and action by the GoJ.

(i) Political leaders, must commit themselves to ending the allocation of the Government's and the political party's resources to Dons in order to reduce the influence of these types of person[s]. In this regard, State funds for use in a constituency (e.g. Constituency Development Fund) should be administered by a representative board rather than at the direction of a Member of Parliament.

(ii) Resources should be targeted at garrison communities to facilitate the development of skills training programmes and remedial schooling for at-risk youths within those communities. We are well aware that there is a tendency to regard garrison communities as being specially deprived areas when, in fact, relative to other poor communities, they tend to be specially favored in the allocation of State funds. The implementation of this recommendation should therefore have regard for and be consistent with the principle of fair allocation of State funds.

(iii) If not currently being done, the Social Development Commission should introduce initiatives to promote and expand the work of youth clubs, sports clubs, and the Boy Scouts and Girl Guides Associations. Such organizations are useful in promoting character-building and fostering respect for discipline.

8. ACTION ON RECOMMENDATIONS OF ECLAC

15.44. Sustainable development is urgently required in addressing the problems in the low-income urban areas. There is a pressing need to attend to the social requirements of the residents, who have limited access to employment, income, housing, health and education. The physical, economic and social challenges in these communities should be attacked aggressively. Programmes directed towards positive changes in the lives of members of each community should be spearheaded by the Government.

15.45. At the request of the GoJ, ECLAC carried out a study on the impact of the events of May 2010 in Jamaica. Its report made a number of specific recommendations, which we do not set forth herein since they are readily available to GoJ. We are content to endorse those specific recommendations for urgent action by GoJ.

15.46. At a macro level, we also endorse the main conclusion of the report that a medium to long-term programme of rehabilitation and revitalization of the affected communities should be developed in order to integrate those communities into Jamaican society. Such a programme must have, at its centre, the creation of mechanisms to train, educate and assist the people in generating wealth from productive activities.

15.47. As part of a programme for inner-city renewal and development we recommend that the Government should vigorously pursue the private sector's assistance by inviting them to embrace the Urban Renewal (Tax Relief) Act. Under section 3 (1) of the Act, the Minister is empowered to declare an area "a special development area." The section reads: "S. 3 (1) The Minister may, by order, declare any area suffering from blight or urban decay to be a special development area for the purposes of the Act."

9. REVIEW AND REFORM OF THE CRIMINAL JUSTICE SYSTEM

15.48. Some memoranda which we received from members of the public tended to list specific areas of concern with discrete parts of the criminal justice system. With respect, the criminal justice system encompasses a series of stages, from investigation of crimes, through various pre-trial processes, trial, sentencing and even post-sentence decisions. We strongly counsel against a piecemeal approach to reform of the criminal justice system. We recommend that there should be a thorough-going holistic review of the existing criminal justice system followed thereafter by appropriate administrative and legislative action.

10. AMENDMENT OF EXTRADITION ACT

15.49. As the law presently stands, there is no time limit within which the Minister responsible for extradition requests must issue an authority to proceed. Extradition proceedings in the Magistrate's Courts do not involve the determination of innocence or guilt, and a fugitive is not stopped from invoking such legal challenges to the request as he/she may be advised.

15.50. We recommend that section 8 of the Extradition Act be amended to make it mandatory that the Minister make a decision on authority to proceed within a finite time.

15.51. It is recommended that where a request for the extradition of a resident or a fugitive is made and the Attorney General intends to sign the Authority to Proceed, this should not be publicized. It is further recommended that immediately upon its execution, the Attorney General should inform the Commissioner of Police.

Source: Report Western Kingston Commission of Enquiry 2016, chapter 15, http://go-jamaica.com /TivoliReport/files/assets/basic-html/page-2.html#.

As one might imagine, the report evoked considerable reaction from domestic and international actors, including a combined response from Amnesty International, a respected international advocacy group, and Jamaicans for Justice, a notable local one. They identified ten factors considered necessary to prevent a recurrence of the TG saga, many of which appeared in the comprehensive list of proposals by the Simmons panel. These included a radical new culture in the operations of the security forces, complete police reform, provision of adequate support and resources for the Independent Commission of Investigations, and assurance of special external oversight of the Mobile Reserve and review of its internal accountability.

The two advocacy organizations also asked for an apology to the residents of Tivoli Gardens, no future use of mortars in the country, counseling for traumatized witnesses and residents, full reparation to all victims, and the dismantling of garrison communities by ensuring that they benefit from state services and protection. They also advocated adherence by Jamaica to fundamental human rights treaties, including the Convention against Torture and Other Cruel, Inhuman, or Degrading Treatment or Punishment; the Convention on the Non-applicability of Statutory Limitations to War Crimes and Crimes Against Humanity; and the International Convention for the Protection of All Persons from Enforced Disappearance, among others (Amnesty International 2016).

An assessment of the governmental adaptations to the findings of the various probes and the societal responses to the aftermath of the Dudus affair is beyond the scope of this case study.[9] Nonetheless, abundant evidence has been provided here of the trauma the society experienced and the inordinate challenge to internal security and public order that this episode represented. Jamaica experienced security and sovereignty under siege, and the region and the rest of the world witnessed it.[10] Regrettably, as the case below reveals, Jamaica's experience of having its security and sovereignty besieged has not been singular, although the circumstances were different and the experience less traumatic.

The 2011 State of Emergency in Trinidad and Tobago

As indicated in chapter 4, a State of Emergency is a suspension of the normal rights of citizens and a modification of the customary functioning of the state, especially in terms of security and judicial procedures and practices. It can suspend or restrict freedoms of movement, through instituting curfews; of assembly, by curtailing or prohibiting street rallies and marches; of speech, by banning certain media or the kind of material they issue; and of due process, by removing probable cause as the basis for arrest, modifying the presumption of innocence in judicial proceedings, and modifying customary arrest, trial, and appeal procedures. Moreover, with an emergency the security forces usually acquire enhanced powers, and sometimes parliamentary business is also suspended or limited. As an extreme governance measure, the SoE is reserved for situations where the ruling officials perceive a threat to normal governance because of civil unrest, armed conflict, high crime, or natural disaster.

Declaration and Extension

The SoE being examined here is not the first one for Trinidad and Tobago; there were earlier ones in 1970 because of the army mutiny, and in 1990 in the aftermath of the Jamaat-al-Muslimeen coup attempt. One also was declared in 1995 when a parliamentary crisis developed over Speaker Occah Seapaul's refusal to vacate her office after having been involved in some litigation, a situation the ruling party deemed injurious to good governance.[11] Unlike the previous SoEs, this one dramatized the dangerous and debilitating nexus between drugs and crime, and it highlighted threats to security and sovereignty—mostly nontraditional, public security, and positive sovereignty, although there were implications for formal-legal sovereignty.

The declaration was guided by the nation's supreme law. As was explained in an FAQ posted to the Trinidad and Tobago Defense Force website at the time of the SoE:

> The Trinidad and Tobago Constitution vests constitutional and legal jurisdiction in the Office of his Excellency the President and Commander-in-Chief of the Republic of Trinidad and Tobago in accordance with section 8 (1) (a) and (b) of the Constitution of the Republic of Trinidad and Tobago to declare the issuance and/or invocation of a "Proclamation" [of] a State of Public Emergency of several grounds such as "an Act of War" under S. 8 (2) (a); a natural disaster for example, "an earthquake" under S. 8 (2) (b) and in the case of the Proclamation dated 21 August 2011 and issued by His Excellency Professor George Maxwell Richards, President and Commander-in-Chief of the Republic of Trinidad and Tobago "a situation of such a threatening nature and extensive scale that is likely to endanger the public safety or deprive the community or any substantial portion of the community of supplies or services essential to life" under S. 8 (2)(c).

Trinidad and Tobago had experienced a 5 percent reduction in reported murders and a decline in overall reported crimes from 2009 to 2010. What, then, precipitated the declaration of the SoE in 2011? In keeping with Section 9 (1) of the constitution, President George Maxwell Richards provided the answer to this question in his August 23, 2011, letter to Speaker Wade Mark. The constitution requires a statement of reasons to be sent to the Speaker within three days of a declaration and a date for parliamentary debate to be set for no later than fifteen days after the declaration. The Speaker sent the statement to the forty-one MPs the day after receiving it.[12]

The president announced that the nation had been witnessing "the tragedy of multiple murders and an upsurge in gang-related violence." For instance, there were eleven murders during one seventy-two-hour period during August 19–21. He cited credible national security intelligence about the escalation in violent crime linked to then-recent counternarcotics activities, one case being a seizure valued in excess of TT$20 million, on August 16, 2011. Consequently, "There is the real risk of reprisal and retaliation by gangs that will compromise and endanger public safety, law and order." He averred, "The present unprecedented escalation in murders and other serious acts of violence and lawlessness warrants the adoption of more decisive and stronger action to ensure the safety of the public. The majority of these murders are occurring in specified geographical areas across Trinidad and Tobago, often committed by members of criminal gangs or persons involved in the drug and arms trade." The president continued: "As a consequence of these events and facts, I am satisfied that the nature and extent of these events endangers public safety to an extent that warrants the declaration of a State of Emergency" (Alexander 2011a).

The president, who also is commander-in-chief, proclaimed the SoE on August 21, initially for fifteen days. The proclamation, shown in figure 6.3, was accompanied by issuance of the Emergency Powers Regulations, 2011. On the basis of the regulations, the following day Acting Commissioner of Police Stephen Williams issued the Emergency Powers (Curfew) Order, 2011, which is shown in figure 6.4.[13] Although the SoE was declared nationwide, the curfew—from 9:00 pm to 5:00 am—was limited to "hot spots" in six areas shown in figure 6.2: Port-of-Spain, San Fernando, Arima, Chaguanas, Diego Martin, and San Juan/Laventille.

FIGURE 6.2 SoE Hot Spots in Trinidad and Tobago in 2011.
Source: Trinidad and Tobago Police Service, 2011.

LEGAL NOTICE NO. 162
REPUBLIC OF TRINIDAD AND TOBAGO
No. 8 of 2011.

By His Excellency Professor GEORGEMAXWELL RICHARDS, T.C., C.M.T., PH.D., President and Commander-in-Chief of the Republic of Trinidad and Tobago.

GEORGE M. RICHARDS
President

A PROCLAMATION

WHEREAS it is enacted by:
(a) section 8(1) of the Constitution that the President may, from time to time, make a Proclamation that a state of public emergency exists; and
(b) section 8(2) of the Constitution that a Proclamation made by the President shall not be effective unless it contains a declaration that the President is satisfied that action has been taken or is immediately threatened by any person, of such a nature and on so extensive a scale as to be likely to endanger the public safety.

Now, therefore, I, GEORGE MAXWELL RICHARDS, President as aforesaid, in pursuance of the powers conferred upon me by section 8(1) of the Constitution hereby declare that:
(a) I am satisfied that action has been taken or is immediately threatened by persons or bodies of persons of such a nature and on so extensive a scale as to be likely to endanger the public safety; and
(b) a state of public emergency exists in the Republic of Trinidad and Tobago.

Given under my Hand and the Seal of the President of the Republic of Trinidad and Tobago, at the Office of the President, St. Ann's, this 21st day of August, 2011.

FIGURE 6.3 Proclamation of the State of Emergency in Trinidad and Tobago 2011.
Source: Trinidad and Tobago Gazette Legal Supplement 50, no. 108, August 31, 2011.

The combined resources of the Trinidad and Tobago Police Service (TTPS) and the Trinidad and Tobago Defense Force (TTDF) were employed, with the TTPS leading. As with any SoE, the security forces had enhanced powers. For example, search and seizure powers did not require search warrants. Besides, TTDF members were permitted to stop and search for firearms; enter and search any premises; arrest and detain individuals; and stop and search any person, vehicle, or vessel. They could arrest and detain people for up to twenty-four hours, after which a magistrate or assistant superintendent of police (or higher rank) could add an extra seven days.

THE EMERGENCY POWERS REGULATIONS, 2011

ORDER

MADE BY THE COMMISSIONER OF POLICE UNDER REGULATION 4 OF THE
EMERGENCY POWERS REGULATIONS, AND BY VIRTUE AND IN EXERCISE
OF ALL OTHER POWERS ENABLING HIM IN THAT BEHALF

THE EMERGENCY POWERS (CURFEW) ORDER, 2011

1. This Order may be cited as the Emergency Powers (Curfew) Order, 2011.

2. This Order applies to the areas described in the Schedules and such areas as are declared Curfew Areas for the purpose of the Emergency Powers Regulations, 2011.

3. Subject to the exemption hereinafter provided, no person shall be out of doors in the areas and at the times specified in the Schedules without a permit in writing of the Commissioner of Police or such other person or authority as may be authorized by him for the purpose and any such permission may be granted subject to such conditions as may be specified therein.

4. A person shall be exempted from the requirement to be in possession of a permit, who, on being required so to do by any police officer or member of the Defense Force in uniform, produces evidence that he is– (a) a police officer or member of the Defense Force who is on duty;

(b) a person who is the holder of a permit as mentioned in paragraph 3.

5. (1) A permit referred to in paragraph 3 may be obtained upon written application to the officer in charge of a police station.

(2) An applicant for a permit referred to in paragraph 3 shall provide to the officer in charge of the police station to whom the application is made, his name, home address and, if employed, work address and telephone number or numbers, if more than one.

FIGURE 6.4 Trinidad and Tobago Curfew Order 2011.
Source: *Trinidad and Tobago Gazette* Legal Supplement 50, no. 109, August 22, 2011.

The SoE was extended on September 4 through December 5. But the curfew was modified: from 11 pm to 4 am. On September 13, authorities added eleven new hot spots. As shown in figure 6.2, the areas are Toco, Carli Bay, Cedros, Moruga, Dow Village, McBean in Couva, Chase Village in Carapichaima, Claxton Bay, Maloney, Windy Hill in Arouca, and La Horquetta. The curfew also was extended along 362 kilometers of coastline within a radius of three nautical miles. The SoE featured in Parliament over several days. It first was debated on September 2, 2011, when the national security minister, Brigadier (Ret.) John Sandy, introduced a motion called "Basis for the Declaration of the State of

> **Motion: Extension of State of Emergency**
>
> **WHEREAS** it is enacted by section 8(1) of the Constitution of the Republic of Trinidad and Tobago that the President may from time to time make a Proclamation declaring that a state of public emergency exists:
>
> **AND WHEREAS** the President has by Proclamation made on the 21st day of August, 2011, declared that a state of emergency exists in the Republic of Trinidad and Tobago:
>
> **AND WHEREAS** it is enacted by section 9(2) of the Constitution that a Proclamation made by the President for the purposes of and in accordance with section 8 shall, unless previously revoked, remain in force for fifteen days:
>
> **AND WHEREAS** it is enacted by section 10(1) of the Constitution that before its expiration the Proclamation may be extended from time to time by resolution supported by a simple majority vote of the House of Representatives, so however that no extension exceeds three months and the extensions do not in the aggregate exceed six months:
>
> **AND WHEREAS** it is necessary and expedient that the Proclamation made by the President on the 21st day of August, 2011 declaring that a state of emergency exists in the Republic of Trinidad and Tobago, should be extended for a further period, not exceeding three months:
>
> **NOW, THEREFORE, BE IT RESOLVED,** that the Proclamation made by the President on the 21st day of August, 2011 declaring that a state of emergency exists in the Republic of Trinidad and Tobago be extended for a further period of three months.
>
> *(By the Minister of National Security)*

First Debated: 03-Sep-2011

Approved on: 4-Sep-2011

Source: Parliament of Trinidad and Tobago

FIGURE 6.5 Motion to Extend the State of Emergency in Trinidad and Tobago 2011.

Source: Parliament of Trinidad and Tobago, 2011. https://www.ttparliament.org/motions/extension-of-state-of-emergency-2/.

Emergency": "BE IT RESOLVED that the House take note of the Statement by the President under Section 9(1) of the Constitution setting out the specific grounds on which the decision to declare the existence of a State of Public Emergency was based."[14] The motion was approved the same day.

Sandy elaborated on aspects of the president's statement of reasons and asserted that if the government had not instituted the SoE, the loss of lives and similar consequences that could have occurred "would have made the events of 1990 look like a garden party" (Alexander 2011b). He mentioned receiving intelligence on Sunday, August 21—the day the SoE was declared—that prompted recommending that the prime minister convene a meeting of the National Security Council. An emergency meeting of the cabinet also was called before the president's concurrence on the SoE was sought (Alexander 2011c). The debate continued the following day, focusing on a motion to extend the emergency for three months. That motion was approved on September 4. During that debate Prime Minister Kamla Persad-Bissessar asserted, "Well before Sunday[,] August 21st, 2011, this country was in a state of emergency. The criminals had declared open war on the citizenry. The majority of the population was living in self[-]imposed curfew, hiding in their own private jails while the criminals who placed them there, roamed free" (Persad-Bissessar 2011).

The prime minister justified the SoE thus:

Renowned politician and Father of the Indian Constitution, Dr. R. Ambedker, reminds us that: "Law and Order are the medicine of the body politic and when the body politic gets sick, medicine must be administered." The paramount obligation of the Government is to protect its citizens and guarantee liberty.

Aristotle, one of the founding fathers of democracy once said "the basis of a democratic state is liberty." A constitutional democracy is essentially a pact between the citizen and the State. When the State breaches this pact because it is unable to fulfill its obligations to guarantee basic fundamental rights and freedoms, such as life, liberty and security, then the rule of law is fractured.

The Constitution is a sacred document however[;] its sanctity is derived from the respect people have for it. However, with the violent and heartless criminal element responsible for rivers of blood that flowed through our streets in the past 10 years[,] we lost our faith in the State's ability to guarantee our rights. The state of emergency is a restoring of the State's ability to guarantee those rights and freedoms to its citizenry. This is a means to an end—the means is the state of emergency and the end is restoration of our rights and freedoms. (Persad-Bissessar 2011)

Prime Minister Persad-Bissessar provided a comparative crime portrait, noting:

- Between 1995 and 2001, there were 789 murders, or 112 per year.
- Between 2002 and 2009, there were 2,853 murders, or 357 per year.
- Between 2002 and 2009, murders increased by 218 percent on average per year compared to between 1995 and 2001.
- Between 2003 and 2009, there were 126,978 serious crimes, of which 3,082 were murders.

(Persad-Bissessar 2011)

Persad-Bissessar used a local adage in her sobering assessment of the nation's crime crucible: "Old wisdom says that, if a frog is placed in boiling water, it will jump out, but if it is placed in cold water that is slowly heated, it will not perceive the danger and will be cooked to death. We were like the proverbial frog being slowly cooked to death by the escalating crime." She added, "Some of us have become so immune to the heat that we are unable to recognize that if we let this state of affairs continue it will eventually render Trinidad and Tobago a 'Failed State,' where crime and violence becomes the norm, and a lawless society takes over, driving law-abiding people out" (Persad-Bissessar 2011).

Rights and Realities

As noted earlier, the potential for infringement of civil and political rights always is a matter of concern in States of Emergency; Trinidad and Tobago was no exception. The prime minister refuted the assertion that citizens lost their rights during the SoE, noting that "apart from the tribunal established by the Chief Justice for detainee[s], their normal rights to access the High Court remains. Persons arrested and charged for criminal offenses still enjoy their Constitutional rights" (Persad-Bissessar 2011). Moreover, she explained that the rights to legal representation, prompt court appearance, and habeas corpus remained intact. Both the prime minister and Minister Sandy refuted allegations of racial profiling during the SoE. Sandy noted that the majority of murder victims and prisoners were people of African descent. "It is people who look like me who are being murdered all the time, people who look like my mother who are weeping and crying for their sons and daughters," he said. Appealing to his "brothers and sisters," he cited a case where one victim in San Juan had left fifteen children as survivors (Alexander 2011b).

Minister Sandy presented some startling data to show the severe impact on Afro-Trinidadians. When his figures are viewed in proportional terms, one finds the following:

- Of the people arrested for murder in 2006, 57.6 percent were Afro-Trinidadians, and of the people imprisoned that year, 57.2 percent were Afro-Trinidadians.
- Of the people arrested for murder in 2007, 78.8 percent were Afro-Trinidadians, and of the people imprisoned that year, 53.7 percent were Afro-Trinidadians.
- Of the people arrested for murder in 2008, 78.1 percent were Afro-Trinidadians, and of the people imprisoned that year, 53.5 percent were Afro-Trinidadians.
- Of the people arrested for murder in 2009, 75.7 percent were Afro-Trinidadians, and of the people imprisoned that year, 57.1 percent were Afro-Trinidadians.

- Of the people arrested for murder in 2010, 67.7 percent were Afro-Trinidadians, and of the people imprisoned that year, 53.9 percent were Afro-Trinidadians.

(Alexander 2011b)[15]

Beyond the charges of racial profiling, there were credible allegations of impropriety by members of the security forces. Sandy acknowledged as much on October 18, 2011, at a training program involving the Police Complaints Authority (PCA) and the Joint Partnership Project on Criminal Justice (Bethel 2011; Kowlessar 2011). Police impropriety predates the SoE, though. For instance, the 2011 Amnesty International's submission to the United Nations cited excessive use of force by TTPS members and several cases of alleged unlawful killings and ill treatment. During 2008 some forty people reportedly were killed by the police; in 2009 the figure was thirty-nine. Many of the killings spawned violent community protests. The report also noted that the PCA's work was hindered by the absence of a director for almost three years, until December 2010; and in February 2011 a backlog of one thousand complaints was identified. It also mentioned the confession in July 2008 by Acting Commissioner of Police James Philbert that "the Police Service owed the nation an apology for the poor quality of policing experienced by some sectors of society over the years" (Amnesty International 2011).

Unless indefinite martial law is imposed, no government could afford an SoE of too long duration or to have an SoE as an end-in-itself strategy. Trinidad and Tobago was no different. December 5 had been set as the endgame, although it could have been be extended. As well, during the September 4 parliamentary debate, the prime minister recounted supplementary criminal justice, social, and other measures and programs intended to mitigate against some of the underlining and ancillary issues involved in their Problems Without Passports. Some of the measures were under way; others were to be developed (Persad-Bissessar 2011).

The prime minister declared, "The State of Emergency is not our last card" (Persad-Bissessar, 2011). Additional efforts were to include continuing to target gang leaders and criminals who peddle drugs and guns, retrieve guns and ammunition, or target "businesses" that support criminal activity or provide "cover" to them. She promised proactive initiatives along with community policing at the end of the SoE. She also cited existing social support measures that aid single mothers, children, and senior citizens and noted the then-impending Morvant-Laventille Initiative as another component of the community support package to be offered as an alternative to the criminality within communities.

As might be expected, there were bumps along the implementation road in relation to some measures, one being in the anti-gang area where there were difficulties with aspects of the Anti-Gang Act passed that year. The difficulties included the fact that the new law created offenses for which there was no local guidance on how to interpret its provisions and absence of clarity regarding what qualifies as proof of the existence of a gang. In one case in September, twenty-one individuals arrested under the new law had to be released after the director of public prosecutions (DPP) acknowledged insufficient evidence to prosecute. On October 16, 2011, Assistant Superintendent of Police (ASP) Joanne Archie reportedly confirmed that some arrests had been halted since September pending the receipt of advice from the DPP. But, said the report, "ASP Archie said there are some pieces of crime legislation which the police need to get the DPP's advice on, but the Anti-Gang Act was not one of these." Deputy Commissioner of Police Jack Ewatski himself admitted the evidence challenge. Indeed, Cedric "Burkie" Burke and his driver, Keon Bain, once considered "big fish" by the police, were among those who were released for insufficient evidence (D. Khan 2011; Alexander 2011a; Baboolal 2011).

The 2011 SoE was extraordinary for several reasons. First, although there have been such cases previously, generally SoE declarations are not prompted by violent crime that is not politically motivated or connected.[16] Second, this SoE was a defining moment for Kamla Persad-Bissessar's eighteen-month-old coalition government, which inherited numerous challenges, crime and violence being among the most serious. The coalition government raised expectations about its ability to deliver "the public goods," of which security—and positive sovereignty—occupied a place of prominence. Third, although Persad-Bissessar downplayed this, she inherited from Patrick Manning the role of CARICOM lead on security, which has occupied a place of prominence within the formal CARICOM architecture having been declared the Fourth Pillar of the Caribbean Community in 2006. Thus, Prime Minister Persad-Bissessar was under the spotlight in that role. Other Caribbean leaders were observing her conduct, looking for a model to emulate or repudiate in their own nations.

Thus, it was natural that security would occupy a place of prominence in the 2012 budget that was presented to Parliament in October 2011 by Finance Minister Winston Dookeran:

> Indeed, it is the Government's duty to protect our citizens and our country. . . . Mr. Speaker, as we look ahead, the policy platform will focus on three priorities. . . . Job creation: with projects for poverty reduction and a range of measures to close the equity gap; Investment: which will include creation of entrepreneurial opportunities and an innovation-driven economy to stimulate growth and competitiveness through public/private investment; and Security: which will involve the continued implementation of strategies for crime reduction, effective containment, and a climate of law and order. (Government of Republic of Trinidad and Tobago 2011, 4, 5–6, 11)

The prominence was reflected tangibly in the line-up of the top six expenditure areas, with national security being ahead of agriculture, housing, and health:

Education and Training: TT$8,717.8 million
Infrastructure (including Works, Public Utilities,
    and Transport):   TT$6,995.4 million
National Security: TT$5,170.5 million
Health: TT$4,724.9 million
Housing: TT$1,970.0 million
Agriculture: TT$1,954.3 million.
           (Government of the Republic of Trinidad and Tobago, 2011, 48)

Results and Risks

Two "r" words—"results" and "risks"—likely would be uppermost on the minds of the political directorate of any nation with a State of Emergency. The SoE attracted broad national support, judging from the results of polls conducted by the *Trinidad Express* and the North American Caribbean Teachers Association and endorsement by corporate, civic, and other leaders (Swamber 2011; *Trinidad Guardian* 2011b; John-Lall 2011). The results between the start of the SoE on August 21 and October 23 included the following:

Gang-related arrests: 449
Drug offenses: 912
Breach of curfew: 405
Traffic offenses: 1,102
Firearms seized: 145
Homicide investigations: 67
Ammunition seized: 12,522 rounds and 31 magazines
Outstanding warrants resolved: 1,338
Total individuals arrested: 5,073 [17]

By the time the SoE ended on December 5, 2011, more than seven thousand people had been detained, some without any charges levied against them. Curiously, the following October, Jack Warner, the new minister of national security, announced that the government would suspend the release of crime statistics for an unspecified period in order to avoid "sensationalizing" crime. However, the acting commissioner of police felt that Minister Warner lacked the authority for such action and signaled his intention to continue releasing relevant information.

The SoE exposed some of the weaknesses in the criminal justice system. For instance, one report issued shortly after the end of the SoE highlighted shortcomings related to the approach to gang control. It noted that during the SoE, "242 persons were arrested under the Anti-Gang Act (2011) of Trinidad and Tobago. The Act, which defines a gang as 'a combination of two or more persons, whether formally or informally organized, that, through its membership or through an agent, engages in any gang related activity' makes it illegal to belong to a gang (2011: p. 3)" (Seepersad and Williams 2012, 61). But, said the report, "all persons detained under this Act were subsequently released, either because there was insufficient evidence or no evidence at all. Quite apart from the circularity of the definition, law enforcement and intelligence capabilities are limited, such that the capacity to deal with crime generally, and gangs specifically, is severely curtailed" (61).

The authorities viewed the following tangibles and intangibles as among the SoE results: the functioning of the National Security Operational Centre and of the Maritime Security Plan; over 50 percent reduction in the homicide rate during the SoE period; the dismantling of gangs and the gathering of intelligence related to gang operations; discovery of a billion-dollar illegal bunkering of diesel racket; seizure and destruction of some one billion dollars' worth of illegal drugs; restoration of a sense of safety by citizens and renewal of the "social contract" between citizens and the state, reflected in the more than eight hundred hotline phone calls received; and independent poll results indicating more than 80 percent support for the SoE.[18]

Skeptics rightly feared that the SoE carried serious risks, including possible subpar achievement of strategic and tactical goals for arresting criminals, disrupting gangs, seizing drugs and guns, and removing the climate of fear. The authorities also risked reduced business activities, with consequent revenue shortfalls (*Trinidad Guardian* 2011b). As well, my own view is that had the SoE been extended beyond December 2011, a siege mentality by citizens likely would have developed, the criminals would have adapted to the new security dispensation, and the equivalent of the law of diminishing security returns would have resulted. Moreover, the longer the SoE was maintained, the greater the likelihood of negative domestic and other impacts, especially on tourism and commerce. The authorities risked stirring societal wrath had the SoE been extended into the Christmas and Carnival seasons. Beyond these risks, regardless of the duration of the SoE and its results, unless the republic's leaders meaningfully address the conditions that conduce to drugs and crime more, SoEs might become necessary in the future.[19]

Earlier chapters have provided undeniable evidence that drugs and crime are clear and present dangers in the Caribbean; they are PWPs with a multiplicity of negatives for the citizens and states of the region. Similarly, this chapter has offered proof positive that the dangers are heightened when guns and gangs are actively involved. Moreover, the decibel levels of security and sovereignty threats are raised considerably when the legitimate rulers are confronted not just with voice but with violence. The two cases examined here were—and are—wake-up calls with many lessons learned, not just for Jamaica and Trinidad and Tobago but for the entire Caribbean, and indeed to nations elsewhere. Evidently, they have been clear manifestations of challenged sovereignty. The security and sovereignty dynamics take on additional features when geopolitics is added to the already multidimensional geonarcotics matrix. Any skepticism about this proposition should be dispelled after we probe some of the "intermestic"—international and domestic—elements in the case of Suriname in the chapter that follows.

7

Dynamics of Geonarcotics and Geopolitics

> Elections, open, free, and fair, are the essence of democracy,
> the inescapable sine qua non. Governments produced
> by elections may be inefficient, corrupt, shortsighted,
> irresponsible, dominated by special interests, and
> incapable of adopting policies demanded by the public
> good. These qualities may make such governments
> undesirable, but they do not make them undemocratic.
> —Samuel Huntington, *The Third Wave:
> Democratization in the Late Twentieth Century*

> Elections in Latin America [and the Caribbean] keep
> showing that the region retains its capacity to surprise
> observers, as well as a potential to generate expectations.
> —Roberto Espíndola, "New Politics, New Parties?"

The late renowned political scientist Samuel Huntington reminds us of the possible imperfections and inherent contradictions of democracy *in practice*, especially when the analysis relates to nations where democracy has experienced uncomfortable roller coaster rides. Suriname is one such nation, and its roller coaster rides have included challenges related to drugs. As well, although Robert Espíndola's analysis does not include Suriname, his observation in the second epigraph above resonates powerfully with that country. The elections of 2010 in Suriname surely had surprising outcomes, the most significant of which was the reemergence of Désiré Delano (Desi) Bouterse as national leader, this time through democratic means.

Bouterse's reemergence has had both internal and external implications. Internally, it has generated hopes about political unity and improved quality of life, among other things. Externally, it has raised geopolitical anxieties because of his colorful history and profile: a two-time coup maker and authoritarian ruler (1980–1987; 1990–1991); the only world leader with the dubious distinction of an eleven-year prison sentence for drug trafficking, issued in absentia by a Dutch court, with extradition foreclosed because Suriname and Holland lack mutual extradition treaties; and defendant (along with others) in a trial for ordering the murder of fifteen political opponents in 1982. The results of the elections raised anxieties in relation to geonarcotics as well as geopolitics. This chapter explores some of these anxieties by discussing some aspects of the country's geonarcotics milieu and some of the geopolitical dynamics of the territorial disputes with Guyana. It then goes on to discuss Bouterse's conviction in November 2019 for murders committed in 1982 and his political demise following the May 2020 elections. But it is essential first to recall the political contestation that brought him to power.[1]

Bouterse's Political Resurrection

In 1996 the late Gary Brana-Shute, cultural anthropologist and Suriname expert, noted the following in a study on Suriname's civil-military relations: "Can we expect any more coups in Suriname? No, I am absolutely sure of that. Will Bouterse and his allies go away? No, I am very certain of that too, now that they have a well-funded political machine—the NDP [National Democratic Party]—that has surprisingly wide support" (Brana-Shute 1996, 482). Brana-Shute was eerily prophetic. Not only did Bouterse not go away, but he returned in 2010 to the pinnacle of political power, this time legitimated through a key democracy factor: elections. I attribute a significant aspect of this outcome to his political acumen in exploiting the country's political circumstances, especially the ethnic plurality and the shortcomings of the incumbent rulers and aggregating various political interests to deliver De Mega Combinatie (Mega Combination) as a coalition force.[2]

In terms of political systems, Suriname is a constitutional republic, with an executive branch headed by a president, a fifty-one-member unicameral legislature called the National Assembly, which is popularly elected for five-year terms on the basis of proportional representation, and a judiciary. The president is elected by a two-thirds majority of the National Assembly or, failing that, by a majority of the People's Assembly, for a five-year term. If at least two-thirds of the National Assembly cannot agree to vote for one presidential candidate, a People's Assembly is formed from all National Assembly delegates and regional and municipal representatives who were elected by popular vote in the most recent national elections. A vice president, normally elected at the same time as the president, needs a simple majority in the National Assembly or People's

Assembly to be elected for a five-year term. The president serves as head of state and head of government and is supreme commander of the armed forces. He also presides over the Council of State, which oversees the execution of government policy, and the National Security Council.[3]

Political Contestation

The May 25, 2010, elections were contested by seven political parties: AC: A Combinatie (A Combination); BVD: Basispartij voor Vernieuwing en Democratie (Basic Party for Renewal and Democracy); MC: Mega Combinatie (Mega Combination); NDP: Nationale Democratische Partij (National Democratic Party); NFDO: Nieuwe Front voor Democratie en Ontwikkeling (New Front for Democracy and Development); PDOE: Partij voor Democratie en Ontwikkeling door Eenheid (Party for Democracy and Development through Unity); and VVV: Volksalliantie voor Vooruitgang (People's Alliance for Progress). As with most elections in the Americas—and elsewhere—over the last few decades, the elections were monitored by international observers from the Organization of American States and CARICOM. The observers found no evidence of fraud, although the OAS team did offer six specific recommendations for future improvement.

As often happens in plural societies where race and ethnicity are just as important as—and sometimes more important than—substantive issues when it comes to interest articulation and voting, race and ethnicity featured in Suriname. The results were widely mixed, with no single majority winner. Seventy-three percent of the 324,490 eligible voters cast their votes. The AC group won 4.7 percent of the votes and seven parliamentary seats; BVD, 5.1 percent and no seats; MC, 40.2 percent and twenty-three seats; NFDO, 31.7 percent and fourteen seats; PDOE, 5.1 percent and one seat; and VVV, 13 percent and six seats.[4]

Thus, since no political party won a decisive mandate, coalition building became necessary. After almost two months of political negotiations, on July 19, 2010, Desi Bouterse emerged as head of the MC slate and the ninth president of the republic, having formed a multiethnic coalition that delivered thirty-six votes. Robert Ameerali, an Independent and former head of the chamber of commerce and industry, was elected as vice president. Ameerali's nomination itself demonstrated Bouterse's acumen; it resulted from a deal stuck with a political nemesis, Ronnie Brunswijk, former head of the guerrilla group called the Jungle Commandos, which battled Bouterse's military government in the 1980s and later became the leader of the AC group (Republic of Suriname 2010; Carroll 2010; *West Indian News* 2010; [Suriname] *Daily Herald* 2010).

One report noted that instead of playing down his past, Mr. Bouterse boldly celebrated it, designating February 25, the date of the coup in 1980, as a national holiday, calling it the "day of liberation and renewal" (Romero 2011). The report also observed that while Bouterse promised not to interfere in the murder case against him, he named one of his codefendants in the trial ambassador to France, showing little deference to the legal cloud hanging over them. Moreover, he placed his wife, Ingrid Bouterse-Waldring, on the government payroll, paying her about US$4,000 a month for her first lady duties, and named his son, Dino Bouterse, who had been convicted in 2005 of heading a cocaine and illegal weapons ring, as part of the command of a new counterterrorism unit. Earlier, Dino also had been arrested in connection with a 2002 weapons theft from Suriname's intelligence agency (Romero 2011).

Bouterse's presidency was guided by pragmatism and national interest rather than ideology. He provided a clue to what he deemed his "development diplomacy" approach during his speech in the National Assembly in October 2010:

> The realization of the national development goals will be central in our interactions with other countries and international organizations, mindful of the policy principle that foreign policy must contribute to national development. The foreign policy will serve to support sectors that are central to the national development, such as agriculture and mining, education, health care, rural development, poverty alleviation and environmental protection. With regard to Suriname this implies a reorientation of the regular diplomacy to a development-oriented diplomacy, with more attention being paid to new subjects such as poverty alleviation, food security, the protection of upcoming business and industries, and the impact of climate change. In this concept the contribution of recognized NGOs and Surinamese will be of great value in the Diaspora. This development diplomacy will be aimed at optimizing effectiveness and productivity of international cooperation on behalf of national development. (Bouterse 2010, 6)

Notwithstanding Bouterse's charisma and campaign skills, his earlier drug entanglements raised a "back to the future" specter in some international quarters. Bouterse's profile included having been a soldier, a coup plotter, a military ruler, a convicted drug trafficker, and, for more than a decade, a fugitive from Interpol. Moreover, for a while he was on trial for the murder of fifteen top opponents. Thus, there was apprehension in some international quarters about aspects of his profile related to drugs, the use of force, and the possible conduct of state affairs. One *New York Times* report captured the skepticism thus: "Now, Mr. Bouterse, 65, is leader of this small South American nation yet again, stirring fears of a possible return to the time when Suriname, once a magnet for Western mercenaries and Colombian drug cartels, was renowned for its openness to criminal enterprise" (Romero 2011). Thus, an analysis of developments on the geonarcotics front is necessary.

On the Geonarcotics Front

Apart from Bouterse's conviction, over time his son and several senior military officials have been implicated in narcotics smuggling. For instance, in 1986 Etienne Boerenven, then the Suriname Defense Force's second in command, was arrested in Miami, convicted of drug trafficking, and sentenced there. He was deported from Florida in May 1991 after serving five years of a twelve-year prison sentence. In March 1998, Ronnie Brunswijk, a former Bouterse bodyguard who later became his nemesis, was convicted of drug trafficking in Holland and sentenced in absentia to eight years in prison.

In April 1999, Brazil's TV Globo reported allegations that Rupert Christopher, Suriname's ambassador in Brazil and a former defense minister under Bouterse, was implicated in the drug trade with Bouterse. Earlier that year, Bouterse's son, Dino, reportedly was recalled from Suriname's embassy in Brazil after authorities found evidence that he had been using his diplomatic immunity to smuggle drugs. In August 1999 Interpol issued an international arrest warrant on Belgium's behalf for Ruben Peiter, commander of the Suriname police mobile unit. Belgium suspected that Peiter was shipping cocaine in timber consignments. In August 2005 Dino Bouterse was convicted in Paramaribo and sentenced to eight years in prison for trafficking in drugs and weapons. He secured an early release (see Griffith 1997; Bohning 1999; Brana-Shute 2000; Kuipers 2010).[5]

Trafficking Entanglements

Marijuana is cultivated in Suriname, although mostly for domestic consumption. However, Suriname produces no cocaine, heroin, or methamphetamines, which feature prominently in trafficking there. Thus, an understandable question in terms of geonarcotics is: What explains Suriname's deep involvement in trafficking? As with any nation so involved, there is no single-factor explanation. Corruption, economic deprivation, and law enforcement resource constraints are relevant factors. Nevertheless, geography is a major factor in several respects.

Suriname is just a stone's throw away from Colombia, a major cocaine and heroin production (and marijuana cultivation) center. It also is close to Venezuela, a major drug conduit, and it shares a 600-kilometer border with Guyana and a 593-kilometer border with Brazil, both of which feature prominently in drug transshipment from South America to the United States, Europe, and Africa, often for rerouting to Europe and the United States. Also, Suriname is less than 3,000 miles away from most popular drug destinations in the United States, a key demand country. For instance, Paramaribo is just 2,154 miles from Miami and 2,655 miles from Washington, D.C. While it is farther away from key drug demand countries in Europe—4,659 miles from Amsterdam and 4,437 miles from London, for instance—commercial and social networks in those countries make the trafficking journeys worthwhile for the illegal drug operators.

Yet, it is not merely a matter of physical geography; social geography is also a factor. Suriname has a little over 600,000 people in its 163,270 square kilometers of territory, as table 2.1 shows. It is four times the size of the Netherlands, its former colonial ruler, and about the same size as the state of Georgia in the United States, which has a little fewer than 10 million people. Thus, Suriname has a very low population density. In addition, as with French Guiana to its east and Guyana to its west, Suriname's population lives mostly along the coast. Consequently—and this is true of Guyana and French Guiana as well—most of the nation's territory is both under-peopled and under-policed. This combination provides vulnerability to drug trafficking (and other illegal activities) as well as opportunity for traffickers and other illegal operators.

Thus, a second understandable question is this: In light of the factors described above, was Bouterse likely to establish a narco state? The salience of this question increased for some individuals with the January 2011 WikiLeaks cable revelation. It was alleged that United States embassy officials in Suriname had filed reports to headquarters that Bouterse had continued his drug dealings even after his 1999 conviction, supposedly until 2006, when he was still a Member of Parliament, and that some of his ventures involved links with Guyanese Roger Khan ([Suriname] *Daily Herald* 2011). Khan, who had been arrested in Suriname in June 2006 and whisked away to the United States through Trinidad and Tobago, was sentenced in October 2009 to forty years in prison in New York, having been convicted on drug trafficking and related charges.

Clearly, with a 2018 unemployment rate of almost 7 percent, a 2018 per capita GDP of under US\$10,000, and almost three-quarters of the population engaged in the low-wage service sector, economic deprivation is still a challenge for Suriname. Indeed, as noted earlier, Bouterse won Suriname's presidency partly because of a pledge to improve the country's economic and social conditions. According to one influential source, in 2015 poverty affected nearly one out of every two people; the official poverty rate at that time was 47 percent.[6] Scott MacDonald, chief economist at Smith's Research and Gradings, explained that bauxite's role in the Surinamese economy was key through the 1980s, but a series of developments impacted the sector negatively. Alcoa and other companies faced increasing competition through the 1970s and into the 1980s, and starting in the 1970s bauxite-producing countries demanded more say over prices and revenues. As if this were not enough, between 1986 and 1992 operations of the bauxite companies were affected by the "Interior War."[7] Thus, by the early years of the twenty-first century, it was becoming clear that Suriname had exhausted its best sources of bauxite, was unable to accommodate the deeper draft ships that typically transport alumina, and faced intense competition from other bauxite producers (MacDonald 2019b, 3).

Global dynamics also factored into the equation; there was a sharp decline in oil and gold prices on the world market, with the result that from 2014 to 2016, the economy contracted by 9 percent while inflation surged, unemployment rose, and government finances deteriorated. Although the International Monetary Fund (IMF) and Suriname worked together to stabilize the situation, there were disagreements that made the relationship more challenging, according to one analyst (MacDonald 2019b, 3). However, there was some economic recovery between 2017 and 2019. Indeed, one economist explained that real GDP went positive again in 2017, at 1.7 percent, and climbed to 2.0 percent in 2018, with the IMF forecasting 2.2 percent for 2019. Moreover, inflation fell back to the single digits, unemployment shifted to more manageable numbers, and the current account balance of payments, which had declined steeply, showed a small surplus in 2018 (MacDonald 2019b, 3).

Understandably, Suriname's economic upturn did not eliminate the corruption there, which is a key facilitator of narcotics production and trafficking. Moreover, the economic, political, and geographic realities of neighboring countries, such as Brazil, French Guiana, Guyana, and Venezuela, did not reduce those countries' contribution to Suriname's vulnerability to trafficking.

Troubling but No Narco State

The 2021 *International Narcotics Control Strategy Report* indicates that Suriname is not a source country for illegal drugs or precursor chemicals but continues to serve as a transshipment point for illicit substances—for South American cocaine en route to Europe and, to a lesser extent, the United States and Africa. As with other places, cargo containers carry most of the illegal product through Suriname, but smaller fishing vessels, commercial and private planes, and human couriers are used as well. Importantly too the country's sparsely populated coastal areas and dense jungles, and weak border controls and infrastructure, conduce to aid the trafficking (U.S. Department of State 2021, 211, 212).

The sidebar, "Suriname Trafficking Portrait, 2006–2020," provides a glimpse of some of the country's geonarcotics realities four years before Desi Bouterse's rise to power and for the duration of his presidency. It paints a troubling portrait in many respects, including the conviction of Bouterse's son and other confidants on trafficking and related infractions, and it highlights some of the clear and present dangers Suriname faces with the drug PWP. Yet, the portrait and the overall discussion offer no evidence that President Desi Bouterse actively facilitated Suriname becoming a narco state, which was a major concern in some quarters at the time of his election, as noted earlier.

text continues on page 212

Suriname Trafficking Portrait, 2006–2020

2006

- 577 kilograms (kg) of cocaine and 42 kg of cannabis were seized; 571 persons were arrested for drug-related offenses.
- While seizures and arrests . . . decreased compared to 2005, law enforcement sources attribute this to the government's focus on targeting major narcotics traffickers. Since 2001, authorities have rounded up eight of the ten known major criminal organizations.
- Through September, GOS law enforcement agencies arrested 112 people who were carrying cocaine in their stomachs. Many who evade detection in Suriname are arrested at the airport in Amsterdam, which since 2004 has implemented a 100 percent inspection of all passengers and baggage arriving from Suriname.
- In a major success in 2006, Surinamese authorities arrested Shaheed "Roger" Khan, a Guyanese national suspected of narcotics trafficking, on charges of false documentation. He was set to return to Guyana via Trinidad and Tobago, but was deported, instead, to the United States. [Khan was later convicted in New York and sentenced in October 2009 to 40 years for drug smuggling and illegal arms possession. Two months later his attorney, Robert Simels, was given 14 years for trying to kill witnesses.]

2007

- 206 kg of cocaine, 131 kg of cannabis, 3,154 MDMA (ecstasy) tablets, and 81 grams of ecstasy powder were seized. A total of 667 people were arrested for drug-related offenses and 462 cases were sent to the Office of the Attorney General for Prosecution.
- While the statistics for cocaine seizures are far below those of last year, the decrease in seizures of cocaine can be attributed to the establishment of the Airport Narcotics Team, as well as anti-narcotics training provided for customs and police officers, which forced traffickers to develop innovative new ways to get narcotics through the airport.

2008

- 228.1 kg of cocaine, 123 kg of cannabis, 785 MDMA (ecstasy) tablets and 3,346.4 grams of heroin [were seized].
- While 2008 seizures were on par with previous year, the GOS Ministry of Justice and Police and law enforcement institutions continued targeting large trafficking rings, (with direct links to South American and European rings). . . . USG law enforcement intelligence shows that traffickers have changed their routes and methods of operations in response to

[the efforts of Surinamese authorities]. The drug trafficking organizations [DTOs] have moved their landing strips further into the interior and changed trafficking tactics, such as using one landing strip for a very short period of time and then moving to another strip.

- A total of 582 people were arrested on drug-related offenses. . . . Law enforcement officials also noted a slight decrease in the number of drug mules arrested, from 99 in 2007 to 66 in 2008. Traffickers continued the use of postal services to mail packages containing household items or foodstuff (ginger roots, noodles, and syrup) laced with or containing narcotics. There was a notable increase of African nationals arrested at Suriname's Johan Adolf Pengel airport carrying narcotics intended for Africa [through Holland]. The most significant arrest trend in 2008 was the arrest of several members of different Surinamese music entertainment groups.

2009

- 238.2 kilograms of cocaine, 158.5 kilograms of cannabis, 4,711.2 grams of hash, and 5.8 grams of heroin [were seized].
- The GOS launched Operation Koetai in the second half of 2009, which focused interdiction on Suriname's western border with Guyana. This operation has resulted in 94.1 kilos of cocaine seized and eight arrests as of October 30. Narcotics traffickers who attempted to bypass Operation Koetai by landing their boats in the district of Saramacca also were apprehended, resulting in seven additional arrests and the seizure of 77.5 kilos of cocaine. Operation Koetai forced an increase in the market price of cocaine from $3,500 to $7,000 per kilo in the area.
- During the year, the GOS installed a urine testing machine at the airport to identify suspected drug mules. Three Dutch-trained dogs were introduced for narcotics detection on flights to Amsterdam. This enhanced effort may have contributed to the downward trend in the number of drug mules arrested—from 99 in 2007, to 66 in 2008, to 49 in 2009. One Surinamese drug mule was arrested at the airport in Holland after having swallowed 182 cocaine capsules, weighing nearly 2.2 kilos.
- Although the majority of the trafficking out of Suriname via the airport occurs mainly on Netherlands-bound flights, drugs were also intercepted on U.S.-bound flights in Trinidad and Tobago, Jamaica, and the United States. For example, drugs were discovered on a U.S.-bound Suriname Airways flight by U.S. Customs in Aruba.
- Nationalities arrested in Suriname in 2009 for drug-related offenses included Filipinos, Spaniards, Dutch, Guyanese, Belgians, British, Brazilians, Ghanaians, Colombians, Venezuelans, and Nigerians.
- As of October 30 that year 454 people were arrested for drug-related offenses of which 323 cases were sent to the Office of the Attorney General for prosecution. As of November 5 of the year, 293 people had been prosecuted for drug-related offenses.

2010

- 342.7 kg of cocaine, 32.5 liters of liquid cocaine, 146 kg of marijuana, 4.5 grams of hashish, and 2 grams of heroin were seized.

- During 2010, 542 people were arrested for drug-related offenses, compared to 454 arrests in 2009. The GOS focuses significant interdiction resources on Suriname's western border with Guyana, a key route for cocaine trafficking by land, air, and water. In 2010 this effort yielded limited success, with fewer interdictions than in 2009. One officer posted at this checkpoint was arrested on corruption charges and this investigation is ongoing.
- A downward trend continued in the number of drug mules arrested—from 99 in 2007, 66 in 2008, 49 in 2009, to 34 in 2010. . . . The use of foodstuff to move drugs out of Suriname continued in 2010, with cocaine discovered in prunes, dried fish, souvenirs, and syrup bottles. The bulk of the cocaine movement out of Suriname to Europe and Africa is via commercial sea cargo, including both larger boats and smaller fishing vessels that carry drugs out to sea and transfer them to larger freight vessels in international waters.
- There were several drug seizures in 2010 of cocaine found in sea cargo originating from Suriname, including: 166 kilos from a container at the port of Tilbury in the United Kingdom, where the drugs were concealed within industrial machinery parts; 266 kilos discovered by Pakistani Customs at the port of Karachi in a shipping container of plywood; and 147 kilos of liquid cocaine discovered by Dutch Customs officials, concealed within a cargo container of syrup.

2011

- 415 kilograms of cocaine, 349 kilograms of cannabis, and 5 grams of hashish were seized.
- Nationalities arrested in Suriname in 2011 for drug-related offenses included Surinamese, Dutch, Brazilians, Colombians, Venezuelans, Guyanese, and Nigerians. The Government of Suriname has yet to initiate a formal investigation into any of the cocaine seizures from 2010 found in containerized cargo originating from Suriname.
- Although the majority of narcotics trafficking by air occurs via Netherlands-bound flights, in 2011 drugs were also intercepted on flights from Suriname to Trinidad and Tobago and Jamaica. The use of foodstuffs to move narcotics out of Suriname continued in 2011. As of October, the Government of Suriname Customs Service had seized 250 packages containing cocaine.
- The bulk of the cocaine movement out of Suriname to Europe and Africa is via container cargo. Smaller fishing vessels also carry drugs out to sea and transfer them to large freight vessels in international waters. In March and August 2011, Jamaica seized 112 and 65 kilograms of cocaine respectively from the ship "Vega Azurit," which is suspected to have been shipped from Suriname to Jamaica.
- Drug trafficking organizations based in Guyana are beginning to use Suriname as a major distribution hub. The cocaine is smuggled into Guyana and then transported to Suriname for safekeeping and distribution.

2012

- 395 kilograms (kg) of cocaine, 102 kg of cannabis, 8,000 ecstasy pills and 80 grams of hashish were seized. Two hundred and sixty-nine people were arrested for drug-related offenses, of which 216 cases were sent to the Office of the Attorney General for prosecution. One hundred and forty-one people were prosecuted for drug-related offenses.

- Suriname is working on legislation to control precursor chemicals, but currently is unable to detect the diversion of precursor chemicals for drug production. The Government of Suriname focuses significant narcotics interdiction resources on the country's western border with Guyana, a key route for cocaine trafficking by land and water.
- The use of foodstuffs to move narcotics through the airport continued in 2012. In October, 57 kg of cocaine were recovered from hollowed-out sweet potatoes.
- The bulk of cocaine smuggled from Suriname to Europe and Africa occurs via container cargo. Smaller fishing vessels also carry drugs out to sea and transfer them to large freight vessels in international waters.

2013

- Between January and October of 2013, KPS counternarcotics units arrested 242 people for drug-related offenses in Suriname, of which 144 cases were sent to the Office of the Attorney General for prosecution. One-hundred and seventy people were prosecuted for drug-related offenses.
- During this 10-month period, KPS counternarcotics units seized a total amount of 191.7 kilograms (kg) of cocaine, 118.3 grams of heroin, 61.53 kg of marijuana, 1.37 kg of hashish and 154 MDMA (ecstasy) tablets.
- At the end of 2013, Surinamese authorities were in the process of drafting legislation to control precursor chemicals.
- The bulk of cocaine smuggled from Suriname to Europe and Africa occurs via containerized cargo. Smaller fishing vessels also carry drugs out to sea and transfer them to large freight vessels in international waters. . . . In September, the Government of Suriname purchased three patrol vessels from France for its Coast Guard, which still lacks legal standing. Suriname does not operate a maritime radar system to track movements at sea.
- In July, KPS counternarcotics units seized and destroyed approximately 808,000 cannabis plants (362 metric tons) and approximately one million cannabis seeds from five cultivating fields. However, there is no additional evidence that cannabis is exported in significant quantities.

2014

- KPS counternarcotics units reported incinerating 319.6 kilograms (kg) of cocaine, 51.5 liters of liquid cocaine, 375.4 kg of marijuana, 42 grams of heroin, 600 grams of hashish, and 27,764 ecstasy tablets seized by Suri-namese authorities during the first 11 months of 2014.
- In late 2013, Surinamese authorities began drafting legislation to control precursor chemicals.
- Top managers at Suriname's Johan Adolf Pengel International Airport continue to work with the Government of Suriname and a Canadian com-mercial partner to implement an automated air-traffic radar and control

system installed in 2010, but still not operational. Interdiction efforts at the airport are run by the Combating International Drug Trafficking (BID) team composed of approximately 32 KPS members. The team focuses almost exclusively on searching passengers and cargo on flights bound for the Netherlands, where it is believed the majority of narcotics trafficked from Suriname is destined.

- Much of the cocaine smuggled from Suriname to Europe and Africa occurs via container cargo. Smaller fishing vessels also carry drugs out to sea for transfer to large freight vessels in international waters.

2015

- There appears to be little political will for vigorous enforcement. Corruption pervades many government offices in Suriname and may also play a role. Criminal investigations of alleged corrupt acts are rare and prosecutions even rarer. . . . Dino Bouterse, son of President Desire Bouterse, was sentenced in March 2015 to prison in New York for drug smuggling and other crimes.
- Cargo containers carry most of the narcotics smuggled through Suriname, but smaller fishing vessels also carry drugs out to sea for transfer to larger freighters.
- During the first nine months of 2015, Surinamese authorities arrested 139 alleged drug traffickers and seized 626.6 kilograms (kg) of cocaine, 33.8 liters of liquid cocaine, 841.7 kg of marijuana, four grams of heroin, 4.3 grams of hashish and 2,878 MDMA tablets. A 32-man Combating International Drug Trafficking (BID) team screens airport passengers on flights bound for the Netherlands. Suriname installed an automated biometrics border control system for travelers at points of entry in 2013 and amended the criminal code to allow DNA as evidence in 2014.
- Suriname has a bilateral maritime counternarcotics enforcement agreement with the United States, as well as similar agreements with the Netherlands, Brazil, Venezuela, and Colombia.

2016

- The National Assembly approved the "Acquisition and Sentence Transfer Enforcement" law in October 2016. This legislation is meant to establish the conditions under which a sentence issued by a foreign court would be applied within Suriname, as well as the conditions involved in applying the verdicts of Surinamese courts abroad.
- Cargo containers carry most of the narcotics smuggled through Suriname, but smaller fishing vessels also carry drugs out to sea for transfer to larger freighters. A U.S.-funded, UN-sponsored Container Control Unit operates at the Terminal of Nieuwe Haven (Port of Paramaribo) and assisted in two drug investigations in 2016. Their operating protocol requires permission and oversight of Surinamese Customs authorities.
- During the first 11 months of 2016, Surinamese authorities arrested 156 suspected drug traffickers and seized 851 kilograms (kg) of cocaine; 8,827 liters of liquid cocaine; 46.3 kg of marijuana; 19,466 MDMA (ecstasy) tablets; and trace amounts of hashish and MDMA in powder form. A

32-person Combating International Drug Trafficking (BID) team screens airport passengers on flights bound for the Netherlands.

- In 2014, lawmakers adopted new legislation allowing treatment for drug addiction as an alternative to criminal sentencing. As of October 2016, implementing protocols for this legislation were still being drafted.

2017

- In July 2017, the U.S.-funded, UN-sponsored Container Control Unit at the Terminal of Nieuw[e] Haven (Port of Paramaribo) assisted Surinamese authorities in detecting and seizing a record of 1.7 metric tons of cocaine in a shipping container destined for Europe.
- Suriname is a party to the Inter-American Convention against Corruption and Migrant Smuggling and the Inter-American Convention on Mutual Assistance in Criminal Matters. Since 1976, Suriname has shared drug-related information with the Netherlands as part of a mutual legal assistance agreement among former Dutch colonies to exchange crime-related data. In 1999, the United States and Suriname completed a comprehensive bilateral maritime counternarcotics enforcement agreement that remains in force. Suriname has also signed bilateral agreements to combat drug trafficking with Brazil, Venezuela, and Colombia.
- Suriname is not a source country for illegal drugs or precursor chemicals, but it continues to be used as a transshipment point for illicit drugs. During 2017, there was an increase in the volume of drugs seized in the country, which may be due to increased drug production in Colombia. Worsening economic conditions in Suriname may also have produced increased incentives for criminal activity. During the first nine months of 2017, Surinamese authorities seized approximately 2.88 metric tons of cocaine; 16.5 liters of liquid cocaine; 57.6 kilograms (kg) of marijuana; three kg of hashish; and 393 MDMA (ecstasy) tablets.

2018

- Suriname is not a source country for illicit drugs or precursor chemicals, but it continues to be a transshipment point for illicit drugs. During the first nine months of 2018, authorities seized approximately 648 kilograms (kg) of cocaine; 16.4 liters of liquid cocaine; 569.1 kg of marijuana; 875 grams of hashish; 524 grams of MDMA (ecstasy) powder; and 504 MDMA tablets. Authorities seized less cocaine, but more marijuana and MDMA compared to the first three quarters of 2017. With support from U.S. authorities, Surinamese law enforcement agencies seized a self-propelled semi-submersible vessel in Saramacca on March 1, 2018, the first ever seized in Suriname. Local authorities seized a Cessna 210 aircraft containing 488 kg of cocaine two weeks later. The Attorney General's Office received 139 drug-related cases from police for additional investigation and brought 71 cases to court.
- The Ministry of Justice and Police included the creation of an Integrated Security Plan in the 2019 draft budget. Under the plan, police, military, and the Directorate of National Security would intensify cooperation on

a variety of security issues, including combatting the trafficking of illicit drugs and strengthening technical investigation skills.

- Drug prevention and control activities are coordinated by Suriname's National Drug Master Plan, developed under the aegis of the National Antidrug Board. This document is supposed to be developed every five years, but the most recent plan expired in 2015. The Government reported that a new plan for the period 2018–2022 was near completion at the end of 2018.

2019

- Suriname is a transit country for South American cocaine en route to Europe, Africa, and, to a lesser extent, the United States. Cargo containers carry most illicit drugs smuggled through Suriname, but smaller fishing vessels, commercial and private air transport, and human couriers also conceal smuggled cocaine. Suriname's sparsely populated coastal region and isolated jungle interior, together with weak border controls and infrastructure, make illicit drug detection and interdiction efforts difficult.
- In January 2019, the U.S.-funded Container Control Unit (CCP) at the Jules Sedney Port identified suspicious containers that contained 2.3 metric tons (MT) of cocaine, Suriname's largest-ever narcotics seizure. The CCP contributed to the seizure of more than 4.5 MT of cocaine since 2016. Beyond the January seizure, the Government of Suriname was unable to provide statistics regarding arrests, seizures, or court cases pertaining to 2019.
- On January 31, the National Anti-Drug Council (NAR) submitted a draft National Drug Master Plan (NDMP) to the Department of National Security (DNV). The Director of the DNV submitted the plan to the President of Suriname on September 19, 2019.

2020

- Suriname is not a source country for illegal drugs or precursor chemicals, but it continues to be a transshipment point for illicit substances. In August 2020, the Container Control Unit assisted in the confiscation of more than 300 kilograms (kg) of marijuana found in a container inbound from China through Jamaica.
- In his July 2020 inaugural remarks, President Santokhi pledged "to change Suriname's image as a drug transit country." In his first annual State of the Republic address in September 2020, he committed his government to strengthening Suriname's Narcotics Brigade. In September 2020, Secretary of State [Mike] Pompeo visited Suriname, where he met with President Santokhi and a number of cabinet ministers. Santokhi's Minister of Justice and Police told local media that cooperation on counternarcotics was a theme of their discussions with the Secretary, and the minister indicated that Suriname wished to strengthen its ties with U.S. law enforcement.

Source: U.S. Department of State, *International Narcotics Control Strategy Report*, various years, https://2009–2017.state.gov/j/inl/rls/nrcrpt/index.htm/.

In relation to the notion of a narco state, although the matter is addressed fully in chapter 8, it is important to share a few observations on the matter here. There is a certain attractiveness to what might be called the two-conditions-test approach to the matter, which posits: "First, a narco state is a country that is economically dependent on [an] illicit drug economy; second, a narco state is a country in which the government elites are complicit in the illicit drug trade" (Paoli, Greenfield, and Reuter 2009, 142). However, I am persuaded that "the three most pertinent criteria by which to judge whether a given country qualifies as a narco state are: the surface area covered by illegal drug crops; the size of the illegal drug economy relative to the overall economy and, most importantly, the state-sponsorship of illegal drug production and/or trafficking" (Chouvy 2016, 35). Pierre-Armand Chouvy also argues persuasively that "for a state to be rightly categorized as a narco state, the illegal drug industry must be state sponsored and must contribute to the majority of a country's overall economy (GDP + illegal economy or, as is now the case within the European Union, GDP that includes the illegal economy)" (35).

Thus, based on the definitional parameters offered above and the evidence presented in the sidebar, I suggest that Suriname is not and never has been a narco state. Considering the discussion above, the fear about the creation of a narco state by Desi Bouterse was not realized and was never likely to be realized. There are several reasons for this. First, the very political acumen that helped Bouterse reemerge legitimately would have enabled him to appreciate the foolhardiness of such a pursuit. Such would hurt both his political self-interest as a world leader and the national interests of his nation. Second, Bouterse must have known of the special spotlight both he and Suriname would have been under. Thus, he was more likely to try to compensate for his history and negative image by being aggressive against trafficking than to become complicit (again) in it. We already saw some of this with the quest for international assistance from Britain, the Netherlands, Bulgaria, Pakistan, and elsewhere (see *Stabroek News* 2011). The sidebar also reveals areas of international collaboration and assistance. Finally, having been born on October 13, 1945, in Paramaribo, Bouterse was almost sixty-five years old at the time of the election in 2010. That is an age when leaders begin to ponder both their mortality and their legacy. Bouterse must have known that enabling the development of a narco state would damage his legacy and complicate the pursuit of his nation's national interests.

However, even if President Bouterse were to compensate for his drug trafficking history and image by being aggressive against traffickers, he might well have wanted to establish a legacy outside the geonarcotics arena. The foreign policy arena could plausibly be that desired legacy area. In such a case, for understandable reasons, his primary zone of engagement would have to be the Caribbean, Brazil, and Venezuela, although Europe and the United States continued to be important for trade, aid, and immigration. Indeed, as part of its South American engagement, in January 2011, less than a year after assuming the presidency, President Bouterse shepherded Suriname into the comity of the Unión de Naciones Suramericanas (UNASUR) or the Union of South American Nations.[8] It is in that context that we turn next regarding some geopolitical dynamics.

On the Geopolitical Front

As was explained in chapter 5, geopolitics refers to the relationship between physical and political geography, on the one hand, and national power, on the other, with key factors being the possession of strategic materials, ownership of or access to strategic waterways, and the possession or location of military bases and other security installations. Among other things, national power competition with Guyana over resource-rich territory has made the relationship with Guyana a key aspect of Suriname's geopolitical dynamics.

Engagements with Guyana

In their shared South American neighborhood, Guyana likely was the nation with the most significant geopolitical anxieties about Bouterse's election for several reasons: the existence of a territorial dispute over the New River Triangle; a then-recently settled dispute over maritime boundaries, which at one point in June 2000 saw the use of military power by Suriname in ejecting a Canadian oil rig that had been granted exploration license by Guyana in its maritime space; and long-standing immigration tensions, among other things. All of this occurred in the context of weakened defense and diplomatic establishments in Guyana.

However, it also is true that precisely because of Bouterse's profile, the anxiety that his election generated, and Suriname's national security interests related to the territorial and other issues mentioned above, Desi Bouterse regarded Guyana as vital to his foreign policy engagement. Thus, it was not entirely surprising that his first international presidential trip was to Guyana: a one-day working visit on September 6, 2010, that touched on several matters, including climate change, information technology, mining, infrastructure development, energy, agriculture, fisheries, and tertiary education. (President Bouterse fell ill with dengue fever a few weeks before the planned visit, but he insisted on making the trip even though he had not fully recovered.)

The long list of topics and paucity of concrete outcomes make for credible conjecture that the summit was more about symbolism than substance. In referring to the communiqué issued at the end of the visit, one observer noted that it amounted to "a literary masterpiece of verbal acuity" that "succeeded in skimming ever so lightly atop every conceivable topic that officials could think about—with the obvious exception of the territorial question—without leaving a trace of the slightest solution to any matter of substance" (*Stabroek News* 2010b). Further, it was noted that "the [President Bharrat] Jagdeo-Bouterse encounter . . . was not the first time that Guyana threw a lifeline to Suriname[,] which was swimming in a sea of international opprobrium" (*Stabroek News* 2010b).

During the visit, Bouterse declared, "Suriname is at a crossroads now and we want to share new ideas with Guyana. We have a special movement and aspiration towards South America and the Caribbean" (*West Indian News* 2010; see also *Stabroek News* 2010c about the visit overall). President Bouterse visited again two months later, on November 20, 2010, this time to Berbice, which borders Suriname, rather than the capital, Georgetown. Jagdeo reciprocated on November 20, 2010, to Nickerie and not the capital, Paramaribo (*Demerarawaves* 2010). Bouterse visited Guyana again on February 26, 2011, on the way back home after attending the CARICOM summit in Grenada.[9]

The matter of lifeline—and an aspect of the anxiety over Bouterse's election, given his profile—surfaced again in January 2011 when President Jagdeo dropped a bombshell during the Guyana Defense Force annual officers' conference. In response to a question following his speech, he declared, "A foreign mission asked us if we will arrest the president of Suriname when he comes here because he is wanted somewhere else, and I said to them 'No'" (*Demerarawaves* 2011). Jagdeo declined to name the nation involved, but his revelation generated understandable speculation about which country had made the request. This led the United States to issue a statement through its embassy in Georgetown indicating that it had not been the nation involved.

Resolved and Unresolved Disputes

At the end of the day, any "life-lining" in Guyana's dealing with Suriname and the geopolitical anxiety occasioned by Bouterse's election are driven by what in essence is the elephant in the room for both nations: the territorial issues and the attendant political heat they generate domestically. There are two sets of issues: one is about land—the unresolved New River Triangle; the other pertains to the maritime dispute that was resolved in 2007 but still has some residual aspects. Figure 7.1 shows the two areas.

The New River Triangle dispute, which involves 15,540 km² (6,000 square miles) of territory, dates to the nineteenth century. The area is resource-rich, with timber and minerals and indications of the presence of bauxite and aluminum. The Border Mixed Commission, established in 1989 as a framework for rapprochement and to move the parties progressively toward resolution,

FIGURE 7.1 Guyana-Suriname Disputed Areas.

Source: Thomas Donovan, "Suriname-Guyana Maritime and Territorial Disputes: A Legal and Historical Analysis," *Journal of Transnational Law* and Policy 23 (Spring), 2003: 41–98.

has been dormant for several years. Meanwhile, over the last few decades there have been many diplomatic and security twists and turns in the territorial saga.[10] Perhaps the most significant development, and the most daring by Suriname, was its action in presenting to the world what it had long done within the country: cartographically portraying the New River area as part of its territory. The occasion was the World Bank Low Carbon Development Strategy Forum, held in October 2009 in Washington, D.C. Suriname upped the ante by including in its submission the map shown in figure 7.2.[11]

Since then Suriname has been depicting itself as inclusive of the New River Triangle domestically, on the website of its embassy in Washington, D.C., and elsewhere.[12] Guyana's feeble protest of this audacious move and its inability to secure a retraction of the map to date reflect its relative diplomatic (and military) ineffectiveness at the time. My worry is this: as Suriname's redefinition of itself has existed for more than a decade, this portrayal will be reproduced, used by others, and slowly become the geographic definition of Suriname in the eyes of some parts of the world.

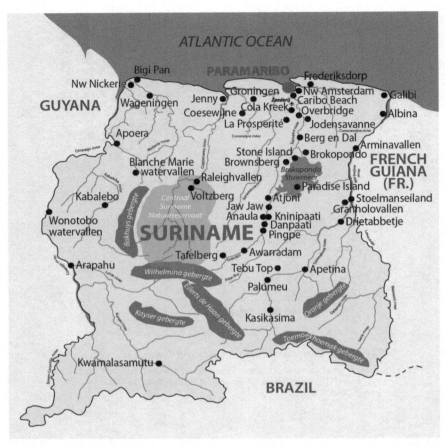

FIGURE 7.2 Suriname Redefined by Suriname.
Source: Bing Images, available at Suriname Country.

The maritime zone's geopolitical value in terms of resources is perhaps greater than that of the New River Triangle given the hydrocarbons there. One study noted:

> The disputed maritime area between Guyana and Suriname, called the Guyana Basin, is an under-explored area on the continental shelf of South America extending from present day Venezuela to Suriname. The Guyana Basin is geographically next to Trinidad and Venezuela, both important oil producers on the Caribbean plateau and the Venezuelan extension, which are two large and productive oil fields. Throughout this area, large commercial petroleum consortiums such as Exxon, Agip, and Burlington have successfully drilled for petroleum.

Limited exploration in the Guyana Basin has been carried out to date. However[,] in June 2000, the United States Geological Survey's World Petroleum Assessment 2000 estimated that the resource potential for the Guyana Basin is 15.2 billion barrels of oil. This estimate indicates that the Guyana Basin is the second most important unexplored region in the world in terms of oil potential. If the potential is reached, it would be the twelfth most productive site in the world. (Donovan 2003, 48)

The zone in question was 31,600 km^2 (5,251 square miles) in size. The dispute over it also witnessed several dramatic high points, perhaps the most notable of which was the ejection in June 2000 by Suriname Defense Force naval vessels of the oil platforms of a Canadian-owned company, CGX Energy Inc., which had been licensed by Guyana to drill in the Guyana Basin. The episode witnessed the humiliation of the Guyana Defense Force—once larger and better trained than the Suriname Defense Force. One report also said, "To add insult to injury, Paramaribo had deployed its naval vessels in the area in a show of strength, declared itself 'the power in the river' and led Georgetown on a meaningless diplomatic waltz which ended on 18 June, with the then Foreign Minister Clement Rohee conceding failure in his quest to restore the status quo ante. The next year, Mr. Rohee was removed from the ministry" (*Stabroek News* 2008).

Interestingly, Suriname's use of force was itself a manifestation of intermestic dynamics. Up until early May 2000, about a year after CGX began its exploration in the area, Surinamese authorities voiced no concern about the presence or purpose of CGX in the basin. Things began to change later that month as the campaign for the impending elections, set for May 25, heated up. Opposition figures began accusing the ruling coalition of condoning Guyana's intrusion into "Surinamese territory" and plundering its oil wealth. As Shridath Ramphal put it, "Political machoism was stirring the nationalist plot; and the Government was not going to be outdone" (Ramphal 2008, 146). On May 11, Suriname delivered a *note verbale* to Guyana through Guyana's ambassador in Paramaribo,[13] demanding that Guyana cease operations in what it deemed its territory.

Guyana replied six days later, asserting that the exploration was being undertaken within its maritime space. Suriname ignored Guyana's response and found it politically expedient not to acknowledge having received it. The May 25, 2000, elections resulted in a loss of power for the ruling coalition and victory for the New Front coalition, although it was sometime before the new National Assembly elected a president. Then on May 31, with the new president not yet agreed on, Suriname's foreign minister—whose president had just lost power—issued a new *note verbale* to Guyana's ambassador. It reasserted its allegation about Guyana's illegal actions, demanded immediate cessation of activities, and promised to use "all avenues" if Guyana did not comply with its demands.

Simultaneously, Suriname ordered CGX to cease operations or face appropriate sanctions. Guyana replied to the May 31 *note verbale* on June 2, offering to host high-level talks within twenty-four hours. That same day, Guyana Defense Force Coast Guard members patrolling the Guyana Basin near the rigs reported Surinamese military aircraft flying threateningly over the rig and Coast Guard vessels. Guyana protested the airspace intrusion and renewed the offer to hold talks, but to no avail. Just after midnight on June 3, the Surinamese navy arrived in the CGX concession area, circled the rig, trained spotlights on the platform, and repeatedly issued the order to "leave the area within 12 hours, or the consequences will be yours" (Ramphal 2008, 149). Understandably fearful for their physical safety and destruction of their equipment, the CGX operators detached the rigs and departed the area under Surinamese naval escort. Suriname also forced oil companies Esso and Maxus to end their operations in the basin.

Incidentally, the affair also highlighted CARICOM's limitations as a dispute-resolution mechanism. CARICOM tried unsuccessfully to resolve the disagreement. Guyana then took the matter to arbitration under the U.N. Convention of the Law of the Sea (UNCLOS) in February 2004. The case took three years, with the composition of the five-member tribunal alone taking nine months. Both sides mounted formidable teams of international lawyers, geographers, and diplomats. Guyana had a twenty-one-member team and Suriname a twenty-five-member team. (For details of the two teams, see Ramphal 2008, 341–42.)[14]

Suriname challenged the tribunal's jurisdiction and the validity of the established international legal principle of equidistance in fixing boundaries, and it attempted to justify the June 3, 2000, use of force. They also pursued a "denial of access" strategy. Although Guyana and Britain allowed Suriname unlimited access to all historical archives, Suriname sought to deny access by Guyana to Dutch archives for the period June 1937 to March 1959, leading the tribunal to declare in its first procedural order, "The Tribunal shall not consider any document taken from a file in the archives of the Netherlands to which Guyana had been denied access" (Ramphal 2008, 222).

Not only did Suriname's approach fail in the extant case, but it also facilitated the strengthening of "the Constitution of the Oceans" in relation to future cases. Indeed, Ramphal asserts, "In all three areas, the UNCLOS Tribunal in this case made decisions of major significance not only to the outcome of the Arbitration, but also to the development of international law generally. The Guyana-Suriname Maritime Award is likely to be an arbitral precedent much drawn upon in international jurisprudence in years ahead" (Ramphal 2008, 17). The tribunal announced the award on September 20, 2007, finding that Guyana was entitled to two-thirds of the disputed zone and Suriname one-third. Beyond this, Guyana felt vindicated in relation to the June 3, 2000, use of force with the tribunal's declaration: "As a result of this Award, Guyana now has undisputed title to the area where the incident occurred" (17).[15]

As with other dispute settlement cases, the tribunal's decision did not remove all frictions. One source indicated, "With the ink barely dry on the historic maritime jurisdiction ruling by the United Nations Conference on the Law of the Sea (UNCLOS) Guyana and Suriname are at it again, this time, following the October 14, 2008[,] seixure [*sic*] by Suriname navel [*sic*] vessels of the Lady Chanrda [*sic*], a privately-owned Guyanese boat on the Corentyne River" (*Stabroek News* 2008). Nevertheless, the settlement enabled resumption of oil exploration by CGX. Joining later was Tullow Oil, a British company, in a joint venture with REPSOL of Spain.

Although Roberto Espíndola's remark in this chapter's epigraph about electoral surprises is quite true, surprises that have national political implications do not originate only at the ballot. Sometimes they derive from actions in the judicial realm. That certainly was the case with the development outlined below.

Judicial Distress and Political Demise

Friday, November 29, 2019, will be recorded in the annals of Suriname's political history as the date when the country's sitting president was convicted by a three-member military court in Paramaribo for the execution of fifteen individuals in December 1982 and sentenced to twenty years in jail. President Bouterse was traveling in China on official business at the time of the ruling. The court ruled that Bouterse had masterminded the operation in which soldiers under his command abducted sixteen leading government critics—including lawyers, journalists, and university professors—from their homes and killed fifteen of them at a colonial fortress in Paramaribo called Fort Zeelandia.[16] Later that day the tribunal convicted six other former military officers of murder for their roles in forcibly removing victims from their homes at night or participating in the massacre (Kuipers 2019; Associated Press 2019; and Fausia 2021).

In a joint statement, the diplomatic missions of the Netherlands, the United States, Britain, Spain, Germany, and France to Suriname advocated that the verdicts be upheld in accordance with the rule of law. One newspaper editorial in neighboring Guyana expressed the supportable opinion that "Friday's decision in Paramaribo was a triumph of the rule of law even if the decision was not handed down by a civilian court as should have been the case. The conviction of a sitting Head of Government by a domestic court in a case of this magnitude and gravity must be recognized as requiring fortitude and courage. Tragically the families of the 15 victims have had to wait for nearly 37 years to gain a sense of justice" (*Stabroek News* 2019b).

The ruling came at an interesting time in the country's political calendar—six months before elections were constitutionally due, in May 2020. Bouterse repudiated calls to step down and reaffirmed his intention to maintain prior plans to contest the 2020 elections. Bouterse's political self-assurance was influenced by the outcome of the 2015 elections and the economic upturn noted above. As well, at the beginning of 2020, the respected *Economist* magazine offered a favorable economic forecast for 2020–2021 (see *Economist* 2020). With regard to the 2015 elections, a total of twenty-five total parties contested power—fifteen as coalitions and ten as independent parties. The National Assembly seat allocation was as follows: National Democratic Party, twenty-six; Progressive Reform Party, eighteen; A Combination, five; and one seat each for the Party for Democracy and Development through Unity and the Progressive Workers' and Farmers' Union. President Bouterse's NDP became the first single party to win a majority in the National Assembly.

As explained earlier, the president is elected indirectly by the National Assembly on the basis of a two-thirds majority. Given the National Assembly allocation noted above, it was predictable that Bouterse would be reelected as president when the assembly met on July 14, 2015, for the vote. Yet, the competence and credibility of the Bouterse government were negatively impacted in the run-up to the May 2020 elections. In February 2020, it was discovered that US$100 million in private citizens' savings had disappeared from the Central Bank. This caused a financial and political furor, especially since the funds had been used without the knowledge of the commercial banks that owned them. The bank's governor was dismissed and a criminal investigation was launched. However, the bank found it difficult to recruit a new leader, from either within or outside the country. Of course, the bank promised to return the missing funds and pledged to keep the Suriname Bankers Association apprised of planned transactions in the future.

Understandably, the entire affair undermined confidence within and beyond the bank. It also had broader national implications. As Scott MacDonald noted, writing in March 2020, "The Central Bank still lacks a governor and the country's financial situation is at risk of further deterioration. . . . The scandal at the Central Bank and the inability to replace [Gov. Robert-Gray] Van Trikt has further eroded confidence in a government that increasingly appears adrift on the policy side. Suriname has a lot of work to do on developing better governance, especially at its Central Bank" (MacDonald 2020a). He also stressed the importance of "getting this right" because of implications for the anticipated oil boom and the importance of a well-respected Central Bank to the management of the oil sector.

Bouterse's self-confidence was misplaced. Seventeen political parties contested the elections on May 25, 2020. His NDP secured only sixteen of the fifty-one seats, while the opposition alliance won thirty-three seats. Even under conditions of the COVID-19 pandemic, the elections process went relatively smoothly, and observers from the OAS and CARICOM deemed the elections free and fair. Bouterse's party demanded a recount in a few districts where they lost. Nonetheless, the electoral authorities declared the new four-party coalition, headed by Chandrikapersad "Chan" Santokhi, leader of the Progressive Reform Party, the winner. Later, on July 13, the National Assembly elected Santokhi as president. The sixty-one-year-old Santokhi, who had served as police commissioner and justice minister between 2005 and 2010, when Ronald Venetiaan served as president, was known for his tough posture against drugs and other criminality. He once engaged in a legal battle with Bouterse, suing him for slander and defamation of character after Bouterse alleged that he was a pawn of drug dealers. Santokhi won the case and Bouterse was forced to withdraw his claims (*Stabroek News* 2020).

Bouterse's return to power in 2010 triggered some geopolitical and geonarcotics anxieties, some of which were misplaced. His replacement as president in 2020 began a new phase of Suriname's democratic trajectory. It is hoped that this trajectory will be sustained. Irrespective of the nature of the democracy experience, the challenges of crime and drugs remain. Yet, as the sidebar in chapter 3 shows, Suriname is pursuing marijuana reform measures. These certainly will add new variables to the country's geonarcotics matrix.

Undoubtedly, Suriname finds itself at a crossroads, driven by geonarcotics and geopolitical circumstances, among other things. Scott MacDonald, for instance, noted that "the geopolitical landscape facing Suriname in both the Caribbean and South America has changed, with the advent of what some analysts are calling a new Cold War between the United States on one side and China, Venezuela, and Russia on the other" (MacDonald 2019b, 1). Their crossroads position also is influenced by the anticipated oil windfall following the January 7, 2020, discovery when American-owned Apache Corp and French-owned Total SA announced a major offshore oil find. It sent Apache's shares surging nearly 27 percent. It is noteworthy that the oil find borders the discoveries in neighboring Guyana that hold some 10 billion barrels of oil. "Apache's agreement with Total included US$100 million upfront payment and expenses incurred in exploration" (S. Khan 2020).

This chapter ends the main conceptual and empirical discourse of this book. It remains only for us to bring finality to this study by interrogating the question that is the fulcrum around which our security and sovereignty concerns revolve. That question is: How secure is security, and how sovereign is sovereignty in the Caribbean? We ponder this question in the next and final chapter.

PART IV

Crucial Contemplation

8

Pondering Challenged Sovereignty

A vital idea set ablaze before the world at the right moment
can, like the mystic banner of the last judgment, stop a fleet
of battleships. . . . We can no longer be a nation of fluttering
leaves, spending our lives in the air, our treetop crowned in
flowers, humming or creaking by the caprices of sunlight or
thrashed and felled by tempests. . . . It is the hour of reckoning
and of marching in unison, and we must move in lines as
compact as the veins of silver that lie at the roots of the Andes.

—José Martí, "Our America"

Sometimes it seems as if small states were like small
boats pushed out into a turbulent sea, free in one sense
to traverse it; but, without oars or provisions, without
compass or sails, free also to perish. Or perhaps, to
be rescued and taken aboard a larger vessel.

—Sir Shridath Ramphal, Opening address of the meeting of
the Commonwealth Experts on Small State Security, 1985

The political and intellectual labors of Caribbean and other statesmen and
scholars in the aftermath of World War II clearly reveal that the notion of
sovereignty was a "vital idea set ablaze before the world," to quote José Martí,
a Caribbean intellectual and literary giant of the colonial era. In advocating
"marching in unison" and movement "in lines as compact as the veins of silver,"
he anticipated the need for unity to cope with the realities of the environment
in which the high ideals of sovereignty might be realized.

In capturing some of the realities that characterize the existence of Caribbean states as small, subordinate, sovereign entities, international statesman
Shridath Ramphal was himself voicing a sentiment of "reckoning" and signaling the necessity for collective action to cope with the extant realities. Some of

those realities are a function of the globalization factor that has enabled Problems Without Passports, as Kofi Annan dubbed them, to impact the security and sovereignty of Caribbean states so as to create what I deem a condition of challenged sovereignty. Hopefully, the foregoing chapters have provided the analytic and empirical evidence to substantiate this proposition. It might be recalled that in chapter 2 we recorded the intent to sketch new designs, present data in relation to four PWPs and their security and sovereignty implications for the Caribbean, and to ask new and pertinent questions. We turn next to one crucial question, which is the fulcrum around which the description and analysis of the new designs and the new data revolve.

How Secure Is Security and How Sovereign Is Sovereignty?

Salience and Strategic Partnerships

The challenges examined in this book are not merely challenges *within the Caribbean*; they are challenges *of the Caribbean*. Stated differently, they are not merely threats and apprehensions faced by a few states and just a few thousand citizens *within the region*. They impact such a large number of states and so many millions of citizens as to constitute threats and apprehensions *of the region*. As was explained in *Caribbean Security in the Age of Terror*, regional salience is a function of threat type and threat intensity, and it is influenced by three main factors: (1) the number of states affected; (2) the definition of the situation by the relevant elites of state and other actors within the region; and (3) the amount of resources being invested in the matter by state (and non-state) actors (Griffith 2004,19–20).

Evidently from earlier chapters and this one, these factors exist in the contemporary Caribbean in that:

- All Caribbean nations are impacted by the PWPs, although threat intensity varies. For instance, drugs and crime stand out in the salience and intensity as *threats of the entire region*. On the other hand, terrorism issues present a narrower regional scope and a lower intensity, although geopolitical dynamics oblige Caribbean and other leaders to place a high regional premium on it. Cyber challenges resonate with lesser threat intensity but have growing region-wide scope, especially because of the implications for tourism and economic survivability.
- The political elites of all Caribbean states and relevant policy and operational leaders of all subregional and regional organizations and similar leaders in the United States, the United Kingdom, Canada, and the European Union—countries with geopolitical, geonarcotics, or geoeconomic

interests in the region—have declared these PWPs threats to their own national or institutional interests.

- Although it is difficult to calculate the total quantum of the national, regional, and international funds expended to combat the PWPs, evidence presented below and elsewhere make it reasonable to suggest that the combined funding has totaled hundreds of millions of U.S. dollars over the last few decades. Moreover, Caribbean countries could not have shouldered that outlay by themselves, and cannot do so in the future, even if the challenges were amenable to unilateral or intra-regional resolution.

The very transnationality feature of the PWPs means that PWP dynamics negatively affect the national self-interest of states outside the region and the institutional interests of non-state actors. Thus, the contributions by non-Caribbean states and international organizations to addressing the PWP realities are not guided by altruism but by geopolitical, geonarcotics, or geoeconomic motivations. Although space limitations preclude an extensive discussion, it is important to note some of the who and the what of the main PWP strategic partners. Strategic partnerships are conducted in what elsewhere have been called Multilateral Security Engagement Zones (MSEZ), defined as geographic spaces for policy and operational collaboration and cooperation by state and non-state actors in relation to defense and security matters. The zones exist at the subregional, regional, hemispheric, and international systemic levels, and they involve states, international governmental and non-state actors, with treaties, protocols, conventions, and memorandums of understanding guiding the various terms of engagement (Griffith 2003, 18–19).

The United States of America, the European Union, the United Kingdom, Canada, the U.N. Office on Drugs and Crime, the Inter-American Development Bank, the World Bank, and the Organization of American States are the region's main strategic partners.[1] Understandably, attention cannot be paid here to all—or even most—of them. Partnership funding takes the forms of grants, purchases, and loans, such as the loan of US$20 million by the Inter-American Development Bank to Jamaica in 2017 to support efforts to measurably increase the conviction rate for murders and other violent crimes. The intent is to help reduce homicides through intensified crime prevention activities and improve the quality and rate of criminal investigations being managed by the Jamaica Constabulary Force. The loan is for a twenty-five-year term, including a five-and-a-half-year grace period.

Some partnership engagements are done bilaterally, others multilaterally. In the case of the United States, the Caribbean Basin Security Initiative (CBSI) is the main umbrella for delivering PWP assistance to the Caribbean. Developed in 2009 to complement the Mérida Initiative, which was launched with

Mexico in December 2008, and the Central America Regional Security Initiative (CARSI), it aims to reduce drug trafficking, advance public safety and security, and promote social justice.[2] President Barack Obama announced the initiative at the fifth Summit of the Americas, which was held in Trinidad and Tobago in April 2009. In June 2017 the United States released a Strategy for Engagement in the Caribbean, which incorporated the CBSI. It articulated priorities aimed at strengthening mutual national security and advancing the citizens' safety through programs to dismantle criminal and terrorist organizations, curb the trafficking of illicit goods and people, strengthen the rule of law, improve citizen security, and counter vulnerability to terrorist threats.

Table 8.1 shows the allocation since the program's inception. Overall, from fiscal year FY2010 through FY2021, Congress appropriated US$751 million for the CBSI countries. For each of FY2018 and FY2019, the Trump administration

TABLE 8.1 CBSI Funding by Foreign Aid Account, FY 2010–FY2021 (U.S.$ millions)

Fiscal Year	ESF	DA	INCLE	NADR	FMF	TOTAL
FY2010	14,000	6,000	27,300	——	14,500	61,800
FY2011	17,000	——	37,500	6,400	16,500	77,400
FY2012	17,000	——	30,000	2,000	15,000	64,000
FY2013	18,802	——	30,000	2,000	9,494	60,296
FY2014	29,200	——	25,000	1,800	7,500	63,500
FY2015	27,000	——	25,000	1,500	5,000	58,500
FY2016	25,000	——	25,221	——	7,500	57,721
FY2017	25,000	——	25,200	——	7,500	57,700
FY2018	25,000	——	25,200	——	7,500	57,700
FY2019	25,250	——	25,250	——	7,500	58,000
FY2020	27,300	——	25,200	——	7,500	60,000
FY2021 (est.)	32,300	——	35,000	——	7,500	74,800
TOTAL	282,852	6,000	335,871	13,700	112,994	751,417

ESF = Economic Support Fund; DA = Development Assistance; INCLE = International Narcotics Control and Law Enforcement; NADR = Nonproliferation, Anti-Terrorism, De-mining and Related Programs; FMF = Foreign Military Financing.

Note: The U.S. federal fiscal year runs from October 1 of the budget's prior year through September 30 of the year being described. For example, FY2021 is between October 1, 2020, and September 30, 2021; and FY2020 is the budget for October 1, 2019, through September 30, 2020. See Fiscal Year: Definition, Federal Budget Examples (thebalance.com).

Source: "In Focus: Caribbean Basin Security Initiative," U.S. Congressional Research Service, November 16, 2021. https://crsreports.congress.gov/product/pdf/IF/IF10789/23/.

requested US$36.2 million, about a 37 percent decrease from FY2017, but Congress rejected those cuts. For FY2018 Congress appropriated US$57.7 million, and for FY2019 it appropriated US$58 million. For FY2020 the Trump administration requested US$40.2 million for the program, about a 30 percent reduction from the amount appropriated in FY2019. Congress agreed to appropriate not less than US$60 million for FY2020, slightly more than was provided the previous year.

In one of his February 2020 blogs, Curtis Ward, former Jamaican envoy to the United Nations, noted that on the tenth anniversary of the CBSI, involving former president Barack Obama's signature security assistance partnership with the region, President Donald Trump's FY2021 budget cut proposal undermined the audacious promises made by Secretary of State Mike Pompeo during his January 2020 visit to Jamaica. Ward observed, "Even as Pompeo was in Jamaica speaking of the increasing security threats to the region and promoting the effectiveness of the CBSI program, his State Department was complicit in proposing significant cuts to the CBSI budget" (Ward 2020). Ambassador Ward also recalled that Trump's FY2021 budget request cut US$28 million from the US$60 million approved by the Congress for FY2020 and was half the level of annual funding during the Obama administration. Ward made the prescient observation that reduced CBSI funding runs contrary to the increasing security threats to the region. Indeed, just before his Jamaica visit, Pompeo had attended the hemisphere's third counterterrorism summit where terrorism threats in the hemisphere were discussed.

Thankfully, the Biden administration has begun to take a different approach. For FY2022 they sought US$66 million for the CBSI, 10 percent more than the amount appropriated in FY2020 and about 12 percent less than that appropriated for FY2021. In July 2021 the House approved its version of the FY2022 foreign aid appropriations bill, which contained not less than US$80 million for the CBSI. In October 2021 the Senate Appropriations Committee introduced its version of the bill, which identified US$74.5 million for the CBSI. According to the Congressional Research Service, the Caribbean Basin Security Initiative Authorization Act ordered reported by the House Foreign Affairs Committee in September 2021 associated US$74.8 million for the CBSI for each fiscal year from FY2022 through FY2026. The full House later approved a similar bill. Regrettably, the Senate did not consider the matter. Interestingly, according to a 2019 Government Accountability Office report, from FY2010 through FY2018, the Dominican Republic received almost 23 percent of the CBSI funding; Jamaica, just over 19 percent; seven Eastern Caribbean countries received 24 percent; and 21 percent was deployed for region-wide activities (U.S. Congressional Research Service 2020).

The Caribbean Basin Security Initiative covers five areas:

1. Maritime and Aerial Security Cooperation, including assistance to strengthen Caribbean maritime and aerial operations capability, improve radar coverage, and sustain those capabilities;
2. Law Enforcement Capacity Building, including assistance to improve law enforcement though police professionalization, anti-corruption training, and community-based policing;
3. Border/Port Security and Firearms Interdiction, including support to improve capacity to intercept drugs, weapons, bulk cash, and other contraband at airports and seaports;
4. Justice Sector Reform, including support to increase the efficacy of prosecutors and criminal courts and reform and strengthen juvenile justice systems; and
5. Crime Prevention and At-Risk Youth, including assistance to populations vulnerable to being victims of crime or at risk of recruitment into criminal organizations.

(U.S. General Accounting Office, 2019;
U.S. Congressional Research Service, 2020)

The United Kingdom is also a key strategic partner, and it has maintained several programs over the years. For example, its Caribbean Anti-Corruption Program, which focuses on Jamaica and the Organization of Eastern Caribbean States member states, is a five-year program (2015–2020) aimed at strengthening their anticorruption framework by building the capacity of select institutions to improve accountability and transparency. Specifically, the project aims to (1) strengthen the capacity of Jamaica's Major and Organized Crime Anti-Corruption Agency to combat corruption and organized crime; (2) provide support to the Financial Investigations Division to recover assets acquired by corruption or organized crime; (3) provide support to Jamaica's Independent Commission of Investigations to hold public officials accountable for their abuse of power; (4) provide support to the government of Jamaica for the establishment of an Integrity Commission to fight corruption and strengthen accountability; and (5) provide support to the Regional Security System to recover assets acquired illegally. The funding was £16,999,993 (US$21,962,290).[3]

Another program, Caribbean Serious Organized Crime, which is funded by the British Conflict, Stability, and Security Fund, was launched in 2017 to assist countries in improving their ability to disrupt serious organized crime, notably by increasing their law enforcement capabilities. The program budget is £3,270,000 (US$4,223,532). Caribbean countries are also beneficiaries of the National School of Government International, which was established in 2018 with a budget of £2,040,564 (US$2,635,592) to improve governance through delivery of short- and long-term programmatic interventions, framing and solving problems identified by counterparts.[4] Of course, this is just a minuscule indication of British engagement.

As for Canada, Roy Price noted that they assist the region through core support to multilateral organizations such as the World Bank, the Inter-American Development Bank, and the International Monetary Fund, and through regional bodies such as the Caribbean Development Bank, in which Canada is the largest non-borrowing shareholder and the largest contributor to the bank's Special Development Fund. In terms of specific programs, Caribbean countries benefit from Canada's Anti-Crime Capacity Building Program (ACCBP), which works to improve the capacity of beneficiary states, government entities, and international organizations to deal with transnational crime.

Although the program has a global mandate, particular attention is paid to Central America, the Caribbean, and Mexico. During the period 2016 to 2017, the ACCBP is reported to have dedicated CA\$13.9 million (US\$10,450,020) to projects in the Americas that tackled issues related to illicit drugs, corruption, human trafficking, migrant smuggling, crime prevention (including cybersecurity), security sector reform, and the proceeds of crime (including money laundering) (Price 2019).

A few other initiatives are worthy of note:

Integrity, Mobilization, Participation, Accountability, Anti-Corruption, and Transparency (IMPACT), which ran from 2016 to 2020, and benefited Jamaica, Trinidad and Tobago, and a few countries outside the Caribbean, with funding of CA\$13,610,805 (US\$10,232,603) to increase the integrity, transparency, and accountability of public institutions and businesses while empowering civil society to advocate for change in policy and practice.

Judicial Reform and Institutional Strengthening, which benefited the Caribbean Court of Justice (CCJ), was offered between 2013 and 2019 at the cost of CA\$19,995,000 (US\$15,028,242). Activities included (1) reengineering the CCJ's business processes; (2) delivering training to court administrators and support staff; (3) developing, introducing, and enhancing appropriate delay and backlog reduction mechanisms; and (4) establishing court administration policies and procedures.

Improved Access to Justice in the Caribbean (IMPACT Justice), administered by the University of the West Indies between 2014 and 2023 with CA\$19,800,000 (US\$14,885,640) worth of funding initially. Headed by former UWI law dean Velma Newton, the project aims to ensure that women, men, youth, and businesses have better access to justice. Its components are (1) to draft and present a gender-equitable and environment-sensitive model to the CARICOM member states; (2) to design, promote, and deliver courses on legislation and treaty drafting for the undergraduate and postgraduate law programs; (3) to conduct a survey of legal education, including accreditation requirements; (4) to deliver training modules to representatives of organizations; and (5) to deliver regional workshops and public education to share knowledge about alternative dispute resolution and restorative justice.

Justice Undertakings for Social Transformation, a two-part project launched in 2008 with a view to concluding in 2020, with Jamaica as the sole beneficiary. Part I was funded with CA$10,601,619 (US$7,969,237) and part II with CA$8,506,000 (US$6,392,259). The program was intended to foster an improved sense of security for Jamaicans, and it had three complementary aspects: (1) order in institutions; (2) order in legislation; and (3) order in society.

Evaluating Alternatives for Imprisonment for Drug-Related Offenses in the Caribbean and Central America, which ran between 2017 and 2019 and was funded with CA$833,127 (US$626,095). The program was intended to assist Barbados, Costa Rica, the Dominican Republic, Jamaica, Panama, and Trinidad and Tobago in improving the ability of personnel involved in drug treatment courts to evaluate court operations as an alternative to adult incarceration for drug-dependent offenders. It was administered by the executive secretariat of the OAS's Inter-American Drug Abuse Control Commission.

(Price 2019)

Sovereignty Stress and Narco State Status

In the discussion about sovereignty in chapter 2, Louis Henkin's proposition noted that "in simpler days, state sovereignty implied several key elements. Primarily, it meant political interdependence. It also meant territorial integrity and virtually exclusive control and jurisdiction within that territory" (Henkin 1999, 2). In the context of things relevant to the Caribbean, we observed that several developments contributed to passage beyond "simpler days." One development was decolonization, which gave rise to the birth of several independent states into a "brave new world" but with such small size and subordinate status in the international scheme of things that their sovereignty was compromised from "birth." The globalization phenomenon also has been a relevant factor.

Nonetheless, as previously noted, even before the advent of decolonization and the spread of globalization, the sovereignty discourse tended to focus on its international, formal-legal dimension: freedom from outside interference; that no authority is legally above a state except that which a state's leaders voluntarily confer on international bodies. However, many scholars and statesmen accepted—especially following decolonization—that a key aspect of sovereignty relates to a nation's internal dynamics. This aspect, called "positive sovereignty," pertains to the holders of state power not only being free from external interference but also having the ability to deliver "political goods" to citizens internally.

Positive sovereignty pertains to governance, and it entails having the economic, public security, and other capabilities to design and deliver public policy.

Curiously, part of the sovereignty stress has been related to a subject that has attracted considerable political emotionalism and journalistic sensationalism over recent years: the matter of Caribbean nations being narco states. Over the last few decades, narco state status has been ascribed by various journalists and local and foreign politicians to Jamaica, Puerto Rico, Guyana, Trinidad and Tobago, the Dominican Republic, Antigua and Barbuda, and Suriname (see Granger 2011; Bybee 2011; Townsend 2010; Pachico 2011b; Ryan 2012; VOXXI 2013). I also am aware that the WikiLeaks reports mentioned Guyana during the tenure of Ronald Bullen, U.S. ambassador to Guyana between 2003 and 2006. Nevertheless, my concern is not merely with the ascription but with whether the evidence bears out this claim.

In broader global terms, the plausible observation has been made that practically every illegal drug-producing or drug-trafficking nation in the world has been called a "narco state" at one time or another or has been warned against becoming such—sometimes by international officials, by counternarcotics officials, by national leaders and other politicians, and by journalists and academics. Although lacking an agreed definition, the term has become exceedingly common. Indeed, one scholar suggests that it would appear that what a narco state is, or is supposed to be, is mostly assumed. Consequently, labeling a country a narco state is relatively easy and often serves the ulterior motives of some state actors interested in delegitimizing particular governments. For Ashley Bybee, "A Narco-State is defined as a state whose political, economic, security or social institutions have been impacted to some extent by the drug trade" (2011, 97).

The phrase "to some extent by the drug trade" gives such elasticity to the definition that it makes so many nations qualify as narco states as to undermine the parsimony of the definition, thereby reducing its explanatory value. Thus, I am persuaded by the proposition that the three most important narco state criteria are (1) the surface area covered by illegal drug crops; (2) the size of the illegal drug economy relative to the overall economy; and (3) the state sponsorship of illegal drug production or trafficking (Chouvy 2016, 35). Pierre-Arnaud Chouvy also argues convincingly that "for a state to be rightly categorized as a narco state, the illegal drug industry must be state sponsored and must contribute to the majority of a country's overall economy (GDP + illegal economy or, as is now the case within the European Union, GDP that includes the illegal economy)" (35).

All things considered, notwithstanding the gravity of the drugs PWP, the narco state ascription to Caribbean nations has been misplaced; no Caribbean nation has ever been a narco state. Chouvy's assertion is particularly relevant to the Caribbean: "No state resorts to illegal drug production or trafficking as part of an official policy as no such ideal narco-state can exist within the international system without becoming a pariah" (30). Caribbean leaders know that their nations are too small, subordinate, subject to multiple vulnerabilities, and dependent on global factors for their survival to risk having them become pariahs. This is not to detract from the seriousness of the situation in many places. There was some credence to the assertion by former Trinidad and Tobago Independent senator Martin Daly that "here in Trinidad and Tobago the slackness of our leaders, not only the political ones, has permitted our country to become narco infiltrated to the point where no one seriously doubts that there are facilitators of the drug trade at every level in the society" (Daly 2011). Of course, over time aspects of this facilitation sentiment have resonated with other places, including Guyana, Suriname, Haiti, the Dominican Republic, Jamaica, and Puerto Rico, given the scope of the drug activities and the corruption there.

The contemporary world faces two incontrovertible realities; the first is that security is not absolute, and the second is that sovereignty is not sacrosanct. Beyond the vicissitudes of economic and security interdependence, there is the powerful factor of information technology. As was argued elsewhere, not only are sovereign boundaries no longer impregnable, but they are also subject to "attack"—and often are "attacked"—by both "enemies" and "friends." All kinds of data move across, over, and through borders as if the borders did not exist. Over-the-horizon radar reaches deep into sovereign airspace of countries with wide geographical expanses, and satellites with high-resolution cameras peer down at military and commercial installations within national boundaries (see Griffith 1995b, 7). Indeed, as indicated in chapter 5, cyber threats take sovereignty vulnerabilities to new heights. Accordingly, as Jarat Chopra and Thomas Weiss asserted several decades ago, "Whether the power structure of sovereign states ever accurately reflected textbook characteristics, sovereignty is no longer sovereign; the world has outgrown it. The exclusivity and inviolability of state sovereignty are increasingly mocked by global interdependence" (Chopra and Weiss 1992, 104).

In my view, the combined effects of global interdependence and impact of the PWPs on Caribbean (and other) states have enabled the mockery of their sovereignty to be taken to new "highs"—or, perhaps, "lows," depending on one's vantage point. The gravity of the manifestations of the four PWPs accentuates the security vulnerability of these nations and further exposes the tenuousness of their sovereignty. The intensity of the threats varies among countries. As such, the nature and extent of the compromise and the siege varies across the region. Much as it might be anathema to some leaders, the harsh reality is that their nations' security is severely compromised, and their sovereignty is under siege. What, then, are some manifestations of compromised sovereignty of Caribbean countries?

Manifestations of Challenged Sovereignty

It is useful here to recall the working definitions of security and of sovereignty that were delineated in chapter 2. *Security* is defined as "protection and preservation of a people's freedom from external military attack and coercion, from internal subversion, and from the erosion of cherished political, economic, and social values." With regard to *sovereignty*, it is taken to mean "the supreme authority of a state over itself, without any interference from foreign entities, unless expressly permitted by the state's authorized officials, that secures its territory and citizens, and possesses the economic, technical, military, and other capabilities to promulgate and execute domestic and foreign policy."

Recall, too, that *challenged sovereignty* was defined as "a condition where the state's vulnerability is exacerbated by internal or external developments that compromise the ability of the supreme authority of the state to promulgate and execute domestic and foreign policy in its own deliberate judgment and on its own terms." It was captured as $CS = \Sigma\ (C1 + C2 + C3)$, where CS is Challenged Sovereignty, C1 is Condition 1, C2 is Condition 2, and C3 is Condition 3.

The conditions themselves were specified as follows:

Condition 1 (C1): The authorized officials of a state can no longer effectively protect the territorial integrity of their state from intruders, whether such intruders are state or non-state actors and irrespective of whether the intruders aim to have a sustained presence in the jurisdiction in question or just transit it.

Condition 2 (C2): The authorized officials of a state face such capability constraints that they are compelled to rely on other states and on international agencies to underwrite public security equipment, training, and other resources and on a sustained basis, such that the absence of those resources jeopardizes the effective maintenance of public security or national defense.

Condition 3 (C3): The authorized officials of a state lack the requisite capabilities to exercise effective internal public order and external sovereign control, which necessitates reliance on external capabilities support; that, in turn, risks further compromising the independence of their actions in promulgating and executing domestic and foreign policies and possibly aggravating the vulnerability of the state.

In the context of the above, it is plausible to posit that, overall, the drugs, crime, terrorism, and cyber PWPs undermine the security and sovereignty of the Caribbean and place the region in a circumstance of challenged sovereignty through the manifestations captured in figure 8.1.

FIGURE 8.1 Manifestations of Challenged Sovereignty in the Caribbean.
Source: Author created.

With regard to these manifestations, the following cases of confiscation and forfeiture are worth noting:

- In October 2013 the properties seized in the Dominican Republic from Puerto Rican kingpin Jose Figueroa Agosto and those of convicted traffickers Manuel Emilio Mesa "El Gringo," Quirino Paulino "El Don," René Sinclair, and Félix Zapata Molet were auctioned though the National Money Laundering Committee. The government raised some RD$150 million (US$2,812,500) from the sale of luxury vehicles, upscale apartments and houses, and lots that had been seized from the convicted individuals (*Dominican Today* 2013b).
- In 2015 in Antigua and Barbuda, Ahmed Williams was convicted of possession with intent to supply and possession with intent to sell after he had been arrested while conducting a drug transaction. He was found in possession of 3.3 kilograms of cocaine, US$16,446, and EC$41,965. After

the conviction, two parcels of land owned by Williams were forfeited to the government (U.S. Department of State, *International Narcotics Control Strategy Report*, 2016b, Vol. 2: 63).

- In 2016 in Jamaica, the Supreme Court froze four high-end properties, valued at nearly J$400 million (US$2,824,000), that were traced by local investigators to a Jamaican couple who had pleaded guilty to drug-trafficking and money-laundering charges in the United States. The properties included a sixteen-unit apartment complex, valued at US$180 million on 20,000 square feet of land in tourism hot spot Montego Bay. The other properties were a ten-unit apartment complex, valued at US$800,000 (J$103 million); another apartment complex, valued at US$500,000 (J$65 million), both in St. James; and a parcel of land being developed in Trelawny (Barrett 2016).

- As noted in chapter 5, in 2017, searches were conducted in Curaçao of homes and business premises owned by Chinese businesspeople as part of an investigation into money laundering and underground banking. One man was arrested and 1 million Antillean guilders (almost half a million euros [US$572,500]) and several cars and buildings, valued at approximately 10 million Antillean guilders (nearly 5 million euros [US$5,725,000]), were seized (van der Veen and Heuts 2018, 40).

- Between 2017 and 2018, twelve people were charged in St. Lucia with money laundering, and in 2018 there were six cash forfeitures totaling US$565,050 (EC$1,527,068) (U.S. Department of State, *International Narcotics Control Strategy Report*, 2019d, Vol. 2: 164).

- In 2018 in Guyana, following the arrest of four Colombians, one Venezuelan, and five Guyanese involved in trafficking, the following items were confiscated: a Toyota Axio car; three speedboats with engines; fifteen cell phones, eleven kilos of cocaine; and a large amount of cash, which included US$87,134, over 1 million Venezuelan bolivares, Colombian pesos totaling US$201,000, 7,362 in Brazilian reals, and G$$82,820 (US$393) (*Kaieteur News* 2018).

As if Caribbean countries did not have enough security and sovereignty stresses because of the PWPs, the COVID-19 pandemic created additional sovereignty stresses, exacerbating the condition of challenged sovereignty. How so? one might ask. Answering this question requires an appreciation of the nature and scope of the region's pandemic exposure.

The COVID-19 Factor

Coronaviruses are a large family of viruses that cause illnesses ranging from the common cold to more serious ones, such as Middle East Respiratory Syndrome (MERS) and Severe Acute Respiratory Syndrome (SARS). A novel coronavirus is a new strain not previously detected in humans. COVID-19 causes pneumonia-like symptoms, including coughs, fever, breathing difficulties, and, in serious cases, organ failure. The name COVID-19 was revealed in February 2020 by the World Health Organization (WHO) (Boseley et al. 2020). The first COVID-19 cases in the Caribbean were reported on March 1, 2020, in St. Martin in a couple who returned from France and in the Dominican Republic in a sixty-one-year-old man visiting from Italy.

COVID-19 has been a significant disease, an equal-opportunity plague that has spared no part of the global commons. We saw in chapter 1 that as of March 10, 2023, the world had endured 676,609,955 infections and 6,881,955 fatalities. When put in Caribbean context, the number of cases worldwide is equivalent to sixty times the 2023 population of Cuba, which is 11.1 million, and the number of deaths worldwide is almost eleven times the population of Suriname, which is 623,236. According to the Caribbean Public Health Agency (CARPHA), the confirmed infections in thirty-five countries and territories as of March 8, 2023, was 4,466,048, while the deaths totaled 37,005.[5] The number of regional deaths amounts to 68 percent of the 2023 population of St. Kitts and Nevis, which was 54,332.

Carissa Etienne, the Pan American Health Organization (PAHO) director, struck several chords of concern in late February 2022. For example, she noted that although COVID-19 deaths have fallen in the Americas for the first time since the beginning of the Omicron variant, the Caribbean remains vulnerable to the virus. Moreover, vaccination rates lagged in many countries at the very time there was a surge in new cases, leading to increases in hospital admissions and deaths. Indeed, more than half of the thirteen PAHO countries that reported increases in deaths were in the Caribbean. In addition, the overall pandemic profile of several countries was troubling at the close of February 2022. In Jamaica, for example, infections surged by 23 percent; in Grenada there was a 50 percent increase in Intensive Care Unit (ICU) admissions; and in Guadeloupe there was a 9 percent increase in ICU admissions (Charles 2022).

The sovereignty stress derives from several factors—notably, the harmful impact on the region's economy, especially on tourism, as noted in chapter 5, along with the pressure on already weak public health systems and heavy reliance on foreign (non-Caribbean) sources to help combat the pandemic. Akin to the circumstances of combating PWPs, significant reliance on international sources for hand sanitizers; testing kits; personal protective equipment, such as face masks and shields; ventilators; and vaccines, is a major indicator of challenged sovereignty. In relation to vaccines, for instance, only Cuba has the capability to develop and administer homegrown inoculations, through five vaccines: Soberana 1, Soberana 2, Soberana Plus, Mambisa, and Abdala. All other Caribbean countries have had to rely on other state and non-state entities. Some of the vaccines are donated and others are purchased. Some of the gifting is done bilaterally, others in multilateral context, through COVAX.

Formed in 2020, COVAX—the COVID-19 Vaccines Global Access system—is co-led by the Coalition for Epidemic Preparedness Innovations, the Global Alliance for Vaccines and Immunization, and the WHO, with UNICEF as a delivery partner. In the Americas, the PAHO Revolving Fund is COVAX's recognized procurement agent and delivery partner. Table 8.2, which shows the gains by Caribbean countries through COVAX, largely reflects U.S. donations to the region, directly and through PAHO. However, the table provides just a partial portrait of the acquisitions by the region, as there has been vaccine diplomacy engagement bilaterally with China, France, India, Denmark, Spain, Russia, and other countries as well (see Griffith 2021b).

TABLE 8.2 COVID-19 Vaccines Secured through COVAX as of June 10, 2022

Country	Vaccine Supplier	Buyer	Quantity (doses)	Arrival
Antigua & Barbuda	AstraZeneca AB	PAHO	24,000	April 8, 2021
	AstraZeneca AB	PAHO	16,800	June 9, 2021
	AstraZeneca AB	PAHO	19,200	Nov. 17, 2021
Bahamas	AstraZeneca AB	PAHO	33,600	March 30, 2021
	AstraZeneca AB	PAHO	33,600	May 11, 2021
	AstraZeneca AB	PAHO	33,600	Aug. 3, 2021
	Pfizer Overseas LLC	PAHO	57,330	Oct. 18,2021
Barbados	AstraZeneca AB	PAHO	33,600	April 6, 2021
	AstraZeneca AB	PAHO	33,600	May 11, 2021
	AstraZeneca AB	PAHO	33,600	Aug. 24, 2021
	Pfizer Overseas LLC	PAHO	14,040	Dec. 16, 2021
Belize	AstraZeneca AB	PAHO	33,600	March 31, 2021
	AstraZeneca AB	PAHO	33,600	May 12, 2021
	AstraZeneca AB	PAHO	33,600	Aug. 3, 2021
	Pfizer Overseas LLC	PAHO	58,500	Oct. 27, 2021
Bermuda	AstraZeneca AB	PAHO	9,600	April 6, 2021
Dominica	AstraZeneca AB	PAHO	28,800	April 6, 2021
	Pfizer Overseas LLC	United States	63,180	Dec. 14, 2021
	Moderna Switzerland	PAHO	30,240	Feb. 4, 2022
Dom. Republic	AstraZeneca AB	PAHO	91,200	April 6, 2021
	AstraZeneca AB	PAHO	187,200	May 14, 2021
	AstraZeneca AB	PAHO	184,800	Aug. 27, 2021

(continued)

TABLE 8.2 (*continued*)

Country	Vaccine Supplier	Buyer	Quantity (doses)	Arrival
Grenada	AstraZeneca AB	PAHO	24,000	April 9, 2021
	AstraZeneca AB	PAHO	21,600	May 26, 2021
	Pfizer Overseas LLC	United States	60,030	Dec. 16, 2021
	Moderna Switzerland	PAHO	5,040	March 23, 2022
	Moderna Switzerland	PAHO	5,040	June 8, 2022
Guyana	AstraZeneca AB	PAHO	24,000	March 29, 2021
	AstraZeneca AB	PAHO	38,400	May 10, 2021
	AstraZeneca AB	PAHO	19,200	Aug. 14, 2021
	AstraZeneca AB	PAHO	38,400	Aug. 14, 2021
	Pfizer Overseas LLC	United States	100,620	Oct. 8, 2021
	Pfizer Overseas LLC	United States	42,120	Dec. 6, 2021
	Janssen	Spain	28,800	Jan. 14, 2022
Haiti	Moderna	United States	500,000	July 14, 2021
	Moderna Switzerland	United States	100,100	Nov. 3, 2021
	Janssen	Denmark	57,600	Dec. 18, 2021
	Janssen	United States	108,000	Dec. 18, 2021
	Pfizer Overseas LLC	United States	39,780	Jan. 11, 2022
	Pfizer Overseas LLC	United States	88,920	Feb. 8, 2022
	Moderna Switzerland	PAHO	151,200	Feb. 14, 2022
Jamaica	AstraZeneca AB	PAHO	14,400	March 15, 2021
	AstraZeneca AB	PAHO	55,200	April 26, 2021
	AstraZeneca AB	PAHO	55,200	May 30, 2021
	AstraZeneca AB	Canada	100,800	Sept. 14, 2021
	AstraZeneca AB	Spain	100,800	Sept. 16, 2021
	AstraZeneca AB	Germany	108,000	Oct. 12, 2021
	Pfizer Overseas LLC	PAHO	100,620	Oct. 29, 2021
	AstraZeneca AB	Canada	369,600	Nov. 1, 2021
	Pfizer Overseas LLC	PAHO	106,620	Nov. 25, 2021
	Pfizer Overseas LLC	PAHO	98,280	Dec. 8, 2021
	Pfizer Overseas LLC	France	250,380	Feb. 7, 2022
	AstraZeneca AB	Canada	100,000	Feb. 22, 2022
	Pfizer Overseas LLC	France	398,970	March 21, 2022
St. Kitts & Nevis	AstraZeneca AB	PAHO	21,600	April 7, 2021

TABLE 8.2 *(continued)*

Country	Vaccine Supplier	Buyer	Quantity (doses)	Arrival
St. Lucia	AstraZeneca AB	PAHO	24,000	April 7, 2021
	AstraZeneca AB	PAHO	26,400	May 12, 2021
	AstraZeneca AB	PAHO	24,000	Sept. 1, 2021
	Pfizer Overseas LLC	United States	115,830	Dec. 14, 2021
	Janssen	Spain	7,200	Dec. 28, 2021
	Moderna Switzerland	PAHO	5,040	March 16, 2022
St Vincent & the Grenadines	AstraZeneca AB	PAHO	24,000	April 7, 2021
	AstraZeneca AB	PAHO	21,600	May 25, 2021
	Pfizer Overseas LLC	United States	70,200	Dec. 15, 2021
Suriname	AstraZeneca AB	PAHO	24,000	March 26, 2021
	AstraZeneca AB	PAHO	28,800	May 10, 2021
	AstraZeneca AB	PAHO	26,400	Aug. 9, 2021
	AstraZeneca AB	Spain	64,800	Dec. 14, 2021
Trinidad & Tobago	AstraZeneca AB	PAHO	33,600	March 30, 2021
	AstraZeneca AB	PAHO	33,600	May 10, 2021
	AstraZeneca AB	PAHO	33,600	Aug. 11, 2021
	Beijing Institute of Biological Products	PAHO	84,000	Nov. 27, 2021

Source: "PAHO Tracker COVAX Initiative Covid-19 Vaccine Deliveries in the Americas," 2022, Microsoft Power BI. https://app.powerbi.com/view?r=eyJrljoiMjA5ZDAxMmEtYTljNC00M2I0LWE5MjUtYWQzZGQx NDc4OThhliwidCI6ImU2MTBlNzljLTJlYzAtNGUwZi04YTE0LTFlNGIxMDE1MTlmNylslmMiOjR9/.

All things considered, the proposition that the Caribbean is facing a circumstance of challenged sovereignty seems well founded. In response to the question "How secure is security?" I offer the inartful but realistic answer: "Not very!" And to the question, "How sovereign is sovereignty?" I also offer a similarly inartful but pragmatic response: "It never really was, and this is obvious now that the sovereignty ship is churning in Category Four hurricane seas." Clearly, the security and sovereignty challenges are far from being overcome. Some two decades ago Prime Minister Ralph Gonsalves of St. Vincent and the Grenadines acknowledged, "It is true that an incidence of being a state is that it has the legitimate monopoly on physical coercion, yet in a growing number of Caribbean countries the dons, the gangs, organized and non-organized criminals challenge this monopoly. In the process, ordinary right-thinking persons begin to question the very legitimacy and relevance of the state itself" (Gonsalves 2003, 32).

Gonsalves then posed the "elephant in the room" question that now is more on the minds—and the lips—of statesmen, citizens, and other individuals within and outside the Caribbean than when he asked it rhetorically nearly two decades ago: "What is the purpose of a nation-state if it cannot guarantee its citizens and visitors, in practice, a condition which protects their security and personal safety?" (32) Yet all is not lost. As noted earlier, the leaders and citizens of the Caribbean, aided by strategic partners, are waging "wars" on various fronts, even though the assets to effectively "wage war," much less to "win war," are woefully inadequate.

The acknowledgment by Jamaica's leader of their funding and other constraints is illustrative of the region-wide dilemma. In addressing the launch of the Global Tourism Resilience and Crisis Management Centre in Montego Bay in January 2019, Prime Minister Holness was candid in relation to cyber challenges: "Security no longer means protecting tourists against physical threats, but also means protecting people against cyber threats, including Internet frauds, identity thefts and others. It is, however, true that *most Caribbean destinations neither have preventive nor remedial systems to manage cyberattacks*" (Davis 2019; emphasis added). Moreover, in his 2020 New Year's Day message, Prime Minister Holness acknowledged the country's inability to manage the high crime and conceded that several factors contributed to their circumstances in that successive governments did not maintain appropriate national security funding, keep abreast with technology, increase the number of investigators and other critical capabilities commensurately, or effectively control police corruption (Holness 2020).

Collaboration Imperative

Although Caribbean countries do not fit the bill as narco states, their circumstances are such that coping with PWP trials and tribulations requires regional and international collaboration and assistance. The late Trinidad and Tobago statesman A.N.R. Robinson articulated this necessity eloquently several decades ago, in noting, "Obviously, it would be foolhardy to depend entirely upon moral suasion and so, the protective services, police and military, play a critical role in ensuring and preserving the physical security of the state and its citizens" (Robinson 1991). Then–prime minister Robinson continued, "However, it is becoming increasingly apparent that no single state, large or small, can in isolation ensure its own security from subversion or external threat. In this era of the interdependence of states, and the globalization of activities relating to almost every sphere of life—economic, cultural, and criminal to name but a few—the preservation of national security can no longer be seen in purely national terms" (Robinson 1991).

The collaboration refrain was echoed by W. Andy Knight, who saw the necessity for Caribbean states to stop substituting one dependence for another, pool their sovereignty by strengthening existing regional institutions, and develop strategic partnerships with entities outside the region (Knight 2019, 406). This study and several others make it easy to concur with him that strategic partnerships are necessary for Caribbean states to cope with the vulnerability and insecurity dynamics of the international environment. Ramphal's reference to "a larger vessel" in the second epigraph to this chapter is noteworthy. For me, regionalism is the only credible "larger vessel," even though it is not a perfect one. Thus, it is disconcerting to see such dithering on regionalism by some Caribbean political elites, especially by leaders of nations that once championed regional integration. Notable here are the leaders of Trinidad and Tobago, the nation once led by champion of regionalism Eric Eustace Williams. These leaders seem unfazed by the contradiction of hosting the Caribbean Court of Justice while not wishing to have the country join the court. This is all the more so when British judicial and political officials have rebuked Caribbean nations for clinging to the Privy Council. Jamaican intransigence on the same issue also is notable. One prime minister—Bruce Golding—not only expressed healthy skepticism about leaving the Privy Council, but he also toyed with the idea of creating a Jamaican court of final appeal rather than embrace the CCJ (*Radio Jamaica News* 2010). Curiously, in May 2023, St. Lucia entered the CCJ's appellate jurisdiction, joining Guyana, Barbados, Dominica, and Belize in forgoing the British Privy Council as the court for its final appeals. The CCJ also exercises an original jurisdiction, in which it interprets and applies the Revised Treaty of Chaguaramas, the agreement that established the Caribbean Community, and serves an international court with compulsory and exclusive jurisdiction in relation to the interpretation of the treaty.

It is especially sad too that these two nations, to which many other Caribbean states look for leadership, would maintain this diffidence more than half a century after attaining their independence, both in 1962, as indicated in table 2.1. Speaking at the July 2011 CARICOM Summit, Prime Minister Ralph Gonsalves voiced what many leaders, citizens, and scholars believe: that the "Big Four" founding members of CARICOM must "in a coordinated way, drive, pull or push the regional juggernaut'" (Gonsalves 2011). The "Big Four" are Barbados, Guyana, Jamaica, and Trinidad and Tobago. With Barbados replacing the British queen as its head of state by becoming a republic on November 29, 2021, Jamaica is the sole remaining member of the Big Four that continues to be constitutionally tethered to the British monarchy. There is reason to hope that status change is in the offing, though. In his 2022 New Year's Day message, Prime Minister Holness remarked, "This year Jamaica will celebrate 60 years of Independence. It is time for us to start the process of redefining our State as a Republic" (Holness 2022).

In a 1996 study commissioned by the U.S. Institute for National Strategic Studies, I deemed survival as sovereign states to be the supreme challenge facing Caribbean states as they grappled with the security problems facing the region on the eve of the twenty-first century. The point also was made that the vulnerabilities to which Caribbean states are subjected, and the threats and apprehensions facing them, make real the question of whether some of them can survive in this century as political and economic entities with more than just a mere modicum of sovereignty (Griffith 1996, 73). This remark still is valid two decades into the twenty-first century.[6] Indeed, in some respects the situation has become graver since I first made the remark because of the impact of PWPs and environmental and other factors. All of this reinforces the necessity for continuous collaborative engagement.

The involvement of foreign strategic partners occasioned by the collaboration imperative does not absolve Caribbean security policy makers and practitioners of the responsibility to adopt a strategy design and delivery posture in coping with the PWPs and their security and sovereignty consequences. Caribbean leaders are to be commended for precisely doing some of this (see CARICOM IMPACS 2013). In terms of strategy engagement posture, propositions made elsewhere are still relevant and worth recalling. In assessing the security landscape in the aftermath of the September 11, 2001, terrorism incident, I suggested that Caribbean security elites should adopt two broad complementary strategies: engagement and adaptation (Griffith 2004).

In relation to the first strategy, I posited the following guiding precept: Caribbean security elites and practitioners should embrace proactive national and regional engagement in order to better cope with extant security challenges, lest the science of muddling through, which is practiced in some places, becomes the regional norm and undermines the security and sovereignty of nations in the region (Griffith 2004, 512–13). The guiding precept for the second one was, similarly, simple: Caribbean security elites and practitioners should undertake periodic threat assessments of their national and regional security landscapes and make adaptations in modes, methods, policies, and practices commensurate with the changing dynamics and needs (521). Needless to say, while thoughts about strategy are necessary, they are not sufficient. It also is necessary to offer some final reflections on this study overall.

Aims Revisited

As noted in chapter 1, this study has aimed to do the following:

- Outline relevant conceptual perimeters of the notions of vulnerability and security.

- Probe some relevant conceptual aspects of sovereignty and postulate the notion of challenged sovereignty.
- Examine some contemporary manifestations and consequences of four Problems Without Passports—the drug phenomenon, crime, terrorism, and cyber threats.
- Analyze the impact on security and sovereignty of the linkages between drugs and crime, with special attention to the 2010–2012 Christopher "Dudus" Coke saga in Jamaica and the 2011 state of emergency in Trinidad and Tobago, controversial cases with region-wide salience.
- Probe the nexus between geonarcotics and geopolitics, focusing on Suriname, where the 2010 election of a former coup maker, who also had the dubious distinction of being the world's only head of state with a drug trafficking conviction and sentence (in absentia), prompted concerns within the U.S. security establishment about the prospects of a narco state being established in Suriname.
- Ponder the question, "How secure is security, and how sovereign is sovereignty in the Caribbean?"

I am both comfortable and confident that these objectives have been fulfilled. Chapter 2 treats the first two aims in offering explorations of vulnerability, security, and sovereignty as well as in postulating the notion of challenged sovereignty. The third objective is addressed in the description and analysis of the four PWPs in three sections of the book—chapters 3, 4, and 5. The sixth chapter facilitates the pursuit of the fourth objective, while the seventh chapter provides the basis for the consideration of the fifth objective. The final objective is addressed above in this chapter. As promised at the end of chapter 2, pursuit of these objectives provided the opportunity for me to ask new questions, sketch new designs, and present data in relation to some of the PWPs that affect the Caribbean and their implications for the security and sovereignty of countries there. In my estimation, this quest has benefited from the provision of copious and credible analytic and empirical data as well as from balanced analysis. But it is for readers—both scholars and non-scholars—to judge how well I have fulfilled the objectives outlined.

I have covered considerable conceptual and empirical ground in this study, although I have not examined all the region's important security and sovereignty issues, such as environmental threats aggravated by the vicissitudes of climate change. Indeed, it was never my intent to examine *all* security and sovereignty challenges. For one thing, there is fertile ground for empirical analysis of the sad irony that crime has been so high and horrendous in the very societies that place such high symbolic value and platitudinous premium on religion.

With regard to the nexus between crime and religion in Jamaica, for example, former national security minister Peter Bunting himself lamented as follows in

Parliament in June 2013: "It has always struck me as paradoxical that Jamaica, according to the *Guinness Book of World Records*, has the most churches per square mile in the world, while also having one of the highest murder rates. I nevertheless continue to have faith that the Church can be one powerful catalyst for changing that sub-culture of violence" (Bunting 2013, 18). Of course, the high crime–deep religion irony applies to other Caribbean countries, and, indeed to the United States and many parts of Latin America. Understandably, too, Bunting's hopefulness that the Church will become a catalyst for change also exists in places other than Jamaica.

This book has offered abundant evidence that the clear and present dangers facing the Caribbean are such that they have resulted in a circumstance of challenged sovereignty for the region. Whether or not the rulers of some states care to acknowledge it, some states enjoy a mere modicum of sovereignty, especially when the perimeter of the sovereignty discourse is extended to the democracy domination and other realms, as the studies by Tom Farer, Linden Lewis, Hilbourne Watson, and other scholars do (see Farer 1996; L. Lewis 2013; Watson 2015). Yet, although despair has been manifesting itself in some places, for the region as a whole fatalism is not an option.

Bear in mind the first epigraph of the first chapter of this book, where President Bill Clinton pronounced on the nature of global interdependence and some of its pitfalls, noting that "many of the world's greatest challenges today are simply modern manifestations of our oldest demons" (Clinton 2012). I contend that drugs, crime, terrorism, and cyber threats, the PWPs examined in this study, are manifestations of some of these old demons. But in that same *Time* magazine opinion, Clinton articulated credible reasons for optimism and hope by the global community—reasons having to do with pursuits in the global commons related to technology, health care, economics, gender equality, and justice. By and large, those reasons for optimism and hope still exist, and they are complemented by others, such as diminution of armed conflict as the primary conflict resolution measure and a growing embrace by state and non-state actors of the collective responsibility to address the world's PWPs.

Beyond the chorus of optimism struck by statesman Bill Clinton and the refrain regarding resilience by scholar-statesman Ralph Gonsalves with prose, it is useful to reflect on chords of defiance and hope struck by a long-dead, distinguished writer with poetry by Jamaican-born Claude McKay, one of the intellectual giants of the Harlem Renaissance.[7] His poem of resistance "If We Must Die" was penned in 1919—not with the Caribbean in mind, though. McKay wrote about racism and the trials and tribulations facing poor and powerless Blacks in the United States. He wrote at a time when individuals and communities faced situations of hopelessness, where personal security and collective identity were under severe threat. However, I consider his words to have deep meaning for the contemporary Caribbean given its extant reality of challenged sovereignty.

> IF we must die—let it not be like hogs
> Hunted and penned in an inglorious spot,
> While round us bark the mad and hungry dogs,
> Making their mock at our accursed lot.
> If we must die—oh, let us nobly die,
> So that our precious blood may not be shed
> In vain; then even the monsters we defy
> Shall be constrained to honor us though dead!
> Oh, Kinsmen! We must meet the common foe;
> Though far outnumbered, let us show us brave,
> And for their thousand blows deal one death-blow!
> What though before us lies the open grave?
> Like men we'll face the murderous, cowardly pack,
> Pressed to the wall, dying, but fighting back!
> —Claude McKay

Extradition Treaty between Jamaica and the United States

LETTER OF TRANSMITTAL

THE WHITE HOUSE, April 17, 1984.

To the Senate of the United States:

With a view to receiving the advice and consent of the Senate to ratification, I transmit herewith the Treaty on Extradition between the United States of America and Jamaica, signed at Kingston on June 14, 1983.

I transmit also, for the information of the Senate, the report of the Department of State with respect to the Treaty.

The Treaty is the first modern United States extradition treaty within the Caribbean region. The Treaty will facilitate United States efforts to prosecute narcotics conspiracies by expressly providing that conspiracies and attempts to commit extraditable offenses constitute extraditable offenses.

The Treaty follows generally the form and consent of extradition treaties recently concluded by this Government. Upon entry into force of this Treaty, the Extradition Treaty between the United States and the United Kingdom signed on December 22, 1931, shall cease to have effect between the United States and Jamaica.

This Treaty will make a significant contribution to international co-operation in law enforcement. I recommend that the Senate give early and favorable consideration to the Treaty and give its advice and consent to ratification.

RONALD REAGAN.

LETTER OF SUBMITTAL

DEPARTMENT OF STATE,
Washington, April 5, 1984.

THE PRESIDENT,
The White House.
THE PRESIDENT: I have the honor to submit to you the Treaty on Extradition between the United States of America and Jamaica, signed at Kingston on June 14, 1983. I recommend that the Treaty be transmitted to the Senate for advice and consent to ratification.

The Treaty is the first modern United States extradition treaty within the Caribbean region. It will supersede the United States–United Kingdom Treaty on Extradition of 1931 which was made applicable to Jamaica in 1935. The Treaty follows generally the form and content of extradition treaties recently concluded by this Government.

Article 1 obligates each State to extradite to the other, in accordance with the terms of the Treaty, any persons charged with or convicted of an extraditable offense by the requesting State. (Extradition shall also be granted, Article 2 explains, for attempts and conspiracies to commit extraditable offenses, as well as for aiding and abetting the commission of such offenses.)

Article 1 further states that extradition shall be granted when the offense for which extradition is requested was committed outside the requesting State provided there is jurisdiction under the laws of both States for the punishment of such an offense in corresponding circumstances.

Article 2 permits extradition for any offense punishable under the laws of both States by imprisonment for more than one year. Instead of listing each offense for which extradition may be granted, as was United States practice until recently, this Treaty adopts the modern practice of permitting extradition for any crime punishable under the laws of both contracting Parties for a minimum period. This obviates the need to renegotiate or supplement the Treaty should both States pass laws covering new types of criminal activity, such as computer-related crimes.

Article 2 also follows the practice of recent United States extradition treaties in indicating that the dual criminality standard should be interpreted liberally in order to effectuate the intent of the Parties that fugitives be brought to justice.

Articles 3 and 6 state mandatory grounds for refusal of extradition. Article 3 provides that extradition shall be denied when the offense for which extradition is sought is a political offense or when it is established that the request is in fact made for the purpose of prosecuting the person sought on account of race, religion, nationality or political opinions or when, for the same reasons, the person sought is likely to be denied a fair trial or punished, detained or restricted in his personal liberty. Article 6 provides that extradition shall be denied where the requesting State's statute of limitation bars prosecution or enforcement of the penalty.

Article 4 states that extradition shall not be precluded by the fact that the requested State has chosen not to prosecute the person sought for the acts for which extradition is requested or has discontinued any pending criminal proceedings.

Articles 3(5) and 5 state discretionary grounds for refusal of extradition. Article 3(5) provides that extradition may be denied for military offenses. Article 5 provides that extradition may be refused when the offense is punishable by death in the requesting, but not the requested, State, unless satisfactory assurances are received that the death penalty, if imposed, will not be carried out.

Article 7 states the obligation of the requested State concerning extradition of its nationals. It provides, in brief, that if extradition is denied on the basis of nationality, the requested State shall, if it has jurisdiction, submit the case to its authorities for prosecution. Extradition shall not be refused, however, if the person sought is a national of both States.

Articles 8–11 specify procedures by which extradition is to be accomplished. The procedures therein are similar to those found in other modern United States extradition treaties.

Article 12 provides that surrender shall be deferred when the person whose extradition is sought is being proceeded against or has been convicted of a different offense in the requested State, unless the laws of the requested State otherwise provide.

Article 13 states that the executive authority of the requested Party shall determine to which country to surrender a person sought by more than one State.

Article 14 expressly incorporates into the Treaty the rule of specialty. This article provides, subject to specified exceptions, that a person extradited under the Treaty may not be detained, tried or punished for an offense other than that for which extradition has been granted.

Article 15 permits surrender without formal proceedings where the person sought agrees in writing to surrender after having been advised by a competent judicial authority of his or her right to a formal proceeding.

Article 16 provides that all property relating to the offense for which extradition is requested may, to the extent permitted under the laws of the requested State, be seized and surrendered to the requesting State. This provision is subject to the rights of third parties.

Article 17 governs expenses in a manner similar to other recent United States extradition treaties. This article further provides that the requested State shall represent the requesting State in any proceeding in the requested State arising out of a request for extradition.

Article 18, like the parallel provision of almost all recent United States extradition treaties, stipulates that the Treaty is retroactive in the sense that it applies to offenses committed before as well as after its entry into force, provided that the offenses were proscribed by the laws of both States when committed.

Article 19 provides that the Treaty will enter into force thirty days after the exchange of the instruments of ratification.

Article 20 provides for termination of the Treaty by either Party upon six months' written notice to the other.

The Department of Justice joins the Department of State in favoring approval of this Treaty by the Senate at an early date.

Respectfully submitted,

GEORGE P. SHULTZ.

EXTRADITION TREATY BETWEEN THE GOVERNMENT OF THE UNITED STATES OF AMERICA AND THE GOVERNMENT OF JAMAICA

The Government of the United States of America and the Government of Jamaica,

Recalling the Treaty for the Mutual Extradition of Criminals between the United Kingdom and the United States of America concluded in London in 1931;

Noting that both the Government of the United States of America and the Government of Jamaica have continued to apply the terms of that Treaty; and

Desiring to provide for more effective cooperation between the two States in the suppression of crime and, for that purpose, to conclude a new treaty for the extradition of offenders;

Have agreed as follows:

ARTICLE I

Obligation to Extradite

(1) The Contracting Parties agree to extradite to each other, subject to the provisions of this Treaty:

(a) persons whom the competent authorities in the Requesting State have charged with an extraditable offense committed within its territory; or

(b) persons who have been convicted in the Requesting State of such an offence and are unlawfully at large.

(2) With respect to an offence committed outside the territory of the Requesting State, the Requested State shall grant extradition, subject to the provisions of this Treaty, if there is jurisdiction under the laws of both States for the punishment of such an offense in corresponding circumstances.

ARTICLE II

Extraditable Offences

(1) An offence shall be an extraditable offence if it is punishable under the laws of both Contracting Parties by imprisonment or other form of detention for a period of more than one year or by any greater punishment.

(2) The following offences shall be extraditable if they meet the requirements of paragraph (1):

(a) conspiring in, attempting to commit, aiding or abetting, assisting, counseling or procuring the commission of, or being an accessory before or after the fact to, an offence described in that paragraph; or

(b) impeding the apprehension or prosecution of a person charged with an offence described in that paragraph.

(3) For the purposes of this Article, an offence shall be an extraditable offence:

(a) whether or not the laws of the Contracting Parties place the offence within the same category of offences or denominate the offence by the same terminology; or

(b) whether or not the offence is one for which United States federal law requires proof of interstate transportation, or use of the mails or of other facilities affecting interstate or foreign commerce, such matters being merely for the purpose of establishing jurisdiction in a United States federal court.

Political and Military Offences

(1) Extradition shall not be granted if the offence for which extradition is requested is of a political character.

(2) Extradition shall also not be granted if:

(a) it is established that extradition is requested for political purposes; or
(b) it is established that the request for extradition, though purporting to be on account of the extraditable offence, is in fact made for the purpose of prosecuting or punishing the person sought on account of his race, religion, nationality, or political opinions; or
(c) the person sought is by reason of his race, religion, nationality, or political opinions, likely to be denied a fair trial or punished, detained or restricted in his personal liberty for such reasons.

(3) It shall be the responsibility of the competent authorities of the Requested State to decide any question arising under paragraph (1). However, it shall be the responsibility of the executive authority of the Requested State to decide any question arising under paragraph (2) or (5) except to the extent that the national laws of that State expressly grant such powers to its courts.

(4) Paragraphs (1) and (2) shall not apply to an offence which is extraditable pursuant to a treaty or convention to which both Contracting Parties are parties, the purpose of which is to prevent or repress a specific category of offences, and which imposes on States an obligation either to extradite the person sought or submit the matter to the competent authorities for decision as to prosecution.

(5) Extradition may be refused for offences under military law which are not offences under ordinary criminal law.

ARTICLE IV

Effect of Decision Not to Prosecute

Extradition shall not be precluded by the fact that the competent authorities in the Requested State have decided not to prosecute the person sought for the acts for which extradition is requested or have decided to discontinue any criminal proceedings which have been initiated against the person sought.

ARTICLE V

Capital Punishment

(1) When the offence for which extradition is requested is punishable by death under the laws of the Requesting State, and the laws of the Requested State do not

permit such punishment for that offence, the executive authority of the Requested State may refuse to grant extradition.

(2) In exercising its discretion pursuant to paragraph (1), the executive authority of the Requested State shall give due and sympathetic consideration to any assurance given by the Requesting State, insofar as the laws of the Requesting State permit, that the death penalty will not be carried out.

ARTICLE VI

Lapse of Time

Extradition shall not be granted when prosecution of the offence for which extradition has been sought, or enforcement of the penalty for such an offence, has become barred by lapse of time according to the laws in the Requesting State.

ARTICLE VII

Nationality

(1) Neither Contracting Party shall be bound to deliver up its own nationals but the executive authority of the Requested State shall, if not prevented by the laws of that State, have the power to deliver them up if, in its discretion, it be deemed proper to do so.

(2) Extradition shall not be refused on the ground that the fugitive is a national of the Requested State if the fugitive is also a national of the Requesting State.

(3) If extradition is not granted for an offence pursuant to paragraph (1), the Requested State shall, if it has jurisdiction over the offence, submit the case to its highest competent authorities for decision as to prosecution, in according with the law of that State.

ARTICLE VIII

Extradition Procedures and Required Documents

(1) The request for extradition shall be made through the diplomatic channel.

(2) The request for extradition shall be supported by:

(a) documents, statements, or other evidence which describe the identity and probable location of the person sought;

(b) a statement of the facts of the case, including, if possible, the time and location of the offence;

(c) a statement of the provisions of the law describing the essential elements and the designation of the offence for which extradition is requested;

(d) a statement of the provisions of the law prescribing the punishment for the offence; and

(e) a statement of the provisions of the law prescribing any time limit on the prosecution or the execution of punishment for the offence.

(3) A request for extradition relating to a person who is sought for prosecution shall also be supported by:

(a) a copy of the warrant of arrest issued by a judge or other judicial authority in the Requesting State; and

(b) such evidence as would justify the committal for trial of that person if the offence had been committed in the Requested State.

(4) When the request for extradition relates to a convicted person, in addition to those items required by paragraph (2), it shall be supported by a certificate of conviction or copy of the judgment of conviction rendered by a court in the Requesting State. If the person has been convicted and sentenced, the request for extradition shall also be supported by a statement showing to what extent the sentence has been carried out. If the person has been convicted but not sentenced, the request for extradition shall also be supported by a statement to that effect.

(5) Statements, depositions and other documents transmitted in support of the request for extradition shall be transmitted through the diplomatic channel and shall be admissible if certified or authenticated in such manner as may be required by the law of the Requested State.

ARTICLE IX

Additional Information

(1) If the executive authority of the Requested State considers that the information furnished in support of the request for extradition is not sufficient to fulfill the requirements of this Treaty, it shall notify the Requesting State in order to enable that State to furnish additional information before the request is submitted to a court of the Requested State.

(2) The executive authority may fix a time limit for such information to be furnished.

(3) Nothing in paragraph (1) or (2) shall prevent the executive authority of the requested State from presenting to a court of that State information sought or obtained after submission of the request to the court or after expiration of the time stipulated pursuant to paragraph (2).

ARTICLE X

Provisional Arrest

(1) In case of urgency either Contracting Party may request the provisional arrest in accordance with the law of the Requested State of any accused or convicted person pending the request for extradition. Application for provisional arrest shall be made through the diplomatic channel or directly between the Department of Justice in the United States of America and the Minister responsible for extradition in Jamaica.

(2) The application shall contain:

(a) a description of the person sought;

(b) the location of that person if known;

(c) such information as would be necessary to justify the issuance of a warrant of arrest had the offence been committed, or the person sought been convicted, in the territory of the Requested State; and

(d) a statement that a request for extradition of the person sought will follow.

(3) On receipt of such an application, the Requested State shall take the appropriate steps to secure the arrest of the person sought. The Requesting State shall be promptly notified of the result of its application.

(4) A person who is provisionally arrested shall be discharged from custody upon the expiration of sixty (60) days from the date of arrest pursuant to the application for provisional arrest if the executive authority of the Requested State has not received the formal request for extradition and the supporting documents required by Article VIII.

(5) The fact that a person is discharged from custody pursuant to paragraph (4) shall not prejudice the extradition of that person if the extradition request and the supporting documents mentioned in Article VIII are delivered at a later date.

ARTICLE XI

Decision and Surrender

(1) The Requested State shall promptly communicate through the diplomatic channel to the Requesting State its decision on the request for extradition.

(2) If the request for extradition is denied by reason of any statutory or treaty prohibition against extradition, the Requested State shall provide such information as may be available as to the reason for the denial.

(3) If the extradition is granted, the competent authorities of the Contracting Parties shall agree on the time and place of the surrender of the person sought.

(4) If the person sought is not removed from the territory of the Requested State within the time prescribed by the law of that State, that person may be discharged from custody and the Requested State may subsequently refuse extradition for the same offence.

ARTICLE XII

Deferred Surrender

If the extradition request is granted in the case of a person who is being prosecuted or is serving a sentence in the territory of the Requested State for a different offence, the Requested State shall, unless its laws otherwise provide, defer the surrender of the person sought until the conclusion of the proceedings against that person or the full execution of any punishment that may be or may have been imposed.

ARTICLE XIII

Requests for Extradition Made by Several States

The executive authority of the Requested State, upon receiving requests from the other Contracting Party and from any other State or States for the extradition of the same person, either for the same offence or for different offences, shall determine to which State it will extradite that person.

Rule of Speciality

(1) A person extradited under this Treaty may only be detained, tried or punished in the Requesting State for the offence for which extradition is granted, or—

(a) for a lesser offence proved by the facts before the court of committal, or in the case of extradition pursuant to Article XV, any lesser offence disclosed by the facts upon which the request is based; or

(b) for an offence committed after the extradition; or

(c) for an offence in respect of which the executive authority of the Requested State, in accordance with its laws, consents to the person's detention, trial or punishment; and for the purposes of this sub-paragraph the Requested State may require the submission of documents mentioned in Article VIII or the written views of the extradited person with respect to the offence concerned, or both; or

(d) if the person—

(i) having left the territory of the Requesting State after his extradition, voluntarily returns to it; or

(ii) being free to leave the territory of the Requesting State after his extradition, does not so leave within forty-five (45) days after the first day on which he was free to do so.

(2) A person extradited under this Treaty may not be extradited to a third State unless—

(a) the Requested State consents; or

(b) the circumstances are such that he could have been dealt with in the Requesting State pursuant to sub-paragraph (d) of paragraph (1).

ARTICLE XV

Simplified Extradition

If the person sought agrees in writing to extradition after personally being advised by a judge or competent magistrate of his right to further extradition proceedings, the Requested State may grant extradition without formal proceedings. Extradition pursuant to this Article shall be subject to Article XIV.

ARTICLE XVI

Seizure and Surrender of Property

(1) To the extent permitted under the laws in the Requested State all articles, instruments, objects of value, documents or other evidence relating to the offence may be seized and such items may be surrendered upon the granting of the extradi-

tion. The items mentioned in this Article may be surrendered even when extradition cannot be effected due to the death, disappearance, or escape of the person sought.

(2) The rights of third parties in such property shall be duly respected.

(3) The Requested State may impose conditions designed to ensure that the rights of third parties are protected and that the property is returned to the Requested State as soon as practicable.

ARTICLE XVII

Expenses and Representation

(1) Expenses related to the transportation of the person sought to the Requesting State shall be paid by that State. All other expenses relating to the apprehension of the person sought and to subsequent proceedings shall be borne by the Requested State. However, expenses which, in the opinion of the Parties, constitute special expenditures shall be borne by the Requesting State.

(2) The Requested State shall also provide for the representation of the Requesting State in any proceedings arising in the Requested State out of a request for extradition.

(3) No pecuniary claim arising out of the arrest, detention, examination and surrender of the person sought under the terms of this Treaty shall be made by the Requested State against the Requesting State.

(4) Paragraph (3) shall not apply to claims arising out of failure of the Requesting State to comply with conditions imposed pursuant to paragraph (3) of Article XVI.

ARTICLE XVIII

Scope of Application

This Treaty shall apply to offences encompassed by Article II committed before as well as after the date this Treaty enters into force if at the time of the act or omission comprising the offence such act or omission constituted an offence under the laws of both States.

ARTICLE XIX

Ratification and Entry Into Force

(1) This Treaty shall be subject to ratification; the instruments of ratification shall be exchanged at Washington as soon as possible.

(2) This Treaty shall enter into force thirty (30) days after the exchange of the instruments of ratification.

(3) Upon entry into force of this Treaty, the Extradition Treaty between the United States of America and the United Kingdom signed at London, December 22, 1931, shall cease to have effect between the United States of America and Jamaica. Nevertheless, the 1931 Treaty shall continue to have effect in relation to any request for extradition made before this Treaty enters into force.

ARTICLE XX

Termination

(1) Either Contracting Party may terminate this Treaty at any time by giving written notice to the other Party, and the termination shall be effective six (6) months after the date of receipt of such notice. (2) Nothing in paragraph (1) shall affect any request for extradition made before the date on which the termination becomes effective.

IN WITNESS WHEREOF, the undersigned, being duly authorized by their respective Governments, have signed this Treaty.

DONE AT KINGSTON, in duplicate, this 14th day of June, 1983.

For the Government of the
United States of America

William A. Hewitt
Ambassador of the United
States of America

For the Government of
Jamaica

Winston Spaulding
Minister of National Security
and Justice

Notes

Chapter 1. Probing Problems Without Passports

1. Of course, developments other than PWPs also can have harmful impacts on people and places across the world and far away from the point of origin of the development. Russia's invasion of Ukraine on February 24, 2022, and its aftermath offer dramatic evidence of this. Thomas Friedman (2022) explains ominously why "the world will never be the same," as the conflict represents "World War Wired—the first war in a totally interconnected world. This will be the Cossacks meet the World Wide Web." R. Evan Ellis (2022) also offers the supportable view that "modern history is punctuated by decisive events that both directly impact the strategic environment and change the calculations of global actors. Russia's February 2022 invasion of the Ukraine is arguably one such event. The impact of the invasion on the global strategic environment, including Latin America and the Caribbean, will be profound and principally negative for Western democracies and the global institutional order that has prevailed since World War II."

2. The Johns Hopkins Coronavirus Resource Center stopped collecting data on March 10, 2023. See Johns Hopkins University Coronavirus Resource Center, https://coronavirus.jhu.edu/. The first COVID-19 cases were detected in China in December 2019. The WHO declared it a Public Health Emergency of International Concern (PHEIC) on January 30, 2020, and a global pandemic on March 11, 2020. The designation was removed just over three years later—on May 5, 2023, to be exact. See https://www.who.int/europe/emergencies/situations/covid-19/.

3. The first edition of *The Alternative World Drug Report* captures succinctly the costs and consequences of drugs in seven areas: (1) wasting billions, undermining economies; (2) undermining development and security, fueling conflict; (3) causing deforestation and pollution; (4) creating crime and enriching criminals; (5) threatening public health, spreading disease and death; (6) undermining human rights; and (7) promoting stigma and discrimination (see Count the Costs 2012). The second edition, which was published in 2016, identified "undermining peace and security" and "undermining development" as separate cost areas. It also added a ninth area: "causing deforestation and pollution."

4. The PCC reputedly was inspired by the Red Command (Comando Vermelho). Both criminal groups were formed by prisoners as self-protection gangs in Brazil's brutal prison system. The PCC, developed in São Paulo in the 1990s, rose to a position of dominance and now is considered Brazil's largest and best-organized criminal entity, with members throughout Brazil and international linkages elsewhere in Latin America and in Europe and Asia (*InSight Crime* 2020).

5. These cases are discussed in Griffith 1997, 154–58. For the investigation into the Antigua and Barbuda case, see Blom-Cooper 1990.

6. For discussion of traditional security issues, see Milfesky 2004; Hall and Chuck-A-Sang 2007; Girvan 2011; and Rodríguez Beruff 2009. Rodríguez Beruff examines both traditional and nontraditional issues.

7. Physical and social geography also conduces to marijuana cultivation, but the relationship between geography and cultivation is not examined in this study. For this, see Griffith 1997, 25–40.

8. The only other place where I have seen the treaty reproduced in full is in Samuels 2011, which is a collection of newspapers articles and documents related to the Coke saga, along with descriptions of related historical and sociological developments. For an excellent analysis of the treaty, see Lewis 2013.

9. The following point is made in one report to the U.S. Senate: "The United States has bilateral extradition treaties with each of the Caribbean nations. However, the Dominican Republic, Haiti and Suriname do not have agreements with the U.S. to extradite their own nationals to the United States. Despite the lack of a formal agreement allowing for the extradition of their own nationals, the Dominican Republic and Haiti have allowed for the extradition of their own nationals for drug-related offenses. While Suriname does not extradite its own nationals, it has not been a serious issue for the U.S. as it has been for the Netherlands and France, which have extradition requests that have not been met" (U.S. Senate 2012, 7).

10. For more on CARICOM IMPACS, see CARICOM IMPACS—The Caribbean Community Implementation Agency for Crime and Security, https://caricomimpacs.org/.

Chapter 2. Understanding Security and Sovereignty

1. For a discussion of various definitions and usages of the term, see Nye and Lynn-Jones 1988; Buzan 1991; McRae and Hubert 2002; and M. Williams 2003.

2. As might be expected, there are many other approaches to sovereignty in the Caribbean. For some rich explorations, see Bishop and Payne 2010; Gilbert-Roberts 2013; L. Lewis 2013; and Watson 2015.

Chapter 3. The Drama of Drugs

1. I asked several colleagues about the meaning of *umara composis*. One of them, sociologist Linden Lewis of Bucknell University, reached out to his network, and on April 1, 2013, he shared a response from someone who noted that "as [a] young dawta

(girl) she used to have to refrain from cooking anytime she had [her monthly] 'umara composis." Thus, it appears Peter Tosh was referring to the use of the herb to alleviate menstrual cramps.

2. These are partial lyrics of "Legalize It," which was recorded in 1975 and released in 1976. Tosh, whose official name was Winston Hubert McIntosh, was a noted Jamaican musician and a devoted Rastafarian. He was killed on September 11, 1987, at age forty-two in a robbery attempt at his home in Kingston, Jamaica, after returning from a tour in the United States. That same year he was bestowed a Grammy Award posthumously for Best Reggae Performance for "No Nuclear War," his last record. Twenty-five years after his death, in 2012, the Jamaican government awarded Tosh the Order of Merit, the nation's fourth-highest national honor. Tosh's evocative song, "Legalize It," is available on YouTube at https://www.youtube.com/watch?v=j6QkVTx2d88/.

3. For a discussion of the use of marijuana and coca leaf in cultural, religious, and medicinal contexts, see Rubin and Comitas 1975; Chevannes 1988; Martin 1970; and CARICOM Regional Commission on Marijuana 2018.

4. Legalization is also gaining traction in South and Central America as revealed by the study commissioned by the OAS in response to a mandate of the 2012 Summit of the Americas. The study, titled "Scenarios for the Drug Problem in the Americas, 2013–2025," was submitted in May 2013 and is available at http://www.oas.org/documents/eng/press/Scenarios_Report.pdf/. I had the honor to serve on the OAS Scenario Team that produced the report.

5. The grandmother, from Georgia in the United States, was convicted in Bermuda for attempting to smuggle US$369,000 worth of cocaine in her girdle into Bermuda aboard a cruise ship. Another interesting granny trafficker case occurred in May 2013 when a fifty-eight-year-old wheelchair-bound woman tried to smuggle cocaine and heroin from Santo Domingo into New York in her wheelchair. Customs officials noticed that she was nervous and that the wheelchair was freshly painted and fragile. The woman, from Boston, confessed to being paid US$12,000 to smuggle the drugs (see Marzulli 2013).

6. In one case in Trinidad and Tobago, National Security Minister Stuart Young is reported as saying, "It shocked me as well to learn that in small TT, we've had interdictions of over 7,000 pills in the last year. We've had people so bold, because it is not on the prohibited list, that they were mailing ecstasy drugs from away [abroad]. That is how boldfaced they are, and the target is our young people and our adolescents" (George 2019).

7. For understandable reasons, this chapter does not address all aspects of the geonarcotics framework. There is only cursory reference to drug production and no attention to money laundering, for example. An aspect of money laundering is discussed in chapter 5 in relation to terrorist financing.

8. For a copy of the agreement, see Griffith 1997, 243–48. The dispute developed added dimensions. Barbados and Jamaica called for "linkage" between shiprider agreements and other matters, including arms trafficking, deportation to the region, and banana-market guarantees. For its part, the United States accused Jamaica of foot-dragging in fighting drugs and threatened economic and other sanctions.

9. See Griffith 1997, 58–61, for detailed information on the distances between (a) twenty-nine Caribbean countries and seven major drug destinations (Atlanta, Baltimore, Boston, Miami, New York, Philadelphia, and Washington, D.C.) in the United States, and (b) twenty-nine Caribbean countries, four South American cities (Bogotá, Cali, Caracas, and Medellín), and three major European drug destinations (Amsterdam, London, and Paris).

10. The other seventeen countries were Afghanistan, Bolivia, Burma, Colombia, Costa Rica, Ecuador, El Salvador, Guatemala, Honduras, India, Laos, Mexico, Nicaragua, Pakistan, Panama, Peru, and Venezuela.

11. See Miroff 2011. Announced in October 2007 and signed into law in June 2008, the Mérida Initiative is a partnership involving the United States, Mexico, Central America, Haiti, and the Dominican Republic to combat transnational crime and drug trafficking. It funds several programs to investigate and prevent corruption within law enforcement agencies; facilitate the sharing of intelligence within and between regional governments; and provide equipment and training, among other things. For more on the crime challenges facing Belize, see López 2013.

12. The commission also suggested that the availability of marijuana for medicine "in the liberalised regime should take into consideration the following: [1.] Access to Medical Marijuana should be made for qualifying conditions in which there is clear evidence of its therapeutic effects and for debilitating, life threatening conditions that are intractable to treatment in which there is evidence of possible benefits, e.g., disastrous and intractable seizures in children; [2.] The smoking of Marijuana should be discouraged except in persons with terminal conditions in which benefits may outweigh the risks; [3.] Measures should be put in place to regulate the market to minimise diversion into the illegal market (e.g. Track and Trace System); [4.] Measures should be put in place to support public health education, prevention and treatment; [5.] Support for research to explore and confirm beneficial and harmful effects of Marijuana; [6.] Mechanisms to identify those who require treatment should be expanded." (CARICOM Regional Commission on Marijuana 2018, 67.)

13. It is noteworthy that Jamaica had contemplated similar measures previously. Fully a decade and a half earlier, the government established a seven-member National Commission on Ganja headed by University of the West Indies sociologist Barry Chevannes. In its August 2001 report, the commission recommended decriminalization to allow ganja to be used for private, personal purposes and for religious sacrament; that there be an accompanying sustained all-media, all-schools education program aimed at demand reduction; that the security forces intensify their interdiction of large cultivation of ganja and trafficking of all illegal drugs; that a Cannabis Research Agency be established, in collaboration with other countries, to coordinate research into all aspects of cannabis, including its epidemiological and psychological effects as well as its pharmacological and economic potential; and that urgent diplomatic initiatives be pursued with CARICOM partners and other countries in order to garner support for Jamaica's posture and to encourage the international community to reexamine the status of cannabis. Regrettably, pressure by the United States prevented the recommendations

from being actualized. See Delano Seiverright, "Chevannes and Ganga Law Reform," *Jamaica Gleaner*, December 12, 2010, https://jamaica-gleaner.com/gleaner/20101212/focus/focus6.html/.

14. In terms of racial distribution, according to the attorney general, of the people between the ages of eighteen and thirty-five charged for cannabis possession, 352 were of African descent, 124 were of East Indian descent, and 185 were mixed race (La Vende 2019). One suspects that a racial distribution of the individuals convicted for drug trafficking and money laundering would reveal a radically different profile.

Chapter 4. The Crucible of Crime

1. Police Commissioner Antony Anderson explained that criminal gangs accounted for almost three-quarters of the homicides in 2021. As well, he indicated that gangs profit from the drugs-for-guns trade, extortion, and scam rings and are connected with international criminal organizations (*InSight Crime* 2022).

2. For a good discussion of transnational organized crime in the Caribbean, see Gunst 1996; Maingot 1999; Griffith 1999; Bagley 2004; Bourne et al. 2017; W. Wallace 2017; Ellis 2018; and Lloyd 2018.

3. For an excellent analysis of homicides, robberies, shootings, burglaries, rapes, and break-ins for twelve Caribbean counties covering the period 2000 to 2010 using official crime data for all countries and victimization survey data for seven of them, see Seepersad 2018. For an excellent analysis of homicides, burglaries, car thefts, assaults, and robberies in Barbados, the Bahamas, Guyana, Jamaica, and Suriname, see Sutton 2017.

4. Phipps was a notorious drug and crime lord who wreaked havoc on the Jamaican society for decades. See "The Donald 'Zekes' Phipps Fact File," *Go-Jamaica*, April 20, 2006, http://go-jamaica.com/news/breaking/read_article.php?id=21.

5. For a useful discussion on the subject, see Lazar 2009; Sheeran 2013; and the Geneva Center for the Democratic Control of Armed Forces Backgrounder, https://www.files.ethz.ch/isn/14131/backgrounder_02_states_emergency.pdf/.

6. On Dominica, see Griffith 1993. On Suriname, see Derooy 1986. For an analysis of early and contemporary SoEs in Jamaica, see Duncan 1991; and Young 2022.

7. With regard to Haiti, see Freed 1994; CNN 2004; Eley 2010; *Haiti Libre* 2019; and Taylor, 2023. On the Dominican Republic and Puerto Rico, see Gardaworld 2019; BBC News 2019; and R. Johnson 2019. On the French SoE, see Osborne 2017.

8. The human rights advocacy group Jamaicans for Justice successfully challenged the constitutionality of the SoE legislation in July 2020 using writs of habeas corpus. Among other things, they argued that the detainees were being unlawfully imprisoned in a detention system that violated the constitution, and they challenged the powers to detain their clients who were neither charged with any criminal offense nor convicted by any court. In September 2020 the Jamaican supreme court invalidated the Emergency Powers Act. This forced the government to pursue revision of the law, which the House of Representatives approved in October 2021. However, the measure was defeated by

one vote in the Senate the following month (see Jamaicans for Justice 2020; Serju 2021; *Jamaica Gleaner* 2021).

9. For the full text of the law, see Jamaican Parliament, "The Law Reform (Zones of Special Operations) (Special Security and Community Development Measures) Act," http://www.japarliament.gov.jm/attachments/article/339/The%20Law%20Reform%20 (Zones%20of%20Special%20Operations)%20(Special%20Security%20and%20 Community%20Development%20Measures)%20Act,%202017.pdf/.

10. For thoughtful critiques of the new measure, see Thompson 2017; and Barnett 2019.

11. For some of this evidence, see Seepersad and Bissessar 2013; Harriott and Katz 2015; Hill and Morris 2018; U.N. Office on Drugs and Crime–World Bank 2007; U.N. Office on Drugs and Crime 2019b; Gunst 1996; Maingot 1999; Duncan 1991; Deosaran 2007; and McElroy and de Albuquerque 1999.

12. Sheridon Hill (2013, 43–47) established a novel three-level hierarchy of gang engagement in violence. Level 1, the highest one, involves a high murder rate and a high level of gang violence, and Jamaica, St. Kitts and Nevis, Trinidad and Tobago, and Belize are identified. Level 2 entails a moderate level of gang violence, and Barbados, Grenada, Guyana, St. Lucia, and the Bahamas are listed. Level 3 indicates a growing trend. Antigua and Barbuda, St. Vincent and the Grenadines, Dominica, and Suriname were identified with this level. Had Hill's unit of analysis been extended beyond the Anglophone Caribbean, he likely would have placed the Dominican Republic and Puerto Rico in Level 1 and Haiti in Level 2. Needless to say, since then the circumstances have changed in many countries.

13. Germany funded the multinational operation, which involved the following countries: Antigua and Barbuda, Bahamas, Barbados, Belize, Bonaire, Curaçao, Dominica, Dominican Republic, France (Guadeloupe and Martinique), Grenada, Guyana, Haiti, Jamaica, Trinidad and Tobago, St. Lucia, St. Kitts and Nevis, Turks and Caicos, St. Vincent and the Grenadines, and Suriname. See https://ibw21.org/news/hundreds-of-firearms -and-12-6-tonnes-of-drugs-seized-in-caribbean-operation/.

14. Anne-Séverine Fabre, Nicolas Florquin, Aaron Karp, and Matt Schroeder, *Weapons Compass: The Caribbean Firearms Study*, April 2023, https://www.smallarmssurvey .org/sites/default/files/resources/CARICOM-IMPACS-SAS-Caribbean-Firearms-Study .pdf/, 18.

15. Fabre, Florquin, Karp, and Schroeder, *Weapons Compass*, 92.

16. Fabre, Florquin, Karp, and Schroeder, *Weapons Compass*, 97–98.

17. "Opening Remarks by Dr. the Hon. Keith Rowley, Prime Minister of the Republic of Trinidad and Tobago to the Regional Symposium: Violence as a Public Health Issue—The Crime Challenge, April 17, 2023," https://caricom.org/opening-remarks -by-dr-the-hon-keith-rowley-prime-minister-of-the-republic-of-trinidad-and-tobago -to-the-regional-symposium-violence-as-a-public-health-issue-the-caricom-challenge -april-1/.

18. "Opening Remarks by Dr. the Hon. Keith Rowley, Prime Minister of the Republic of Trinidad and Tobago to the Regional Symposium: Violence as a Public Health Issue—The Crime Challenge, April 17, 2023."

19. Georges Fauriol, "Haiti's Humanitarian and Political Crash," Global Americans Report, May 10, 2023, available at https://theglobalamericans.org/2023/05/haitis-humanitarian-and-political-crash/.

20. See Reuters, "Around 70% of Haitians back international force to fight gangs, survey says," February 3, 2023, https://www.reuters.com/world/americas/around-70-haitians-back-international-force-fight-gangs-survey-says-2023-02-04/.

21. Although the IDB study does not address the impact of crime on tourism, this relationship is a crucial one in terms of lost revenue for both businesses and the government, on brand and image of tourism destinations, among other things. Space limitations in this chapter preclude attention to this matter, but for excellent examination of the subject, see McElroy and de Albuquerque 1999; Mohammed and Sookram 2015; and C. Morris 2019.

22. For a discussion of Caribbean civilization, see Gonsalves 2003; and Bolland 2004, especially his introduction.

23. For some interesting interview responses by both inmates and prison officers in several nations about institutional conditions and experiences, see Lancaster-Ellis 2018, 104–109).

24. For the lyrics of Peter Tosh's powerful equality and criminal justice anthem, see https://genius.com/Peter-tosh-equal-rights-lyrics/.

25. As if to add insult to injury, in January 2015 Sergeant Lall was promoted to inspector of police and Constable Dolai was promoted to police corporal. Shortly after the change of government in May 2015, the new minister of home affairs, Khemraj Ramjattan, ordered the dismissal of Corporal Lall from the police force. However, he was legally precluded from firing the inspector and made a recommendation to that effect to the Police Service Commission. Interestingly, Ramjattan, who is an attorney by profession, had provided pro bono legal representation to Thomas prior to becoming a government minister (see *Kaieteur News* 2015).

Chapter 5. The Trauma of Terror and Cyber Threats

1. The GTI world regions are the Middle East and North Africa (MENA), South Asia, sub-Saharan Africa, Asia-Pacific, Russia and Eurasia, Europe, South America, North America, and Central America and the Caribbean.

2. The GTI ranks 163 countries based on four indicators weighted over five years. A country's annual score is based on a scoring system that accounts for the relative impact of incidents in the year. The four factors counted in each country's yearly score are (1) total number of terrorist incidents in a given year; (2) total number of fatalities caused by terrorists in a given year; (3) total number of injuries caused by terrorists in a given year; and (4) a measure of the total property damage from terrorist incidents in a given year. Each factor is weighted between zero and three, and a five-year weighted average is applied in order to reflect the latent psychological effect of terrorist acts over time (see Institute for Economics and Peace 2019, 90).

3. The institute explains that its economic impact model includes the costs from four categories: deaths, injuries, property destruction, and the GDP losses. The GDP losses included in the model are a country's losses in economic activity as a result of

terrorism. GDP losses are included when the total of all terrorism incidents within a country, in a year, caused more than a thousand deaths. Deaths from terrorism form the largest category in the model, accounting for 58 percent of the global economic impact of terrorism, which is equivalent to US$19.3 billion in 2018. GDP losses are the second-largest category, contributing to 39 percent of the total, or US$12.9 billion (see Institute for Economics and Peace 2019, 30).

4. The discussion in the next section draws on Griffith 2021, *Conventional and Health Geopolitics in the Contemporary Caribbean*, Occasional Paper, Perry Center for Hemispheric Defense Studies, National Defense University, September 2021, https://www.williamjperrycenter.org/sites/default/files/publication_associated_files/Conventional%20and%20Health%20Geopolitics.pdf/.

5. SA stands for Société Anonyme, a public limited company, a category of corporate entities in France.

6. Tourism and terrorist financing are not the only relevant geoeconomic factors. Foreign direct investment also is important. On this, see De Groot and Pérez Ludeña 2014. While unrelated to Western financing, see Bernal 2016. Also important is critical infrastructure, such as telecommunication and electrical grids, air and seaports, bridges, water supply and treatment facilities, and hospitals and health facilities.

7. According to Sanjaya Baru, "Geo-economics may be defined in two different ways: as the relationship between economic policy and changes in national power and geo-politics (in other words, the geopolitical consequences of economic phenomena); or as the economic consequences of trends in geopolitics and national power. Both the notion that 'trade follows the flag' (that the projection of national power has economic consequences) and that 'the flag follows trade' (that there are geopolitical consequences of essentially economic phenomena) point to the subject matter of geo-economics" (Baru 2012, 47). For an excellent analysis of the theoretical and conceptual literature on the subject, see Scholvin and Wigell 2018.

8. The borrowing member countries are Anguilla, Antigua and Barbuda, the Bahamas, Barbados, Belize, British Virgin Islands, Cayman Islands, Dominica, Grenada, Guyana, Haiti, Jamaica, Montserrat, St. Lucia, St. Kitts and Nevis, St. Vincent and the Grenadines, Suriname, Trinidad and Tobago, and Turks and Caicos Islands.

9. *New York Carib News*, "Jamaica's Minister of Tourism Announces One Million Visitor Arrivals to Date for 2023," May 12, 2023, https://nycaribnews.com/2023/05/jamaicas-minister-of-tourism-announces-one-million-visitor-arrivals-to-date-for-2023/.

10. For more on narcotics money laundering, see Maingot 1998; MacDonald and Zagaris 1992; Griffith 1997; United States Senate 1989; and Beaty and Gwyne 1993.

11. These numbers have not changed radically over the last decade. See the entries for individual Caribbean countries at Global Religious Futures.org, http://www.globalreligiousfutures.org/regions/latin-america-caribbean/religious_demography#/?affiliations_religion_id=16&affiliations_year=2020/.

12. For some of the copious literature on the coup attempt, see Ryan 1991; Deosaran 1997; Pantin 2007; and Government of Trinidad and Tobago 2014. The leader of the coup attempt, Yasin Abu Bakr, collapsed at home and later died in the hospital on October 21, 2021, two days after celebrating his eightieth birthday (Mendes-Franco 2021).

13. *Hijra* refers to the journey of the prophet Muhammad and his followers from Mecca to Medina in 622 A.D., which marks the beginning of the Muslim Era. The Islamic new year, known as Al-Hijra, begins on Friday and marks the beginning of Muharram, the first month of the Muslim lunar calendar.

14. For full descriptions and variations of these methods, see Jeff Melnick, *Top 10 Most Common Types of Cyber Attacks*, https://blog.netwrix.com/2018/05/15 /top-10-most-common-types-of-cyber-attacks/.

15. On reading the first draft of this chapter, my friend Dr. Holger Henke remarked on March 18, 2020, that "the most recent report I am getting from my computer anti-virus program is that since it was installed on this new computer last August (2019) it has blocked over 35,000 bad connections! In the last week alone, it recorded ca. 1,600 such intrusive connection attempts."

16. See "Distribution of IoT Attacks Worldwide from August 2021 to December 2022, by Country of Origin," https://www.statista.com/statistics/1364419/share -of-iot-attacks-by-country-of-origin/.

17. For excellent studies of the economic costs of cybercrime, see J. Lewis 2018; IDB 2016; and Bissell and Ponemon 2019.

18. See "Estimated Cost of Cybercrime Worldwide from 2016 to 2027 (in trillion U.S. dollars)," https://www.statista.com/statistics/1280009/cost-cybercrime-worldwide/.

19. According to the IDB report, the Police Information Technology unit does not have a digital forensics laboratory and sends evidence to Antigua and Barbuda for analysis; however, it has recently acquired some equipment to develop laboratory capacity within the country. Quite interestingly, also, it noted that companies are not required to report breaches in cybersecurity to the authorities.

20. See "Number of Web Application Attacks in the Energy and Utilities Sector in the Caribbean in June 2019, by Target Country," https://www.statista.com/statistics/1066539 /number-web-attacks-energy-utilities-sector-caribbean-country/. It is reasonable to suspect that petro-power-in-the-making Guyana soon also will be the target of attacks on operations there.

21. For more on the ICJ decision and the hacking episode, see Ivelaw Lloyd Griffith, "Guyana and Venezuela: A David and Goliath Match Up?" *OilNOW*, April 22, 2023, https://oilnow.gy/featured/guyana-and-venezuela-a-david-and-goliath -match-up/; Denis Chabrol, "Guyana Govt's Petroleum Website Hacked Apparently by Venezuelans," *Demerarawaves*, April 9, 2023, https://demerarawaves.com /2023/04/09/guyana-govts-petroleum-website-hacked-apparently-by-venezuelans/; and "Guyana's Petroleum Portal Back Up after Hacking Spurred by Court Ruling on Border Case," *OilNOW*, April 18, 2023, https://oilnow.gy/featured/guyanas -petroleum-portal-back-up-after-vandalism-by-venezuela-hackers/.

Chapter 6. Security and Sovereignty Under Siege

1. Thompson, a Rhodes Scholar, distinguished attorney, and Pan Africanist, served Jamaica as a diplomat as well as minister of national security and of foreign affairs. Born in Panama in January 1917, he died in New York in January 2012, at age ninety-five. The

year before his death, the African Union announced that it would award him their first Citizen of Africa Award, with an accompanying passport.

2. Miss Patsy died on August 22, 2011, within a month of her sixty-fifth birthday, and was buried on September 14, 2011. Among the many prominent citizens who attended the funeral and eulogized her were former JLP leader and prime minister Edward Seaga; Tivoli Gardens MP for forty-three years, Kingston mayor Desmond McKenzie; and JLP senator and onetime Dudus lawyer, Tom Tavares-Finson. One of her grandchildren, Christopher Coke Jr., also read a letter from his father, then on trial in New York (Dennis 2011). Interestingly, Miss Patsy was buried the same day Enid Golding, the mother of Prime Minister Golding, died.

3. The Rev. Dr. Miller, the popular pastor and founder of Fellowship Tabernacle Church in St. Andrew, later was arrested and charged with attempting to pervert the course of justice. He was found guilty in June 2016 and sentenced to J$1 million or one year in prison (see *The Star* 2016).

4. "Christopher Coke's Letter to Sentencing Judge," September 21, 2011, *New York Times*, http://www.nytimes.com/interactive/2011/09/21/nyregion/21coke-letter .html?ref=nyregion/.

5. The timeline and other information come from several sources, including Henry 2010; Chaplin 2011; Goldstein 2011; *Jamaica Observer* 2011a; George Commission of Inquiry 2011; and Simmons Commission of Inquiry 2016.

6. For a reaction of the seventy-year old Kenneth Baugh, who was Golding's deputy prime minister, see Thaffe 2011. Regarding the Holness selection, see Padgett 2011; and Virtue 2011.

7. Distinguished Jamaican political scientist Rupert Lewis puts the Tivoli Gardens contract figure at over J$140 million (US$912,800). As well, in an October 10, 2011, email to me he noted, "Contracts were awarded by the PNP up to 2007 and [by the] JLP when they took power."

8. The panel recorded its outrage with some of its experiences, noting, "With much regret, we must comment on some of the Counsel taking part in the Inquiry. . . . Some Counsel were aggressive and rude. They behaved outrageously to some of the witnesses and some were even rude to the Commissioners. . . . Conduct of this kind was not only reprehensible but did not assist the Commission in its search for the truth, it merely prolonged the Inquiry and gave to it an element of unpleasantness" (George Commission of Inquiry 2011, 54).

9. For excellent analysis on related aspects, see Meikle and Jaffe 2015; and Y. Campbell 2018.

10. As we saw in chapter 4, gangs continue to wreak havoc in Jamaica. One of the country's most significant gang trials began in September 2021. It involved thirty-three members of the One Don Gang faction of the Klansman gang, who were charged with criminal organization, murder, arson, extortion, and illegal possession of firearms. Incidentally, despite its name, the gang has no relation to the United States white supremacist Ku Klux Klan. The trial is reputedly a landmark trial because it involves the largest number of defendants ever to be tried simultaneously under a single indictment in Jamaica's history (see Gorder 2021). In March 2023, ten of the defendants were acquitted of the

murder charges. However, they were not released from custody, as they faced other charges (*Jamaica Observer* 2023).

11. For a discussion of these cases, see Griffith 1993, chs. 4, 8; and *Houston Chronicle* 1995.

12. The democracy thrust worldwide over that last six decades has evoked a deep concern about the impact of SoEs on human rights (see United Nations 2001). Under Article 4 (3) of the Covenant on Civil and Political Rights, States Parties to the Covenant are required to inform the other States Parties, through the U.N. secretary-general, whenever an SoE is declared and the reasons for it. Trinidad and Tobago complied with this provision when its permanent representative in New York, Rodney Charles, sent a five-page notification to Secretary-General Ban Ki-moon on September 28, 2011.

13. Both National Security Minister Sandy and Commissioner of Police Dwayne Gibbs were criticized over the fact that Gibbs as well his Canadian deputy, Jack Ewatski, were out of the country at the time the SoE was declared. Gibbs was at a conference in Brazil, and Ewatski was vacationing back in Canada. Gibbs cut short his Brazil trip and returned to Port-of-Spain on August 23 (see Seelal 2011).

14. Parliament of the Republic of Trinidad and Tobago, http://www.ttparliament.org/chamber_business.php?mid=11&id=220/.

15. For a critique of racial profiling in Trinidad and Tobago, see David Muhammad (2012), who noted: "While Black teenagers were being arrested wholesale[,] so-called 'big-fish' criminals who are responsible for importing guns and drugs were not being caught and allowed to continue to have their illegal business flourish. For example, it was reported September 15, 2011, that a quantity of marijuana weighing 2,000-pounds was discovered at the Point Lisas Port in Trinidad. It was valued at $34.6 million, sent from the United States and addressed to a businessman in Central Trinidad who merely told the police it did not belong to him and was allowed to go free."

16. Although the Tivoli Gardens violence was not politically motivated per se, it had deep political ramifications. As mentioned earlier in this chapter, Dudus was not just a criminal entrepreneur but also a power broker. His garrison was politically aligned and was critical to JLP power pursuits. Garrison political partisanship and clientelism have been staples of Jamaican politics for decades. Elsewhere in the Americas, SoE declarations were precipitated by violent crime in the Brazilian state of Minas Gerais in January 2011.

17. Email from National Security Minister John Sandy to author on October 23, 2011, with "Summary for August 21 to October 23, 2011."

18. Email from National Security Minister John Sandy to author on October 23, 2011, with "Critical Success Factors: The Results."

19. Of course, this applies to other nations as well. At the time of the SoE, St. Lucian leaders acknowledged having considered declaring one, and the opposition party in St. Kitts and Nevis called for one there. Also noteworthy is that the leaders in Antigua and Barbuda, Grenada, and Guyana publicly endorsed the SoE in Trinidad and Tobago.

Chapter 7. Dynamics of Geonarcotics and Geopolitics

1. Parts II and III below draw on my "Political Acumen and Geopolitical Anxiety in Suriname," *Security and Defense Studies Review* 12, nos. 1/2 (2011): 47–72.

2. By "political acumen" I mean the use of a mixture of shrewdness, charisma, and organizational skills to gain political outcomes both for Bouterse and the individuals and groups whose interests he represents.

3. For a discussion of the structure and operation of Suriname's political system and some contemporary political aspects, see Dew 1994; Sedoc-Dahlberg 1997; Singh 2007; MacDonald 2019b; Hoefte and Veenendaal 2019; and Inter Parliamentary Union, https://www.ipu.org/parliament/SR/.

4. Understandably, the results also reflected the plural society nature of the nation. The National Assembly comprised seventeen Hindustani, eleven Creole, ten Maroon, nine Javanese, two Amerindian, and two Chinese. Interestingly, as well, thirty-one of the fifty-one new parliamentarians were elected for the first time.

5. With regard to geonarcotics, the international spotlight was more on trafficking and less on production, consumption-abuse, and money laundering, although a director of the Suriname Central Bank once was indicted (in absentia in Holland) for money laundering (see Brana-Shute 2000, 107).

6. See the Borgen Project's "Poverty in Suriname," https://borgenproject.org/poverty -suriname/.

7. As two Dutch scholars have explained, the Interior War was a conflict between the country's army and Maroon insurgency groups, which rallied behind Ronnie Brunswijk's Jungle Commando. The conflict pertained to control over the resources and cocaine trafficking networks in the country's interior. Among the war crimes committed by both sides was the killing of thirty-nine innocent Maroon civilians in the village of Moiwana by the military in 1986. Although the Maroons earlier had played no consequential role in the country's politics, the Interior War and the socioeconomic and other dislocations stimulated their political awareness. This contributed to the nation's political fragmentation (see Hoefte and Veenedaal 2019, 182).

8. The other members of UNASUR are Argentina, Bolivia, Brazil, Chile, Colombia, Ecuador, Guyana, Paraguay, Peru, Uruguay, and Venezuela.

9. Bouterse and Jagdeo reportedly discussed the bridging of the Corentyne River, crime, and immigration. On immigration, they agreed to regularize the riverboat system whereby Guyanese land in Suriname and Surinamese land in Guyana through the unregulated speedboat system (Newspress 2011).

10. For a discussion of the historical antecedents and legal and political dynamics of this dispute, see Donovan 2003; Ferguson 2007; Pollard 2007; and *Stabroek News* 2010a.

11. It is worth nothing that President Jagdeo allowed himself to be humiliated in January 2002 when, as part of an official visit to Suriname, he was invited to address the National Assembly and spoke from a position in the assembly where the map of Suriname with the New River Triangle as part of Suriname was part of the backdrop (see *Guyana Chronicle* 2002).

12. See Suriname embassy, http://www.surinameembassy.org/. This is a variation of Venezuela's approach where it portrays Essequibo, the five-eighths of Guyana it claims as part of its territory, as *la Zona en reclamación*. See, for example, "Map of Venezuela," Venezuelatuya.com, http://www.venezuelatuya.com/geografia/mapavenezuela.htm/.

Noteworthy too is the fact that in June 2011 President Bouterse reasserted the claim to the New River Triangle.

13. A *note verbale* is a form of communication used in the diplomatic community that is unsigned and written in the third person. It is less formal than a *note* but more formal than an *aide-mémoire*.

14. Interestingly, CGX footed most of Guyana's legal bill. According to one report, "Toronto-based CGX Energy Inc. paid $8.9 million in fees—the majority of Guyana's legal bill—incurred in a maritime border dispute with Suriname over rights to the undersea basin, President Bharrat Jagdeo said late Monday. 'This is no secret,' Jagdeo told reporters outside his offices [in] Georgetown. 'I'm very grateful to CGX for footing the bill, because it didn't come from the treasury. But that doesn't mean that they have any preferences'" (Associated Press 2007).

15. For the case's historical, political, and legal dynamics, see Ramphal 2008. Shridath Ramphal is an international lawyer with a distinguished career: former attorney general and then foreign minister of Guyana, and former commonwealth secretary general. He led Guyana's team. Suriname's team was led by then–minister of foreign affairs, Lygia Kraag-Keteldijk.

16. The victims were Cyril Daal, chairman of the Moederbond, Suriname's largest trade union confederation; Kenneth Gonçalvez, dean of the bar association; journalists Bram Behr, Leslie Rahman, and Frank Wijngaarde; Jozef Slagveer, director of the Informa news agency; Andre Kamperveen, owner of the ABC radio station and former minister of culture and sport; Gerard Leckie, dean of the University of Suriname; Suchrim Oemrawsingh, a university lecturer; and businessman Robby Sohansingh. Two of the victims, Soerindre Rambocus and Jiwansingh Sheombar, were former army officers who had been in military detention, accused of involvement in an attempted coup in March 1982. The remaining three victims, John Baboeram, Eddy Hoost, and Harold Riedewald, were their defense attorneys (see *Stabroek News* 2019b).

Chapter 8. Pondering Challenged Sovereignty

1. China also has begun to extend its engagement with the region in this area. See Montoute 2013; Bernal 2016; Tannenbaum 2018; Ellis 2020; and MacDonald 2022.

2. The thirteen partner countries are Antigua and Barbuda, the Bahamas, Barbados, Dominica, the Dominican Republic, Grenada, Guyana, Jamaica, St. Kitts and Nevis, St. Lucia, St. Vincent and the Grenadines, Suriname, and Trinidad and Tobago. Belize receives assistance under CARSI, and Haiti does so bilaterally. I had the honor of being invited to testify before the U.S. House of Representatives in December 2009 after the CBSI proposal was submitted by the Obama administration to Congress. See Griffith 2009.

3. See United Kingdom Development Tracker, at https://devtracker.dfid.gov.uk /regions/380/projects.

4. See United Kingdom Development Tracker, at https://devtracker.dfid.gov.uk/ regions/380/projects.

5. CARPHA is a regional public health agency that was established in July 2011 and became operational in January 2013. The member states are Anguilla, Antigua and Barbuda, Aruba, Bahamas, Barbados, Belize, Bermuda, Bonaire, St. Eustatius, Saba, British Virgin Islands, Cayman Islands, Curaçao, Dominica, Grenada, Guyana, Haiti, Jamaica, Montserrat, St. Kitts and Nevis, St. Lucia, Sint Maarten, St. Vincent and the Grenadines, Suriname, Trinidad and Tobago, and the Turks and Caicos Islands (CARPHA 2023).

6. Sill valid too is the proposition by Matthew Bishop and Anthony Payne that "the way in which the notion of sovereignty is understood, projected, discussed and practiced in the Caribbean is somewhat at odds with the region's existential situation" (Bishop and Payne 2010, 13).

7. The Harlem Renaissance was an African American intellectual, social, and artistic explosion that ran from 1918 through the mid-1930s. It was centered in Harlem, New York, but also included urban sections of the Northeast and Midwest United States that were affected by the migration of African Americans from the South and by people from parts of the Caribbean, Africa, and Europe. McKay's poem is available at https://www.poetryfoundation.org/poems/44694/if-we-must-die/.

Bibliography

Books, Monographs, Journal Articles

Allen, Dudley. 1980. "Urban Crime and Violence in Jamaica." In *Crime and Punishment in the Caribbean*, edited by Rosemary Brana-Shute and Gary Brana-Shute. Gainesville: University Press of Florida.

Bagley, Bruce M. 2004. "Globalization and Transnational Organized Crime: The Russian Mafia in Latin America and the Caribbean." In *The Political Economy of the Drug Industry*, edited by Menno Vellinga. Gainesville: University of Florida Press.

Bagley, Bruce M., and Rosen, Jonathan D., eds. 2017. *Drug Trafficking, Organized Crime, and Violence in the Americas*. Gainesville: University of Florida Press.

Baradaran, Shima, Michael Findley, Daniel Nielson, and Jason Sharman. 2014. "Funding Terror." *University of Pennsylvania Law Review* 162, no. 3: 477–536.

Barclay, Corlane. 2017. "Cybercrime and Legislation: A Critical Reflection on the Cybercrimes Act, 2015, of Jamaica." *Commonwealth Law Bulletin* 43, no. 1: 77–107.

Baru, Sanjaya. 2012. "Geo-economics and Strategy." *Survival* 54, no. 3: 47–58.

Beaty, Jonathan, and S. C. Gwynne. 1993. *The Outlaw Bank: A Wild Ride into the Secret Heart of BCCI*. New York: Random House.

Bishop, Matthew Louis, and Anthony Payne. 2010. *Caribbean Regional Governance and the Sovereignty/Statehood Problem*. Caribbean Paper No. 8, Center for International Governance Innovation. https://www.files.ethz.ch/isn/112276/Caribbean%20Paper%208.pdf/.

Bissell, Kelly, and Larry Ponemon. 2019. *The Costs of Cybercrime: Ninth Annual Cost of Cybercrime Study Unlocking the Value of Improved Cybersecurity Protection*. Ponemon Institute LLC and Accenture. https://www.accenture.com/_acnmedia/PDF-96/Accenture-2019-Cost-of-Cybercrime-Study-Final.pdf#zoom=50/.

Blom-Cooper, Louis. 1990. *Guns for Antigua*. London: Duckworth.

Bolland, O. Nigel, ed. 2004. *The Birth of Caribbean Civilization: A Century of Ideas about Culture and Identity, Nation and Society*. Kingston, Jamaica: Ian Randle Publishers.

Bourne, P. A., M. S. Peterkin, Ronald Anderson, Marsha Pabarue, and Dave Higgins. 2017. "Organized Crime in the Caribbean and Latin American Region." *International Journal of Insights & Transformations in Law, Crime & Justice* 1, Issue 1: 43–64. http://science.eurekajournals.com/index.php/IJITLCJ/article/view/21/15/.

Bowling, Ben. 2010. *Policing the Caribbean: Transnational Security Cooperation in Practice*. Oxford: Oxford University Press.

Brana-Shute, Gary. 1996. "Suriname: A Military and Its Auxiliaries." *Armed Forces and Society* 22, no. 3: 469–84.

Brana-Shute, Gary. 2000. "Narco-Criminality in the Caribbean." In *The Political Economy of Drugs in the Caribbean*, edited by Ivelaw Lloyd Griffith. London: Palgrave Macmillan.

Bryan, Anthony T., J. Edward Greene, and Timothy M. Shaw, eds. 1990. *Peace, Development, and Security in the Caribbean*. New York: St. Martin's Press.

Bybee, Ashley Neese. 2011. "Narco State or Failed State? Narcotics and Politics in Guinea-Bissau." PhD diss., George Mason University.

Buzan, Barry. 1991. *People, States, and Fear*. Boulder, CO: Lynne Rienner.

Campbell, Yonique, ed. 2018. *Citizenship on the Margins: State Power, Security and Precariousness in 21st-Century Jamaica*. London: Palgrave.

Chami, Georgina, Jerome Teelucksingh, and Marlon Anatol, eds. 2022. *Managing New Security Threats in the Caribbean*. London: Palgrave Macmillan.

Chevannes, Barry. 1988. *Background to Drug Use in Jamaica*. Institute of Social and Economic Research Working Paper No. 34. University of the West Indies, Jamaica.

Chopra, Jarat, and Thomas Weiss. 1992. "Sovereignty Is No Longer Sovereign: Codifying Humanitarian Intervention." *Ethics and International Affairs* 6: 95–117.

Chouvy, Pierre-Armand. 2016. "The Myth of the Narco-State." *Space and Polity* 20, no. 1: 26–38.

Clarke, Nigel. 2021. "Preparing Jamaica to Recover Stronger: Opening of the 2021/2022 Budget Debate, March 9." https://jis.gov.jm/media/2021/03/MOF-Opening-Budget-Debate-2021-22-with-cover-17.03.21.pdf/.

Cornell, Svante E., and Niklas Swanström. 2006. "The Eurasian Drug Trade: A Challenge to Regional Security." *Problems of Post-Communism* 53, no. 4: 10–28.

Cottee, Simon. 2019. "The Calypso Caliphate: How Trinidad Became a Recruiting Ground for ISIS." *International Affairs* 95, Issue 2: 297–317. https://academic.oup.com/ia/article/95/2/297/5366526/.

Cronin, Audrey Kurth. 2002–2003. "Behind the Curve: Globalization and International Terrorism." *International Security* 27, no. 3: 30–58.

Dawson, Maurice, and Pedro Manuel Taveras Nuñez. 2018. "Issues in Cybersecurity: Security Challenges and Problems in the Dominican Republic." *Land Forces Academy Review* 23, no. 3 (91): 173–80. https://www.researchgate.net/publication/328212096_Issues_in_Cybersecurity_Security_Challenges_and_Problems_in_the_Dominican_Republic/.

de Haan, Leah. 2019. "ISIS, Foreign Fighters, and Trinidad and Tobago." *International Affairs Blog*. October 21. https://medium.com/international-affairs-blog/isis-foreign-fighters-and-trinidad-and-tobago-caf96ab3adb9/.

Deosaran, Ramesh. 1997. *A Society under Siege*. St. Augustine, Trinidad and Tobago: University of the West Indies Press.

Deosaran, Ramesh, ed. 2007. *Crime, Delinquency, and Justice*. Kingston, Jamaica: Ian Randle Publishers.

Desch, Michael C., Jorge I. Domínguez, and Andrés Serbin, eds. 1998. *From Pirates to Drug Lords: The Post–Cold War Caribbean Security Environment*. Albany: State University of New York Press.

Dew, Edward M. 1994. *The Trouble in Suriname, 1975–1993*. Westport, CT: Praeger.

Domínguez, Jorge I. 1998. Introduction to *From Pirates to Drug Lords: The Post–Cold War Caribbean Security Environment*, edited by Michael C. Desch, Jorge I. Domínguez, and Andrés Serbin. Albany: State University of New York Press.

Domínguez, Jorge I., ed., 1999. *The Future of Inter-American Relations*. Washington, DC: Inter-American Dialogue.

Donovan, Thomas. 2003. "Suriname-Guyana Maritime and Territorial Disputes: A Legal and Historical Analysis." *Journal of Transnational Law and Policy* 13 (Spring): 41–98.

Dookeran, Winston. 2022. *The Caribbean on the Edge: The Political Stress of Stability, Equality, and Diplomacy*. Toronto: University of Toronto Press.

Dreyfus, Pablo Gabriel. 2002. "Border Spillover: Drug Trafficking and National Security in South America." PhD thesis, University of Geneva, Switzerland.

Duncan, Neville. 1991. "Political Violence in the Caribbean." In *Strategy and Security in the Caribbean*, edited by Ivelaw Lloyd Griffith. New York: Praeger.

Dunn, Hopeton S., and Indianna D. Minto-Coy. 2010. *The Communications Industry in the Caribbean: Issues, Challenges, and Opportunities*. The Centre for International Governance Innovation, Caribbean Paper No. 9, May. https://www.cigionline.org/sites/default/files/caribbean_paper_9.pdf/.

Ellis, R. Evan. 2018. *Transnational Organized Crime in Latin America and the Caribbean*. Lanham, MD: Lexington Books

Ellis, R. Evan. 2020. "China's Advance in the Caribbean." Woodrow Wilson Center. October. https://www.wilsoncenter.org/sites/default/files/media/uploads/documents/China%E2%80%99s%20Advance%20in%20the%20Caribbean.pdf/.

Ellis, R. Evan. 2022. "The Impact of Russia's Invasion of Ukraine on the Global Strategic Environment and Latin America." Peruvian Army Center for Strategic Studies. February 28. https://ceeep.mil.pe/2022/02/28/the-impact-of-russias-invasion-of-ukraine-on-the-global-strategic-environment-and-latin-america/?lang=en/.

Espíndola, Roberto. 2009. "New Politics, New Parties?" In *Latin American Democracy: Emerging Reality or Endangered Species?*, edited by Richard L. Millett, Jennifer S. Holmes, and Orlando J. Pérez. New York: Routledge.

Farer, Tom, ed. 1996. *Beyond Sovereignty: Collectively Defending Democracy in the Americas*. Baltimore: Johns Hopkins University Press.

Farer, Tom. 1999. *Transnational Crime in the Americas*. Oxford: Routledge.

Ferguson, Tyrone. 2007. "The Guyana-Suriname Territorial Conflict: Is the Moment Opportune for Third Party Intervention?" In *Intervention, Border and Maritime Issues in CARICOM*, edited by Kenneth Hall and Myrtle Chuck-A-Sang. Kingston, Jamaica: Ian Randle Publishers.

Feuer, Will. 2021. "WHO Says Pandemic Has Caused More 'Mass Trauma' Than WWII." CNBC. March 5. https://www.cnbc.com/2021/03/05/who-says-pandemic-has-caused -more-mass-trauma-than-wwii-and-will-last-for-years.html/.

Figueira, Darius. 2004. *Cocaine and Heroin Trafficking in the Caribbean: The Case of Trinidad and Tobago, Jamaica, and Guyana*. Lincoln, NE: iUniverse.

Figueira, Darius. 2012. *Cocaine Trafficking in the Caribbean and West Africa in the Era of Mexican Cartels*. Bloomington, IA: iUniverse Books.

Fowler, Michael Ross, and Julie Marie Bunck. 1995. *Law, Power, and the Sovereign State: The Evolution and Application of the Concept of Sovereignty*. University Park: Penn State University Press.

Franzese, Patrick W. 2009. "Sovereignty in Cyberspace: Can It Exist?" *Air Force Law Review* 64, no. 1: 1–42.

Friedman, Thomas L. 2005. *The World Is Flat: A Brief History of the Twenty-First Century*. New York: Farrar, Straus, and Giroux.

Gilbert-Roberts, Terri-Ann. 2013. *The Politics of Integration: Caribbean Sovereignty Revisited*. Kingston, Jamaica: Ian Randle Publishers.

Girvan, Norman. 2011. "ALBA, PetroCaribe, and Caricom: Issues in a New Dynamic." In *Venezuela's Petro-Diplomacy: Hugo Chávez's Foreign Policy*, edited by Ralph S. Clem and Anthony P. Maingot. Gainesville: University Press of Florida.

Granger, David A. 2011. *Public Security: Criminal Violence and Policing in Guyana*. Georgetown, Guyana: Institute for Security and International Studies.

Griffith, Ivelaw Lloyd, ed. 1991. *Strategy and Security in the Caribbean*. Westport, CT: Praeger.

Griffith, Ivelaw Lloyd. 1993. *The Quest for Security in the Caribbean: Problems and Promises in Subordinate States*. Armonk, NY: M. E. Sharpe.

Griffith, Ivelaw L. 1993–1994. "From Cold War Geopolitics to Post–Cold War Geonarcotics." *International Journal* (Canada) 49 (Winter): 1–36.

Griffith, Ivelaw L. 1995a. "Caribbean Security: Retrospect and Prospect." *Latin American Research Review* 30, no. 2: 3–32.

Griffith, Ivelaw L. 1995b. "The Implications of Information Technology on Sovereignty." *U.N. Institute for Disarmament Research Newsletter*, no. 30, 7–8.

Griffith, Ivelaw Lloyd. 1996. *Caribbean Security on the Eve on the 21st Century*. Washington, DC: National Defense University Press.

Griffith, Ivelaw Lloyd. 1997. *Drugs and Security in the Caribbean: Sovereignty under Siege*. University Park: Pennsylvania State University Press.

Griffith, Ivelaw L. 1999. "Organized Crime in the Western Hemisphere: Content, Context, Consequences, and Countermeasures." *Low Intensity Conflict and Law Enforcement* 8, no. 1 (Spring): 1–33.

Griffith, Ivelaw Lloyd, ed. 2000. *The Political Economy of Drugs in the Caribbean*. London: Macmillan-Palgrave.

Griffith, Ivelaw L. 2003. "The Caribbean Security Scenario at the Dawn of the 21st Century: Continuity, Change, Challenge." *North-South Center Agenda Paper*, no. 65, September.

Griffith, Ivelaw Lloyd, ed. 2004. *Caribbean Security in the Age of Terror: Challenge and Change*. Kingston, Jamaica: Ian Randle Publishers.

Griffith, Ivelaw L. 2011. "Political Acumen and Geopolitical Anxiety in Suriname." *Security and Defense Studies Review* 12, nos. 1/2: 47–72.

Griffith, Ivelaw Lloyd. 2021a. *Conventional and Health Geopolitics in the Contemporary Caribbean*. Occasional Paper, William J. Perry Center for Hemispheric Defense Studies, National Defense University. September. https://www.williamjperrycenter.org /sites/default/files/publication_associated_files/Conventional%20and%20Health %20Geopolitics.pdf/.

Griffith, Ivelaw L. 2021b. "Vaccination and Vaccine Diplomacy in the Caribbean." Global Americans Special Report. December 9. https://theglobalamericans.org/2021/12 /vaccine-diplomacy-in-the-caribbean/.

Grayson, Kyle. 2008. *Chasing Dragons: Security, Identity, and Illicit Drugs in Canada*. Toronto: University of Toronto Press.

Gunst, Laurie. 1996. *Born Fi Dead: A Journey through the Jamaican Posse Underworld*. New York: Henry Holt.

Guyana Times. 2022. "Seizure of 'Guyana-Registered Vessel': Interpol Alerted as Probe Launched into Arms, Ammo Find in Senegal." January 22.

Haass, Richard N. 2009. "Sovereignty." *Foreign Policy*. October 20. https://foreignpolicy .com/2009/10/20/sovereignty/.

Hall, Kenneth, and Myrtle Chuck-A-Sang, eds. 2007. *Intervention, Border, and Maritime Issues in CARICOM*. Kingston, Jamaica: Ian Randle Publishers.

Harriott, Anthony, Farley Braithwaite, and Scott Wortley, eds. 2004. *Crime and Criminal Justice in the Caribbean*. Kingston, Jamaica: Arawak Publishers.

Harriott, Anthony, and Charles M. Katz, eds. 2015. *Gangs in the Caribbean: Responses of State and Society*. Kingston, Jamaica: University of the West Indies Press.

Haughton, Suzette A. 2011. *Drugged Out: Globalization and Jamaica's Resilience to Drug Trafficking*. Lanham, MD: University Press of America.

Heine, Jorge, and Leslie Manigat, eds. 1988. *The Caribbean and World Politics*. York: Holmes and Meier.

Henkin, Louis. 1999. "That 'S' Word: Sovereignty, and Globalization, and Human Rights, Et Cetera," *Fordham Law Review* 68, no. 1 (October): 1–14.

Hill, Sheridon. 2013. "The Rise of Gang Violence in the Caribbean." In *Gangs in the Caribbean*, edited by Randy Seepersad and Ann Marie Bissessar. Newcastle upon Tyne: Cambridge Scholars Publishing.

Hill, Sheridon, and Patrice K. Morris. 2018. "Drug Trafficking and Gang Violence in the Caribbean." In *Crime, Violence, and Security in the Caribbean*, edited by M. Raymond Izarali. New York: Routledge.

Hoefte, Rosemarijn, and Wouter Veenendaal. 2019. "The Challenges of Nation Building and Nation Branding in Multi-Ethnic Suriname." *Nationalism and Ethnic Politics* 25, no. 2: 173–90. https://www.tandfonline.com/doi/full/10.1080/13537113.2019.1602371/.

Huntington, Samuel P. 1991. *The Third Wave: Democratization in the Late Twentieth Century*. Norman: University of Oklahoma Press.

Izarali, M. Raymond, ed. 2018. *Crime, Violence, and Security in the Caribbean*. New York: Routledge.

Jackson, Robert H. 1990. *Quasi States: Sovereignty, International Relations, and the Third World*. New York: Cambridge University Press.

Jasper, Scott, and James Wirtz. 2017. "Cyber Security." In *The Palgrave Handbook of Security, Risk, and Intelligence*, edited by Robert Dover, Huw Dylan, and Michael S. Goodman. London: Palgrave Macmillan.

Jenkins, Brian. 1975. *International Terrorism: A New Mode of Conflict*. Los Angeles: Crescent Publications.

Kegley, Charles W., Jr. 1993. "The Neoidealist Moment in International Studies? Realist Myths and the New International Realities." *International Studies Quarterly* 37 (June): 131–46.

Kincaid, Douglas A., and Eduardo A. Gamarra. 1996. "Disorderly Democracy: Redefining Public Security in Latin America." In *Latin America in the World Economy*, edited by Roberto Patricio Korzeniewicz and William C. Smith. Westport, CT: Greenwood Press.

King, Gary, Robert O. Keohane, and Sidney Verba. 1994. *Designing Social Inquiry: Scientific Inference in Qualitative Research*. Princeton, NJ: Princeton University Press.

Kissinger, Henry A. 2020. "The Coronavirus Pandemic Will Forever Alter the World Order." *Wall Street Journal*, April 3.

Klein, Alex, Marcus Day, and Anthony Harriott, eds. 2004. *Caribbean Drugs: From Criminalization to Harm Reduction*. London: Zed Books.

Knight, W. Andy. 2019. "The Nexus between Vulnerabilities and Violence in the Caribbean." *Third World Quarterly* 40, no. 2: 405–424.

Krasner, Stephen D. 1999. *Sovereignty: Organized Hypocrisy*. Princeton, NJ: Princeton University Press.

Krasner, Stephen D. 2001. "Sovereignty." *Foreign Policy*, No. 122 (Jan.–Feb.): 20–22, 24, 26, 28, 29.

Lancaster-Ellis, Karen. 2018. "Prisons in the Caribbean: Structures, Conditions, and Effectiveness." In *Crime, Violence, and Security in the Caribbean*, edited by M. Raymond Izarali. New York: Routledge.

Lazar, Nomi Claire. 2009. *States of Emergency in Liberal Democracies*. New York. Cambridge University Press.

Lewis, Kenneth L., Jr. 2013. "The Extradition Treaty between Jamaica and the United States: Its History and the Saga of Christopher 'Dudus' Coke." *University of Miami Inter-American Law Review* 45, no. 1 (Fall): 63–90.

Lewis, Linden, ed. 2013. *Caribbean Sovereignty: Development, and Democracy in an Age of Globalization*. New York: Routledge.

Lewis, Vaughan A. 1976. "The Commonwealth Caribbean and Self-Determination in the International System." In *Size, Self-Determination, and International Relations: The Caribbean*, edited by Vaughan A. Lewis. Kingston, Jamaica: Institute of Social and Economic Research.

Lloyd, Marshall. 2018. *Transnational Crimes in the Americas: Law, Policy, and Institutions*. London: Anthem Press.

Lutz, Brenda J., and James M. Lutz. 2018. "Terrorism and Tourism in the Caribbean: A Regional Analysis." *Behavioral Sciences of Terrorism and Political Aggression* 12, no. 1: 55–71. https://doi.org/10.1080/19434472.2018.1518337/.

MacDonald, Scott B., and Bruce Zagaris. 1992. "Caribbean Offshore Financial Centers: the Bahamas, the British Dependencies, the Netherlands Antilles and Aruba." In

International Handbook of Drug Control, edited by Scott B. MacDonald and Bruce Zagaris. Westport, CT: Greenwood Press.

MacDonald, Scott B. 2022. *The New Cold War and the Caribbean: Economic Statecraft, China, and Strategic Realignments*. London: Palgrave Macmillan.

Maguire, Edward R., William R. King, Devon Johnson, and Charles M. Katz. 2010. "Why Homicide Clearance Rates Decrease: Evidence from the Caribbean." *Policing and Society* 20, no. 4 (December): 373–400.

Maharaj, Sanjay Badri. 2017. "Globalization of the Jihadist Threat: Case Study of Trinidad and Tobago." *Strategic Analysis* 41, no. 2:1–17. https://www.tandfonline.com/doi/abs /10.1080/09700161.2017.1278880?journalCode=rsan20/.

Maingot, Anthony P. 1998. "Laundering the Gains of the Drug Trade: Miami and Caribbean Tax Havens." *Journal of Interamerican Studies and World Affairs* 30, Issue 2–3 (Summer): 167–88.

Maingot, Anthony P. 1999. "The Decentralization Imperative in Caribbean Criminal Enterprises." In *Transnational Criminal Enterprise in the Americas*, edited by Tom Farer. New York: Routledge.

Maingot, Anthony P. 2000. "Changing Definitions of 'Social Problems' in the Caribbean." In *Security in the Caribbean Basin: The Challenge of Regional Cooperation*, edited by Joseph S. Tulchin and Ralph H. Espach. Boulder, CO: Lynne Rienner.

Manigat, Leslie. 1988. "The Setting: Crisis, Ideology, and Geopolitics." In *The Caribbean and World Politics*, edited by Jorge Heine and Leslie Manigat. New York: Holmes and Meier.

Martin, Richard T. 1970. "The Role of Coca in the History, Religion, and Medicine of South American Indians." *Economic Botany* 24: 422–38.

McCoy, John, and W. Andy Knight. 2017. "Homegrown Violent Extremism in Trinidad and Tobago: Local Patterns, Global Trends." *Studies in Conflict and Terrorism* 40, no. 4: 267–99.

McDavid, Hilton A. 2011. "Security Challenge and Threats in the Caribbean." In *Rewiring Regional Security in a Fragmented World*, edited by Chester A. Croker, Fen Osler Hampson, and Pamela Aall. Washington, DC: United States Institute of Peace.

McElroy, Jerome, and Klaus de Albuquerque. 1999. "A Longitudinal Study of Serious Crime in the Caribbean." *Caribbean Journal of Criminology and Social Psychology* 4, nos. 1/2: 32–70.

McRae, Rob, and Don Hubert, eds. 2002. *Human Security and the New Diplomacy*. Montreal: McGill-Queens University Press.

Meikle, Tracian, and Rivke Jaffe. 2015. "'Police as the New Don?' An Assessment of Post-Dudus Policing Strategies in Jamaica." *Caribbean Journal of Criminology* 1, no. 2 (August): 75–100. https://pdfs.semanticscholar.org/7418/9dcb226b8f83992a4e15 debeb5f769181f15.pdf/.

Milfesky, Raymond J. 2004. "Territorial Disputes and Regional Security in the Caribbean Basin, in *Caribbean Security in the Age of Terror: Challenge and Change*, ed. Ivelaw Lloyd Griffith. Kingston, Jamaica: Ian Randle Publishers.

Mohammed, Anne-Marie, and Sandra Sookram. 2015. "The Impact of Crime on Tourist Arrivals: A Comparative Analysis of Jamaica and Trinidad and Tobago." *Social and Economic Studies* 64, no. 2: 153–76.

Monaco, Lisa, and Vin Gupta. 2018. "The Next Pandemic Will Be Arriving Shortly." *Foreign Policy*. September. https://foreignpolicy.com/2018/09/28/the-next-pandemic-will-be -arriving-shortly-global-health-infectious-avian-flu-ebola-zoonotic-diseases-trump/.

Montoute, Annita. 2013. "Caribbean-China Economic Relations: What Are the Implications?" *Caribbean Journal of International Relations and Diplomacy* 1, no. 1 (February): 110–126. https://journals.sta.uwi.edu/ojs/index.php/iir/article/view/344/304/.

Morris, Michael. 1994. *Caribbean Maritime Security*. New York: St. Martin's Press.

Nadelmann, Ethan A. 1993. *Cops across Borders*. University Park: Pennsylvania State University Press.

Naím, Moises. 2005. *Illicit: How Smugglers, Traffickers, and Copycats Are Hijacking the Global Economy*. New York: Anchor Books.

Nye, Joseph S., Jr., and Sean Lynn-Jones. 1988. "International Security Studies: A Report of a Conference on the State of the Field." *International Studies Quarterly* 12 (Spring): 5–27.

Nye, Joseph S., Jr. 2020. "Post-Pandemic Geopolitics." Project Syndicate, October 6. https://www.project-syndicate.org/commentary/five-scenarios-for-international -order-in-2030-by-joseph-s-nye-2020-10/.

Pantin, Raoul, A. 2007. *Days of Wrath: The 1990 Coup in Trinidad and Tobago*. Lincoln, NE: iUniverse.

Paoli, Letizia, Victoria A. Greenfield, and Peter Reuter. 2009. *The World Heroin Market. Can Supply Be Cut?* Oxford: Oxford University Press.

Patel, Akshat. 2021. "A Tale of Two Seas: The Caribbean and South China Sea in Great Power Perspective." Center for International Maritime Security, May 11. https:// cimsec.org/a-tale-of-two-seas-the-caribbean-and-south-china-sea-in-great-power -perspective/.

Perl, Raphael. 1989. "International Narcopolicy and the Role of the U.S. Congress." In *The Latin American Narcotics Trade and U.S. National Security*, edited by Donald Marby. Westport. CT: Greenwood Press.

Phillips, Dion. E. 2022. *The Military of the Caribbean: A Look at the Armed Forces of the Anglo Caribbean, 1958–2022*. Bridgetown, Barbados: Caribbean Chapters Publishers.

Pollard, Duke E. E. 2007. "The Guyana/Suriname Boundary Dispute in International Law." In *Intervention, Border, and Maritime Issues in CARICOM*, edited by Kenneth Hall and Myrtle Chuck-A-Sang. Kingston, Jamaica: Ian Randle Publishers.

Ramphal, Shridath. 1985. "Opening address of the meeting of the Commonwealth Experts on Small State Security." In *Commonwealth Study Group, Vulnerability: Small States in a Global Society*. London: Commonwealth Secretariat.

Ramphal, Shridath. 2008. *Triumph for UNCLOS: The Guyana-Suriname Maritime Arbitration: A Compilation and Commentary*. London: Hansib Publishers.

Ramsey, Russell, W. 2003. *Essays on Latin American Security*. Bloomington, IA: 1st Books Library.

Rapley, John. 2006. "The New Middle Ages." *Foreign Affairs* 85, no. 3 (May–June). https:// www.foreignaffairs.com/articles/2006-05-01/new-middle-ages/.

Reichel, Philip, and Ryan Randa, eds. 2018. *Transnational Crime and Global Security*. Santa Barbara, CA: Praeger.

Rodríguez Beruff, Jorge, and Humberto García Muñiz, eds. 1996. *Security Problems and Policies in the Post–Cold War Caribbean*. London: Macmillan.

Rodríguez Beruff, Jorge. 2009. "La Seguridad en el Caribe en 2008: Huracanes, Crimen, Rusos y Soft Power." In *Seguridad Regional en America Latina y el Caribe: Anuario 2009*, edited by Hans Mathieu and Paula Rodríguez Arredondo. Bogota: Friedrich Ebert Stiftung.

Rosenau, James N. 1980. *The Scientific Study of Foreign Policy*. London: Francis Pinter.

Rosenau, James N. 1995. *Multilateral Governance and the Nation State System: A Post–Cold War Assessment*. Inter-American Dialogue Occasional Papers in Western Hemisphere Governance, No. 1, September.

Rosenau, James N. 1997. *Along the Domestic-Foreign Frontier: Exploring Governance in a Turbulent World*. Cambridge: Cambridge University Press.

Rubin, Vera, and Lambros Comitas. 1975. *Ganja in Jamaica: A Medical Anthropological Study of Chronic Marijuana Use*. Scotch Plains, NJ: Mouton.

Ryan, Selwyn. 1991. *The Muslimeen Grab for Power: Race, Religion, and Revolution in Trinidad and Tobago*. Port-of-Spain, Trinidad: Caribbean Imprint.

Sáenz Rovner, Eduardo. 2009. *The Cuban Connection: Drug Trafficking, Smuggling, and Gambling in Cuba from the 1920s to the Revolution*. Chapel Hill: University of North Carolina Press.

Samuels, K. C. 2011. *Jamaica's First President 1992–2010: His Reign, His Rise, His Demise*. Kingston, Jamaica: Pageturner Publishing House.

Sanders, Ronald. 1993. "The Drug Problem: Policy Options for Caribbean Countries." In *Democracy in the Caribbean*, edited by Jorge I. Domínguez, Robert A. Pastor, and R. Delisle Worrell. Baltimore: Johns Hopkins University Press.

Scholvin, Sören, and Mikael Wigell. 2018. "Power Politics by Economic Means: Geoeconomics as an Analytical Approach and Foreign Policy Practice." *Comparative Strategy* 37, no. 1: 73–84.

Sedoc-Dahlberg, Betty N. 1997. "Democracy and Human Rights in Suriname." In *Democracy and Human Rights in the Caribbean*, edited by Ivelaw Lloyd Griffith and Betty N. Sedoc-Dahlberg. Boulder, CO Westview Press.

Seepersad, Randy, and Ann Marie Bissessar, eds., 2013. *Gangs in the Caribbean*. Newcastle upon Tyne: Cambridge Scholars Publishing.

Seepersad, Randy, and Dianne Williams. 2016. *Crime and Security in Trinidad and Tobago*. Kingston, Jamaica: Ian Randle Publishers.

Seepersad, Randy. 2018. "Crime, Violence and Public Safety in the Caribbean." In *Crime, Violence, and Security in the Caribbean*, edited by M. Raymond Izarali. New York: Routledge.

Seiverright, Delano. 2010. "Chevannes and Ganga Law Reform." *Jamaica Gleaner*. December 12. https://jamaica-gleaner.com/gleaner/20101212/focus/focus6.html/.

Setty, Sudha. 2011. "What's in a Name? How Nations Define Terrorism in Ten Years after 9/11." *University of Pennsylvania Journal of International Law* 33, no. 1: 1–63.

Sheeran, Scott, P. 2013. "Reconceptualizing States of Emergency under International Human Rights Law: Theory, Legal Doctrine, and Politics." *Michigan Journal of International Law* 34, no. 3: 491–557.

Shelley, Louise I. 1995. "Transnational Organized Crime: An Imminent Threat to the Nation-State?" *Journal of International Affairs* 48, no. 2 (Winter): 463–89.

Shuldiner, Henry. 2022. "Dominican Republic Cybercrime Ring Shows Extent of Caribbean's Financial Fraud Crisis." *InSight Crime*. March 9. https://insightcrime.org/news/dominican-republic-cybercrime-ring-extent-caribbean-financial-fraud/.

Singh, Chaitram. 2007. "Reining in the Military: Re-Democratization in Suriname." *Journal of Third World Studies* 24, no. 1: 73–96.

Smith, Jacob. 2022. "Jamaica: Well-Known Businesswoman Shot Dead along with Her Domestic Help in Westmoreland." Writeups. January 13, https://writeups24.com/jamaica-well-known-businesswoman-shot-dead-along-with-her-domestic-help-in-westmoreland/.

Strange, Susan. 1996. *The Retreat of the State: The Diffusion of Power in the World Economy*. Cambridge: Cambridge University Press.

Szabo, Liz. 2021. "The Pandemic Caused the Biggest Decline in U.S. Life Expectancy since World War 2. Black and Hispanic Americans Have Suffered the Most." *Time*. June 23. https://time.com/6075295/covid-19-life-expectancy-decline/.

Taylor, Luke. 2023. "Haiti Faces 'Hunger Emergency' Amid Escalating Gang Violence and Surging Inflation." *The Guardian*. March 24. https://www.theguardian.com/global-development/2023/mar/24/haiti-faces-hunger-emergency-amid-escalating-gang-violence-and-surging-inflation/.

Thomas-Johnson, Amandla. 2018. "Caribbean to 'Caliphate': On the Trail of the Trinidadians Fighting for the Islamic State." *Middle East Eye*. March 1. https://www.middleeasteye.net/big-story/caribbean-caliphate-trail-trinidadians-fighting-islamic-state/.

Townsend, Dorn. 2010. "Trouble in Paradise: Welcome to the World's Newest Narcostate." *Foreign Policy*. March 11. https://foreignpolicy.com/2010/03/11/trouble-in-paradise-2/.

Tulchin, Joseph S., and Ralph H. Espach, eds. 2000. *Security in the Caribbean Basin*. Boulder, CO: Lynne Rienner.

Ullman, Richard H. 1983. "Redefining Security." *International Security* 8: 129–53.

Väyrynen, Raimo. 2001. "Sovereignty, Globalization, and Transnational Social Movements." *International Relations of the Asia-Pacific* 1: 227–46.

Vellinga, Menno, ed. 2004. *The Political Economy of the Drug Industry*. Gainesville: University Press of Florida.

Wallace, Wendell, C. 2017. "An Exploratory Study on the Impact of Organized Crime on Societies in Small Island Developing States: Evidence from Five (5) Caribbean Countries." *Perspectivas*. March. https://www.williamjperrycenter.org/sites/default/files/publication_associated_files/Perspectivas%203.pdf/.

Wang, Lidong, and Cheryl Ann Alexander. 2021." Cyber Security during the COVID-19 Pandemic." *AIMS Electronics and Electrical Engineering* 5, no. 2: 146–5 https://doaj.org/article/712723435519449994566ff98c84e411 7.

Watson, Hilbourne A., ed. 2015. *Globalization, Sovereignty, and Citizenship in the Caribbean*. Kingston, Jamaica: University of the West Indies Press.

Williams, Michael C. 2003. "Words, Images, Enemies: Securitization and International Politics." *International Studies Quarterly* 47, no. 4: 511–31.

Young, Alma H., and Dion E. Phillips, eds. 1986. *Militarization in the Non-Hispanic Caribbean*. Boulder, CO: Lynne Rienner.

Young, Germaine. 2022. "States of Exception as Paradigms of Government: Emergency and Criminal Justice in Jamaica?" *Canadian Journal of Latin American and Caribbean Studies* 47, no. 2: 235–60.

Zagaris, Bruce. 2020. "Former Barbados Minister and Parliamentarian Convicted of Receiving and Laundering Bribes from Barbados Insurance Company While Company Must Disgorge." *International Enforcement Law Reporter* 36, no. 1 (January 25). http://www.ielr.com/node?page=2/.

Newspaper and Online Sources

Abdul, Fausia S. 2021. "Former Surinamese President Dési Bouterse Convicted of Murder for the Second Time—But Will He Go to Prison?" Global Voices.org. September 19. https://globalvoices.org/2021/09/19/former-surinamese-president-desi-bouterse -convicted-of-murder-for-the-second-time-but-will-he-go-to-prison/.

Alexander, Gail. 2001. "Pres: $30M Gang Bust and Fear of Gang Warfare." *Trinidad Guardian*. August 27.

Alexander, Gail. 2011a. "Arrests under Anti-Gang Act Halted." *Trinidad Guardian*. October 18. http://www.guardian.co.tt/news/2011/10/17/arrests-under-anti-gang -act-halted/.

Alexander, Gail. 2011b. "Sandy Calls on Manning to Share Info—Who Is Mr. Big?" *Trinidad Guardian*. September 3.

Al-Marashi, Ibrahim. 2020. "The Geopolitics of the Coronavirus Outbreak." Pacific Council on International Policy. February 21. https://www.pacificcouncil.org /newsroom/geopolitics-coronavirus-outbreak/.

Alvarez, Lizette. 2011. "Puerto Rico Prodded to Get Tough with Police." *New York Times*. October 5.

Andreas, Peter. 1993. "Profits, Poverty, and Illegality: The Logic of Drug Corruption." *NACLA Report on the Americas* 27 (November-December): 22ff.

Asmann, Parker. 2019. "Arrests Thrust Dominican Republic's Top Drug Lord into Spotlight." *InSight Crime*. September 13. https://www.insightcrime.org/news/analysis /arrests-dominican-republic-drug-lord-spotlight/.

Associated Press. 2007. "Oil Company Paid Guyana's Legal Fees." October 10.

Associated Press. 2019. "Suriname President Convicted in 1982 Killings." *New York Times*. November 29.

Associated Press. 2022. "Official Says Puerto Rico's Senate Targeted by Cyberattack." January 26. https://apnews.com/article/technology-business-caribbean-puerto-rico -1fba92d4872254d3e9a6134844f15375.

Baboolal, Yvonne. 2011. "Evidence Against Gangs Hard to Come By—Ewatski." *Trinidad Guardian*. October 20. http://www.guardian.co.tt/news/2011/10/20/evidence-against -gangs-hard-come-ewatski/.

Barnett, Lloyd. 2019. "States of Emergency, ZOZOs, and the Fundamental Rights of Individuals." *Jamaica Observer*. January 20. http://amp.jamaicaobserver.com/news

/states-of-emergency-zozos-and-states-of-emergency-zozos-and-the-fundamental
_154611?profile=1444/.

Barrett, Livern. 2016. "Seized! Court Places Clamp on $400m in Property Traced to J'can
Couple Jailed in the US." *Jamaica Gleaner.* December 8. http://jamaica-gleaner.com
/article/lead-stories/20161208/seized-court-places-clamp-400m-property-traced
-jcan-couple-jailed-us/.

BBC News. 2018. "St Kitts and Nevis Profile—Timeline." May 28. https://www.bbc.com
/news/world-latin-america-20033469/.

BBC News. 2019. "Tropical Storm Dorian: Puerto Rico Declares Emergency." August
28. https://www.bbc.com/news/amp/world-us-canada-49486154/.

Bethel, Camille. 2011. "Lucky: Report Police Brutality Cases to PCA." *Trinidad Express.*
September 23.

Bnamericas. 2019. "Corruption and Electricity Costs: The Bane of the Caribbean." October 28. https://www.bnamericas.com/en/news/corruption-and-electricity-costs-the
-bane-of-the-caribbean/.

Bohning, Don. 1999. "Arms-for-Sale Deals Rise: Suriname Military at Focal Point."
Miami Herald. September 12.

Bryan, Anthony T. 2021. "Rivalry in the Guyana Suriname Basin, the Holy Grail of Oil &
Gas." OilNOW. March 1. https://oilnow.gy/featured/rivalry-in-the-guyana-suriname
-basin-the-holygrail-of-oil-ga/.

Bryan, Christopher. 2015. "Cybercrime—An Emergent Global Phenomenon with Implications for the Caribbean." *Jamaica Observer.* June 6. https://www.jamaicaobserver
.com/columns/cybercrime-an-emergent-global-phenomenon-with-implications
-for-the-caribbean/.

Campbell, Edmond. 2020. "PM: Crime 'above our capacity' . . . But investments in Personnel, Tech Will Bear Fruit, Says Holness." *Jamaica Gleaner.* February 27. http://
jamaica-gleaner.com/article/lead-stories/20200227/pm-crime-above-our-capacity
-investments-personnel-tech-will-bear-fruit/.

Caribbean 360. 2011. "Cuba and Jamaica Partner in Fighting Organized Crime." September 7.

Caribbean Business. 2021. "Over 150 Million Cyber-Attacks Registered in Puerto
Rico Last Year." March 3. https://caribbeanbusiness.com/over-150-million-cyber
-%E2%80%8B%E2%80%8Battacks-registered-in-puerto-rico-last-year/.

Caribbean National Weekly. 2020a. "Another State of Emergency Declared in Kingston,
Jamaica." January 26. https://www.caribbeannationalweekly.com/caribbean-breaking
-news-featured/another-state-of-emergency-declared-in-kingston-jamaica/.

Caribbean National Weekly. 2020b. "St. Kitts Moves Closer to Establishing a Cannabis
Industry." February 13. https://www.caribbeannationalweekly.com/news/caribbean
-news/st-kitts-moves-closer-to-establishing-a-cannabis-industry/.

Caribbean Times NYC. 2017. "'Dudus' Moved to Low-Security Prison." May 20. https://
caribbeantimesnyc.com/2017/05/dudus-moved-to-low-security-prison/.

Carroll, Rory. 2010. "Suriname President Promises Not to Interfere in His Own Murder Trial." *The Guardian.* July 22. http://www.guardian.co.uk/world/2010/jul/22
/suriname-president-murder-trial/.

Caymans Compass. 2019. "Customs Makes Record Ecstasy Bust." June 28. https://www.caymancompass.com/2019/06/28/customs-make-record-ecstasy-bust/.

Chabrol, Dennis Scott. 2011. "Breaking News: High Court Awards $$millions to Tortured Teen." *Demerarawaves.* June 17.

Chaplin, Ken. 2011. "Bruce's Cabinet Reshuffle." *Jamaica Observer.* July 5.

Charles, Jacqueline. 2019. "Jamaica Allows Medical Marijuana, But Now What? 'We're not going to be like Colorado.'" *Miami Herald.* June 26.

Charles, Jacqueline. 2022. "COVID Is Still Surging in the Caribbean, Where Rising Deaths, Low Vaccination Continue." *Miami Herald.* February 23.

Charles, Jacqueline. 2023. "Caribbean Is a Top Smuggling Destination for Illegal Arms. U.S. Lawmakers Want Answers." *Miami Herald.* April 4. https://www.msn.com/en-us/news/world/caribbean-is-a-top-smuggling-destination-for-illegal-arms-us-lawmakers-want-answers/ar-AA19tAtJ/.

Clavel, Tristan. 2017. "Haiti's Hellish Prisons Symbolize Broken Justice System." *InSight Crime.* February 21. https://www.insightcrime.org/news/brief/haiti-hellish-prisons-symbolize-broken-justice-system/.

Clinton, Bill. 2012. "The Case for Optimism." *Time.* October 1.

CNN. 2004. "State of Emergency Declared in Haiti: Rebel Leader Agrees to Lay Down Arms." CNN. March 3. https://www.cnn.com/2004/WORLD/americas/03/03/haiti.rebels/.

Coke, Christopher. 2011. "Christopher Coke's Letter to Sentencing Judge." *New York Times.* September 21.

Cooper, Carolyn. 2011. "Dudus Sings and Bruce Croaks?" *Jamaica Gleaner.* October 2. http://jamaica-gleaner.com/gleaner/20111002/cleisure/cleisure3.html/.

Cullinan, Jeanna. 2011. "Jamaica, Honduras Sign Security Pact to Fight Organized Crime." *InSight: Organized Crime in the Americas.* September 22. http://insightcrime.org/insight-latest-news/item/1606-jamaica-honduras-sign-security-pact-to-fight-organized-crime/.

Daily Herald (Suriname). 2010. "Desi Bouterse Sworn In as Suriname President." August 12.

Daily Herald (Suriname). 2011. "Bouterse Was Involved in Drugs after Conviction, Says WikiLeaks Cables." January 24.

Daly, Martin. 2011. "Our Narco Infiltrated State." *Trinidad Express.* December 3.

Daniels, Joe Parkin. 2021. "'Haitians are kidnapped every day': Missionary Abductions Shed Light on Growing Crisis." *The Guardian.* October 20. https://www.theguardian.com/world/2021/oct/20/haiti-kidnapping-abduction-missionaries/.

Davis, Garwin. 2019. "PM Says Region Must Guard against Terrorism and Cybercrimes." Jamaica Information Service. January 29. https://jis.gov.jm/pm-says-region-must-guard-against-terrorism-and-cybercrimes/.

Dawkins, Colleen. 2021. "Gov't Bolstering Cybersecurity—Minister Vaz: Speech Declaring Open Cybersecurity Awareness Month." Jamaica Information Service. October 1. https://jis.gov.jm/govt-bolstering-cybersecurity-minister-vaz/.

Demerarawaves. 2010. "Absence of Foreign Ministry in Talks with Suriname Criticized." November 20.

Demerarawaves. 2011. "Guyana Was Asked about Arresting Suriname's President." January 25.

Demerarawaves. 2022. "New York–Bound Man Held with Cocaine-in-Fried Rice—CANU." February 22.

den Held, Douwe. 2022. "US Guns Fuel Arms Trafficking in the Dominican Republic." *InSight Crime*. June 3. https://insightcrime.org/news/us-guns-fuel-arms-trafficking-in-the-dominican-republic/.

den Held, Douwe, and Gavin Voss. 2023. "A History of the Caribbean's Most Powerful Drug Kingpins." *InSight Crime*, May 12. https://insightcrime.org/news/history-caribbean-most-powerful-drug-kingpins/.

Dennis, Denise. 2011. "Seaga, McKenzie among Mourners Praising Dudus's Mom." *Jamaica Observer*. September 15.

Derooy, Fernand. 1986. "State of Emergency Declared in Suriname." United Press International. December 2. https://www.upi.com/Archives/1986/12/02/State-of-emergency-declared-in-Suriname/1424533883600/.

Dig Jamaica. 2017. "What Are 'Zones of Special Operations'?—In Layman's Terms." July 12. http://digjamaica.com/m/blog/what-are-zones-of-special-operations-in-laymans-terms/.

Dominica News Online. 2010. "Magistrate Shot by Masked Assailants in St. Lucia." April 8. https://dominicanewsonline.com/news/homepage/news/crime-court-law/magistrate-shot/.

Dominican Today. 2011. "Official's Slaying Reveals the Country's Booming Auto Theft Business." September 22.

Dominican Today. 2013a. "Dominican Republic Puts 5 Drug Traffickers' Seized Assets on the Block." September 10. https://dominicantoday.com/dr/local/2013/09/10/dominican-republic-puts-5-drug-traffickers-seized-assets-on-the-block/.

Dominican Today. 2013b. "Energy Subsidy, Theft, Cost Dominican Republic Taxpayers US$1.24B." September 9. https://dominicantoday.com/dr/local/2013/09/09/energy-subsidy-theft-cost-dominican-republic-taxpayers-us1–24b/.

The Economist. 2011. "Jamaica's Prime Minister Golding Goes." October 1. http://www.economist.com/node/21531033/.

The Economist. 2014. "Drug Trafficking in the Caribbean: Full Circle." May 24. https://www.economist.com/the-americas/2014/05/24/full-circle/.

The Economist. 2016. "Blue Seas, Black Holes; Caribbean Prisons." March 12. https://link-gale-com.udel.idm.oclc.org/apps/doc/A450872107/EAIM?u=udel_main&sid=EAIM&xid=7dc0e3/.

The Economist. 2020. "Suriname: Economic Growth." January 1. https://country.eiu.com/article.aspx?articleid=48901188&Country=Suriname&topic=Economy&subtopic=Forecast&subsubtopic=Economic+growth&aid=1&oid=128901196#/.

Eley, Tom. 2010. "Death Toll at 200,000: US Military to Enforce State of Emergency in Haiti." World Socialist Website. January 19. https://www.wsws.org/en/articles/2010/01/hait-j19.html/.

Ellington, Owen. 2013. "Dealing Effectively with Guns and Drugs for Improved Public Safety." *Jamaica Observer*. June 2. http://www.jamaicaobserver.com

/columns/Dealing-effectively-with-guns-and-drugs-for-improved-public-safety_
14390368/.

Fauriol, Georges. 2023. "Haiti's Humanitarian and Political Crash," *Global Americans Report*. May 10. https://theglobalamericans.org/2023/05/haitis-humanitarian-and
-political-crash/.

Fox News Latino. 2013. "Drug Trafficking Up in Caribbean, Assistant Secretary of State Says." June 27. https://www.foxnews.com/world/drug-trafficking-up-in-caribbean
-assistant-secretary-of-state-says/.

Freed, Kenneth. 1994. "Haiti Puppet President Declares Emergency: Caribbean: No Unusual Military Activity Is Evident. U.S. Diplomats Warn about Treatment of Americans." *Los Angeles Times*. June 13.

Friedman, Thomas L. 2022. "We Have Never Been Here Before." *New York Times*. February 25.

Gardaworld. 2019. "Dominican Republic: State of Emergency Declared as Tropical Storm Dorian Approaches." August 28. https://www.garda.com/crisis24/news
-alerts/262136/dominican-republic-state-of-emergency-declared-as-tropical-storm
-dorian-approaches-august-28/.

GEOExPro. 2019. "The Caribbean Hots Up!" *Geoscience* 16, no. 4. https://assets.geoexpro
.com/uploads/cc3874f6–0d54–4c55–82a2-a09fe3d024fa/Geoscience_Magazine
_GEO_ExPro_V16i4_2019.pdf/.

George, Kinnesha. 2019. "Young Wants to Ban Ecstasy Drug." *Trinidad and Tobago Newsday*. July 25. https://newsday.co.tt/2019/07/25/young-wants-to-ban-ecstasy-drug/.

Goldstein, Joseph. 2011. "Jamaican Kingpin Pleads Guilty in New York." *New York Times*. August 31.

Gorder, Gabrielle. 2021. "Klansman Trial Reveals Jamaica's Sophisticated Gang Dynamics." *InSight Crime*. November 16. https://insightcrime.org/news/klansman-trial-
reveals-jamaicas-sophisticated-gang-dynamics/.

Griffith, Ivelaw Lloyd. 2010. "Jamaica's Sovereignty Saga, Crisis in the Caribbean Nation." *New York Carib News*. June 10.

Griffith, Ivelaw Lloyd. 2020. "Elections and Geopolitical Neighborhoods in Guyana." CNG Media. February 29. https://www.caribbeannewsglobal.com/elections-and
-geopolitical-neighborhoods-in-guyana/.

Guyana Chronicle. 2002. "An Unfortunate Map Display." November 6. https://www
.landofsixpeoples.com/news022/nc21106.htm/.

Haiti Libre. 2019. "Haiti—Politic: Texts of the Resolution of the State of Emergency and the 11 Measures." February 7. https://www.haitilibre.com/en/news-26868-haiti
-politic-texts-of-the-resolution-of-the-state-of-emergency-and-the-11-measures
.html/.

Hall, Arthur, and Nedburn Thuffe. 2011. "Corruption Choking Courts." *Jamaica Gleaner*. October 10. https://jamaica-gleaner.com/gleaner/20111010/lead/lead5.html/.

Hamilton, Brad, and Cathy Burke. 2010. "The Brutal Rise of Drug Lord Christopher Coke and the Fight to Bring Him to Justice." *New York Post*. June 27. http://www
.nypost.com/p/news/international/drug_lord_brutal_rise_LDn1aR3kSTCsJQIiNZ
UL2H#ixzz1Zt0V7La.

Hanson, Vicki. 2016. "2015 the Year of Ganja in Jamaica." *TNI Drug Law Reform*. January 29. http://www.druglawreform.info/en/weblog/item/6729–2015-the-year-of-ganja -in-jamaica/.

Henry, Paul. 2010. "'Dudus' in NY Court Today." *Jamaica Observer*. June 25. http://www .jamaicaobserver.com/news/-Dudus—in-NY-court-today/.

Henry, Paul. 2011. "'Dudus' Didn't Squeal—Speculation 'Disturbs' Coke's Lawyer." *Jamaica Observer*. September 22. https://www.stabroeknews.com/2011/09/22 /news/guyana/dudus-didnt-squeal-speculation-'disturbs'-coke's-lawyer/.

Henry, Paul, and Harold Bailey. 2012. "VIDEO: 23 Years! 'Dudus' Gets Maximum Sentence in New York Court: Anger, Shock, Tears in Tivoli." *Jamaica Observer*. June 9. https://www.jamaicaobserver.com/news/video-23-years-dudus-gets-maximum -sentence-in-new-york-court/.

Hernández Cabiya, Yanira. 2020. "Cyberattacks on Puerto Rico Government Offices Have Been Recurrent." *Caribbean Business*. February 13. https://caribbeanbusiness .com/cyberattacks-on-puerto-rico-government-offices-have-been-recurrent/.

Herrington, A. J. 2019. "St. Kitts and Nevis to Introduce Legislation Decriminalizing Marijuana." *High Times*. August 5. https://hightimes.com/news/st-kitts-nevis-introduce -legislation-decriminalizing-marijuana/.

Hines, Horace. 2013. "GG's Wife Rocked by Cop's Murder." *Jamaica Observer*. April 12. https://www.jamaicaobserver.com/news/ggs-wife-rocked-by-cops-murder/.

Ho, Solarina. 2019. "Jamaica Extends 'State of Emergency' Travel Warning over High Levels of Violent Crime." CTVNews.ca. August 13. https://beta.ctvnews.ca/national /world/2019/8/13/1_4547466.html/.

Houston Chronicle. 1995. "Trinidad Speaker Held as Emergency Declared." August 8.

InSight Crime. 2020. "First Capital Command—PCC." March 9. https://insightcrime .org/brazil-organized-crime-news/first-capital-command-pcc-profile/.

InSight Crime. 2022. "InSight Crime's 2021 Homicide Round-Up." February 1. https:// insightcrime.org/news/insight-crimes-2021-homicide-round-up/.

InSight Crime. 2023. "InSight Crime's 2022 Homicide Round-Up." February 8. https:// insightcrime.org/news/insight-crime-2022-homicide-round-up/.

Internet World Stats: Usage and Population Statistics. Americas—Internet Usage Statistics. Various dates. www.internetworldstats.com/stats2.htm/.

Interpol. 2022. "Hundreds of Firearms and 12.6 Tonnes of Drugs Seized in Caribbean Operation." October 13. https://www.interpol.int/en/News-and-Events/News/2022 /Hundreds-of-firearms-and-12.6-tonnes-of-drugs-seized-in-Caribbean-operation/.

Jamaica Gleaner, 2010. "Who Is Dudus?" May 24. https://jamaica-gleaner.com/gleaner /20100524/lead/lead4.html.

Jamaica Gleaner. 2013. "Editorial—Tyranny in the Ghetto." April 27. https://jamaica -gleaner.com/gleaner/20130427/cleisure/cleisure1.html.

Jamaica Gleaner. 2018a. "A Closer Look at All Jamaica's States of Emergency." January 19. http://digjamaica.com/m/blog/a-closer-look-at-all-jamaicas-states-of-emergency/.

Jamaica Gleaner. 2018b. "Jamaica Makes First Shipment of Medical Marijuana to Canada." September 27. https://jamaica-gleaner.com/article/news/20180927/jamaica -makes-first-shipment-medical-marijuana-canada.

Jamaica Gleaner. 2020. "Jamaica National Hit by Major Cyberattack." March 20. https:// jamaica-gleaner.com/article/news/20200320/jamaica-national-hit-major-cyber-attack.

Jamaica Gleaner. 2021. "Golding's Gamble: PNP Risks Popularity with SOE Move; President Willing to Pay Price." November 27. https://jamaica-gleaner.com/article/lead -stories/20211127/goldings-gamble/.

Jamaica Gleaner. 2023. "Jamaica Recorded 1,498 Murders in 2022." January 3. http:// cmslocal.gleanerjm.com/article/news/20230103/jamaica-recorded-1498-murders -2022.

Jamaica Information Service. 2017. "The Law Reform (Zones of Special Operations) (Special Security and Community Development Measures) Law." October 26. https:// jis.gov.jm/information/get-the-facts/law-reform-zones-special-operations-special -security-community-development-measures-law/.

Jamaica Loop News. 2019. "St. Andrew South Police Division a Hotbed of Violence— Commissioner." July 8. https://jamaica.loopnews.com/content/st-andrew-south -police-division-hotbed-violence-commissioner/.

Jamaica Loop News. 2021. "Seven States of Emergency Declared by Gov't to Address Crime Wave." November 14. https://jamaica.loopnews.com/content/seven-states -emergency-declared-govt-address-crime-wave/.

Jamaica Observer. 2011a. "CARICOM Chairman Scoffs at Jamaica's Position on CCJ." January 29.

Jamaica Observer. 2013. "'A dark night of the soul': Full Text of What National Security Minister Peter Bunting Said." April 17. http://www.jamaicaobserver.com/news/A -dark-night-of-the-soul_14082950/.

Jamaica Observer. 2016. "Jamaica Homicides Jump 20 Per Cent, Highest Level in 5 Years." January 10. http://www.jamaicaobserver.com/NEWS/Jamaica-homicides-jump-20 -per-cent--highest-level-in-5-years_48331/.

Jamaica Observer. 2021. "Throats of Elderly Sisters Slashed in St Catherine." November 3. https://www.jamaicaobserver.com/latest-news/throats-of-elderly-sisters-slashed -in-st-catherine/.

Jamaica Observer. 2022. "Jamaica Ends 2021 with 1,463 Murders." January 4. https:// www.jamaicaobserver.com/news/jamaica-ends-2021-with-1463-murders/.

Jamaica Observer. 2023. "10 Alleged Klansman Gangsters Found Not Guilty in Several Murders." March 2. https://www.jamaicaobserver.com/latest-news/10-alleged -klansman-gangsters-found-not-guilty-in-several-murders/.

John-Lall, Raphael. 2011. "Big Businesses Support State of Emergency." *Trinidad Guardian*. September 1. https://www.guardian.co.tt/article-6.2.449679.f30a988df1/.

Johnson, R. J. 2019. "Puerto Rico Declares State of Emergency as Hurricane Dorian Approaches." August 28. iHeart Radio. https://www.iheart.com/content/2019-08 -28-puerto-rico-declares-state-of-emergency-as-tropical-storm-dorian-approaches/.

Kaieteur News. 2009. "Tortured Teen Taken to Hospital—after Four Days of Hell." November 1. http://www.kaieteurnewsonline.com/2009/11/01/tortured-teen-taken -to-hospital-after-four-days-in-hell/.

Kaieteur News. 2011. "Bouterse Makes Brief Stop-Over." February 28. https://www .kaieteurnewsonline.com/2011/02/28/bouterse-makes-brief-stop-over/.

Kaieteur News. 2015. "Leonora 'Torture Cop' Kicked Out of Force." June 3. https://www
.kaieteurnewsonline.com/2015/06/03/leonora-torture-cop-kicked-out-of-force/.

Kaieteur News. 2016. "17 Dead . . . after Inmates Set Prison Block on Fire." March 4.
https://www.kaieteurnewsonline.com/2016/03/04/17-deadafter-inmates-set-prison
-block-on-fire/.

Kaieteur News. 2018. "Cocaine, Millions $$ Seized in Multi-Region Drug Operation."
January 6. https://www.kaieteurnewsonline.com/2018/01/06/cocaine-millions-seized
-in-multi-region-drug-operation/.

Khan, Daniel. 2011. "Legal Issues with Prosecuting Gangs." *Trinidad Express*. September
28.

Khan, Shariq. 2020. "Apache Shares Jump 27% on Major Discovery in Suriname
with Total." Reuters. January 7. https://www.reuters.com/article/us-total-apache
-idUSKBN1Z61EC/.

King, Kemol. 2019. "Lands and Surveys Commission Faces Cyber Attacks . . . Police Called
In." *Kaieteur News*. December 10. https://www.kaieteurnewsonline.com/2019/12/10
/lands-and-surveys-commission-faces-cyber-attacks-police-called-in/.

Kowlessar, Geisha. 2011. "Cops' Action in Emergency Under Scrutiny—Volney." *Trinidad Guardian*. October 19. http://www.guardian.co.tt/news/2011/10/19/cops-actions
-emergency-under-scrutiny-volney/.

Krauss, Clifford. 2021. "Suriname Could Be Latest Big Oil Find as Industry Cuts Costs."
New York Times. January 20.

Kuipers, Ank. 2010. "Suriname MPs Elect Strongman as President." *Star Online*. July 20.

Kuipers, Ank. 2019. "Suriname President Bouterse Convicted of Murder for 1982 Executions." *US News and World Report*. November 29.

Lamers, Matt. 2019. "Barbados Medical Cannabis Law Clears Final Hurdle in Parliament."
Marijuana Business Daily. December 3. https://mjbizdaily.com/barbados-medical
-cannabis-law-clears-final-hurdle-in-parliament/.

Lewis, Emma. 2021. "Controversial Jamaican Pastor Dies in Car Crash on the Way to
Being Charged for 'Cult' Deaths." *Global Voices*. October 26. https://globalvoices.org
/2021/10/26/controversial-jamaican-pastor-dies-in-car-crash-on-the-way-to-being
-charged-for-cult-deaths/.

La Vende, Jensen. 2019. "Weed Is Legal." *Trinidad and Tobago Newsday*. December 22.
https://newsday.co.tt/2019/12/22/weed-is-legal/.

Linton, Latonya. 2019. "Consistent Reduction in Criminal Case Backlog." Jamaica Information Service. May 23. https://jis.gov.jm/consistent-reduction-in-criminal-case
-backlog/.

López, Julie. 2013. "Organized Crime and Insecurity in Belize." Inter-American Dialogue
Working Paper. January 15. https://ambergriscaye.com/art2/IAD9014_Belize_Lopez
_Paper_FINAL.pdf/.

Lord, Nate. 2019. "What Is Cyber Security? Definition, Best Practices, and Examples."
Digital Guardian. July 15. https://digitalguardian.com/blog/what-cyber-security/.

Los Angeles Times. 2011. "Hotel Owner Sought in Dominican Journalist Killing." August
18.

Luhnow, David, and José de Cordoba. 2009. "The Perilous State of Mexico." *Wall Street
Journal*. February 21.

Mahfood, John. 2020. "Theft of Electricity and Its Impact on Crime and Violence in Jamaica." *The Gleaner*. February 12. https://jamaica-gleaner.com/article/commentary/20200212/john-mahfood-theft-electricity-and-its-impact-crime-and-violence-jamaica.

Marder, Michael. 2020. "The Coronavirus Is Us." *New York Times*. March 3.

Marzulli, John. 2013. "Grandma Sneaks Drugs into U.S. from Dominican Republic in Wheelchair." *New York Daily News*. May 30.

Medina, Irene. 2013. "Dirty Money: $.6b in Suspicious Transactions in T&T from 2011–2012." *Trinidad Express*. March 2.

Mejia, Camilo, 2014. "Trinidad Attorney Killed by International Drug Gang: US." *InSight Crime*. June 26, https://www.insightcrime.org/news/brief/trinidad-attorney-assassinated-international-organized-crime/.

Melnick, Jeff. 2018. "Top 10 Most Common Types of Cyber Attacks." *Netwrix* Blog. May 15. https://blog.netwrix.com/2018/05/15/top-10-most-common-types-of-cyber-attacks/.

Memesita. 2021. "The US Asks to Delay the Trial of Deputy Miguel Gutiérrez Díaz until 2022." September 9.

Mendes-Franco, Janine. 2021. "Yasin Abu Bakr, Leader of Trinidad & Tobago's Attempted Islamist Coup, Dies 31 Years after Failed Insurrection." Global Voices. October 22. https://globalvoices.org/2021/10/22/yasin-abu-bakr-leader-of-trinidad-tobagos-attempted-islamist-coup-dies-31-years-after-failed-insurrection/.

Miroff, Nick. 2011. "Mexico's Drug War Comes to Belize." *Globalpost*. October 11. https://theworld.org/stories/2011-10-11/mexicos-drug-war-comes-belize/.

Morris, Ainsworth. 2019. "States of Public Emergency Declared in St. James, Westmoreland and Hanover." Jamaica Information Service. April 30. https://jis.gov.jm/states-of-public-emergency-declared-in-st-james-westmoreland-and-hanover/.

Morris, Catherine. 2019. "The Costs of Crime." *St. Lucia Star*. March 23. https://stluciastar.com/the-cost-of-crime/.

Muhammad, David. 2012. "'Gangster' Profiling, Black Males and Afro-Trinidad's Future." *Final Call*. April 18. www.finalcall.com/artman/publish/perspectives_1/article_8739.shtml/.

Munnings, Lynaire. 2023. "Davis Decries 'Epidemic' of Violence in Caribbean." *Tribune 242*. April 18. http://www.tribune242.com/news/2023/apr/18/davis-decries-epidemic-violence-caribbean/.

Nabe, Cedric. 2020. "The Impact of COVID-19 on Cybersecurity." *Deloitte*. December. https://www2.deloitte.com/ch/en/pages/risk/articles/impact-covid-cybersecurity.html/.

Nelson, Jaevion. 2013. "A Divine Intervention for Crime and Violence." *Jamaica Gleaner*. April 18. http://mobile.jamaica-gleaner.com/gleaner/20130418/cleisure/cleisure4.php/.

Neves, Yuri, and Mónica Betancur. 2019. "PCC-'Ndrangheta, the International Criminal Alliance Flooding Europe with Cocaine." *InSight Crime*. August 8. https://insightcrime.org/news/analysis/pcc-ndrangheta-criminal-alliance-flooding-europe-cocaine/.

New York Post. 2012. "Jamaican Drug Lord 'Dudus' Coke Sentenced to 23 Years in Prison." June 8. https://nypost.com/2012/06/08/jamaican-druglord-dudus-coke-sentenced -to-23-years-in-prison/.

News Caribbean Jamaica. 2019. "A Third State of Emergency Declared in Jamaica." September 5. https://www.caribbeannationalweekly.com/caribbean-breaking-news -featured/a-third-state-of-emergency-declared-in-jamaica/.

OilNOW. 2020. "Guyana Will Become Just the 11th Nation in History to Reach Million Barrel a Day Milestone—WoodMac." March 10. https://oilnow.gy/featured /guyana-will-become-just-the-11th-nation-in-history-to-reach-million-barrel-a-day -milestone-woodmac/.

Osborne, Samuel. 2017. "France Declares End to State of Emergency Almost Two Years after Paris Terror Attacks." *The Independent.* October 31.

Pachico, Elyssa. 2011a. "Cuba Releases 2010 'Drug War' Statistics." *InSight Crime.* February 16. http://insightcrime.org/insight-latest-news/item/570-cuba-releases-2010 -drug-war-statistics/.

Pachico, Elyssa. 2011b. "Is Puerto Rico Becoming a Narco-State?" *Christian Science Monitor.* December 16.

Padgett, Tim. 2011. "Can a Young Prime Minister Reform Jamaica's Old Criminality?" *Time.* October 6.

Padgett, Tim. 2022. "Guns of the Caribbean: Haiti, U.S. Virgin Islands Flooded with Firearms—Often from Florida." WLRN 91.3 FM. March 22. https://www.wlrn.org /news/2022-03-22/guns-of-the-caribbean-haiti-u-s-virgin-islands-flooded-with -firearms-often-from-florida/.

Paynter, Mellany. 2020. "Jamaica Corruption Increases." *Jamaica Gleaner.* January 29. https://www.nycaribnews.com/articles/jamaica-corruption-increases/.

Phillips, Dion E. 1991. "Terrorism and Security in the Caribbean: The 1976 Cubana Disaster Off Barbados." *Terrorism: An International Journal* 14, no. 4: 208–219.

Phillips, Dion E. 2008. "Terrorism and Security in the Caribbean Before and After 9/11." *Armed Forces and Conflict Resolution: Sociological Perspectives* 7: 97–138.

Pickering, Clinton. 2021. "Human Sacrifice Is the Gruesome End to This Cult's Creepy History." *Daily Beast.* October 20. https://culteducation.com/group/1357-pathways -international-kingdom-restoration-ministries/36209-human-sacrifice-is-the -gruesome-end-to-this-cult-s-creepy-history.html/.

Radio Jamaica News. 2010. "Golding Faces Regional Ire for Jamaican Court Proposal." December 24. http://radiojamaicanewsonline.com/local/golding-faces-regional-ire -for-jamaican-court-proposal/.

Ramdass, Ann. 2023. "War on Illicit Weapons." *Trinidad Express.* April 19. https:// trinidadexpress-tto.newsmemory.com/?publink=14b59ca41_134ab37/.

Ramdass, Rickie. 2020. "10 to Stand Trial for Dana Seetahal Murder." *Sunday Express.* July 23. https://trinidadexpress.com/newsextra/10-to-stand-trial-for-dana-seetahal -murder/article_fc10054a-cd21-11ea-8d90-5b4b769d0102.html/.

Rattray, Garth A. 2010. "Don't Dehumanize Prisoners." *Jamaica Gleaner.* September 1. http://mobile.jamaica-gleaner.com/gleaner/20101101/cleisure/cleisure2.php/.

Reid, Tyrone. 2011a. "Different without Dons—Commish Profiling 'Criminal Actors.'" *Jamaica Gleaner*. October 9. https://jamaica-gleaner.com/gleaner/20111009/lead /lead5.html/.

Reid, Tyrone. 2011b. "Prostitutes Hooked on Ecstasy—Jamaican Sex Workers Abusing Party Drug as Coping Mechanism." *Jamaica Gleaner*. October 2. https://jamaica -gleaner.com/gleaner/20111002/news/news3.html/.

Reid, Tyrone, and Marcella Scarlett. 2011. "Costly Abuse: Government Pays Hundreds of Millions for Human Rights Violations." *Jamaica Gleaner*. October 16.

Rolle, Krystel. 2011. "Figures Confirm Sharp Rise in Violent Crime." *Nassau Guardian*. October 20.

Romero, Simon. 2011. "Returned to Power, a Leader Celebrates a Checkered Past." *New York Times*. May 2.

Rout, Deepak. 2015. "Developing a Common Understanding of Cybersecurity." *ISACA Journal*. Vol. 6. https://www.isaca.org/resources/isaca-journal/issues/2015/volume-6 /developing-a-common-understanding-of-cybersecurity.

Ryan, Selwyn. 2012. "Gangsters and the Emergent Narco-State." *Trinidad Express*. February 25.

Sanchez, Ray. 2010. "First Medical Marijuana Ad Airs in California." ABC News. September 3. http://abcnews.go.com/Business/medical-marijuana-commercial-airs -california/story?id=11547326#.UZmZRPLD-M8/.

Saturday Express. 2023. "The Murder of State Attorney Dana Seetahal." March 17. https://trinidadexpress.com/newsextra/the-murder-of-state-attorney-dana-seetahal /article_1bf8d7f4-c4f7-11ed-88b1-4738cb11616e.html/.

Savage, Charlie, and Lizette Alvarez. 2011. "Police in Puerto Rico Are Accused of Abuses by Justice Dept. Report." *New York Times*. September 8.

Searchlight. 2022. "SVG to Export 110 Pounds of Medicinal Marijuana to Germany." January 11. https://www.searchlight.vc/news/2022/01/11/svg-to-export-110-pounds -of-medicinal-marijuana-to-germany/.

Seelal, Nalinee. 2011. "Where Is Gibbs?" *Trinidad and Tobago Newsday*. August 24. http:// www.newsday.co.tt/news/0,146114.html/.

Seelal, Nalinee. 2014. "Assassinated." *Trinidad and Tobago News*. May 5. http://www .trinidadandtobagonews.com/blog/?p=8184t/.

Serju, Christopher. 2021. "PM, Chuck Tangle with Golding as Amended SOE Law Passed." *Jamaica Gleaner*. October 27. https://jamaica-gleaner.com/article/lead -stories/20211027/pm-chuck-tangle-golding-amended-soe-law-passed/.

Smith, Robert W. 2004. "Jamaica's Maritime Claims and Boundaries." *Limits in the Seas*, no. 125. February 5. https://2009–2017.state.gov/documents/organization/57677.pdf/.

South Florida Caribbean News. 2019. "St. Kitts and Nevis among the 10 Countries with the Highest Murder Rate." February 12. https://sflcn.com/st-kitts-and-nevis-among -the-10-countries-with-the-highest-murder-rate/.

Stabroek News. 2008. "Nervous Neighbours: Guyana and Suriname." November 5. https:// www.stabroeknews.com/2008/11/05/guyana-review/nervous-neighbours-guyana -and-suriname/.

Stabroek News. 2010a. "Frontiers: Why Should Guyana Trust Suriname." August 31. http://www.stabroeknews.com/2010/guyana-review/08/31/frontiers-why-should -guyana-trust-suriname/.

Stabroek News. 2010b. "Suriname Desperately Seeks Acceptability." September 30. http:// www.stabroeknews.com/2010/guyana-review/frontiers/09/30/suriname-desperately -seeks-acceptability/.

Stabroek News. 2011. "Suriname Seeks International Help in Drug Seizures." February 22. http://www.stabroeknews.com/2011/news/breaking/02/22/suriname-seeks -international-help-on-drug-seizures/.

Stabroek News. 2019a. "Presence and Sale of Ecstasy in Schools 'Disturbing,' CANU Says Drug Discovered in Five Institutions." June 15. https://www.stabroeknews .com/2019/06/15/news/guyana/presence-and-sale-of-ecstasy-in-schools-disturbing -canu-says/amp/.

Stabroek News. 2019b. "President Bouterse Must Step Down." December 2. https:// www.stabroeknews.com/2019/12/02/opinion/editorial/president-bouterse-must -step-down/.

Stabroek News. 2020. "Suriname's Electoral Authority Confirms Bouterse Defeat." June 16. https://www.stabroeknews.com/2020/06/16/news/guyana/surinames-electoral -authority-confirms-bouterse-defeat/.

The Star. 2016. "$1M or 12 Months Imprisonment . . . Al Miller Sentenced for Role in Dudus Affair." September 15. http://jamaica-star.com/article/news/20160915/1m-or -12-months-imprisonment-al-miller-sentenced-role-dudus-affair/.

St. Lucia Star. 2010. "PM's Constituency Office Is Latest Murder Scene." September 20.

St. Lucia Times. 2022. "680 Kilos of Cocaine Seized in Caribbean Sea." February 7.

Swamber, Keino. 2011. "Seethal Supports State of Emergency." *Trinidad Express*. August 22.

Tatone, Michael. 2013. "Caribbean Will See Trafficking Revival: State Department." *InSight Crime*. April. http://www.insightcrime.org/news-briefs/caribbean-will-see -trafficking-us-brownfield.

Thaffe, Nedburn. 2011. "Baugh Rebukes Golding." *Jamaica Gleaner*. October 3.

Thompson, Canute. 2017. "Zones of Special Operations." *Jamaica Observer*. July 23. http://amp.jamaicaobserver.com/colmns/zones-of-special-operations_105609 ?profile=1096/.

Treisman, Rachel. 2021. "All of the Kidnapped Missionaries in Haiti Have Now Been Released." *NPR News*. December 16. https://www.npr.org/2021/12/16/1064842364 /haiti-kidnapped-missionaries-released-free/.

Trinidad Express. 2020. "Senior Cops Charged with Child Trafficking, Supporting Gang." February 24. https://trinidadexpress.com/newsextra/senior-cops-charged-with -child-trafficking-supporting-gang/article_34812f9e-5770–11ea-bf01-cff8e387feal .html/.

Trinidad Guardian. 2011a. "Growing Prison Population Raises Security Concern." September 5. http://www.guardian.co.tt/news/2011/09/05/growing-prison-population -raises-security-concerns/.

Trinidad Guardian. 2011b. "$1M Lost Due to State of Emergency." September 30. http://www.guardian.co.tt/news/2011/09/30/1m-lost-due-state-emergency/.

Trinidad Guardian. 2011c. "Poll: Strong Support for SoE, Curfew." October 2. http://www.guardian.co.tt/news/2011/10/02/poll-strong-support-soe-curfew/.

Trinidad and Tobago Newsday. 2010. "Well Done, Verna." March 21.

Turner, Rasbert. 2020. "Rats Chase Inmates out Spanish Town Lock-Up; Jail Ordered Closed as Rodents 'Big Like Puss' Bite Detainees." *The Gleaner*. January 30. http://jamaica-gleaner.com/article/lead-stories/20200130/rats-chase-inmates-out-spanish-town-lock-jail-ordered-closed-rodents/.

Virtue, Erica. 2011. "My Contract with Jamaica." *Jamaica Gleaner*. October 10. https://jamaica-gleaner.com/gleaner/20111010/lead/lead1.html/.

VOXXI. 2013. "COPOLAD: Dominican Republic Is the Command Center for Drug Trafficking." VOXXI.com. January 22. https://www.huffpost.com/entry/dominican-republic-emerge_n_2533210/.

Wallace, Alicia. 2015. "45th SW Says Farewell to Antigua Air Station." *United States Space Command News*. July 13. https://www.afspc.af.mil/News/Article-Display/Article/731131/45th-sw-says-farewell-to-antigua-air-station/.

Ward, Curtis A. 2020. "Trump's Security Assistance Cuts and Pompeo's Jamaica Promises Diverge." *Ward Post*. February 25. https://thewardpost.com/trumps-security-assistance-cuts-and-pompeos-jamaica-promises-diverge/.

Washington Post. 2011. "Gunmen Kill Army Colonel Serving as Aide to Top Anti-Drug Official in Dominican Republic." September 20.

Weaver, Jay. 2022. "Exdiputado Gutiérrez Díaz declarado en Miami 'incompetente' para ser juzgado por narcotráfico." *El Nacional*. June 1. https://elnacional.com.do/exdiputado-gutierrez-diaz-declarado-en-miami-incompetente-para-ser-juzgado-por-narcotrafico/.

West Indian News. 2010. "'We Are More Attracted to Guyana'—Says Bouterse as Guyana and Suriname Concretize Relations." September 7.

WIC News Reporter. 2019. "Medical and Small Amount of Marijuana Decriminalized in St. Kitts-Nevis." February 20. https://wicnews.com/caribbean/medical-small-amount-marijuana-decriminalised-st-kitts-nevis-493516721/.

Wilburg, Kiana. 2018. "GPL Lost US$450M in 19 Years to Electricity Theft, Poor Networks." *Kaieteur News*. December 10. https://www.kaieteurnewsonline.com/2018/12/10/gpl-lost-us450m-in-19-years-to-electricity-theft-poor-networks/.

Wilkinson, Bert. 2019. "Caribbean Countries Ramp Up Oil Exploration." *Amsterdam News*. September 5. http://amsterdamnews.com/news/2019/sep/05/caribbean-countries-ram-oil-exploration/.

Wyss, Jim. 2021. "Dominican Lawmaker Arrested in Miami on Drug Trafficking Charges." *Bloomberg News*. May 18. https://www.bnnbloomberg.ca/dominican-lawmaker-arrested-in-miami-on-drug-trafficking-charges-1.1605282/.

Xinhuanet. 2019. "Chinese Technology Helps Cuba Drill for Offshore Oil." April 17. http://www.xinhuanet.com/english/2019-04/17/c_137984456.htm/.

Government and International Documents and Speeches

Amnesty International. 2011. "Human Rights Concerns in Trinidad and Tobago: Submission to the UN Periodic Review." October. http://www.amnesty.org/en/library/asset/AMR49/005/2011/en/8214dbd7-c7b7-4b8f-914e-ff70dbd992e1/amr490052011en.html.

Amnesty International. 2016. "Jamaica: State of Emergency 2010—Ten Things the Government Must Learn and Ten Things It Must Do." June. https://www.amnesty.org/download/Documents/AMR3843372016ENGLISH.PDF/.

Annan, Kofi. 2000. Preface to *World Drug Report 2000*. New York: U.N. Office on Drug Control and Crime Prevention.

Anthony, Kenney. 2012. "Affirming Our Common Future, Our Common Faith: Remarks from the Incoming Chairman of the Caribbean Community at the Thirty-Third Regular Meeting of the Conference of Head of Governments of the Caribbean Community." Gros Islet, St. Lucia, July 4.

Arthur, Owen. 2002. "Address" at the Inaugural Session of the 32nd General Assembly, Organization of American States. Bridgetown, Barbados. June 2.

Benmelech, Efraim, and Esteban F. Klor. 2016. "What Explains the Flow of Foreign Fighters to ISIS?" National Bureau of Economic Research Working Paper No. 22190, April 2016. https://www.nber.org/papers/w22190.pdf/.

Bernal, Richard L. 2016. *Chinese Foreign Direct Investment in the Caribbean: Potential and Prospects*. IDB Technical Note No. 1113. https://publications.iadb.org/publications/english/document/Chinese-Foreign-Direct-Investment-in-the-Caribbean-Potential-and-Prospects.pdf/.

Bouterse, Désiré Delano. 2010. "Cross Roads: Together Towards Better Times." Statement of Government Policy 2010–2015 Delivered in the National Assembly on Friday 1 October 2010 by his Excellency D. D. Bouterse.

Caribbean Council. 2023. "CARICOM States Join Mexico's Anti-Gun Lawsuit in the US." March 31. https://www.caribbean-council.org/caricom-states-join-mexicos-anti-gun-lawsuit-in-the-us/.

Caribbean Development Bank. 2017. *Tourism Industry Reform: Strategies for Enhanced Economic Impact*. https://www.caribank.org/sites/default/files/publication-resources/CDB_Tourism_Industry_Reform_Web_FINAL.pdf/.

Caribbean Financial Action Task Force. 2016. *Anti-Money Laundering and Counter-Terrorist Financing Measures: Trinidad and Tobago Mutual Evaluation Report*. June. https://www.fatf-gafi.org/media/fatf/documents/reports/mer-fsrb/cfatf-4mer-trinidad-tobago.pdf/.

CARICOM. 2001. *Nassau Declaration on International Terrorism*. The CARICOM Response at the Conclusion of the Special (Emergency) Meeting of the Heads of Government of the Caribbean Community. October 11–12. The Bahamas.

CARICOM. 2016. *The CARICOM Cyber Security and Cybercrime Action Plan*, developed in Gros Islet, St. Lucia. March. https://www.caricomimpacs.org/Portals/0/Project%20Documents/CCSAP.pdf/.

CARICOM. 2018. *The CARICOM Counter-Terrorism Strategy*, adopted at the Twenty-Ninth Inter-Sessional Meeting of the Conference of Heads of Government of the Caribbean Community (CARICOM), Port-au-Prince, Haiti, on 26–27 February. https://www.caricomimpacs.org/Portals/0/Documents/CARICOM%20 COUNTER%20TERRORISM%20STRATEGY%20Final.pdf?ver=2018-08-30-143014 -403&timestamp=1584015494707/.

CARICOM IMPACS. 2013. *CARICOM Crime and Security Strategy 2013: Securing the Region*, Adopted at the 24th Inter-Sessional Meeting of the Conference of Heads of Government of CARICOM, 18–19 February 2013, Port-au-Prince, Republic of Haiti.

CARICOM Regional Commission on Marijuana. 2018. *Waiting to Exhale: Safeguarding Our Future through Responsible Socio-Legal Policy on Marijuana Use*. https://caricom .org/documents/report-of-the-caricom-regional-commission-on-marijuana-2018 -waiting-to-exhale-safeguarding-our-future-through-responsible-socio-legal-policy -on-marijuana/.

CARICOM Secretariat. 1990. "Address by L. Erskine Sandiford, Prime Minister of Barbados to 1990 CARICOM Summit." In "Communiqué and Addresses—Eleventh Meeting of the Heads of Government of the Caribbean Community."

CARICOM. 2023. "Declaration by Heads of Government on Crime and Violence as a Public Health Issue." April 18. https://caricom.org/declaration-by-heads-of -government-on-crime-and-violence-as-a-public-health-issue/.

CARPHA (Caribbean Public Health Agency). 2022. "CARPHA Situation Report No. 232, June 6, 2022, Coronavirus Disease (COVID-19) Pandemic." https://carpha.org /Portals/0/Documents/COVID%20Situation%20Reports/Situation%20Report %20232%20-%20June%206%202022.pdf/.

CARPHA. 2023. "COVID-19 Situation Report No. 262." March 8, https://www .carpha.org/Portals/0/Documents/COVID%20Situation%20Reports/Situation %20Report%20262%20-%20March%208%202023.pdf/.

Chang, Horace. 2022. "Advancing Citizen Security." Budget Sectoral Presentation. June 1, https://jis.gov.jm/speeches/2022–23-sectoral-presentation-by-minister-of-national -security-hon-dr-horace-change-cd-mp/.

Commonwealth Advisory Group. 1997. *A Future for Small States: Overcoming Vulnerability*. London: Commonwealth Secretariat.

Commonwealth Study Group. 1985. *Vulnerability: Small States in the Global Society*. London: Commonwealth Secretariat.

Count the Costs. 2012. *The Alternative World Drug Report: Counting the Costs of the War on Drugs*. http://www.countthecosts.org/sites/default/files/AWDR.pdf/.

Count the Costs. 2016. *The Alternative World Drug Report: Counting the Costs of the War on Drugs*, 2nd ed. https://transformdrugs.org/product/the-alternative-world -drug-report-2nd-edition/.

Couture, Stéphane, and Sophie Toupin. 2018. "What Does the Concept of 'Sovereignty' Mean in Digital, Network and Technological Sovereignty." Paper for Giganet 2017 Conference. https://papers.ssrn.com/sol3/papers.cfm?abstract_id=3107272/.

DEA (Drug Enforcement Administration). 2021. "International Drug Trafficking Organization Member Sentenced for Trafficking Over a Thousand Kilograms of Cocaine." December 3. https://www.dea.gov/press-releases/2021/12/03 /international-drug-trafficking-organization-member-sentenced-trafficking.

De Groot, Olaf, and Miguel Pérez Ludeña. 2014. *Foreign Direct Investment in the Caribbean: Trends, Determinants and Policies*. ECLAC Studies and Perspectives 35. https://repositorio.cepal.org/bitstream/handle/11362/36620/S2014046_en.pdf.

ECLAC (Economic Commission for Latin America and the Caribbean). 2010. "Jamaica: Report on the Macro Socio-Economic Effects of the Events in Western Kingston Jamaica Area, 22 May-7 June, 2010," LC/CAR/L.271/Rev.1, 27 October.

Erez, Noam. 2018. "Cyber Attacks Are Shutting Down Countries, Cities, and Companies. Here's How to Stop Them." *World Economic Forum Agenda*. June 22. https://www.weforum.org/agenda/2018/06/how-organizations-should-prepare-for-cyber-attacks-noam-erez/.

García Zaballos, Antonio, and Félix González Herranz. 2013. "From Cybersecurity to Cybercrime: A Framework for Analysis and Implementation." IDB Technical Note No. IDB-TN-588. September. https://www.contexto.org/pdfs/IDBcybersec.pdf/.

George Commission of Inquiry. 2011. *Report of the Commission of Inquiry into the Extradition Request for Christopher Coke*. June 6. https://jis.gov.jm/media/Manatt-Final-Report-1.pdf/.

Global Action on Cybercrime Extended. 2019. *Report on the Regional Conference on Cybercrime Strategies and Policies and Features of the Budapest Convention for the Caribbean Community*, 12–14 June. Santo Domingo, Dominican Republic, Jointly Organized by the GLACY+ Joint Project of the Council of Europe and the European Union, the Ministry of Presidency of the Dominican Republic and CARICOM IMPACS. https://rm.coe.int/3148–1–1–3-final-report-dr-reg-conference-cy-policies-caribbean-comm-1/168098fb6c/.

Golding, Bruce. 2011a. "Budget Debate Presentation, Tuesday, May 10, 2011, by the Hon. Bruce Golding, MP, Prime Minister of Jamaica." 25–26.

Golding, Bruce. 2011b. "National Broadcast by the Hon. Bruce Golding, Prime Minister of Jamaica, Sunday October 2, 8:00 pm." http://www.opm.gov.jm/files/Address-JamaicasPrimeMinisterBruceGolding-Embargoed-JamaicaTime8p.m.October2-2011.pdf/.

Gonsalves, Ralph. 2003. "Our Caribbean Civilization and Its Political Prospects." Inaugural Lecture in the Distinguished Lecture Series Sponsored by CARICOM to Commemorate Its Thirtieth Anniversary, Port-of-Spain, Trinidad, February 12.

Gonsalves, Ralph. 2011. "'Big Four' Must Provide Focused Leadership—Prime Minister Gonsalves." CARICOM Press Release, July 5.

Gonsalves, Ralph. 2012. "Budget Presentation to Parliament by Prime Minister Ralph Gonsalves of St. Vincent and the Grenadines, Delivered January 9."

Government of Jamaica, Ministry of Justice. 2015. "Fact Sheet on the Dangerous Drug (Amendment) Act 2015." https://moj.gov.jm/sites/default/files/Dangerous%20Drugs%20Amendment%20Act%202015%20Fact%20Sheet_0.pdf/.

Government of Trinidad and Tobago. 2011. "Budget Statement 2012: From Steady Foundation to Economic Transformation, Safety, Jobs, Investment." Presented to Parliament by Winston Dookeran, Minister of Finance, October 10.

Government of Trinidad and Tobago. 2014. *Report of the Commission of Enquiry Appointed to Enquire into the Events Surrounding the Attempted Coup D'état of 27th of July 1990.* Government of the Republic of Trinidad and Tobago, March. http://www.ttparliament.org/documents/rptcoe1990.pdf/.

Grenade, Kari, and Allan Wright. 2018. "Macro-Critical Issues and Implications for the Financial Sector in CARICOM." IDB Policy Brief No. 272, April. https://publications.iadb.org/publications/english/document/Macro-Critical-Issues-and-Implications-for-the-Financial-Sector-in-CARICOM.pdf/.

Griffith, Ivelaw Lloyd. 2009. "New Directions or Old Path? Caribbean Basin Security Initiative." Congressional Testimony of Dr. Ivelaw Lloyd Griffith, Professor of Political Science Provost and Senior Vice President for Academic Affairs York College of the City University of New York before the Subcommittee on the Western Hemisphere of the Committee on Foreign Affairs, U.S. House of Representatives, December 9. https://foreignaffairs.house.gov/2009/12/new-direction-or-old-path-caribbean-basin-security-initiative-cbsi.

Holness, Andrew. 2017. "Contribution to the 2017/18 Budget Debate by Prime Minister Andrew Holness." March 21. https://jis.gov.jm/media/PM-Contribution-to-the-2017-2018-Budget-Debate.pdf/.

Holness, Andrew. 2019. "Presentation by the Most Honourable Andrew Holness ON, MP Prime Minister in Parliament on the State of Emergency." May 7. https://opm.gov.jm/statement/presentation-by-the-most-honourable-andrew-holness-on-mp-prime-minister-in-parliament-on-the-state-of-emergency/.

Holness, Andrew. 2020. "New Year Message 2020 Prime Minister, The Most Hon. Andrew Holness." January 1. https://jis.gov.jm/speeches/new-year-message-2020-prime-minister-the-most-hon-andrew-holness/.

Holness, Andrew. 2022. "New Year Message 2022 Prime Minister, The Most Hon. Andrew Holness." January 1. https://jis.gov.jm/speeches/2021-new-years-day-message-by-the-prime-minister-the-most-hon-andrew-holness-on-pc-mp/.

IDB (Inter-American Development Bank). 2016. *Cybersecurity: Are We Ready in Latin America and the Caribbean?* https://publications.iadb.org/publications/english/document/Cybersecurity-Are-We-Ready-in-Latin-America-and-the-Caribbean.pdf/.

IDB. 2017. "Jamaica to Strengthen Efforts to Combat Violent Crime with Help from the IDB." News Release, November 22. https://www.iadb.org/en/news/jamaica-strengthen-efforts-combat-violent-crime-help-idb/.

Information Systems Audit and Control Association. 2019. *State of Cybersecurity 2019.* http://www.isaca.org/Knowledge-Center/Research/Documents/cyber/state-of-cybersecurity-2019-part-1_res_eng_0319.pdf?regnum=535517/.

Institute for Economics and Peace. 2017. *Global Terrorism Index 2017.* http://visionofhumanity.org/app/uploads/2017/11/Global-Terrorism-Index-2017.pdf/.

Institute for Economics and Peace. 2019. *Global Terrorism Index 2019.* https://reliefweb.int/sites/reliefweb.int/files/resources/GTI-2019web.pdf/.

Institute for Economics and Peace. 2020. *Global Terrorism Index 2020.* https://www.economicsandpeace.org/wp-content/uploads/2020/11/GTI-2020-web-2.pdf/.

International Institute for Strategic Studies. 2021. *The Military Balance 2021.* London: International Institute for Strategic Studies, 2021.

International Telecommunication Union (ITU). 2019. *Global Cybersecurity Index 2018*. https://www.itu.int/dms_pub/itu-d/opb/str/D-STR-GCI.01–2018-PDF-E.pdf/.

International Telecommunication Union (ITU). 2021. *Global Cybersecurity Index 2020*. https://www.itu.int/dms_pub/itu-d/opb/str/D-STR-GCI.01–2021-PDF-E.pdf/.

Jaitman, Laura, ed. 2017. *The Costs of Crime and Violence: New Evidence and Insights in Latin America and the Caribbean*. Washington, DC: Inter-American Development Bank. https://publications.iadb.org/publications/english/document/The-Costs-of-Crime-and-Violence-New-Evidence-and-Insights-in-Latin-America-and-the-Caribbean.pdf/.

Jamaica National Group. 2019. *Director's Report and Financial Statement*. https://www.jngroup.com/wp-content/uploads/2019/11/Annual-Report-People-First_2019-WEB.pdf/.

Jamaica Tourist Board. 2019. *Annual Travel Statistics 2018*. https://www.jtbonline.org/report-and-statistics/.

Jamaica Tourist Board. 2021. *Annual Travel Statistics 2020*. https://www.jtbonline.org/wp-content/uploads/Annual-Travel-Statistics-2020.pdf

Jamaicans for Justice. 2020. "Supreme Court Rules Detentions under States of Emergency (SOE) Unconstitutional." September 25. https://jamaicansforjustice.org/soe-detentions-unconstitutional/.

Jessop, David. 2016. "Action Needed to Address Caribbean Cyber Security: The View from Europe." Caribbean Council. October 30. https://www.caribbean-council.org/wp-content/uploads/2016/10/The-View-From-Europe-Oct-31-Action-needed-to-address-cyber-security.pdf/.

King, Stephenson. 2010. "Address to the Nation on the Crime Situation in Saint Lucia and Government's Response by Prime Minister the Honorable Stephenson King." May 30.

Lewis, James. 2018. *Economic Impact of Cybercrime—No Slowing Down*. Center for Strategic and International Studies (CSIS) Report. February. https://assets.website-files.com/5bd672d1924b9893a632c807/5c171d5e85ed62697a79e351_economic-impact-cybercrime.pdf/.

Lewis, Rupert. 2010. "Notes on the Western Kingston Crisis and Party Politics." Symposium by the University of the West Indies and Duke University, Mona, Jamaica, June 16–18. https://www.mona.uwi.edu/cct/sites/default/files/cct/u3/Rupert%20Lewis%20Politics%202010%20for%20web.pdf/.

Maharaj, Ramesh. 2000. "Remarks by the Hon. Ramesh Lawrence Maharaj, Attorney General and Minister of Legal Affairs of the Republic of Trinidad and Tobago at the Opening of the Caribbean–United States–European–Canadian Ministerial (Criminal Justice and Law Enforcement) Conference," Port-of-Spain, Trinidad, June 12–13.

MacDonald, Scott B. 2019a. "Is There a 'New Normal' for De-risking in the Caribbean?" Center for Strategic and International Studies (CSIS) Report, October 16. https://www.csis.org/analysis/there-new-normal-de-risking-caribbean/.

MacDonald, Scott B. 2019b. "Suriname at a Crossroads." Center for Strategic and International Studies (CSIS) Report. August. https://csis-prod.s3.amazonaws.com/s3fs-public/publication/190731_MacDonald_Suriname_v1.pdf/.

MacDonald, Scott B. 2020a. "Suriname and the Need for Good Governance." *Global Americans*. March 4. https://theglobalamericans.org/2020/03/suriname-and-the-need-for-good-governance/.

MacDonald, Scott B. 2020b. "Suriname's Changing of the Guard?" *Global Americans*. June 17. https://theglobalamericans.org/2020/06/surinames-changing-of-the-guard/.

Marczak, Jason, and Wazim Mowla. 2022. "Financial De-Risking in the Caribbean: The US Implications and What Needs to Be Done." Atlantic Council Financial Inclusion Task Force Report. March 1. https://www.atlanticcouncil.org/in-depth-research-reports/report/financial-de-risking-in-the-caribbean/.

Nippon Telegraph and Telephone. 2019. *Global Threat Intelligence Report 2019*. https://www.nttsecurity.com/docs/librariesprovider3/resources/2019-gtir/2019_gtir_report_2019_uea_v2.pdf/.

Nippon Telegraph and Telephone. 2021. *Global Threat Intelligence Report 2021*. https://services.global.ntt/en-us/insights/2021-global-threat-intelligence-report/.

OAS (Organization of American States). 2003. "Declaration on Security in the Americas." OEA/Ser.K/XXXVIII, CES/DEC. 1/03 rev. 1. October 28. http://www.oas.org/documents/eng/DeclaracionSecurity_102803.asp/.

OAS. 2013. *The Drug Problem in the Americas*. May. http://www.oas.org/documents/eng/press/Introduction_and_Analytical_Report.pdf/.

OAS Inter American Drug Abuse Control Commission. 2010. "Comparative Analysis of Student Drug Use in Caribbean Countries 2010." http://www.cicad.oas.org/Main/pubs/StudentDrugUse-Caribbean2011.pdf/.

OAS Secretariat for Multidimensional Security. 2011. *Report on Citizen Security in the Americas 2011*. June. http://www.oas.org/dsp/alertamerica/Alertamerica_2011.pdf/.

Office of the Prime Minister, Jamaica. 1996. "Speaking Notes for the Hon. P. J. Patterson, QC, MP, at the Opening of the Regional Drug Training Center." Twickenham Park, St. Catherine, September 27.

Persad-Bissessar, Kamla. 2011. "Speaking Notes of the Hon. Kamla Persad-Bissessar, Prime Minister of Trinidad and Tobago on the Extension of the Emergency, September 4, 2011."

Price, Roz. 2019. "Mapping Security and Justice Activities in the Caribbean." Institute of Development Studies, Brighton, United Kingdom. August 30. https://assets.publishing.service.gov.uk/media/5d9b5d46ed915d354c1af102/658_Mapping_Security_and_Justice_Activities_in_the_Caribbean.pdf/.

Republic of Suriname. 2010. "Legislative Elections of 25 May 2010." http://psephos.adam-carr.net/countries/s/suriname/suriname2010.txt/.

Riley, Ingrid. 2019. *Sun, Sea, and Sensi—Guide to Current Caribbean Cannabis Laws*. https://IngridRiley.com/2019/08/27/sun-sea-and-sensi-guide-to-current-caribbean-cannabis-laws/. August 27.

Robinson, A.N.R. 1991. "Speech by Prime Minister of Trinidad and Tobago to Regional Seminar on Security." May 31. Port-of-Spain, Trinidad and Tobago.

Sáenz, Esteban G. 2020. "Panama Canal: Redefining World Trade." https://aapa.files.cms-plus.com/2019Seminars/Shifting/Esteban%20Saenz.pdf/.

Sanders, Ronald. 2016. "The Commonwealth of Nations: Its Role for Global Good." Presentation by Sir Ronald Sanders at the Global Leadership Forum on 10th November 2016 in Nassau, Bahamas. http://www.sirronaldsanders.com/Docs/The%20Commonwealth%20of%20Nations%20Its%20role%20for%20Global%20Good.pdf/.

Satchell, Nicola. 2020. *Survey of Individuals Deprived of Liberty: Caribbean 2016–2019, Jamaica Country Report.* IDB Discussion Paper No. IDB-DP—821. October. https://publications.iadb.org/en/survey-individuals-deprived-liberty-caribbean-2016-2019-jamaica-country-report.

Schott, Paul Allan. 2006. *Reference Guide to Anti-Money Laundering and Combating the Financing of Terrorism.* Washington, DC: The World Bank. http://documents.worldbank.org/curated/en/558401468134391014/pdf/350520Referenc1Money01OFFICIAL0USE1.pdf/.

Seepersad, Randy, and Dianne Williams. 2012. *A Report on Citizen Security, Trinidad and Tobago 2012: Human Development and the Shift to Better Citizen Security.* https://www.undp.org/sites/g/files/zskgke326/files/migration/tt/UNDP_TandT_Citizen_Security_Survey_2012.pdf/.

Simmons Commission of Inquiry. 2016. *Report of the Western Kingston Commission of Enquiry.* https://moj.gov.jm/news/report-western-kingston-commission-enquiry-2016/.

Simon, Henderson. 1998. "Statement by Minister Henderson Simon of Antigua and Barbuda to the Third Defense Ministerial, Cartagena, Colombia, November 1998." http://www.oas.org/csh/english/docministerialsStatem.asp/.

Sutton, Heather. 2017. "Unpacking the High Cost of Crime in the Caribbean: Violent Crime, the Private Sector, and the Government Response." In *The Costs of Crime and Violence: New Evidence and Insights in Latin America and the Caribbean*, edited by Laura Jaitman. Washington, DC: Inter-American Development Bank.

Tannenbaum, Ben. 2018. "Filling the Void: China's Expanding Caribbean Presence." Council on Hemispheric Affairs. April 3. http://www.coha.org/filling-the-void-chinas-expanding-caribbean-presence/.

Transparency International. 2019. *Global Corruption Barometer Latin America and the Caribbean 2019 Citizens' Views and Experiences of Corruption.* https://www.transparency.org/files/content/pages/2019_GCB_LatinAmerica_Caribbean_Full_Report.pdf/.

Transparency International. 2020. *Perceptions Corruption Index 2019.* https://www.transparency.org/cpi2019/.

United Nations (U.N.). 2001. See "General Comment No. 20, States of Emergency (Article 4), International Convenant on Civil and Political Rights, CCPR/C/21/Rev.1/Add.11." August 31.

U.N. Office on Drugs and Crime. 2011a. *Global Study on Homicide: Trends, Contexts, Data.* http://www.unodc.org/documents/data-and-analysis/statistics/Homicide/Globa_study_on_homicide_2011_web.pdf/.

U.N. Office on Drugs and Crime. 2011b. *World Drug Report 2011.* http://www.unodc.org/documents/data-and-analysis/WDR2011/WDR2011-web.pdf/.

U.N. Office on Drugs and Crime. 2012. *World Drug Report 2012*. http://www.unodc.org/documents/data-and-analysis/WDR2012/WDR_2012_web_small.pdf/.

U.N. Office on Drugs and Crime. 2013. *World Drug Report 2013*. http://www.unodc.org/unodc/secured/wdr/wdr2013/World_Drug_Report_2013.pdf/.

U.N. Office on Drugs and Crime. 2019a. *Global Study on Homicide*, https://www.unodc.org/documents/data-and-analysis/gsh/Booklet1.pdf/.

U.N. Office on Drugs and Crime. 2019b. *World Drug Report 2019*. https://www.unodc.org/documents/data-and-analysis/gsh/Booklet1.pdf/.

U.N. Office on Drugs and Crime. 2021. *World Drug Report 2021*. https://www.unodc.org/unodc/data-and-analysis/wdr2021.html.

U.N. Office on Drugs and Crime. 2023. *Haiti's Criminal Markets: Mapping Trends in Firearms and Drug Trafficking*. https://www.unodc.org/documents/data-and-analysis/toc/Haiti_assessment_UNODC.pdf.

U.N. Office on Drugs and Crime–World Bank. 2007. *Crime, Violence, and Development: Trends, Costs, and Policy Options in the Caribbean*. https://www.unodc.org/documents/data-and-analysis/Caribbean-study-en.pdf/.

U.S. Congress. 2023. "Legislative Request to the Government Accountability Office." April 3. https://castro.house.gov/imo/media/doc/Castro-Meeks-Durbin%20Letter%20to%20GAO.pdf/.

U.S. Congressional Research Service. 2020. "In Focus: Caribbean Basin Security Initiative." January 30. https://fas.org/sgp/crs/row/IF10789.pdf/.

U.S. Department of Justice. 2022. "Eight Members of Puerto Rico–Based Drug Trafficking Organization Sentenced." Press Release. February 25. https://www.justice.gov/usao-mdfl/pr/eight-members-puerto-rico-based-drug-trafficking-organization-sentenced/.

U.S. Department of State. 2009. "Declaration of Commitment of Port-of-Spain." April 19. https://2009-2017.state.gov/p/wha/rls/123028.htm/.

U.S. Department of State. 2013. *International Narcotics Control Strategy Report*. March 5. https://2009-2017.state.gov/j/inl/rls/nrcrpt/2013/index.htm/.

U.S. Department of State. 2016a. *Country Reports on Terrorism 2015*. June. https://2009-2017.state.gov/j/ct/rls/crt/2015/index.htm/.

U.S. Department of State. 2016b. *International Narcotics Control Strategy Report*. March 28. https://2009-2017.state.gov/documents/organization/253983.pdf/.

U.S. Department of State. 2018. *Country Reports on Terrorism*. https://www.state.gov/country-reports-on-terrorism-2/.

U.S. Department of State. 2019a. *2018 Country Reports on Human Rights Practices: Haiti*. https://www.state.gov/wp-content/uploads/2019/03/HAITI-2018.pdf/.

U.S. Department of State. 2019b. *2018 Country Reports on Human Rights Practices: Trinidad and Tobago*. https://www.state.gov/wp-content/uploads/2019/03/TRINIDAD-AND-TOBAGO-2018.pdf/.

U.S. Department of State. 2019c. *Country Reports on Terrorism 2018*. October. https://www.state.gov/wp-content/uploads/2019/11/Country-Reports-on-Terrorism-2018-FINAL.pdf/.

U.S. Department of State. 2019d. *International Narcotics Control Strategy Report*. March 28. https://www.state.gov/2019-international-narcotics-control-strategy-report/.

U.S. Department of State. 2021. *International Narcotics Control Strategy Report*. March. https://www.state.gov/2021-international-narcotics-control-strategy-report/.

U.S. Energy Information Administration. 2021. "U.S. Natural Gas Imports by Country." https://www.eia.gov/dnav/ng/ng_move_impc_s1_a.htm/.

U.S. General Accounting Office. 2019. *Security Assistance: U.S. Agencies Should Establish a Mechanism to Assess Caribbean Basin Security Initiative Progress*. Report to Congressional Requesters, February. https://www.gao.gov/assets/700/697137.pdf/.

U.S. Institute for National Strategic Studies. 2000. *Strategic Assessment 1999: Priorities for a Turbulent World*. Washington, DC: National Defense University Press.

U.S. Secret Service. 2022. "Former Government Official in the Dominican Republic Sentenced to 15 Years for Conspiring to Import Cocaine into the United States." Press Release. March 16. https://www.secretservice.gov/newsroom/releases/2022/03/former-government-official-dominican-republic-sentenced-15-years/.

U.S. Senate. 1989. *Drug Money Laundering, Banks, and Foreign Policy*. Hearings Before the Subcommittee on Narcotics, Terrorism, and International Operations. 101st Cong. 2d sess., September 27, October 4, and November 1.

U.S. Senate. 2012. *Preventing a Security Crisis in the Caribbean: A Report by the United States Senate Caucus on International Narcotics Control*, 112th Congress, Second Session, September. https://www.feinstein.senate.gov/public/_cache/files/9/0/90bb66bc-3371-4898-8415-fbfc31c0ed24/82FE9908E85FB144D84F73F217DAC7A6.caribbean-drug-report.pdf/.

U.S. Southern Command. 2020. "Cooperative Security Locations." https://www.southcom.mil/Media/Special-Coverage/Cooperative-Security-Locations/.

van der Veen, Henk, and Lars Franciscus Heuts. 2018. "National Risk Assessment on Money Laundering and Terrorist Financing for the Caribbean Netherlands (Bonaire, Sint Eustatius and Saba)." Research and Documentation Center, Ministry of Justice and Security, The Netherlands. https://www.wodc.nl/binaries/Cahier%202018-17a_2689g_Full%20text_tcm28-379590.pdf/.

Vaz, Daryl. 2022. "Building Our Jamaica: Creating an Enduring Legacy in Science, Energy, and Technology." Sectoral Presentation 2022–2023. May 10. https://jis.gov.jm/media/2022/05/BUILDING-OUR-JAMAICA-Full-reduced.pdf/.

West Indian Commission. 1992. *Time for Action: Report of the West Indian Commission*. Black Rock, Barbados: West Indian Commission.

Index

Christopher, Rupert, 202
Chuck, Delroy, 115–16, 170
Clarke, Nigel, 137
Clinton, Bill, 3, 5, 246
cocaine, 7, 8, 40, 46, 48–52, 54, 69–70, 91, 116, 201, 202, 204, 205–11, 236–37
coca leaf, 38, 48
Coke, Christopher "Dudus," 10, 15–17, 43, 80–81, 84, 86, 166–85
Coke, Lester, 167
Cold War: impact on perceptions of security, 20, 24, 40–41; realist paradigm and, 25, 40
collaboration imperative, 242–44
Colombia: arms trafficking and, 8; drug activity and, 44, 48, 202, 210
Commissions of Inquiry (COI), Dudus Affair (Jamaica), 169, 170, 174–85
Computing Technology Industry Association, *State of Cybersecurity,* 6
Cooperative Security Location (CSL), 130–31
Cornell, Svante, 41
corruption, 111–17; Caribbean Anti-Corruption Program, 230; drugs-driven, 17, 38, 46, 111, 116; police officer impunity and, 17, 113–15; Transparency International and, 112–13; types of, 111–12. *See also* money laundering
Costa Rica, terrorism and, 122
Cottee, Simon, 144, 146–47
Count the Costs Initiative, *The Alternative World Drug Report,* 6
COVID-19 pandemic, 237–42; anti-vaxxers, 82–83; Caribbean infections and deaths, 4, 238; challenged sovereignty and, 4–5, 238–42; cybercrime and, 151, 152, 159; global infections and deaths, 4, 238; origins of, 238, 261n2; strategic partnerships and, 239–42; tourism and, 132, 137
crack cocaine, 46, 51
crime, 71–117; armed gangs (*see* gangs/armed gangs); assassinations/attempted assassinations, 81–82, 97–98; civilizational implications of, 72–81; clearance rates, 83–84, 101; context for, 88–94; corruption, 111–17; cybercrime (*see* cybercrime); daring and dastardly forms of, 81–84; domestic violence, 72, 74, 79–80, 97, 114; drugs and (*see* drugs); economic and social costs of, 99–103; electricity theft, 102–3; extradition treaties, 16, 17t, 169, 170, 174, 175, 249–59, 262n9; guns and (*see* firearms/guns); homicides (*see* homicides); kidnapping, 82, 97–99; money laundering (*see* money laundering); organized crime

groups, 38, 74, 81–82, 91–92, 131, 158, 165, 230–31; prisons and (*see* prisons); States of Emergency and (*see* States of Emergency); terrorism (*see* terrorism); tourism and, 80, 124, 127, 139–40, 267n21
criminal organizations, 7, 8, 230
CrowdStrike, *Global Threat Report,* 6
Cuba: China and, 128; drug activity and, 44; homicide and, 75t; marijuana reforms, 62; marijuana use/consumption in, 53; money laundering and, 52; physical geography of, 48; strategic materials, 128, 129; terrorism and, 122; tourism and, 132, 133; U.S. strategic installations and, 130
Curaçao: marijuana reforms, 62–63; money laundering and, 142–43, 237; social geography of, 49; strategic installations, 130–31; strategic materials, 129
cybercrime, 148–61; attack methods, 149, 150–53; Caribbean attacks, 153–61; costs of, 153, 158; COVID-19 pandemic and, 151, 152, 159; cybersecurity importance and, 148–49, 152–53, 234; cybersecurity innovations and, 30–31; defined, 149; global cases, 151–53, 160–61; international reporting on, 6, 150–53, 158, 159; local-global nexus and, 6; vulnerability to, 30–31

Dalmau, José Luis, 158
Daly, Martin, 234
Davis, Phillip, 93
Dawson, Maurice, 158–59
decolonization: impact on sovereignty, 28–29, 232–33; post-World War II, 20, 120
de Haan, Leah, 144
Dolai, Mohanram, 114
domestic violence, 72, 74, 79–80, 97, 114
Domínguez, Jorge, 12
Dominica: drug activity and, 50–52; marijuana reforms, 63; money laundering and, 52; terrorism and, 125t, 126t
Dominican Republic: arms trafficking and, 7; assassinations, 81–82; banking and financial services, 140; corruption in, 113, 116; cybercrime and, 158–59; drug activity and, 17, 40, 51–52, 53, 73, 233, 234; electricity theft, 102; guns originating in the U.S., 91; homicide and, 75t, 76t, 78, 79; marijuana reforms, 63; marijuana use/consumption in, 53; money laundering and, 52, 236; prisons in, 105–8; State of Emergency (SoE), 85; strategic materials, 128; terrorism and, 122; tourism and, 132, 133

Lord, Nate, 148
Lutz, Brenda, 132
Lutz, James, 132

MacDonald, Scott, 203–4, 220, 221
Macron, Emmanuel, 85
Maguire, Edward R., 83–84
Mahfood, John, 102–3
Mahraj, Ramesh, 72–73
Maingot, Anthony, 32–33, 265n2, 266n11, 268n10
Manigat, Leslie, 124
Manley, Michael, 86
Manning, Patrick, 194
marijuana/cannabis, 54–70; CARICOM Regional Commission on Marijuana, 14, 54–58, 69–70; consumption/use of, 51, 53; country legalization efforts, 58–70; cultural and religious uses of, 38, 54, 57–61, 64, 66, 68, 264–65n13; ganja, 39, 58–59, 64, 264–65n13; medicinal cannabis, 56, 58, 60–67, 264n12; production of, 46–47, 53, 202; reforms concerning, 38–39, 56–70, 264–65nn12–14; trafficking in, 57, 68–69, 205
Mark, Wade, 186
Marley, Bob, 54, 58
Martí, José, 225
Martinique: marijuana reforms, 64; social geography of, 49, 85
Mayotte, 85
McCoy, John, 144–46, 147
McKay, Claude, 246–47
Medellín cartel leaders, 8
medicinal cannabis, 56, 58, 60–67, 264n12
Melnick, Jeff, 150
mercenary training, 8
Mérida Initiative, 53, 227–28, 264n11
Merkel, Angela, 30
methamphetamines, 49, 202
Mexico: Anti-Crime Capacity Building Program (ACCBP, Canada), 231–32; arms trafficking and, 92–94, 95; counternarcotics measures, 52; crackdown on drug cartels, 74; Mérida Initiative, 53, 227–28, 264n11; terrorism and, 122; tourism and, 134
Miller, Merrick "Al," 169, 270n3
Minto-Coy, Indianna, 154
Moïse, Jovenel, 97
money laundering, 138–43; Caribbean cases, 142–43; confiscation and forfeiture of property and, 236–37; defined, 138; drugs

and, 40, 41–43, 46, 52, 53, 57, 73, 140; major money laundering countries, 52; mechanisms of, 138–40; risks of, 140–42; terrorism and, 138–43; tourism and, 139–40
Montserrat: marijuana reforms, 64; social geography of, 49
Moreno, Luis Alberto, 153
multidimensionality, 6; crime and, 72; cyber threats and, 118–19; drug activity and, 38, 40, 41–44, 45; of security, 26–27; terrorism and, 118–19
Multilateral Security Engagement Zones (MSEZ), 227

Nadelmann, Ethan, 111–12
Naím, Moisés, 3, 5
narco state status, 11, 15, 46, 203–5, 212–13, 232–34, 245
nationalism, as corollary of sovereignty, 32
natural resources/strategic materials, 128–29, 203–4, 214–19
Netherlands: Caribbean territories and, 17t, 21–23t, 49, 62–64, 131, 141f, 142–43, 199, 204–6, 210, 218; cybercrime and, 152; money laundering and, 142–43
Nevis. See St. Kitts and Nevis
New River Triangle (Suriname), 213, 214–19
Newton, Isaac, 19
Newton, Velma, 231–32
Nicaragua: strategic materials, 128; terrorism and, 122–23
Nigeria: Boko Haram and, 120; cybercrime and, 152; drug activity and, 8–9; terrorism and, 120, 121, 123–24
Nippon Telegraph and Telephone Corporation, 6, 150–52
nongovernmental organizations (NGOs), 43–45
Núñez, Endy and Danny, 116

Obama, Barack, 130, 148, 228, 229, 273n2
oil, 128–29, 143, 148, 160, 204, 213, 214–19, 221
Operation Trigger VII, 91–92
Organization of American States (OAS), 16; *Declaration on Security in the Americas,* 26–27; election monitoring by, 200, 220–21; Inter-American Drug Abuse Control Commission, 50–52, 232
organized crime groups, 7, 8, 38, 74, 81–82, 91–92, 131, 158, 165, 230–31

IVELAW LLOYD GRIFFITH is a Fellow of the Caribbean Policy Consortium and of Global Americans and a Senior Associate of the Center for Strategic and International Studies. His books include *Strategy and Security in the Caribbean, The Quest for Security in the Caribbean, Drugs and Security in the Caribbean, The Political Economy of Drugs in the Caribbean,* and *Caribbean Security in the Age of Terror.*

The University of Illinois Press
is a founding member of the
Association of University Presses.

———————————————————

University of Illinois Press
1325 South Oak Street
Champaign, IL 61820-6903
www.press.uillinois.edu